The Wandering Herd

The Medieval Cattle Economy
of South-East England c. *450–1450*

Andrew Margetts

WIND*gather*
PRESS

Windgather Press is an imprint of Oxbow Books

Published in the United Kingdom in 2021 by
OXBOW BOOKS
The Old Music Hall, 106-108 Cowley Road, Oxford, OX4 1JE

and in the United States by
OXBOW BOOKS
1950 Lawrence Road, Havertown, PA 19083

Paperback Edition: ISBN 978-1-91118-879-7
Digital Edition: ISBN 978-1-91118-880-3 (epub)

A CIP record for this book is available from the British Library

Printed in Malta by Gutenberg Press

Typeset by Versatile PreMedia Service (P) Ltd.

For a complete list of Windgather titles, please contact:

United Kingdom
OXBOW BOOKS
Telephone (01865) 241249
Email: oxbow@oxbowbooks.com
www.oxbowbooks.com

United States of America
OXBOW BOOKS
Telephone (610) 853-9131, Fax (610) 853-9146
Email: queries@casemateacademic.com
www.casemateacademic.com/oxbow

Oxbow Books is part of the Casemate group

Front cover: Cattle in woodland (photo by the author)
Back cover: Longhorn cattle at Knepp (image courtesy of Pip Stephenson)

Contents

List of plates and figures

List of tables

Abbreviations

ACM	Arundel Castle Manuscripts
TNA	The National Archives
BL	British Library
Box. Chart.	Fleming, L. (ed.) 1960: *Chartulary of Boxgrove Priory, 12th–14th Centuries*. Lewes: Sussex Record Society, vol. 59
Cal. Chart.	Calendar of Charter Rolls
Cal. Close	Calendar of Close Rolls
Cal. Inq. p. m.	Lyte, H.C. 1910: *Calendar of Inquisitions Post Mortem and other analagous documents. Preserved in the Public Record Office, vol. VI. Edward II*. Hereford: His Majesty's Stationary Office
Cal. Pat.	Calendar of the Patent Rolls
Cart. Sax. 1885	Birch, W. de G. (ed.) 1885: *Cartularium Saxonicum: A collection of charters relating to Anglo-Saxon history. vol. 1, AD 430–839*. London: Whiting and Co.
CCA	Canterbury Cathedral Archives
CDC	Chichester District Council
Cell. Batt.	Searle, E. and Ross, B. (eds) 1967: *The Cellarers' Rolls of Battle Abbey: 1275–1513*. Lewes: Sussex Record Society, vol. 65
Chi. Chart.	Peckham, W.D. (ed.) 1942: *The Chartulary of the High Church of Chichester*. Lewes: Sussex Record Society, vol. 46
CPD	Career and Personal Development
Cust. Cant.	Redwood, B.C. and Wilson, A.E. 1958: *Custumals of the Sussex Manors of the Archbishop of Canterbury, 1285–1330*. Lewes: Sussex Record Society, vol. 57
Cust. Chi.	Peckham, W.D. (ed.) 1925: *Thirteen Custumals of the Sussex Manors of the Bishop of Chichester*. Lewes: Sussex Record Society, vol. 31
Cust. Lau.	Wilson, A.E. 1961: *Custumals of the Manors of Laughton, Willingdon, and Goring*. Lewes: Sussex Record Society, vol. 60
DAERA	Department of Agriculture, Environment and Rural Affairs
ESCC	East Sussex County Council
ESRO	East Sussex Record Office
HER	Historic Environment Record
Hist. Franc.	*Historia Francorum*
Laws of Ine	Attenborough, F.L. (ed.) 1922: *The Laws of the Earliest English*

	Kings. London: Cambridge University Press
ME	Middle English
MSU	Michigan State University
NHLE	National Heritage List for England
NMR	National Monument Record
P.N.E 1956a	Smith, A.H. 1956a: *English Place-name Elements: Part 1, The Elements A–IW, Maps.* Cambridge: English Place-Name Society, vol. 25
P.N.E 1956b	Smith, A.H. 1956b: *English Place-name Elements: Part 2, The Elements JAFN–YTRI Index and Maps.* Cambridge: English Place-Name Society, vol. 26
Pipe. R.	Cannon H.L. 1908: *The Great Roll of the Pipe for the twenty-sixth year of the reign of King Henry the second, A.D. 1179–1180.* London: The Pipe Roll Society, vol. XXIX
P.N.Sr 1934	Mawer, A. and Stenton, F.M. (eds) 1934: *The Place-Names of Surrey.* London: English Place-Name Society, vol. 11
P.N.Sx 1929:	Mawer, A. and Stenton, F.M. (eds.) 1929: *The Place-Names of Sussex: Part 1.* Cambridge: Cambridge University Press, English Place-Name Society, vol. 6
P.N.Sx 1930:	Mawer, A. and Stenton, F.M. (eds.) 1930: *The Place-Names of Sussex: Part 2.* Cambridge: Cambridge University Press, English Place-Name Society, vol. 7
P.N.Y. 1961	Smith, A.H. 1961: *Place-Names of the West Riding of Yorkshire. Part 3: The Wapentake of Morley.* Cambridge: Cambridge University Press, English Place-Name Society, vol. 32
Rec. Lew.	Taylor, A.J. (ed.) 1940: *Records of the Barony and Honour of the Rape of Lewes.* Lewes: Sussex Record Society, vol. 44
SERF	South East Research Framework
SHC	Surrey History Centre
SRS	Sussex Record Society
Txt. Roff. 1720	Hearne, T. (ed.) 1720: *Textus Roffensis,* Oxford
VCH	Victoria County History
WCR	Wakefield Court Rolls
WSRO	West Sussex Record Office

Acknowledgements

The author would like to thank his Ph.D. supervisor Professor Stephen Rippon for his help and support; Greg Chuter and Chris Greatorex (Archaeologists East Sussex County Council) for supplying the OSL dates of the Belle Tout enclosures; Jim Waterson (Senior Lecturer in Crop and Environment Sciences at Harper Adams University) for specialist contacts advice; Peter Aspin of the Shropshire Agroforestry Project for information regarding the possible medicinal benefits of browse to cattle; James Brown (Head Dairyman at Dedisham Farm) for advice regarding cattle husbandry practice; and Brian Short (Emeritus Professor of Geography at the University of Sussex) for information regarding medieval livestock pasturing on Ashdown Forest. He would also like to thank Naomi Sykes (The Lawrence Professor of Archaeology University of Exeter) and Mark Gardiner (Associate Professor in Heritage University of Lincoln) for their comments on an earlier iteration of this work.

He would also like to thank Archaeology South-East (UCL Institute of Archaeology) for access to their project databases. Thanks are due to Jon Butler (Post-Excavation Manager at Pre-Construct Archaeology) and David Bowsher (Director of Research Museum of London Archaeology; MoLA) for supplying grey literature reports. Thanks are also due to Lucy Sibun (Senior Forensic Archaeologist and Osteologist Archaeology South-East) for advice regarding small animal bone assemblages.

CHAPTER I

Introduction

....

1.1 Introduction

> The late medieval sheep of Britain have so engaged the attention of the agrarian
> historians that other aspects of stock husbandry appear to have been neglected.
> Our knowledge of cattle of the period, and of how they were kept, is somewhat
> sketchy. (Trow-Smith 1957, 88)

Trow-Smith's perceptive observation that our understanding of the cattle
economy lagged behind that of other livestock is still true today. At a national
level, pastoral facets of agrarian history are still dominated by medieval sheep
husbandry and in South-East England these biases are particularly acute. Here,
archaeologists and historical geographers have been so concerned with the
importance of medieval sheep, and to a slightly lesser extent pigs, that no
systematic examination of the region's cattle economy has ever been undertaken.
This preoccupation with sheep husbandry as well as swine pannage is strange
for during the time we know as the medieval period South-East England was
home to a cattle economy that not only supplied the region's populace with
meat for the table, but also facilitated the production of crops through traction
and manure. Cattle were a commodity by which wealth was measured, tax was
paid and wars could be fought. In life cows could supply dairy by way of milk,
butter and cheese, and following death cattle could produce hides, bones, fat
and hooves. From these by-products a multitude of items were born. Tallow
would light the scribe's manuscript written on vellum parchments made from
the skin of a calf, while clothing, tools and glue were other secondary products
of an all-pervasive but never static economy.

If we travelled back some 1,200 years, the region's wide, un-metalled
droveways would have been thronged by herds on their way from the coast and
downland to well-watered summer pastures in the Weald. Local woods would
have echoed to the lowing of herds feeding on browse as contentedly as they
had done on the grass of Romney Marsh or the chalkland hills. This was an
economy that played a fundamental role in the shaping of the historic landscape
and the evolution of the rural settlement pattern, and yet in comparison to other
aspects of agriculture, it has been one of the most under-researched elements of
the region's past. In the rare instances where discussion of the area's medieval
pastoralism has been undertaken, a focus on sheep pasturing or swine pannage
has been the norm (*e.g.* Pelham 1934; Du Boulay 1961; Turner and Briggs 2016).
This emphasis on livestock apart from cattle may have been partly influenced by
the iconic nature of the landscapes of sheep farming, but may also be reflective

of scholars' historic reliance on information provided by the Domesday Survey. Within this document, a given woodland is measured in the number of pigs it could support in pasture. Whilst it is undoubted that the pannage of swine was an important aspect of the South-East's medieval economy, it must be remembered that this was only one part of a wider livestock regime that may not have been recorded in the same level of detail. A similar bias may have been introduced by the nature and distribution of surviving medieval documents. These are overwhelmingly focused on the arable areas of the region and those landscapes where the keeping of sheep for the burgeoning later medieval wool trade was customary. Areas traditionally suited to the pasturing of cattle (such as the Weald and the North Downs) were landscapes of 'secondary settlement', which did not receive anything like the same degree of documentation until the end of the medieval period (Everitt 1986).

A combination of place-name and landscape evidence, utilised together with documentary and archaeological information, may illuminate the South-East's medieval cattle economy and the form which this took. The so-called marginality of the Weald meant that historically cow-keeping, pig-rearing and coppice-cutting were the most advantageous methods of farming (Brandon 1988). Thus the Old English place-names of the region often came to reflect a pastoral model of settlement with names such as fold (*fald/falod*), *denn* (a forest retreat put to pastoral use), *gesell* (herdsmen's buildings) and *wic* (dairy farm or specialised settlement) (*P.N.Sx* 1929; 1930; *P.N.E.* 1956b) serving to highlight areas in which pastoral economies dominated.

Thus far, the only two areas to receive any in-depth investigation of large-scale medieval cattle husbandry have been the north of England and Dartmoor (Winchester 2000; Fox 2012). The former is characterised by the great demesne and ecclesiastical cattle ranches or vaccaries (*vaccaria*) that have been seen as a fundamental part of medieval land-use and settlement evolution (Winchester 2000). Though sheepcotes, the specialised equivalent of cattle ranches, have received dedicated study at a national level (Dyer 1995; see section 2.5) vaccaries have only seen limited regional or local attention, and then mainly from a historical perspective (*e.g.* Higham 1968; Smith 1999, 21–23; Kissock 2001; Winchester 2003; Smith 2007). Resolving this disparity needs attention as vaccaries were as important as sheep farms (beccaries; Aston 1993, 82).

To date, few archaeological remains in the south of England have been interpreted as vaccary sites, although medieval documentary evidence for cow-housing and dairying does exist. Vaccaries have been recorded in southern England since the time of the Domesday Survey when, for instance, three manors comprising *vaccaria* or *wica* were mentioned in the Vale of the White Horse (Berkshire/Oxfordshire border):

> At Sparsholt Henry de Ferrers has deprived the Crown of a dairy (*vaccaria*) producing six weys of cheese; at Shellingford the dues of cheese (*consuetudines caseorum*) are worth to Abingdon Abbey no less than £4 16s 8d; at Buckland bishop Osbern has a dairy farm (*wica*) producing ten weys of cheese, which are worth £1 12s 4d. (Ditchfield and Page 1906, 305)

Though vaccary farms have largely been seen as a feature of northern, upland pastoral landscapes their occurrence in a lowland context should be better recognised. Vaccaries were an element in the pastoral usage of the Weald from at least the early medieval period (Everitt 1986) and the recent discovery of *The Hayworth* on the manor of Trubwick (Haywards Heath, West Sussex; Margetts 2017) may represent the first archaeologically recognised vaccary in the South-East, and perhaps the most thoroughly excavated example nationally. An appraisal of the presence of vaccary sites in the Weald and elsewhere is, therefore, long overdue and has implications for our understanding of medieval economy and society as well as patterns of settlement evolution.

Earlier investigations by the author (Margetts 2017) have shown that the cattle economy may have had a strong influence on the region's historic settlement pattern as well as its landscape development, communities and infrastructure. In marginal areas, such as the Weald or Romney Marsh, settlement was often tied to pastoral exploitation, which acted as a driver of colonisation based initially on seasonal usage and subsequently on more permanent occupation. These so-called marginal landscapes comprise some of the least well-understood aspects of the medieval period (see section 2.5) and the Weald in particular represents one of the most archaeologically understudied parts of the country. Whilst the key aim of this book is to redress the imbalance in the study of the region's agriculture and highlight how important the keeping of cattle has been to regional development, it will also aim to further knowledge of the history of the Weald and other marginal areas, thus responding to research objectives at both regional (SERF 2008) and national levels (see section 2.5).

Seasonal settlement within the South-East has often been discussed in relation to the practice of transhumance (the movement of people and animals to grazing grounds on a seasonal cycle). This was conducted between more favourable landscapes and areas which comprised wooded commons or un-reclaimed wetlands. Despite the area's national and European-wide importance for transhumance studies, the actual specifics of this economy are currently not well understood. This is particularly in relation to the type and relative composition of livestock which underwent the seasonal movement, but also in terms of the traces this economic model left on the physical fabric of the countryside. Though key elements such as droveways and enclosures thought to be related to the practice have been studied (Chatwin and Gardiner 2005; Margetts 2017; 2018a), a more in-depth analysis is also required. By attempting to fulfil this research objective, this book will provide a detailed study of elements of the region's landscape in order to show how the medieval cattle economy may have functioned and how landscape elements were articulated within associated outlying pastoral systems. The study will aim to shed light on the origins of Wealden commons and later appropriated pastures. The latter may be defined by oval or arc-shaped boundaries (Chatwin and Gardiner 2005; Margetts 2017; 2018a), areas highlighted as requiring further research (Thomas 2019). From peasant to royal level, this book will attempt to demonstrate the fundamental significance of enclosure to cattle husbandry and landscape evolution. Work will include a survey of potential vaccary sites as well as discussion of cattle enclosures within open pastures, commons, arable areas and parks.

Subject to specific legal status and utilised as elite hunting grounds, Forest and Chase's importance for grazing at both demesne and leased level has only recently been explored at any depth (Winchester 2010; Fox 2012); the author attempts to produce comparable work here. By undertaking these objectives, it will be possible to explore what we can learn from medieval cattle husbandry practice and to investigate the medieval cattle economy's relevance to our understanding and future management of landscape. It is clear that past grazing regimes and traditional breeds of cattle hold value for both biodiversity and nature recovery. As part of agri-environmental schemes, cattle grazing, informed by ancient practice, may provide one of the key methods of enhancing the countryside and changing our approach to farming. Only by understanding the methods of the past can we hope to gain a clearer picture of how landscape can be managed in the future.

1.2 The study area

Natural areas and settlement regions

South-East England comprises the modern counties of Kent, Surrey and East and West Sussex as well as part of Greater London (Figure 1.1). While it cannot be claimed to comprise sharply contrasting geographical zones to the degree of some parts of northern and western Britain (Gardiner 2012b, 100), it nevertheless contains multiple *Character Areas* that transcend modern county boundaries. It is a region of varied underlying geologies, topography and environments that have given rise to a number of *pays* apparent through differing landscape types. The idea of *pays*, taken from the French term for an area of culturally and environmentally distinctive territory (Everitt 1986), provides units by which the historic landscape can be studied. The *pays* of the South-East, as they are defined here, are represented in Plate 1.1.

A glance at Plates 1.1 and 1.2 will show that the South-East is divided into banded zones with a central core comprising the Weald surrounded by a 'horseshoe' of the downs and Greensand. The North Downs are situated in Kent and extend into Surrey. They are well-wooded, and this is partly due to superficial deposits of intractable Clay-with-Flints. These heavy soils, with frequent large flint nodules, must have been discouraging to early cultivation, although parts of the well-wooded western South Downs, where this geology is also widespread, have recently been shown to preserve extensive prehistoric or Romano-British field-systems (Carpenter *et al.* 2016). In these areas the downland is dominated by managed woodland, a land-use type that is largely a legacy of the medieval Forest of Arundel. In the east, however, the South Downs are characterised by famously sweeping, open vistas created and maintained through livestock husbandry. The South-East's most fertile and tillable lands are the Brickearth Head deposits of the Sussex Coastal Plain and north-eastern

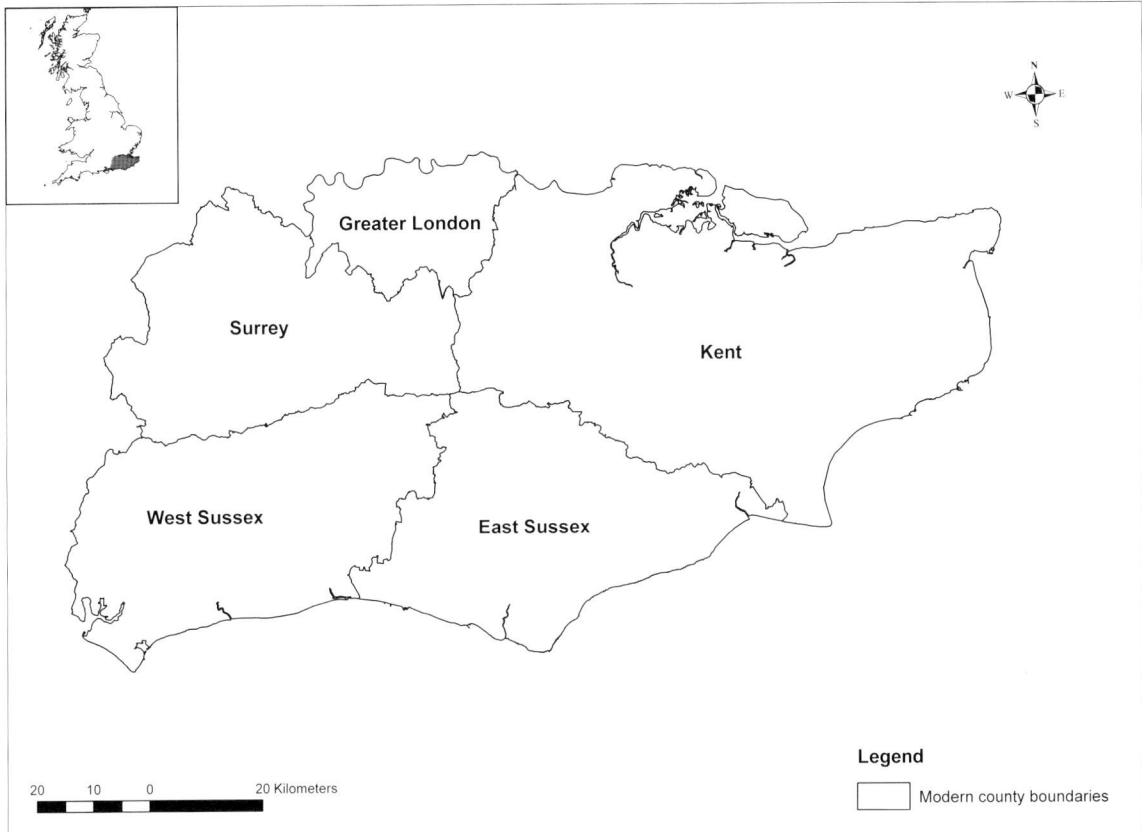

FIGURE 1.1: Modern
county boundaries of
South-East England
(drawn by the author.
Contains material
covered by © Crown
copyright and database
rights 2019 Ordnance
Survey, Educational
Service Provider licence
number v2.1)

Kent. In contrast, part of the Thames Basin and northern Kent are occupied by heavy London Clays or thin sands. Bordering the English Channel, the marshes of Walland and Romney as well as the Pevensey Levels have distinctive coastal histories linked to the exploitation of wetland or reclaimed land.

Encompassing the majority (over 60%) of the South-East's landmass and centrally situated in the great bowl formed of the opposing chalk escarpments of the North and South Downs (Figure 1.2), the Weald (named from the Old English for forest; Hooke 2013) is the region's poorest arable area. It is traditionally divided between the elevated, predominantly sandstone, High Weald and the largely clay Low Weald. From the early medieval period and possibly before, this area comprised a pastoral and woodland resource in which a system of transhumance prevailed. Early 'pioneering' communities utilised a network of droveways and based their agricultural exploitation of this marginal area on parent settlements situated within areas of greater arable potential (see sections 2.5, 4.2, 5.1). Traces of the pastoral economy can be seen in modern-day road networks, field boundaries and enclosures of the Wealden landscape, and through careful examination of the evidence, an evolution of rural society and settlement patterns from seasonal occupation to permanent farming communities and/or villages may be seen (Witney 1976; Everitt 1986; Brandon and Short 1990).

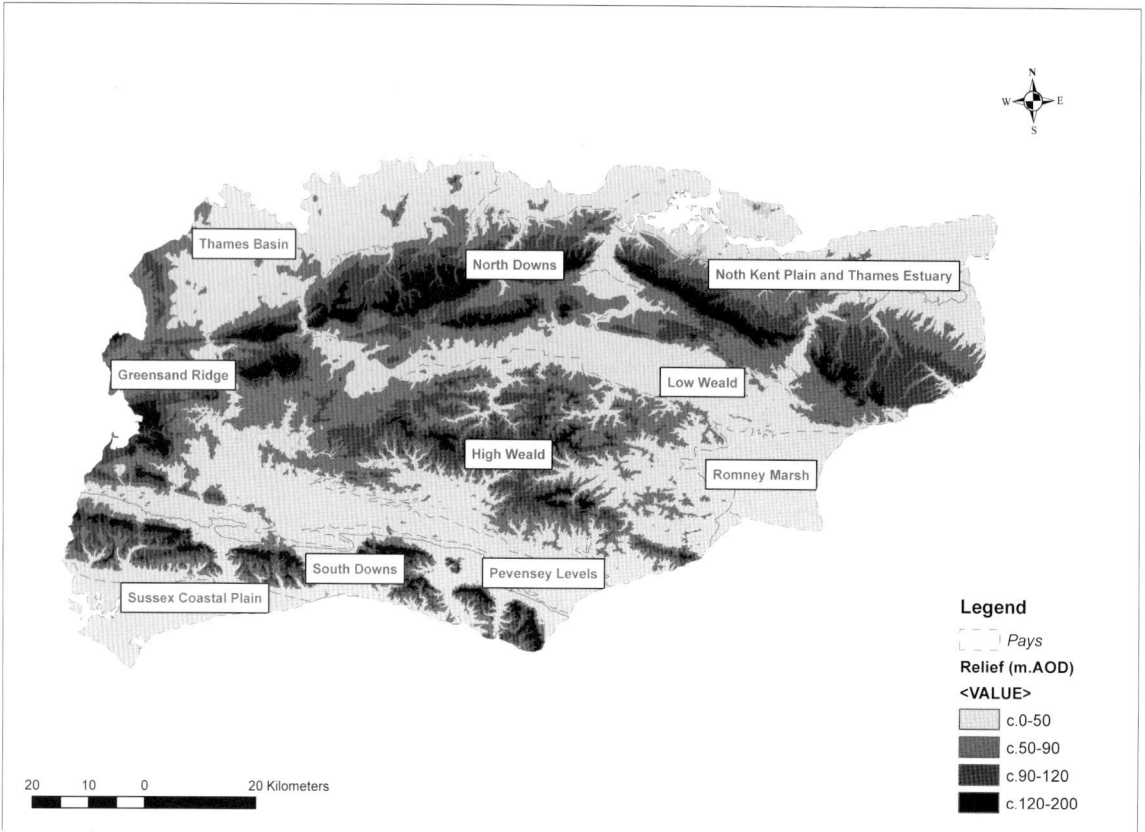

The historic formation of the study area

During the early medieval period the South-East was dominated by the two rival kingdoms of Kent and Sussex. Surrey, however, appears to have been a subordinate district, its name coming from *Sūþrīge* or the 'southern region' (Blair 1989; 1991), a probable reference to it being within the sphere of tribal groupings to the north such as the Middle Saxons of the Thames Valley. Later it would become a contested area surrounded by more powerful kingdoms such as Kent, Essex and Mercia, finally being absorbed into Wessex during the early 9th century. In contrast to Surrey, Kent emerged as one of the most powerful early Anglo-Saxon kingdoms, a status no doubt encouraged by its proximity to the continent and reflected in the rich grave goods of its many excavated cemeteries. These sites have produced distinctive early Anglo-Saxon or so-called Jutish material culture, artefacts which have strengthened traditional perceptions of a widespread replacement of the South-East's native British population with Germanic incomers. This view of discontinuity is also corroborated by the region's place-name evidence. In Sussex there was an almost complete replacement of British place-names (*P.N.Sx* 1929, xvi) and in Surrey surviving 'Celtic' elements are limited to a

FIGURE 1.2: The South-East, showing major topographical zones as well as *pay* boundaries (drawn by the author. Contains material covered by © Crown copyright and database rights 2019 Ordnance Survey, Educational Service Provider licence number v2.1)

few rivers such as the Wey and Mole (previously known as the *Emene*), as well as a small number of settlement names (*P.N.Sr* 1934, xvii–xviii). The traditional explanation for this change was based largely upon problematic documentary sources such as *The Anglo-Saxon Chronicle* which for Sussex tells of the early creation of the kingdom and the destruction of a surviving Romano-British population by a Germanic war band led by Aelle (first king of the South Saxons).

Current perceptions of post-Roman Britain include both an influx of Germanic migrants and survival of a so-called native Romano-British population. Scientific approaches tend to favour the idea of an English settlement characterised as much by acculturation as migration with the majority of the population comprised of indigenous Britons (Higham and Ryan 2013, 105). Recent studies have shown how there may have been some continuity in the landscape of post-Roman Britain (Rippon, Smart and Pears 2015), something also attested in the field and enclosure boundaries, if not the settlement of the Sussex Weald (Margetts 2018a; 2018b). Certainly, within the wider region archaeological evidence appears to suggest that the distribution of settlement changed little from the end of the Roman period until the 7th and 8th centuries, at least in the fertile lowlands of eastern Kent, southern Sussex and the Thames Valley. This emerging picture of continuity, or rather partial continuity, may be reflected in the name of King Aethelwalh of the South Saxons, the element *walh* suggesting some British connection (Drewett, Rudling and Gardiner 1988, 265). Aethelwalh existed at a time when Sussex was most likely divided between two or more kings as well as distinctive folk groups such as the *Hæstingas* (*P.N.Sx* 1929, xxiv).

Despite sporadic wars, and Offa of Mercia's final subjugation of the kingdoms of Kent and Sussex in the late 700s, the 7th to 9th centuries were a time of relative prosperity and population growth. The population expansion, facilitated in part by the intensification of agriculture and increasing socio-political organisation, is most evident in an apparent advance in settlement within the Weald. It is thought that by the 11th century the area had become thoroughly, though sparsely, settled (Drewett, Rudling and Gardiner 1988, 291), largely as a result of the break-up of large estates and the parcelling out of land. This evolution of Wealden settlement has often been portrayed as a battle between frontier colonisers and unforgiving dense woodland with its unproductive and heavy soils (Loyn 1962, 69, 343), with the region's centre – the High Weald – occupied only during later centuries (Witney 1976; Brandon 1978). This diffusionist view has been challenged by Gardiner, who noted the lack of evidence and regarded the expansion of Late Anglo-Saxon settlement not as a physical movement into new territory but as an increasing density of population and the uptake of previously unoccupied land (Drewett, Rudling and Gardiner 1988, 291; Gardiner 1995b).

Following the Norman Conquest, Anglo-Saxon estate structures were subject to changes in both tenurial and administrative organisation. William granted the land previously held by English nobles such as the Godwins to his own followers, and this fragmentation of Anglo-Saxon power was institutionalised in post-Conquest Sussex by the division of the county into five rapes, each of which had its own lord and sheriff (Salzman 1935, 352). These linear administrative districts were very likely based on pre-Conquest examples, similar to early strip-like territories know as lathes that existed in Kent and perhaps Surrey (Drewett, Rudling and Gardiner 1988, 278; Brooks 1989, 67–84; Blair 1991, 12–24). Their adoption, albeit in modified form, in the Norman administration of the South-East may be indicative of the persistence of earlier methods of land tenure and usage. Indeed, it is thought that the boundaries between the counties of Kent, Sussex and Surrey as they existed at Domesday were largely a reflection of the earlier kingdoms and the territory of Surrey as they were in the 7th or 8th century (Gardiner 1997a, fig. 2; Figure 1.3). This said, place-name evidence and the Domesday folios suggest some fluidity between the boundaries within wooded district on the Surrey–Sussex border (Lloyd 1962, 364; Chatwin and Gardiner 2005, 35) and it is likely that the county boundary was only strictly defined within a few decades of 1086 (Lloyd 1962, 364).

Until the demographic reversals of the 14th century, the subsequent later medieval period (AD 1066–1350) was a time of continued agrarian innovation and demographic growth. Within the South-East this was manifest in the increased reclamation of coastal marshes, the pushing up of cultivation onto the thin soils of the downland (which in places such as Bullock Down had not been ploughed since the 6th or 7th century: Bell 1983) and, perhaps most notably, the assarting and permanent settlement of the central Weald. Beyond the areas already occupied this resulted in the previously mentioned clearance and cultivation but also in enclosure of former areas of waste and land still utilised as manorial *denn* (see section 1.1). New peasant, freeholder and higher-status holdings sprang up and the period also witnessed the creation of further monastic estates, lordly deer parks and moated sites.

The transect study area

As well as the wider study area outlined above it was also necessary to introduce a nested transect study area. This was done with the objective of creating a more intensively examined part of the South-East, facilitating analysis of aspects of the landscape (such as roads and enclosures; Chapters 5 and 6) that would not be achievable at the regional level. The transect study area was defined between the Thames and the English Channel with the aim of encompassing as many of the *pays* of the South-East as possible (Plate 1.3). Whilst portions of the majority (seven of the ten *pays*) were included, there were by necessity several omissions. These included the North Kent Plain and Thames Estuary, Romney Marsh and the Pevensey Levels. The drawbacks of these omissions are perhaps limited when it is considered that the coastal marshes as depicted on 19th-century mapping (one of the primary datasets utilised by this work) owe much of their character to the historic landscapes of post-medieval reclamation rather than the 5th to

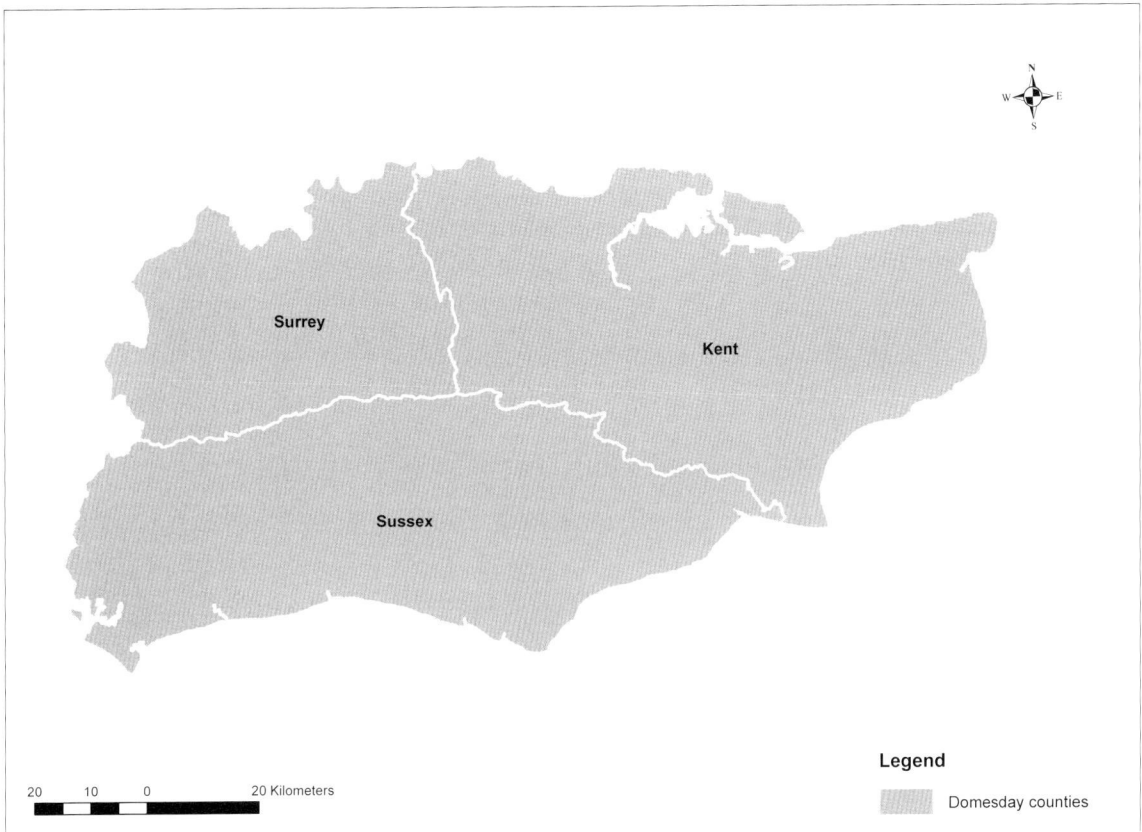

FIGURE 1.3: The county
boundaries of the
South-East at Domesday
(AD 1086) recreated
in reference to the
Domesday Geography
and Phillimore
Domesday (after Darby
and Campbell 1962;
Morris 1975; 1976; 1983;
drawn by the author)

mid-15th centuries with which we are concerned here. Some of this investigation will also be based at the county (Chapter 3) or *pay* level (Chapter 7).

1.3 Scope of the project and organisation of the book

To complete this study, it is necessary to explore the cattle economy from a landscape perspective, as it is only through a holistic interdisciplinary approach that such a complex economy can be adequately understood. In order to highlight cattle establishments as well as remaining aspects of the economy, it is necessary to undertake a cohesive multi-disciplinary approach utilising diverse sources. Within modern landscape archaeology it has been consistently highlighted that this is the most advantageous method for studying a region and it is the intention of the author that this research should include historical work, discussion of place-name evidence, historic landscape analysis, study of bone assemblages and the incorporation of excavation results and field survey. In this manner, the vast majority of available evidence for the cattle economy will be considered and brought together to provide the first critical evaluation of its importance within the South-East. Furthermore, this approach will be the first of its kind at a national level. Whilst earlier works have focused on one or two of these aspects in detail (*e.g.* Biddick 1989; Fox 2012) this book will give equal weight to all elements potentially related to cattle husbandry.

This work makes use of the most modern aids to interpreting historic landscapes, such as LiDAR and GIS, but will also require application of more traditional methods of analysing historic place (such as toponymic and documentary evidence). The approach will be based around investigation of the physical structure of the historic landscape as depicted on 19th-century maps (including tithe maps and the OS 1st Edition), which provides a framework within which to integrate a wide variety of other resources. These will be drawn together within an ArcGIS format in order to analyse multiple aspects of the historic landscape holistically and at a landscape scale.

As a key element of the cattle economy, vaccaries were essentially a later medieval innovation tied to the agricultural revolution of the High Middle Ages; however, they may have grown out of early medieval or even older livestock establishments. In order to examine earlier elements of the cattle-related landscape as well as contemporary methods of husbandry, the utilisation of toponymic evidence will greatly enhance the rather meagre early medieval documentary sources. The study of place-names remains an important contributor to historic landscape analysis (Rippon 2004, 28) and use of toponymy is key to this study, place-names often acting as indicators of past farming practices (Gelling 1984).

Place-names are particularly helpful in highlighting areas in which early medieval seasonal pasturing and transhumance occurred. These methods of exploitation have been studied around the country and have included scholarly work by Fox on Dartmoor (2012) and the Wolds (2000), Herring in Cornwall (1996; 2012) Gardiner in the Irish uplands (2012a), Winchester in the north of England (2000; 2012), Rippon in wetlands (2000) and Everitt in the Weald (1986). In relation to the cattle economy, transhumance often involved the practice of summering. The work consisted of dairying on open pastures populated by small hut-like settlements sometimes known as shielings (see section 2.5). The herds grazed on these pastures would have comprised cows and their calves, whereas open pasturing of young steers and oxen may have taken place in alternative areas and have been a male preserve (rather than the female associations ascribed to dairying; Fox 2012, 155). These seasonal forms of exploitation in areas of so-called secondary settlement sometimes evolved into more permanent patterns (*e.g.* Margetts 2017; 2018a).

The settlements that developed in both the early and later medieval period included farmsteads and areas utilised for pasture, each of which were often defined by various types of enclosure. These could occur in both landscapes commonly thought of as marginal, which in the South-East include the Weald, Romney Marsh and the Pevensey Levels, as well as more habitable zones where arable agriculture was widespread, such as the Sussex Coastal Plain or parts of north-east Kent. Categories of enclosure in remote and pastoral areas comprise seasonal pastures or permanent farmsteads as well as smaller stock enclosures or temporary pounds. Within arable zones the primary concern was to prevent cattle from straying. Animals could be pastured on the fallows, within open fields, separated by a temporary barrier from precious crops beyond. They were kept in small peasant holdings or crofts, as well as closes within hedged field-scapes.

In order for herds to reach pasture the medieval cattle economy relied on a network of droveways and tracks. The need to move animals between grazing or to market was as true for the later medieval period, when seasonal pasturing was much more restricted geographically, as it was for the period of early medieval transhumance when cattle could be moved 15 to 20 km or more in search of summer grazings. A systematic analysis of the South-East's historic road system has the potential to illuminate landscapes utilised for seasonal and specialised pasture. If droveway destinations could be identified within a routeway dataset, this would facilitate analysis of territorial links between grazing lands and their home settlements. In addition, investigation of routeways and commons has the potential to highlight the areas within the South-East which were utilised as a pastoral resource. These are the landscapes in which specialised elements of the cattle economy could be expected and it is postulated that these would have included landscapes designated as medieval Forest and Chase. The existence of agisted cattle on Ashdown Forest is recorded in a survey of 1273 (TNA SC 12/15/46) and their prevalence is also recorded in the end of the 13th century when 2,000–3,000 cattle were grazed (Penn 1984, 115). This was at a time when sheep were completely excluded from the Forest (Brian Short, pers. comm.) and specialised vaccaries were developing on its fringes (Margetts 2017). Further elements of enclosure tied to the cattle economy are medieval parks. These are often wrongly assumed to have functioned solely as hunting preserves of the medieval elite. In fact, such areas were frequently considered as an important pastoral resource. Following payment of an agistment fee (a payment made in exchange for the permission to take cattle to graze), manorial tenants could sometimes graze their animals alongside those of the lord within the park bounds. The *pale* would have therefore functioned not only as an important barrier for keeping deer in, but also herds of livestock pastured on the launds and woodlands/wood-pasture of the parkland landscape.

The most tangible evidence of cattle as individuals is provided by bone assemblages made available through excavation. This study explores some of the largest and most up-to-date medieval bone assemblages from the South-East including data produced from both urban (*e.g.* Swift in prep.) and rural (*e.g.* Stevenson 2013b) contexts as well as high-status and lowly peasant sites. Care will also be given to analyse assemblages from all the various *pays* of the South-East, although within some of these areas bone preservation is poor and data may not be available.

It has already been signalled above that incorporation of excavation results and field survey will be an important part of this work. The amalgamation of excavated evidence with other strands of inquiry will create a holistic approach. Apart from the bone assemblages it is also important to analyse the archaeological and landscape features relating to sites concerned with the cattle economy. Where relevant, the excavation reports of others will be utilised in this regard; however, it is also the intention of the author to provide details of his own research papers as case studies to aid understanding of the cattle economy. Two studies are proposed, *The Hayworth* and *The Wickhurst*. These include excavation results detailed within a *Medieval Archaeology* article (Margetts 2017) and a multi-period monograph (Margetts 2018a). This material will be incorporated within the narrative as a précis. The work will begin with a historiography of the medieval cattle economy and a review of current understanding of related medieval landscape research (Chapter 2).

This will provide context and further highlight the book's place in current scholarly approaches to studying medieval agriculture and settlement. This will be followed by the main body of results (Chapters 3–8), which will be organised with their own methodology sections. This is required as the interdisciplinary approach necessitates tailored attempts at how to tackle the particular sources being examined. The results will commence with an indicative thematic exploration of historical and documentary evidence (Chapter 3) based at a county level but drawing on evidence from the remainder of the study area and further afield. A study of place-names will be utilised in Chapter 4 to highlight locations in which cattle farming was undertaken as well as the types of pasture or enclosure that may have been related to their husbandry. Such work is essential for providing a framework for understanding the nature of the early medieval countryside (Jones and Hooke 2012, 36). Chapter 5 will explore roads, commons, Forest and Chase, whilst Chapters 6 and 7 will investigate oval enclosures, medieval parks and so-called valley entrenchments (a distinctive form of small, often rectilinear, embanked enclosure). Bone assemblages from the various *pays* of the South-East will be analysed in Chapter 8. Chapter 9 will detail the case studies based on the author's previous fieldwork, which will be followed by a wide-ranging discussion (Chapter 10) and a short conclusion (Chapter 11).

CHAPTER 2

Related medieval landscape research

2.1 Introduction

> A stranger coming into a wold one evening in the seventh century or the eighth would have entered a wood-pasture … a landscape dominated by those two types of land use rather than by ploughland. He would have seen clumps of wood casting long shadows over the great open spaces and, everywhere on the pastures, domestic animals of all kinds. Now people come into view, the keepers of those animals returning to their summer dwellings as night closed in. (Fox 2000, 51)

In Fox's imaginings of pastoral life within the wolds during the early medieval period we can glimpse aspects of the landscape that were fundamental to contemporary grazing regimes. Elements of the countryside, such as wood-pasture, open grassland and summer habitations, are features of the historic landscape that continue to be studied. The interdisciplinary nature of this book builds upon a body of former research from diverse elements of medieval scholarship and agrarian history (see section 1.3). Though at its core (Chapters 3–8) this work includes discussion of specific elements of related research (*e.g.* place-names and the study of historic roads) the chapter below attempts to review work from the broader field of landscape study. This has been undertaken to provide an appraisal of current understanding of cattle's role in creating historic landscapes, as well as their place within the medieval economy and settlement development more generally. While a historiography of certain categories of research (*e.g.* investigation into marginal landscapes) is examined, effort has also been made to provide a focused and critical study of past work on specialised vaccaries. The chapter concludes with an evaluation of where this study may fit within national and more local research agendas.

2.2 The history of research into the medieval landscape

It would be Hoskins, following publication of *The Making of the English Landscape* (1955), who could perhaps be considered as the father of modern landscape history. His work marked a move away from the simple descriptive texts of early topographic writers discussed by Darby (1954) and put the countryside itself forward as a historical resource. Though some of his interpretations can now be classed as outdated, the work remains an early innovation through its interdisciplinary approach, combining documentary sources with the evidence contained within maps, standing buildings and other components of the landscape as it survives today (what we now call the historic landscape). Hoskins would go on to inspire the Leicester School of landscape historians, authors such as Fox, Thirsk and, most importantly in the context of the South-East, Everitt. As highly important as the Leicester School's work has been, it has lacked application of archaeological evidence. Though such work occasionally utilised archaeology in an illustrative manner, it was certainly not at the forefront of the approach. Since the discipline of landscape archaeology (see below) emerged to complement these historic methods the theories of landscape historians have begun to be tested.

Another important advance in the 1950s was Darby's *Domesday Geography* series (*e.g.* Darby and Campbell 1962; Darby 1977). This significant study set out to map and reconstruct the geographical information contained within Domesday Book. It utilised the historical data contained within William the Conqueror's great survey to attempt to illustrate the local variations in the countryside and the economy. The works provide an early glimpse of distinctive districts, and they remain an invaluable resource for both archaeologists and historians interested in Domesday and regionality. Despite its importance this series of studies is not without problems, not least that Domesday was not a uniform record across England, as each area had its own peculiarities differing from the next in terms of what was recorded. In the South-East, for instance, there was no record of livestock, apart from the number of pigs paid as an annual rent for the right of pasturage, a factor that has obvious consequences as to how we view the pastoral economy. Other elements of Domesday do, however, have the ability to shed light on this aspect of 11th-century agriculture, such as the distribution of pasture, woodland and meadow.

It was not until the 1970s, with a growing interest in deserted medieval villages and the implementation of large-scale systematic field surveys, such as Wade-Martins' (1980) survey of the Launditch Hundred in Norfolk, and Shennan's (1985) East Hampshire survey, that landscape archaeology really started to emerge as a concept (Rippon 2008, 7–8). Aston and Rowley (1974), with the publication of *Landscape Archaeology*, first attempted to merge the discipline of landscape history with archaeology. This was in order to understand cultural landscapes and move away from a narrow site-based view of archaeology. The study of medieval landscapes has gradually increased from the 1970s until the present day. This occurred in tandem with the realisation that, in order to undertake the most effective research possible, multi-disciplinary work encompassing many methodologies was desirable.

By the 1990s the post-processual approach to landscape archaeology had become dominant. With an emphasis on social agency and the implementation of techniques such as phenomenology, scholars including Johnson (2007) began to reject the role environmental influences had on the formation of cultural landscapes as well as perceived materialist interpretations of the past. Such trends have not been without challenge (see Fleming 2006) and currently environmental influences on landscape character are once again being considered (*e.g.* Williamson 2013). Alongside the post-processual emphasis, former medieval landscape research has suffered from a 'Midland-centric' bias with landscapes characterised by nucleated settlements (villages) and vast open fields (Rippon 2008; and see Partida, Hall and Foard 2013 and Williamson 2013 for a continuation of this trend). In recent years there has been a movement towards redressing this imbalance by examining areas outside of Roberts and Wrathmell's 'Central Province' (2000; see section 2.4; *e.g.* Fox 2012; Winchester 2000).

Prior to these more recent attempts at studying landscape there was often a tendency to examine the development of the countryside in a way that was defined by rather arbitrary modern administrative boundaries. Hoskins' influence, and his particular interest in Devon, led to an approach that was concerned with the study of individual counties (*e.g.* Sussex: Brandon 1974). These works could be argued to be parochial or even sentimental in approach and they often suffer from divisions that strike across more distinctive culturally or environmentally cohesive areas. Also constrained by boundaries imposed by administration, investigations of parishes have often been undertaken. While these benefit from the detailed application of fieldwork and/or documentary evidence (*e.g.* Shapwick: Gerrard and Aston 2007) so that a defined local area can be more fully understood, they are often hampered by the fact that the areas being examined are not typical of the wider landscape (Rippon 2012, 8). As the subjects of landscape archaeology and history developed, scholars started studying the landscape at different scales. Though it can be claimed that more geographically restricted studies provide the building blocks that allow wider-ranging evaluations of variation in historic landscape character, region- or *pays*-based studies aid understanding of cultural landscapes with distinctive physical characteristics (*e.g.* Everitt 1986; Brandon 1998; Rippon 2012). This book, with its regional focus, perhaps fits within the latter category and it is hoped that a detailed study of the cattle economy will aid future thematic studies and contribute to mapped datasets that characterise modern landscape research (see Rippon 2008, 26–27).

2.3 Medieval agricultural history

Investigation into any aspect of the agricultural economy of the medieval period will obviously be significantly influenced by historical work. Though medieval landscape archaeology was slow to emerge as a discipline, medieval history, including that of agrarian history, has been established for some time. The British Agricultural History Society was formed in 1953 in response to a growing awareness of the economic importance of agriculture, stimulated by efforts to feed the British population during the two world wars (Thirsk 2002, 156). The society was created in order to encourage the study of agricultural history, rural society and the landscape of Britain and Ireland. It has regularly published its annual journal, *Agricultural History Review*, and continues to provide an important avenue for discussion and research into medieval rural life.

An early founder of the society was Trow-Smith, who not long after its formation published the significant work *A History of British Livestock Husbandry to 1700* (1957). Though aspects of this volume are now out of date, it remains highly significant for our understanding of medieval techniques of livestock husbandry. A further criticism of the work would be the over-emphasis placed on the management of sheep as opposed to cattle, a factor influenced by the use of sources preoccupied with the medieval trade in wool.

The enlivened interest in British agricultural history brought about by creation of the society would be harnessed by Finberg and Thirsk in order to produce the highly influential works that comprise the *Agrarian History of England and Wales*. The medieval coverage in the series (Finberg 1972a; Hallam 1988a; Miller 1991) extends from the end of the Roman period to the Early Modern era and the volumes provide a deep history of agrarian regions based on documentary evidence, the evidence of Domesday and local studies. Though, like most historical works, the volumes could be criticised for a lack of application of archaeological data, the medieval volumes are successful in conveying the distinctiveness of Britain's farming regions. This was largely thanks to the energies of Thirsk, whose interest in the regionalisation of agriculture was initially applied to the early post-medieval period (Thirsk 1987) but these ideas have subsequently been influential in the field of medieval landscape study (*e.g.* Rippon, Smart and Pears 2015). In formulating her ideas on regionalisation, Thirsk (2002, 160) has acknowledged the importance of Tupling's book on *The Economic History of Rossendale* (1927), which is also significant for the study of medieval cattle husbandry (see section 2.6).

Perhaps the most valuable work on British agricultural history of more recent times has been Campbell's *English Seigniorial Agriculture: 1250–1450* (2000). This weighty volume draws on the evidence of manorial accounts and *inquisitiones post mortem* to analyse in detail the farming practices used on both ecclesiastical and lay demesne farms, including animal husbandry regimes. Regional variation is again apparent within this volume but it suffers due to the huge levels of detail presented in tables and is a somewhat difficult book to use.

2.4 Far from the madding crowd: medieval 'marginal lands'

Certain methods of exploitation explored within this book, such as seasonal pastoralism and transhumance, are a particular feature of so-called marginal landscapes, which themselves comprise an important facet of modern landscape research. Medieval Britain can in part be said to have comprised areas of land that to modern sensibilities seem unsuited to settlement and farming. Such a view had an impact on how landscape researchers understood medieval colonisation and land-use. Postan (1972) saw such areas as marginal mainly in a physical sense. Landscapes that suffered from poor soils, legal and administrative restrictions and a geographical distance from areas of denser settlement (*ibid.*, 19) were thought to be colonised relatively late and only at times of population pressure. This rather disparaging view was influenced by Ricardian economics (Svensson and Gardiner 2009, 22), including *The Law of Diminishing Returns*, and can be said to have had a major influence on the study of medieval rural landscapes up until the 1990s. This view began to be redressed following the publication of Bailey's *A Marginal Economy* (1982). This work suggested alternative ways of viewing marginal landscapes and in particular brought their 'resource potential' (Rippon 2000) to the fore. Previously, scholars had focused too heavily on the arable prospects of regions without considering non-agricultural employment such as industry or indeed the pastoral economy. It must be remembered that areas often considered marginal, in fact often comprised huge reserves of pasture (whether grassland, saltmarsh or wood-pasture), useful for areas where this resource was restricted (which in the South-East included eastern Surrey between the Thames and the Weald and parts of the Sussex Coastal Plain: Campbell 2000, 111). Indeed, 'in over 40 per cent of southern England there was only half as much pasturage, by value, as there was demesne arable' (*ibid.*).

Svensson and Gardiner (2009) have highlighted that marginality has been confused with a geographical distance from the social and economic core. To them, marginality was not a spatial concept but a 'social and cultural idea', dependent on the judgement of individuals within medieval society and those who viewed their contemporaries as living 'unusual lifestyles' outside of the mainstream (*ibid.*, 21). As a relative principle it is perhaps important to treat the term flexibly, for the concept is still invaluable to our understanding of medieval rural settlement and land-use. Poor soils and a lack of cultivation did not mean that regions were economically underdeveloped. So-called marginal landscapes could provide alternative resources and the potential for specialised 'alternative agriculture' (Thirsk 1997). An example of the latter can be provided by Williamson's (2007) study of medieval rabbit warrens, which has shown how relatively poor agricultural landscapes could provide foodstuffs that at one time were considered a high-status commodity.

Areas such as upland and woodland, which in the past were considered marginal, are often (but not always) characterised by a dispersed settlement pattern. These landscapes are regarded as being comprised of scattered isolated farmsteads rather than the nucleated villages of the Midlands model. In the past the latter have been the subject of far more scholarly attention. These works have often been located within Roberts and Wrathmell's 'Central Province' (2000). These authors' attempts at mapping settlement patterns was based on analysis of 19th-century cartographic evidence and succeeded in showing that the Central Province was surrounded by areas that display a much more dispersed nature to their settlement pattern (the 'Northern and Western Province' and the 'South-Eastern Province'). A glance at the mapping of their dataset (*ibid.*, 8, fig. 3; Figure 2.1) shows that areas that are often perceived as marginal (Dartmoor and Exmoor, for example) are sited beyond the Central Province and show extremely low densities of both nucleation and dispersion. They could potentially be

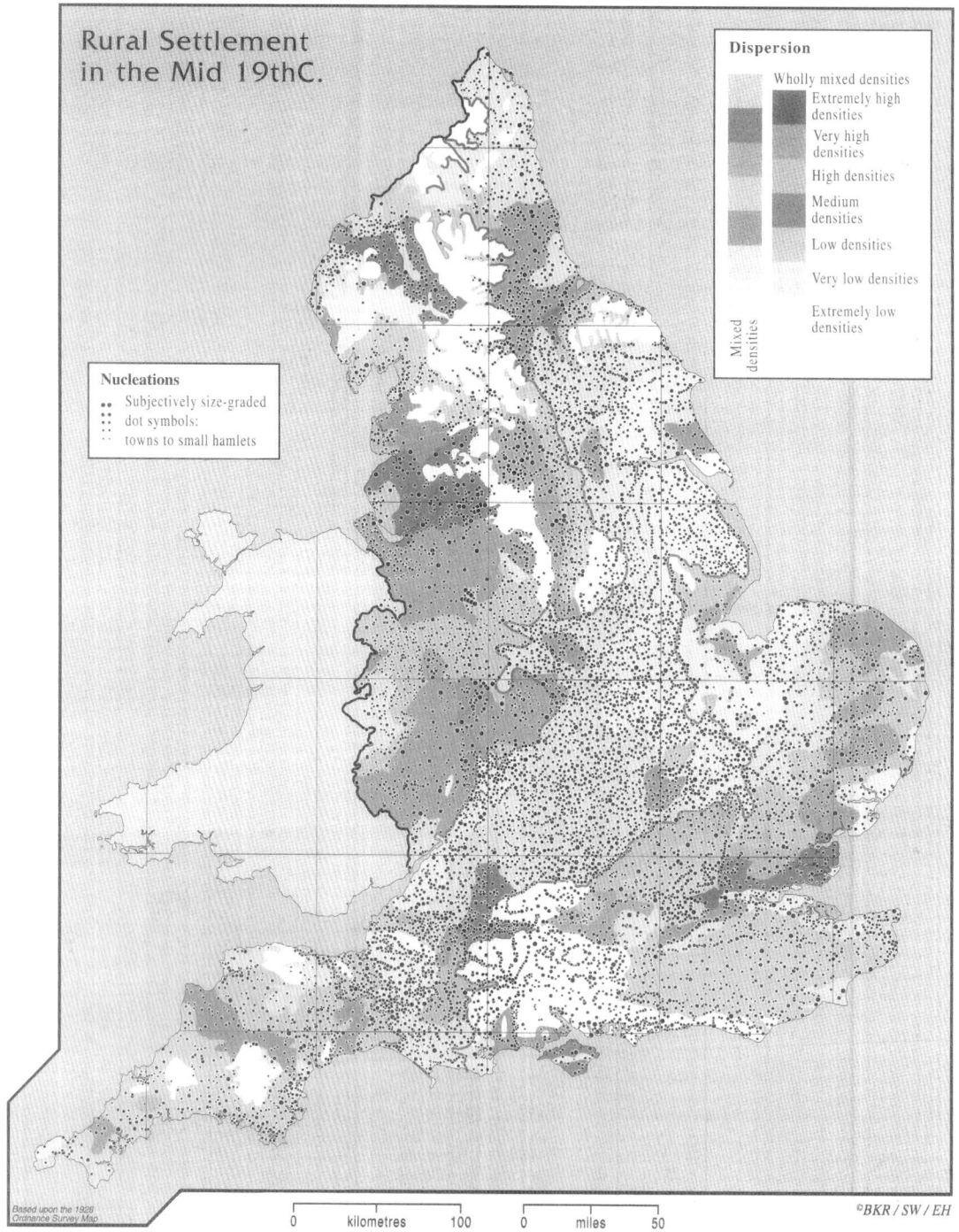

FIGURE 2.1: Rural settlement in the mid-19th century showing variation in settlement character across England (source: Roberts and Wrathmell 2000, fig. 3; reproduced courtesy of Stuart Wrathmell and Brian Roberts)

perceived as relatively unsettled and of little agricultural value. Other marginal areas, such as the Weald, can be characterised by scattered nucleation and high densities of dispersion, thus indicating a settlement pattern based on isolated farms. The need for an understanding of the settlement history of areas that display such patterns has been steadily growing in momentum over the years and this work relies on knowledge of the various settlement components that contributed to their formation. Through the study of differing settlement types (including pastoral settlements) that went into creating cultural landscapes we may gain knowledge of the subtle intricacies that brought about such patterns.

2.5 Specialised settlements

Over the years authors have sought to highlight the presence of specialised settlements that were thought to have been a product of so-called 'multiple' or 'federative estates' (Jones 1961; 1979). This concept, linked to the system of outliers or detachments, relies on the exploitation of various ecological zones or resources by the implantation of specialised settlements. These could then distribute some of the resultant products within the estate. Operation of these 'outstations' could help manage risk by diversifying resources across contrasting environmental zones (Ward 1997). An alternative view could be that such specialisation would perhaps lead to a reliance on markets where interdependence on other, specialised parts of the manor or estate either failed or never existed.

In the 'federative estate' model, the vast majority of the specialist settlements were involved in some form of agriculture (albeit often seasonal). A class of these specialised seasonal settlements are known as shielings. These constituted the summertime habitations of grazers whilst they pastured their livestock on the commons. The shelters themselves comprised huts, or groups of huts, usually within upland contexts; however, similar classes of settlement are known from wetland and woodland zones (*e.g.* Barber and Priestley-Bell 2008, 65–66; James 2015; Margetts 2018a). Though the term is most often applied to the seasonal settlements of northern Britain (*e.g.* Ramm, McDowell and Mercer 1970; Winchester 2000, 90–93), they have their equivalent in the *hafods/havos* of Wales and Cornwall (Miller 1967; Davies 1985; Herring 1996; 2012) and the booley huts of Ireland (Gardiner 2008). Place-names of the South-East include elements of Old and Middle English that have equivalent or similar meanings to the Scandinavian words (*sǽtr, erg, skali/shele*) that denote these summer pastures or temporary settlements. The Old English elements *(ge)sell* ('a shed, a shelter for animals, a herdsman's hut') and *scydd/scedd* ('a hovel, a shed, a pig-sty') are reasonably common in both Kent and Sussex (*P.N.E.* 1956b, 117–18, 115; Chapter 4) and indicate similar seasonal exploitation (linked with transhumance) of wooded landscapes.

One of the earliest references to shielings comes from the antiquary William Camden, who in 1599 described transhumance in operation in Carlisle:

All over the Wastes (as they call them,) as well as in Gillesland, you would think you see the ancient Nomades; a Martial sort of people that from April to August, lie in little Hutts (which they call Sheales and Shealings) here and there among their several Flocks. (Camden 1722, 1079; Ramm *et.al.* 1970, 1)

Though as an activity shieling clearly continued into the post-medieval period, it is thought to have originated in the early medieval period or before.

Since the time of Camden there have been many studies of transhumance and this type of specialised seasonal settlement that accompanied it (*e.g.* Rathbone 2009; Fox 2012; Herring 2012). The system essentially provided a means of utilising marginal pastures while alleviating pressure on grazing land close to the home settlements. Though much scholarly attention has been applied to the largely upland phenomenon of these summer settlements, it is clear that equivalent sites existed within the lowland zone. Perhaps the most obvious examples are the *denns* of the Weald of South-East England, where swine but also cattle were grazed (Everitt 1986). The use of these pastures appears to have largely been a product of the 10th and 11th centuries and was well past its peak by the 1200s when exploitation for pannage went into major decline. Whilst scholarship concerning these Wealden pastures, and their equivalent, the '*falods*' of Sussex, has been largely focused on the study of swine pasturing (*e.g.* Du Boulay 1961; Turner and Briggs 2016), it is also apparent that cattle were taken to Wealden pasture in the summer months (Everitt 1986). Indeed, it has been speculated during an in-depth local study by Turner (1997, 10) that use of the Wealden commons could have originated as cattle shieling grounds rather than the pig pastures for which the Weald is more famous.

By the later medieval period, lords and ecclesiastical establishments began to attempt to increase the efficiency and output of their seigneurial and monastic estates by attempting greater specialisation. Pastoral producers made the most of environmental and circumstantial advantages, and concentrated upon what they produced best. In this manner they maximised not only their own output but also that of the agricultural system as a whole (Campbell 2000, 14). The product of this specialisation were the great sheep and cattle ranches, the *beccaria* and *vaccaria* recognisable in contemporary documentation. They essentially comprised outlying centres of pastoral production, which aided the maximisation of estate resources. Beccary sites, or sheepcotes, have been investigated in a seminal paper by Dyer (1995). His exploration marked a departure from the rather disparaging views of medieval agriculture that existed until the early 1980s (see section 2.4) and succeeded in showing the levels of investment and the careful husbandry that occurred during the period. The sites were revealed to be characterised by complexes of enclosures and buildings, including long narrow examples interpreted as sheepcotes used for shelter, storage, as a source of manure and as centres for the management of sheep-farming. Their use changed in the late medieval period with the decline of the great estates and the rise of leasehold farms. 'They were the only settlements in some upland areas, and even then only in certain seasons, but [they] can be seen as representing a phase of upland land use different from that prevailing both before and after the Middle Ages' (Dyer 1995, 162).

Despite the historical focus on the species, the archaeology of sheep farming has been little studied in the South-East, perhaps in part due to difficulties in recognising archaeological elements linked to their husbandry. During the period much of the South Downs was covered in open sheep-walk and, whilst specialised sheepcotes or *beccaria* undoubtedly existed (such as the sheepcote of the Earl of Arundel at Preston or the sheepfold (*bergeria*) in Bishopstone: *Chi Chart* 1942, 35, 41), no detailed study of these specialised elements of the region's livestock economy have been undertaken. In many ways these specialised sheep establishments were likely to have been similar to those of cattle, both being associated with complexes of buildings (including long examples) and enclosures (Dyer 1995, 138; Newman 2006, 125; Margetts 2017, 139–40).

Though pastoral elements were the most common feature of specialised settlements, it must be remembered that not everyone was employed directly (or even all year round) in farming practices during the medieval period. A clear example of non-agricultural settlement was that connected to salt production. Salt would have been a vital commodity in the past and could be utilised for a multitude of purposes not least as a preservative in food preparation. Following decline (or even a hiatus) of production at the start of the early medieval period the industry seems to have been re-invigorated from around the 8th century (Rippon 2000, 42–46) and would have clearly been a beneficial component of any federative estate. Salt is key to the dairy process and access to good quality (Bridbury 1955, 109) and cheap supplies would have been advantageous within any estate that also contained enterprises concerned with the manufacture of dairy produce. Indeed, the by-product of the salt industry, the salterns that still dot coastal marshes around the country, may have also had indirect benefits to dairying in acting as raised drier locations in which the process could take place as well as refuges for livestock in times of flood (Rippon 2000, 98). Within Kent, salt-pans are mentioned in connection with 24 places at Domesday, with three areas of salt-making discernible. These are Romney Marsh, the former Wantsum Channel and the North Kent Marshes (Darby and Campbell 1962, 539).

The myriad forms of industry that existed in the medieval period (see Blair and Ramsey 1991; Zell 1994) were in part composed of rurally sited occupations that required a settlement of some kind, be it seasonal or permanent. Quarrying, iron-working, mining, glassmaking, potting, turf-cutting, charcoal burning and woodland management are just some of the industrial activities that occurred in marginal landscapes.

An additional category of specialised non-agricultural site that is not often discussed in the context of the medieval settlement pattern is the high-status establishment linked to medieval hunting. Medieval parks were often a feature of marginal wooded landscapes, although they could also be found in prime agricultural areas (Liddiard 2007). The establishments incorporated what could be referred to as settlements in the form of hunting lodges as well as ancillary sites such as kennels. Parks could also exist within a royal Forest or baronial Chase (Langton and Jones 2010) and should be considered within the context of any settlement analysis connected to marginal or pastoral landscapes. While the beneficial relationships arising from implementation of (often seasonal) specialised non-agricultural settlements are well recognised, the potential conflicts that could occur within such a system have received less attention. The struggle between those grazing herds in areas of 'royal' Forest also utilised for the preservation of game is well represented in contemporary documents but the loss of pasture to industries such as mining and turf-cutting is also worthy of consideration (Fox 2012, 101–02). The competition to exploit resources in marginal lands created harmony in society as well as tension, but the dominant grouping (at least in terms of prevalence) could be seen as those engaged in pastoralism.

2.6 Cattle husbandry and vaccaries

As mentioned in Chapter 1, the only areas to receive in-depth investigation of large-scale medieval cattle husbandry have thus far been the north of England (Winchester 2003; 2010) and Dartmoor (Fox 2012). Fox's publication of *Alluring Uplands* (*ibid.*) comprises a posthumous but highly influential work showing the importance of seasonal pastoralism and transhumance. These methods of exploitation effectively tied a marginal upland landscape to the surrounding lowlands. This work was also successful in tracing the movement from early medieval 'personal' to later medieval 'impersonal' transhumance, as well as highlighting the importance of place-names indicating summer dairying (*butere* and *smeoru*) and seasonal settlement. Fox's work is of further relevance to this study due to his identification of Sir John Cary's demesne farm at Northlew (*ibid.*, 218–19). This establishment clearly acted as a vaccary, a little-studied category of specialised medieval cattle ranch.

Vaccaries are largely viewed as a 12th- and 13th-century feature of marginal upland areas and they have to date been mainly encountered in parts of Wales, Cumbria, Yorkshire and Lancashire (Tupling 1927; Atkin 1985; Winchester 2000; 2010; Kissock 2001). Nevertheless, Fox's (2012, 218–19) example cited above complements work by Biddick (1989, 16, fig. 3) on the estate of Peterborough Abbey, which showed the presence of specialised breeding herds and a vaccary at Oxney. These instances, and an example excavated by the author (Margetts 2017), demonstrate that vaccaries exist beyond the traditional northern heartlands and in lowland as well as upland zones.

Vaccaries were part of the lord's Forest demesne, whether or not they were (or were still) farmed directly for his benefit (Winchester 2010). The cattle were run on areas that comprised two major landscape elements, an enclosed plot of wood and/or meadow and an expanse of open grazing. The enclosures, which seem to be the defining landscape features of a vaccary (Winchester 2000, 69, 115), had at least one stock funnel or driftway allowing the herd to move between the site and nearby open pasture (Newman 2006, 124–25). Several farm buildings were clustered together within the enclosure's interior (*ibid.*, 124) and these included a dwelling for the cow-keeper (*vaccarii*) and his family, the cow-house (*vaccaria*), and possibly (as in the case of the Gatesgarth vaccary, Buttermere) a house for hay and calves (Winchester 2003, 114).

Further details of these enclosure systems have been illustrated through important landscape research in Lancashire. This has shown that vaccary establishments can be characterised by a landscape form of 'double-oval' (Atkin 1993). These comprised two large, often adjacent enclosures, each up-to half a mile across. Their bounds are frequently defined by footpaths or lanes as well as large banks, ditches or streams. The double-oval consisted of a larger pastoral unit with stock funnels leading onto upland with a smaller oval that contained field divisions intended for arable, pasture and convertible land (Atkin 1985, 173–175). It is clear that the ovals acted as self-contained units (Atkin 1993) and they seem to have been deliberately sited so that a watercourse runs through their centre.

The requirement of vaccaries to be sited near expanses of open grazing led to a distribution close to royal Forest or baronial Chase. They are often located in side valleys (Newman 2006, 124) and appear to be associated with areas of dispersed settlement (Atkin 1985), ones that had a cultural history of seasonal exploitation. Indeed, historic records associated with some vaccaries show a gradual transition from a pasture in the Forest to a fully functioning *vaccaria* (Winchester 2010, 115). Vaccaries have been viewed as an element in the pastoral usage of the Weald from early medieval times (Everitt 1986) and manors such as Shere Vachery (Malden 1911) on the Surrey–Sussex border and Chelwood Vachery (Ashdown Forest, East Sussex) (Brandon 2003; Chapters 4 and 6) provide recognised but little-studied instances of medieval cattle ranches in both a Low and High Wealden context.

The recent discovery of a vaccary site, *The Hayworth*, part of the manor of Trubwick (Haywards Heath, West Sussex; Margetts 2017; Chapter 9), represents the first archaeologically excavated vaccary site within the South-East as well as the most extensively excavated example nationally. Remains encountered at the site facilitated not only the investigation of the nature and workings of this type of manorial cattle ranch, but also exploration of the transition from a seasonal pasture utilised in common to a permanent 12th-century establishment held in severalty. Interpretation of the site was hampered through a lack of bone survival, although painstaking documentary research together with landscape analysis showed that particular enclosures could be ascribed vaccary functions and status on the fulfilment of a number of criteria. The excavation of the site has fuelled an interest not just in this specialised form of livestock establishment, but also the wider cattle economy in which they were a component. Further sites of this type will be sought within the South-East region and the role of vaccaries will be assessed within the context of settlement development and landscape formation.

Fox (2012, 228), in his monograph concerning medieval pastoral management on Dartmoor, called for further comparable work to be undertaken elsewhere and the importance of livestock and in particular cattle to the understanding of landscapes more generally has been highlighted as an area for further research (Evans and Yarwood 1995; Sellick and Yarwood 2013). The appreciation that vaccaries are recognisable within the South-East's landscape is perhaps a new theme (Margetts 2017) and this book hopes to address the need for a wider-ranging survey to aid their recognition. Such establishments may be seen as a seigniorial imposition on the landscape but their subsequent leasing in areas such as Cumbria also led to the creation of new peasant communities (Winchester 1987). The study of these demesne, or formerly demesne, pastures can therefore aid knowledge of the complex interplay between differing social groups or hierarchies. This is especially important given that vaccaries were often located near to, or within, areas of royal Forest or baronial Chase (Winchester 2010). The benefits and conflicts that may arise between lords or their tenants by having specialised livestock concerns located near to areas also utilised for the preservation of game are many and varied but need to be understood.

Cattle rearing or dairying may provide the South-East's most archaeologically recognisable form of organised animal husbandry. Medieval cattle required shelter in the winter, protection from the wolf, and networks of droveways and stock funnels to move them between pasture. Pig rearing, by contrast, was connected to the practice of pannage and often comprised the turning out of domestic animals on areas of Forest, Chase and common. As such, the livestock were relatively free to roam and, apart from possible remains of the attendant swine-herds dwellings, or toponymic evidence of where such activities were centred (*i.e.* the *stye* place names of the central Weald) (*P.N.Sx* 1929; 1930; Brandon and Short 1990), such an economy would have conceivably left little archaeological trace.

2.7 Landscape research within the South-East

While there is a long record of medieval archaeology and landscape history in the different counties that make up the region, there have been few scholarly syntheses of research into the South-East during the medieval period. Gardiner's contribution within *The South-East to AD 1000* (Drewett, Rudling and Gardiner 1988), his chapter within *Medieval Rural Settlement* (2012b), together with Brandon and Short's (1990) work on the medieval historic environment, currently remain the most recent and wide-ranging analyses of the medieval period of the region. In addition to these, a regional landscape history for the South-East has been undertaken by Short (2006) as part of a set of volumes published by English Heritage intended to provide a national, standardised series. These books have received some degree of criticism, although this is in no way the fault of the individual authors. Taylor (2007) has rightly perceived English Heritage's attempt, while admirable, as fundamentally flawed in its definition of regions. The South-East, for instance, includes southern Essex, extends as far west as Dorset and incorporates London, which could probably have been included elsewhere, or even had a volume of its own. While this study area is understandable, especially in the light of Roberts and Wrathmell's 'South-Eastern Province' (2000), it will be rejected here in favour of the more traditional, county-based definition of the region outlined above (section 1.2) and followed by the majority of scholars.

More successful in defining study area are Brandon's works on the North (2005) and South Downs (1998) and the Weald (2003). These *pay*-focused studies, while not encompassing the region as a whole, transcend the convenience of administrative boundaries to individually examine these more culturally and physically distinct areas. Combined, the texts go some way to examining the character of the South-East's historic landscape in the vein of Hoskins and the Leicester School of landscape historians (see section 2.2). While this has many benefits (an engaging narrative, for example) it does not place archaeology at the forefront and can suffer in the eyes of some scholars as being regarded old-fashioned.

At a county level, Kent-focused scholarship has been influential in the study of medieval settlement at both a regional and national scale. This is in part due to a relative wealth in surviving medieval documents but is also due to the completion of some major works of historical geography. The earliest of these can be ascribed to Jolliffe, whose publication of *Pre-Feudal England: The Jutes* (1933) was highly important in the investigation of early medieval royal estates. Though his study was a product of its time and thus included interpretations of the past that were heavily influenced by race and ethnicity, it introduced a concept that has been fundamental to the study of medieval settlement of the region – that is, the antiquity of the Kentish lathes. These administrative territories developed out of early royal centres or *villae regales* and are paralleled in the rapes of Sussex (Gardiner 1988, 278). Despite apparent failings within his work (such as disregard for contrary evidence), Jolliffe's scholarship would go on to inspire authors whose focus was more strongly in the landscape rather than historic social institutions that had interested him. His ideas were developed by Witney in *The Jutish Forest* (1976), a work that possessed a far stronger landscape element, enabling effective investigation of Kentish *denns* (detached pastures usually associated with swine, see section 2.5).

Perhaps the single most important study for the understanding of medieval settlement in the South-East is Alan Everitt's *Continuity and Colonization* (1986). Within this book Everitt proposes that Kent can be divided between landscapes of 'continuity' in more habitable areas (such as Holmesdale and the Foothills) and 'colonisation' in less favourable zones (such as the Weald and Kentish Marshes). A member of the Leicester School of landscape historians,

Everitt would utilise the concept of *pays* to thoroughly investigate the landscape history of the county and the evolution of its settlement. Though he could be criticised for using archaeology only in an illustrative manner, the study remains an important piece of landscape history.

Brandon could perhaps be considered the county of Sussex's foremost landscape scholar. His work would begin with a Ph.D. thesis on the Sussex Commons and Wastes (1963) followed by a study of arable farming on the Coastal Plain (1971). It would be his later material, however, that defined him as an author. The publication of *The Sussex Landscape* (1974) was clearly influenced by Hoskins and the Leicester School and he would follow this success as editor of the volume *The South Saxons* (1978). This book would bring together writers on many aspects of early medieval Sussex, and although some of the contributions are now out of date the work remains an interesting and engaging attempt at examining an early medieval kingdom. Brandon (1998; 2003; 2005) also produced *pay*-based works, although these have been discussed in more detail above.

Also highly significant in the study of the historic landscape of Sussex, and the medieval South-East more generally, has been Gardiner. His Ph.D., *Medieval Settlement and Society in the Eastern Sussex Weald before 1420* (1995b), essentially showed the complex economic, environmental and social processes at work in the development of Wealden settlement. Though it built on the work of earlier writers such as Jolliffe, the thesis challenged some of past scholarship's more simplistic theories on how the Weald came to be occupied. Prior to completing this Ph.D. he had already developed a significant body of commercial archaeological work together with a number of other Sussex-based landscape studies. As well as his contributions to an *Historical Atlas of Sussex* (1999b) and regional syntheses (1988; 2012b) discussed above, he has also completed studies of economy and landscape on both a county-wide and more restricted scale (1984; 2003; 2011).

For Surrey, important works have been undertaken by Blair, the earliest of which comprised an essay on the Anglo-Saxon origins of the county (1989), and the second was largely a work of landscape history based on his D.Phil. thesis (1991). The latter could be considered as the definitive county-based study of its type, in the same way as Everitt's (1986) work was for Kent and Brandon's (1974) for Sussex. Within *Early Medieval Surrey; Landholding, Church and Settlement* (1991), Blair convincingly showed that the hundredal geography of the county was based on older territorial units or *regios* that revolved around the Weald. He also analysed linear earthworks such as the *fullingadic* and related these to territorial disputes between the early medieval kingdoms. Like Sussex (*P.N.Sx* 1929; 1930), Surrey benefits from the production of a definitive English Place-Name Society volume (*P.N.Sr* 1934). The existence of these volumes is especially welcome when it is considered that no such comparable work has been undertaken for the county of Kent (see Chapter 4).

2.8 Conclusion

This review has shown that both nationally and within the South-East there has been a growing interest in the study of pastoral landscapes, particularly those that occurred in less settled districts beyond more habitable zones. As was shown in Chapter 1, the region of the South-East is defined by contrasts. Although this statement may have become a cliché in landscape archaeology, the differing nature of the various *pays*, geologies and topographies has never been lost on the region's scholars. The fact that subtle differences in the natural environment have had major influences on medieval settlement evolution and land-use has never really fallen from favour as it has done elsewhere (for example, see Johnson 2007), a fact that reveals the fundamental influence these variables have had on the region's landscape evolution.

The concepts of marginality and dispersion have been considered as these are the areas in which we may expect vaccaries to have existed. Regions that are, or were, perceived as marginal have been shown to incorporate specialised non-agricultural settlements that would have existed alongside any pastoral economy. Studies beyond the Central Province are still required, especially in a pastoral context, and whilst some have been undertaken (*e.g.* Fox 2012) these are few in number and have often been restricted to upland zones. The importance of livestock in shaping cultural landscapes is beginning to be better recognised and it is hoped this study will aid understanding of the complex but traceable imprint that medieval cattle husbandry has had on our landscape.

The region has been well served by both landscape historians and archaeologists whose work has gone on to be influential in much wider spheres than this south-easterly corner of the British Isles (*e.g.* Everitt and Gardiner). It is, however, immediately clear that there has been a distinct lack of literature dealing with the medieval period of the region as a whole. County- and *pay*-based studies have been far more extensively published over the years, and while some synthetic attempts have been made, those that exist are either out of date or suffer from governmentally imposed classification of study area. This situation is desperately in need of remedying, as we have shown that the region is formed by a highly cohesive set of *pays* that are carved up in an arbitrary way by the historic counties. To really understand the region, it needs to be studied in its entirety, an approach that will be undertaken here. As well as this lack of up-to-date synthetic coverage there is also a noticeable discrepancy in the locations where archaeological fieldwork has been completed. Medieval sites have largely been excavated on the more habitable *pays* as compared to the Weald. This is due to a number of factors such as site recognition and a persistent lack of developer-funded work (see Margetts 2018a).

What is also clear is that the earlier part of the period, the phase often termed Anglo-Saxon in the South-East, has received more attention than the later medieval period. Perhaps this is due to the 'glamour' of the 5th–7th centuries, with their cemeteries and rich grave goods, that have so often shaped understanding of settlement and society in the region. Or maybe it is related to the fact that the early medieval period was one of social and agrarian innovation, a time that landscape historians and archaeologists have termed the 'long 8th century' (Hansen and Wickham 2000; Rippon 2008, 27). Whatever the reasons for this bias, the balance needs to be redressed. Work on the later medieval period should no longer be limited to the higher-status sites that have so often characterised the fieldwork of archaeologists, but should look towards the everyday rural settlements in which the great majority of the contemporary population lived. Only in this way will we understand the wider historic landscape of the South-East, how its countryside and settlements evolved.

In the past it has been shown how the study of medieval agriculture has been so dominated by arable regions. Where study of the pastoral economy has been undertaken it is overwhelmingly based on the history and archaeology of sheep husbandry, a trend that continues to this day (*e.g.* the recent publication of Rose 2018). Though within the South-East the economy of pig husbandry has also received study, the production of medieval cattle has thus far been completely neglected. This may in part be influenced by factors such as an over-reliance on primary sources (particularly Domesday) that give little clue as to the pastoral rather than arable economy (see the discussion of the Domesday Geography series in section 2.2). Whilst the practice of pig pannage is highly prominent within the historical studies of the South-East, the keeping of cattle largely slides from view, a trend noticeable in this chapter that will be more fully explored below.

CHAPTER 3

A historical and documentary perspective

....

3.1 Introduction

> Far off the pearly sheep
> Along the upland steep
> Following the shepherd from the wattled fold,
> With tinkling bell-notes falling sweet and cold
> As a stream's cadence, while a skylark sings
> High in the blue with eager, outstretched wings,
> Till the strong passion of his joy he told. (Watson, *On the Downs*, 1891)

The pastoral identity of Sussex is synonymous with the economy of sheep pasture made famous by the iconic images of the South Downs and Walland Marsh. Such a strong perception could, however, mask a pastoral heritage based on cattle traceable in the surviving documentation. To date, no systematic examination of the cattle economy of the county has ever been undertaken. This is not to say that cattle have not featured in historical analysis of the rural economy in general (Gardiner 1999, for example) or investigation of particular *pays* (see Brandon 1971), but cattle have, on the whole, been relegated to a subordinate element of the pastoral economy. In order to redress this balance and shed new light on this under-researched element of medieval South-East England, and Sussex in particular, an exploration of the medieval historical and documentary evidence was undertaken. It is not the intention of this study to provide a definitive chronological map, for such a feat would be neither practical nor possible given the irregular survival of sources and what they record. What is presented is a contextualisation of the available records within a historical narrative. This was based on themes related to the wider agendas of society, pastoralism and landscape and incorporates national evidence as well as sources from the wider study area of the South-East.

3.2 Methodology

The earliest datable written references that may be related to livestock of the South-East comprise Anglo-Saxon charters as well as the laws of Ine (*c*. AD 688–694). King of Wessex in the late 7th century, Ine enjoyed varying degrees of hegemony over the study area during his lifetime and his laws show that there was already in existence a market for livestock, as well as systems of compensation and law governing theft (*Laws of Ine* 1922, 165; Trow-Smith 1957, 48). It is the late 11th-century Domesday Survey (1086), however, which is most often analysed for information on the rural economy of pre-Conquest England, although in a south-eastern context the application of data is not without problems. Domesday makes little systematic reference to the livestock of Kent, Sussex and Surrey apart from plough oxen and swine pannage. This fact was not lost on Darby (1962, 555–56), but this renders his important work, *The Domesday Geography of South-East England*, of limited use to this study (see section 2.2). It is not until the later medieval period, and the associated increase of documentary records in the 13th and 14th centuries, therefore, that we can really hope to gain an adequate picture of the cattle economy.

Cattle farming in Sussex, as elsewhere, was based on a number of key components such as dairying, meat production and plough teams. Analysis of these components within an historical and documentary context will provide further avenues for exploring the wider nature of cattle husbandry in the medieval period. Key themes such as the location of specific activities, who was farming cattle, what the methods of husbandry were and the nature of the issues facing the medieval herdsman will be explored.

As well as a generally unsystematic search of key secondary sources, it was determined that an orderly examination of the National Archives catalogue would be undertaken to highlight sources related to cattle. This was followed by analysis of the Sussex Record Society volumes, in particular the 'Accounts of the Cellarers of Battle Abbey' (*Cell. Batt.* 1967), various custumals (*Cust. Chi.* 1925; *Cust. Cant.* 1958; *Cust. Lau.* 1961), cartularies (*Chi. Chart.* 1942; *Box. Chart.* 1960) and court records (*Rec. Lew.* 1940). Where translations of original sources were not available, care was taken to search for Old or Middle English terms for cattle (*e.g. cū, oxa, hridra, P.N.E.* 1956a; 1956b; *cōu, kīen,* Kurath 2007). Of course, many if not all historical documents must be studied with caution and the innate bias of such records is well known. It should be noted that the exploration attempted here is indicative and not exhaustive.

3.3 Pasture

The grazing and type of pasture available to the medieval husbandman suited particular aspects of the economy more than others. An exploration of the pastoral resources of Sussex, their particular benefits, disadvantages and functions, is in part achievable through examination of the documentary evidence. Wetlands were utilised for their rich grass and saltmarsh vegetation and in arable areas fallows, stubbles and leguminous crops could be grazed at certain times of the year. While some parts of Sussex were characterised by open grassland or by enclosed fields devoted to grazing, the most extensive pastoral resource comprised wood-pasture. The use of wood-pasture has in the past been most often associated with the pannage of swine (Du Boulay 1961; Jørgensen 2013a); however, the importance of the practice has sometimes been called into question and other livestock species, including cattle, were also present within these environments (Hooke 1989, 117; Rackham 2003, 62). Although wooded commons decreased in size and importance though the medieval period, they remained an abundant, though much reduced, type of grazing land into the 18th century (Brandon 2003). By this time these assets had become much maligned by the agricultural improvers of the day (see Marshall 1798).

The mutual benefits between the arable and cattle economies of Sussex is fully explored below; however, so-called open-fields were also a contributor to the pastoral resource. Situated on the Gault Clay and Lower Greensand, Ringmer, or rather the number of small settlements that make up the parish, are noted for their open-field systems (Brandon and Short 1990, 60) and the fallows of these fields presumably formed the pasture for peasant oxen and cows mentioned during the mid-14th century at Ashton (ESRO GLY/1175; GLY/1181; GLY/1182). That some strip fields or furlongs were devoted to cattle pasture within these systems is clear from a feoffment dated AD 1356 where a land parcel named 'longacre' provided feeding (*pasturam*) for six peasant cattle (ESRO GLY/1175).

That primarily arable areas made these provisions for the cattle economy is also visible in the landscape of the Coastal Plain. By 1300 the demesnes of this part of Sussex were largely cultivated in severalty, although they were not always separated by a physical barrier from the common fields of the servile tenantry (Brandon 1971, 121). Where the demesne open-fields were enclosed this was often by way of a ditch, although hedgerows (*rewes*) were also an important component of land division and these formed a useful resource to the medieval tenant, for they were often planted with trees to afford grazing for their cattle (*ibid.*, 122).

Settlement of marshland landscapes often originated as detached, seasonal settlement (Everitt 1986, 66; Rippon 2000), and Sussex, being coastal, was reasonably well endowed with such areas in the form of Winchelsea Marsh, the Pevensey Levels (Plate 3.1) and numerous estuarine coastal wetlands. That such pasture was highly prized for its grazing is shown in Walter of Henley's Treatises where it is stated that two cows fed on saltmarsh would yield the same (a wey of cheese and half a gallon of butter) as three cows fed on wood-pasture, stubbles or meadow after it had been cut (Oschinsky 1971, 332–5). The worth of marsh as dairy grazing was also encouraged by the proximity of the salt industry, the produce of which was necessary for making butter and cheese (Rippon 2000, 42). The value of marshland for dairying occasionally meant that land was chosen to be left un-reclaimed (*ibid.*, 203).

That the potential of marshland was realised by the people of Sussex is apparent in the documentary records of the later medieval period. Mention is made of marshland pasture belonging to the manor of Leasam (probably in the vicinity of Leasam Wood) near Rye. The manor held 24 cows and a bull in AD 1418 (ESRO amsg/AMS5592/99), a herd sufficient for a dairy establishment exploiting pasturage on the marshes perhaps on a seasonal basis. The monks of Battle Abbey also exploited the grazing benefits of marshland for the Cellarers' Rolls of the mid-14th-century record oxen, heifers and cows kept at Dengemarsh (*Cell. Batt.* 1967, 54). The full stock list provided in an account of the manor of Denge in 1356–57 lists 20 horses, 96 cattle, 178 sheep and 39 swine (Mark Gardiner, pers. comm.).

After marshland and wood-pasture (see below) the third most important feature of the early medieval agrarian landscape was the *feld*. This comprised land free from trees that was utilised as common pasture, characterised by rough grassland and sometimes used by multiple settlements (Finberg 1972, 406). In Sussex the *feld* was scattered across the county (Dodgson 1978, 62) but could be said to be mainly found on the Greensand Ridge and the lighter soils of the Weald. It is highly probable that cattle were pastured in these communal acreages from an early date. By post-Conquest times pastures were still used in common by all the settlements of a hundred, but it is not until the areas of *feld* had been subjected to the advances of the plough that the word acquired the sense of unenclosed land held in common for cultivation (Finberg 1972, 406).

During the later medieval period, common grassland pastures were still utilised for cattle and often such land was in a semi-upland context. It seems that grassland pasture specifically for cattle was provided for the people of Eastbourne and was located on the hill of Grovedown that was part of the common of '*Medese*' (Meads?). Rights to pasture two bullocks and a cow were granted in AD 1333 (ESRO SAS-CP/11/1/266) and one and a third oxen and one cow in AD 1363 (ESRO SAS-CP/11/1/267). In addition, pasture for a cow was also granted at Southdown, which was also part of the wider common (*ibid.*). That these downland pastures were used for cattle (and in Grovedown's case probably for them only) in an area that would usually be considered sheep country is illustrative of the lack of attention cattle have received in the context of pastoralism of the South Downs (Plate 3.2).

Meadow provided an additional grassland resource that figures in medieval documentary evidence from the earlier part of the period. At this time it is distinguished by the term *prata* from pasture known as *pascua*. The meadows were mown for their valuable hay crop, which provided what was often only a portion of the required winter fodder. Subsequent to the mowing of the hay the aftermath provided additional grazing for cattle (Finberg 1972, 406–07). By the time of Domesday, meadow was still in relatively short supply and even small acreages were often of considerable value. The hay produced on these meadows has been judged as vital to the maintenance of a healthy plough team as well as other animals on the manor (Harvey 1988, 122). Meadow retained its importance into the medieval period and exchange of parcels between lords and commoners often features in the records of Sussex in the 14th century (ESRO GLY/1181; GLY/1182; GLY/1189; RYE/136/35). The value of meadow meant that its ownership was often in dispute, as records from 12th century Battle show:

> Robert of Icklesham and his mother Matilda seized a meadow that lay within the boundary of the manor. They attempted to carry off the hay by force, but the abbot had been warned and, gathering a number of men, met force with force. (Searle 1980, 219)

The role of wood-pasture and the rights and customs attached to it were of fundamental influence to the evolution of settlement in Kent (Everitt 1986) and the wider South-East. Although pastoral exploitation of the woodland resource is often investigated through the pannage of swine, wood-pasture for cattle also played an important role in the early agrarian economy (Witney 1990, 25). Tracing this economy using solely documentary evidence is, however, extremely difficult. Kent has received more attention than Sussex and it is here that woodland cattle pasture is mentioned in a number of pre-Conquest documents. In AD 805 Cuthred King of Kent granted *hridra leah*, or the cattle glades, near Petham in the Buckholt forest to the Archbishop of Canterbury (Sawyer 40; *Cart. Sax.* 1885, 450–51) and in AD 724 Minster was granted a right to pasture in Blean, Buckholt and Oxney ('the ox enclosure') (Sawyer 1180; *Cart Sax* 1885, 206–07; Witney 1990, 26). These examples are a rarity and the importance of wood-pasture for cattle has usually relied on other forms of evidence (such as place-names) rather than purely documentary investigation (Figure 3.1).

Through a multidisciplinary approach Everitt (1986) was able to show that woodland vaccaries together with open sheep walks were distinguishing characteristics of the Kentish downland both up to and after the Norman Conquest (Witney 1990, 25–26). No subsequent work on the wood-pasture vaccaries of Kent has thus far been undertaken and the cattle economy of Sussex has been even more neglected. This is strange as, apart from the need to secure a water supply, the nature of downland woods makes them well suited to cattle pasture. Oak was less prevalent here than in the Weald and the woodland was comprised of a wider range of species. Acorns are known to be harmful to cattle, and even during summer oak woods were best avoided (Everitt 1986, 163; Witney 1990, 26). That the wooded western downs of Sussex were also utilised for cattle is clear from two late 12th-century documents. The earlier of these concerns infringements of wood-pasture and herbage rights at Slindon (CCA-DCc-ChAnt/S/354) while the later concerns a grant by the Bishop of Chichester of pasture rights for 12 oxen belonging to the 'men of *la Wudecota*' in '*Godiuawuda*' (Goodwood) (*Box. Chart.* 1960, 21).

By the 13th century, coppice with standards had become a prevalent land-use in both the downland and the Weald where it came to replace the less profitable use as pannage (Witney 1990). Cattle were pastured in these woodlands as soon as the stools of the trees had regrown to height beyond which they could browse. The cattle would only be removed when the herbage of the woodland floor was shaded out by the canopy. They would then be transferred to a compartment that had been more recently cut. This form of husbandry required a woodbank and ditch of four feet in width as well as a thick live hedge to act as an efficient fence (Brandon 2003, 53–54). Perhaps population pressure and its resultant increased demand for wood as well as conversion of large areas of the Weald for coppice facilitated wider cattle pasturing than had previously been attempted. Could more glades have existed as a result of increased clearance and could regular coppice cutting have decreased the amount of acorn mast, creating a more favourable environment for the animals? Unfortunately, as is the case with Sussex wood-pasture for cattle in general, the documents are largely silent.

An exception to this rule is the evidence for cattle keeping in the wood-pasture environments of parks and forests. Both are now recognised for their use as livestock grazing grounds (Liddiard 2007; Winchester 2010; Plate 3.3) and this is visible in the documentary records for Sussex, which are rich with accounts of such activities. The medieval parks of Sussex were mainly located on the poorer soils of the Weald and western downs (Gardiner 1999, 38–39) where animals, including cattle, upon payment of an agistment fee, could be pastured outside of the fence-month (Brandon 2003, 77). This was the case at Henfield Park where both the lord and others could take advantage of the available grazing as long as there was enough pasture left for the deer (*Cust. Chi.* 1925, 123). Pasture in parks could also be granted by way of a right, as is attested by Bartholomew de Ellested's provision for seven oxen of the monks of Boxgrove Priory (*Box. Chart.* 1960, 93) and Richard de Wych, Bishop of Chichester's for 12 beasts for monks in the park of Cuckfield (*Chi. Chart.*

FIGURE 3.1: A remnant of wood-pasture. The Sun Oak, St Leonard's Forest near Horsham, West Sussex. See Fleming (2012) for a discussion of how veteran trees such as this can provide clues to the presence of vanished medieval wood-pasture (source: the author)

1942, 57). As well as woods, the parks of Sussex were also amply provided with *launds*, which comprised open grassed areas with trees. At Henfield Park there were 80 acres of pasture at '*la Westlaund*' and 15 acres, full of bracken, called '*la Estlaund*' (*Cust. Chi.* 1925, 123).

An intriguing late 13th-century record from the manor of Willingdon (*Cust. Lau.* 1961, 30–31), near Eastbourne, mentions the imparkment of what must have been a huge head of cattle, for it comprised those of the lord of the manor and the tenants of the whole hundreds of Willingdon and Eastbourne. This custom, known as *lep*, was presided over by the reeve and beadle of the manor at any time between Michaelmas and Martinmas. Each tenant had to pay 1d. for each beast, whereas the beasts of the lord were exempt. This custom was said to be worth sometimes 10s. and sometimes half a mark, perhaps indicating a gathering well in excess of 80–120 cattle. The custom may have been an old one as it had been neglected by the time of its recording and it is also possible that the cattle being gathered were being seasonally grazed perhaps in

relation to dairying. The anonymous writer of *Hosebonderie* records the period between Michaelmas and Martinmas as the time in which to make cows cheese (Oschinsky 1971, 430–31); however, it is unclear whether the cattle were being gathered in a park or some other form of enclosure.

Royal Forests and baronial Chase have been investigated as areas used for livestock pasture as well as for hunting and other activities. Forests such as Dartmoor (Fox 2012) and Skipton (Winchester 2010) have been recognised as agistment grounds, areas of seasonal grazing and landscapes where specialised cattle establishments or vaccaries were located. In Sussex, Forests and Chases were located within the Weald, and on the South Downs and in these areas of the South-East, as in other areas that have received more attention, cattle were pastured. Cattle were evidently located in St Leonard's Forest in the 13th century as tithes of calves and cheese were mentioned in 1247 (Hudson 1987, 26). The existence of agisted cattle on Ashdown Forest is also recorded by way of a survey dating to 1273 (TNA SC 12/15/46); the prevalence of these animals is noted at the end of the 13th century when 2,000–3,000 cattle were grazed (see section 1.3; Penn 1984, 115). As well as the commoners' certain ecclesiastical estates had pasture rights in Ashdown Forest, for example at the ancient enclosure of Vachery, near Chelwood Gate (Brandon 2003, 79).

3.4 Cattle and arable

Medieval pastoralism cannot be studied in complete isolation from other rural practices. Cattle often formed part of mixed farming economies and had much to lend to arable cultivation. The most obvious link between cattle and crop production is the fact that in medieval England oxen, not horses, were the dominant plough animal. Indeed, in parts of Sussex the ox was not overtaken by the horse until the early 19th century (Brandon 2003, 191). Teams of anything between one and eight oxen were harnessed to the plough, dependent on the heaviness of the particular soil. It is even possible that teams numbering above eight individuals were sometimes used. That the eight-ox team was, however, the norm is not in dispute and it is likely that teams of this size were usually recorded in Domesday (Trow-Smith 1957, 68–69).

Medieval Sussex was particularly well furnished in arable lands in the form of the brickearths of the Coastal Plain. Here the soils were both fertile and tillable and this is reflected in the high average wealth of 14th-century coastal Sussex, the prosperity of the area only exceeded by the arable districts of north and east Kent (Glasscock 1965, 66–68). This relationship between the affluence of the Coastal Plain and its soils is also visible in the Domesday records for the number of plough-teams per square mile. The better soils of the central and eastern Coastal Plain were recorded as having the largest number of plough-teams in the county, with 45 and over recorded for much of the area (Darby and Campbell 1962, 432, fig. 124; Figure 3.2).

The numbers of plough oxen kept on the coastal manors of Sussex is also noticeable throughout the later medieval documents. 'The Chartulary of the High Church of Chichester' (*Chi. Chart.* 1942) records the Bishop of Chichester's livestock on the manors that comprise his estate. Of those on the coast, Cakeham is fairly typical where livestock including 36 oxen, 24 cows and a bull were recorded, together with around 600 sheep and a small number of horses, pigs, geese and chickens (*ibid.*, 223). Oxen at Cakeham numbered 46 in 1220 (*Chi. Chart.* 1942, 61–62); these high numbers on a manor that did not even have access to the best soils in the area and which was in part characterised, like much of the Manhood Peninsula, by woodland-common (Brandon 1978, 8), may indicate that this manor was intended to supply draught oxen to the neighbouring arable.

The Coastal Plain, encouraged by good soils and access to seaborne trade, was an area of agricultural innovation in medieval England. Here, by the 13th and 14th centuries, it is certain that advanced round-course systems were adopted in preference to the orthodox three-course husbandry long used elsewhere (Brandon 1971, 129; 1988, 318). The round course was largely based on a three-year rotation of wheat, barley (or oats) and legumes (Brandon 1971, 129; 1988, 320) and, although the latter of these crops replaced the important grazing land provided by the earlier fallows, the benefits of an increased fodder crop may well have led to more intensive livestock husbandry than the earlier system had allowed.

FIGURE 3.2: Sussex: Domesday plough-teams by densities. Domesday boroughs are indicated by initials: A, Arundel; C, Chichester; H, Hastings; L, Lewes; P, Pevensey; R, Rye; S, Steyning. The southern boundary of Weald Clay is shown (source: Darby and Campbell 1962, fig 124)

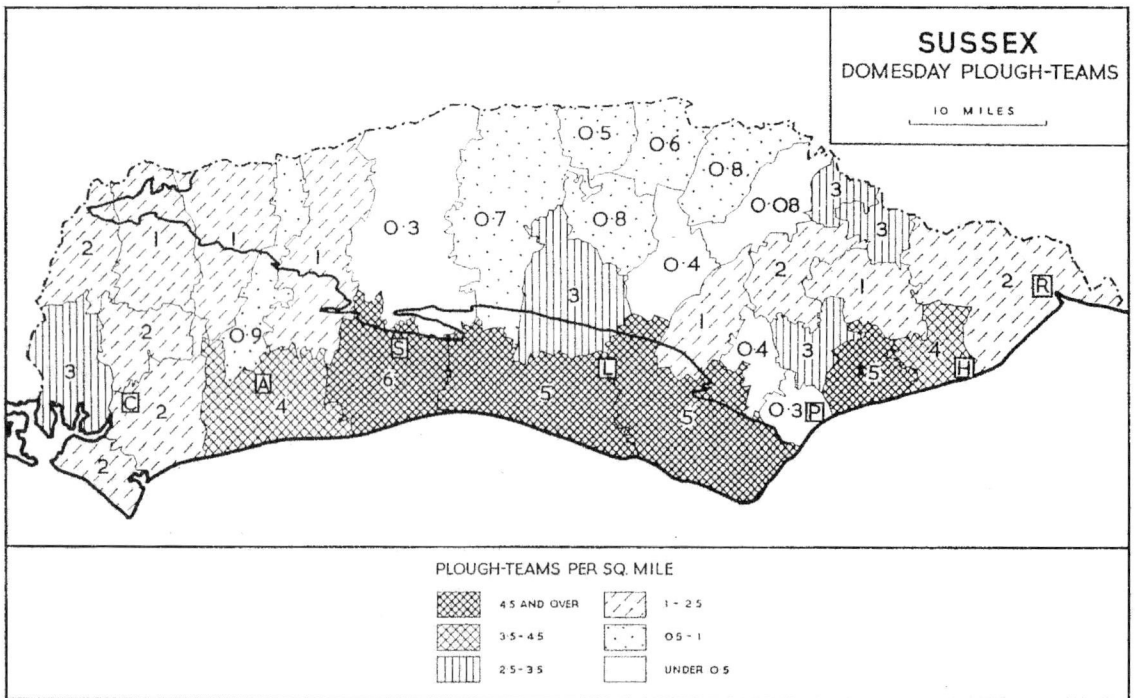

Another benefit of the growing of legumes was its use as a nitrogen giving fertiliser; this was a role it shared with the sheepfold in a method known as sheep-corn husbandry. It is often assumed that sheep provided the favoured means of manuring land not in cultivation and this is certainly backed up by the documentary evidence. Use of folded sheep as a source of dung dominates the livestock references of the 'Sussex Custumal of the Bishop of Chichester' (*Cust. Chi.* 1925). There are, however, also reasonably frequent references to cattle. Mention of oxen in arable country such as this would obviously be expected, but cows, bullocks and calves are also recorded, and manure from their cow-houses, barns and byres was utilised to rejuvenate the fertility of the land (Brandon 1988, 322).

That the role of cattle as a manure source may, at least to some degree, have been underplayed in the past is noticeable from Bosham, near Chichester in 1295/6. Here, when 126 acres were under legumes, a further 35.5 acres were manured with dung brought in from the barns by cart, 16 acres were spread with slush (ditch mud) and only an acre treated by the sheepfold (TNA SC 6/1020/23; Brandon 1971, 130). Carting dung was, as one can imagine, not always a popular business. The Estreats of the Court of Cakeham (Wednesday, 18 June 1315) records an argument as to whether certain members of the manor were obliged to cart the lord's dung with the other customers of the 'Hallmote' (*Cust. Chi.* 1925, 12).

Cattle manure was of paramount importance elsewhere in medieval Sussex. The Weald at this time was one of the most difficult places in all of Britain in which to produce an arable crop. The poor soils needed a massive input of labour and cultivation in order to grow cereals or pulses and the stiff, cold, intractable clays were exceedingly hungry, needing heavy dressings of dung to maintain fertility (Brandon 2003, 59). Apart from pigs, cattle were the dominant livestock kept on the medieval Wealden manors (Gardiner 1999, 38) and it is therefore likely that they would be looked to as the primary source of manure.

That lords maintained seigneurial dung hills (*mixen*), which were required to be added to by the tenants' livestock, is attested by the 'Custumal of Bishopstone' (*Cust. Chi.* 1925, 94). Here it is recorded that a certain William Newman was obliged to have one cow 'at the lord's *mixen*'. This rare reference suggests that medieval landholders were well aware of the necessity of maintaining adequate stockpiles of manure that were so necessary for maintenance and improvement of the soil's fertility. The importance of manure in the history of human development and social cohesion has been recognised and well argued (Jones 2009; 2012).

Thus far, the examined historical and documentary records are skewed towards seigneurial agriculture, although records do exist of the later medieval peasant and his livestock. It seems that cattle were kept not just by the bishops and lords but also by those at the lower end of the social scale. By examining the custumals of four coastal manors of the Bishop of Chichester's estate (Selsey, Cakeham, Preston and Ferring, detailed in *Cust.*

Chi. 1925), the peasants on average were allowed to pasture three beasts with those of the bishop. While most peasants were able to pasture two beasts on the manors of Selsey and Preston, certain peasants were allowed to pasture four. Peasants were also permitted to pasture their animals after grazing by the bishop's herd; the average number of beasts allowed in this case was one over the four manors.

As we have seen, the existence of a cattle economy alongside one based primarily on arable had mutually beneficial effects. Arable regimes allowed pasture on fallows as well as fairly intensive methods of husbandry based on fodder crops. In return, cattle provided the traction necessary for cultivation as well as vast quantities of manure for fertiliser. Nonetheless, cattle are regarded as playing a subsidiary role to sheep on the Coastal Plain where the latter animal provided the key role in the sheep-corn husbandry that dominated the area (Brandon 1971, 122). Documentary evidence from Domesday may, however, show that numbers of coastal plough teams often exceeded the size of the plough-lands that were available (at Barnham, for example; Darby and Campbell 1962, 431). Though it must be treated with caution as there is no consensus on the true meaning of a plough-land (see Harvey 1985; 2014, 223–26; Roffe 2007, 18, 206–07), this picture of higher quantities of cattle than may be expected is also reflected in the number of cows and bulls recorded on the Bishop of Chichester's estate for the later medieval period. Of seven Coastal Plain manors recorded in a chartulary entry for a single year (detailed in *Chi. Chart.* 1942, 223–24), cows were recorded on six. Of these an average of 18 cows were kept, with the maximum number being 24 and the minimum six, and these were always attended by a bull. It is therefore likely that breeding stations, probably intended to supply replacements for the plough teams, existed on these arable lands during the medieval period. Such a heritage may well have formed the basis for the switch to an economy that was dominated by cattle from the end of the 14th century (Brandon 1971, 134).

3.5 Dairying

Records of dairying and dairy products are widespread throughout the documentary evidence that survives for the medieval period; indeed, commodities such as cheese and butter were likely key components of the medieval diet from the early through to the later part of the period (Woolgar 2006). The traditional view, based almost entirely on documentary evidence and exemplified by Trow-Smith (1957), is that sheep were overwhelmingly favoured as a dairy animal in pre-Conquest times. Historians perceived 11th-century evidence of cattle dairying as a fairly recent phenomenon. It was thought that Domesday mentions of *vaccaria* and *wica*, such as those known from the Vale of the White Horse (Ditchfield and Page 1906, 305), were representative of a new stage of dairying in which the cow began to be seen as a viable large-scale alternative to the ewe and the she-goat (Trow-Smith 1957, 73).

More recent adoption of multidisciplinary approaches has allowed a more balanced view of early medieval dairying than documentary evidence alone could achieve (Everitt 1976; Fox 2012) and it is now thought certain that dairying based on cattle was, in localities with a history of transhumance, common: for example, the shielings of Cumbria (Winchester 1987) and summering on Dartmoor (Fox 2012). The earliest datable written references related to the dairy industry of the region may be contained in the laws of Ine. Law 38 of Ine's code declares:

> If a husband has a child by his wife and the husband dies, the mother shall have her child and rear it, and [every year] 6 shillings shall be given for its maintenance- a cow in summer and an ox in winter; the relatives shall keep the family home until the child reaches maturity. (*Laws of Ine* 1922, 48)

Summer is the traditional time of dairying and it is likely that the cow mentioned in the text was intended as a milk and dairy animal. Though such glimpses of cattle dairying are somewhat vague, slightly more concrete references are made in 9th-century charters of the period. The Anglo-Saxon charters of Sussex are largely silent concerning the dairy economy; however, early medieval documents from neighbouring Kent (which may have shared much in common with early land-uses of Sussex) are more informative. Wetlands have often been associated with dairy farming (*e.g.* Rippon 2000) and Trow-Smith (1957, 60–61) has cited the AD 858 exchange of the high yielding marshlands, including the dairy farms of the people of Wye, between Ethelbert, King of Kent, and one of his thanes, Wulflaf, as an indicator of the predominance of sheep within the dairies of pre-Conquest England (Sawyer 328).

Although references to sheep dairying may have received more attention, dairying based on cattle is not unknown. Archbishop Wulfred's high payment for a tract of marshland between Faversham Creek and Graveney (both in Kent) known as 'the king's cow-land' (Sawyer 1615; *Cart. Sax.* 1885, 485–86) may be indicative of cattle dairies in a wetland context. The charter is a conflated version of Sawyer 40 (AD 805) and Sawyer 177 (AD 814), the earlier of which refers to the purchase of an estate that included land known in Latin as '*campus armentorum*' and in English as '*hridra leah*' (Sawyer 40; *Cart. Sax.* 1885, 450–51). That *hridra* is the Old English for cattle (or oxen) has allowed Finberg (1972, 410) to hint that cattle pasturing may have been more important in the early medieval South-East than is immediately obvious.

Domesday may also indicate early medieval dairying based on cattle, although once again evidence for Sussex must be extrapolated from information we can glean for Kent. The problems associated with Domesday data are well known and perhaps the largest concern for the study of the late 11th-century dairying in the South-East is the fact that the folios described in Exchequer Domesday Book do not make any systematic reference to cattle apart from plough-teams and ploughing oxen (Darby and Campbell 1962, 555). Entries for Kent do, however, hint at Domesday-era cattle dairying. Pasture for

300 sheep and 31 cattle is recorded at Wickhambreux (Domesday 5,124) and a total of 56½ weys of cheese (*pensae caseorum*) appear in the entry for Newington (Domesday 13,1) as a due from the manor of Milton Regis (Darby 1962 556). 'Wick' place-names are known to be associated with dairying (*P.N.E.* 1956b, 260–61) and medieval dairy products could sometimes be made from a mixture of cows' and ewes' milk (Hallam 1988c, 358). The manor of Milton Regis was associated with intensive cattle dairying during the later medieval period (CCA-DCc-ChAnt/M/244A; see section 3.7 below) and it could be suggested that this late 11th-century reference to cheese may be founded on a manor that had a lasting legacy of cow keeping for the dairy.

Thus far exploration of medieval cattle dairying in Sussex has relied heavily on evidence from Kent, which is better served by the documentary record. It is not until the 13th century, with its vast increase in the available sources, that we can investigate medieval cattle dairying in Sussex with any confidence. Uplands, like wetlands, may be associated with dairying and records of cow pasturing from these landscapes may therefore indicate such activities. Of a systematic search of the sources it is immediately apparent that the eastern downs were overwhelmingly regarded (as one would expect) as sheep country. The only reference to any quantity of cows was from the Bishop of Chichester's manor of Bishopstone (*Chi. Chart.* 1942, 224), though it is more probable that this concentration is due to other reasons (see section 3.8 below).

The picture for the western downs is different. An explicit reference to dairying based on cattle was dated AD 1237 from West Dean. The document includes the important instance of tithes of cows 'consisting in milk without cheese' together with tithes of calves (*Chi. Chart.* 1942, 64). The western downs are often capped with Clay-with-Flints, the curse of the medieval ploughman. These deposits are more widespread than in the east and in part this geology led to a more wooded landscape (Brandon 1998) with a superficial geology that was capable of retaining water. These environmental factors may be of some importance, for the western downs share similarities to the North Downs of Kent, which are known to be associated with medieval cattle dairying (Everitt 1976).

The above evidence may suggest that wooded landscapes played an important part as cattle pasture. Though Witney (1990) judged wood-pasture for cattle as less nutritious than either marsh, meadow or fescue grassland, it was significant for it was more extensive (*ibid.*, 25). So should we expect later medieval dairying in that greatest of woodland resources, the Sussex Weald? Once again the custumal of the Bishop of Chichester is our most informative source (*Chi. Chart.* 1942, 223–24). Three Wealden manors are mentioned in the custumal – Drungewick, Stretham and the coastal manor of Bexhill. All three show excessive numbers of cows in comparison to manors located elsewhere. The average for the 13 recorded holdings is 20 cows, whereas Drungewick and Bexhill are known to have pastured 30 each and Stretham maintained a herd of

40 cows. What may at first appear as Wealden dairying based on wood-pasture shows on closer inspection to perhaps be more linked to the presence of fertile riverside pastures and a permanent source of water, Stretham, has access to rich pasturage on the Adur floodplain while Drungewick could take advantage of pasture in proximity to the headwaters of the River Arun. Bexhill, however, although Wealden in terms of its geology, is actually located on the coast. It is likely that the proximity of the Pevensey Levels provided the wetland dairy resource exploited by this manor.

Riverine pasture may have been of some importance elsewhere in Sussex. The Arun River Valley and its associated pasture seem to have been highly valued for the grazing of cattle. Numerous mentions of the Amberley Brooks are made in association with cattle and these extensive pastures are located just north of the South Downs within the Arun gap. One Sussex custumal for the manor of Amberley is particularly enlightening; it states:

> William Pulayn and William Ailmer hold 1 yardland and render 15d. … They two shall have in Cowbrook (*in pastura vaccarum*) 6 oxen and 2 horses, and in *Wildebrok* they shall have all their own *avers*. (*Cust. Chi.* 1925, 44)

This 'Cowbrook' was important for other members of society, too, as the *Chichester Chartulary* documents the bishop as having 24 cows and a bull in the same pasture, as well as 24 oxen in 'Oxbruke' during the summer (*Chi. Chart.* 1942, 274). A separate record for the manor of Amberley records the numbers of cattle as 20 oxen, one bull and 20 cows (*Chi. Chart.* 1942, 223). Such large numbers of cattle under ecclesiastical control surely indicate a breeding station and the likely location of a vaccary.

3.6 Meat

Beef and veal must be considered as one of the most important by-products of the cattle economy. Documentary evidence for their consumption in Sussex is, however, of a limited nature. Records for the early medieval period are virtually non-existent, but oxen's value as meat is perceptible as early as the 7th century within the documentary record, for Ine's law states:

> If a husband steals a beast and carries it into his house, and it is seized therein, he shall forfeit his share [of the household property] – his wife only being exempt, since she must obey her lord. If she dare declare, with an oath, that she has not tasted the stolen [meat], she shall retain her third of the [household] property. (*Laws of Ine* 1922, 55–57; Finberg 1972, 410)

That aged oxen were important for the table is highly probable, and, although the evidence for this practice is limited to this single regional source, records for the later medieval period confirm the continuation of the practice. John Loteby of the manor of Stretham is recorded in the Sussex custumal as being required to help drive the lord's oxen 'fatted for the house larder' to other manors on the Bishop of Chichester's estate (*Cust. Chi.* 1925, 114).

Stretham has already been discussed for its potential as a manor linked to dairying on the Adur floodplain, although this reference implies that at least some of the 20 oxen recorded in the *Chichester Chartulary* (*Chi. Chart.* 1942, 223–24) may have been specifically pastured there for rich grazing in order to create a herd of fat-stock. Documentary evidence for animals raised specifically for meat and not, as is the case for oxen, for meat after their use as working animals, is available nationally even from the early medieval period. Possible instances of stalled bullocks (*faldhriera* or *fal'd'reere*) and grazing bullocks (*feldhryer*) are sometimes mentioned within the contemporary record, although the two terms may have the same general meaning. *Fal'd'rere* has been translated as a 'beast kept in a fold', and this does not necessarily mean that they were not outdoor animals (Trow-Smith 1957, 59). The most likely explanation for the two terms is that bullocks designated *fal'd'reere* were pastured within enclosures and those termed *feldhryer* were grazing open land.

No early medieval references for such a practice has been encountered for Sussex and it is equally impossible to judge the levels of beef consumption for the period from documentary evidence alone. Where documents simply record the numbers of livestock it is impossible to say whether such sources reflect meat consumption or are rather more indicative of patterns of production (Woolgar 2006, 89). Analysis of the Domesday plough team data is potentially illustrative of this point. Holdings that record excessive numbers of oxen in comparison to plough-lands are known from Sussex and include Ditchling with 60 plough-lands with 99.5 teams, and South Malling with 50 plough-lands with 94 teams (Darby and Campbell 1962, 430, 566). Though the problems with the precise meaning of plough-lands has already been mentioned, do such places indicate beef enterprises and are they indicative of high levels of beef consumption on these manors? The only possibility for judging consumption is where specific records of larders, stores and meals are recorded.

On a national scale meat consumption prior to the Black Death was at generally low levels in the countryside even amongst the middling and wealthy peasant households. Post-1349, a different situation, with many more livestock available per capita, prevailed (Mate 1987). This was tied to a well-documented growth in the stocking of cattle and increase in the meat trade (Woolgar 2006, 90), which may in turn be linked to the increasing number of non-producers (Trow-Smith 1957, 92), growth of urbanisation and general development of a market economy. Aristocratic households were already avid meat consumers prior to the Black Death, and by the 15th century the quantities had become excessive. These families acted as leaders of culinary fashion and may have had influence over consumption in gentry and richer peasant households as well as monasteries (Woolgar 2006, 91). Evidence for beef consumption for the latter has been encountered for Sussex and is available from the *Cellarers' Rolls of Battle Abbey* (*Cell. Batt.* 1967).

The observances of different monastic orders placed varying emphasis on meat consumption. Whereas meat had come to play a significant role in the Benedictine diet in the later medieval period, the Cistercians aimed to avoid flesh (Woolgar 2006, 98). As a Benedictine Abbey, Battle was open to a central position for beef in the diet of its monks, and Searle and Ross (*Cell. Batt.* 1967, 18) who examined the Cellarers' Rolls regarded the beef consumption of the community as one befitting of the 'cattle country of the Sussex Weald'. Ten cattle carcasses valued at £4 12d. were recorded in the cellarer's office in AD 1351–52 (*Cell. Batt.* 1967, 54) and mention of both full-grown steers and yearlings being brought on as steers was recorded in AD 1407–08 (*Cell. Batt.* 1967, 99).

The early 15th-century reference mentioned above also provides evidence that calves were being consumed as veal at Battle Abbey. A single calf 'of produce', meaning that it had been raised by the Abbey's herd and not purchased from the market, 'was used in the household' (*ibid.*). By this time younger, tender meat was becoming fashionable and this was reflected in aristocratic households where some beef was drawn from stock, but increasing amounts, especially of veal, were bought fresh in the market. Where such households were recorded they often consumed one calf on most meat days (Woolgar 1992; 2006, 92). Evidence that Battle Abbey sold some of its meat produce was also encountered. The profits of the Cellarer's Office dated AD 1369–70 recorded the entrails of cattle being sold for 62s. 2d. (*Cell. Batt.* 1967, 61); such records of the marketability of offal are something that we can gain by documentary work alone.

3.7 Cattle housing

It is largely in the north of England that historical analysis of medieval cattle housing has thus far been undertaken. Documentary studies show cow-houses to have been long structures, for example at Gatesgarth vaccary (Buttermere) the cow-house built in AD 1282–83 was 67 feet (20.5 m) in length (Winchester 2003, 114). Despite the lack of scholarship, documentary evidence for vaccary buildings certainly exists in the South-East. A 'Report of Inquisition' (CCA-DCc-ChAnt/M/244A) within the Canterbury Cathedral Archives records one such Kentish example:

> Philippa of Hainault, formerly queen of England and lady of the manor of Milton Regis, and all previous lords of the manor and their tenants of the hundred of Marden should repair the house of a cow-pasture ('*vaccaria*'), called '*Cowhous*' in the manor of Milton Regis. The tenants of Marden should repair the part called '*Somerhous*' which is 18 feet wide and 48 feet long, and should make cheese, butter and dairy products for the serjeant ('*serviens*') called 'le day'. The tenants have built more than they should, 18 feet wide and 48 feet broad, because the steward compelled them … (*ibid.*)

Evidence from Sussex shows cattle housing is often only referred to when building work was required. Within the *Cellarers' Rolls of Battle Abbey* (*Cell. Batt.* 1967, 135) an account exists of the amount of timber and manpower required to build a cow-shed:

> … for 1 man hired to cut down timber at le Rette for a new cow-shed of this office, for 6 days, 3s., at 6d. Per day for salary and food. And for 3 carpenters hired to trim the timber for the said cowshed for 3 days, 4s sharing among them 16d. per day for salary and food. And for 3 wagons hired to carry the said timber from le *Rette* to the *monastry*, for 1 day, 2s 6d, namely for the wagon 10d per day. (*ibid.*)

Three wagonloads of wood cut over six days and three carpenters' work over three days must indicate a substantial and well-constructed building for the cattle of the monks of the abbey.

In West Sussex, too, we hear of William Trancheuent and John Burgays, yardlanders who were required to make and repair the barn, byre and hayloft at Amberley. This was done at their own cost but they would be aided in their endeavour by a master carpenter hired by the lord. Interestingly, and relevant to an earlier section of this study (see section 3.4 on dairying above), are provisions given to the men for their work. As well as grain and bacon the men were given '*i caseum de pis' cicestr*' or one cheese of a wey of Chichester (*Cust. Chi.* 1925, 54). Perhaps this reference is to a specific type or regionally distinctive cheese.

The references to the well-built cow-houses above are from ecclesiastical estates where such buildings may be expected; however, it is also noticeable that those lower down the later medieval social scale also provided housing for livestock. William Newman, whose addition of a cow to the lord's dung heap was mentioned previously (see section 3.4 above), owned a croft 'on which he should build a byre'. When elected oxherd for the manor he was to keep the bishop's oxen 'in grazing and in byre' (*Cust. Chi.* 1925, 94). Peter Copere of the manor of Preston held four acres of land 'and a house for the byre' (*ibid.*, 85).

3.8 Losses, legality and conflict

Livestock losses were an all-too-common feature in the world of medieval husbandry. Deaths from natural causes were covered by the word *murrain*, and this term incorporated every source of loss except theft and deliberate slaughter (Trow-Smith 1957, 129). The word is perhaps most associated with diseases of medieval livestock and, while little can be gleaned from the documentary evidence as to the specific pathogens (Atkin 1994, 7), what can be said is that illness among cattle was less common than in pigs and far rarer than in sheep (*ibid.*, 129). Bovine abortion seems to have been a particularly widespread problem; however, whether the cow aborted because she was too weak in late winter to carry her calf or because of brucellosis infection it is impossible to say.

Where stocking rates were heavy and where stock were herded in common sickness must have spread quickly, but outbreaks were usually local except on the few occasions where widespread epidemics of murrain are recorded (*ibid.*, 130).

Murrain could cover losses apart from disease, and wolves may have been a problem in Sussex (especially in the Weald) as they were in the Forest of Rossendale, Blackburnshire (Atkin 1994, 8). The documents do not refer to wolf attacks in Sussex but they do indicate other forms of 'accident'. Richard atte Founte is recorded as making a plea of trespass against John Hammyng in the 'Records of the Barony and Honour of the Rape of Lewes' (*Rec. Lew.* 1940, 59) due to the death of one of his cows caused by a particularly 'ill-tempered and dangerous' bull. Richard believed that John deliberately allowed it to go where Richard's cows were grazing and where the former had no rights of common; however, John pleaded that his bull was grazing in the adjacent pasture of the Lady Countess, which was not separated by either a hedge or ditch, and that he did not know or maliciously allow the bull to trespass with the other beasts.

Such disputes are relatively commonplace in manorial records but medieval pastoral life was well provided for and regulated by complex legal frameworks. Common, herbage, pasture and tithe rights are perhaps the most frequently referred to elements of pastoral legislation, but as mentioned previously evidence of agistment in parks and forests is also often found. At Maresfield, for instance, the Bishop of Chichester had the right to agistment of cattle 'both from foreigners and natives' (*Chi. Chart.* 1942, 269–70) and such payments must have been a welcome and profitable addition to the estate.

Agistment payments may have been resented by villeins attempting to pasture cattle; however, it must also be remembered that such fees allowed access to valuable additional pasture. The payment of heriot, however, must have surely been universally disliked by those at the lower end of the social scale. Heriot essentially comprised a duty paid to the lord on the death of one of his villeins, and in Sussex the heriot very often comprised the best ox or cow owned by the peasant. The customs of the manor of Loventon (dated AD 1285) are a good example of the restrictions placed on the medieval villein where livestock as well as other aspects of their life were concerned:

> if he be reeve he shall be quit of his works for labour and of his rent for wages, and he shall have in the lord's pasture with the oxen 1 horse and 3 cows, and in another pasture 50 ewes and 1 ram, and he shall have his food in harvest. And he cannot marry himself, his sons or daughters, nor sell his young colt foaled by him nor ox calved by him, without leave, and after his death the lord shall have the best ox or cow, or 5s. as a heriot if there be not one. (*Cust. Cant.* 1958, 18)

If heriots were refused by tenants the lord could seize beasts via distraint. This seizure of cattle could be utilised to compel attendance in court, payment of a debt or the rendering of a service and was obviously a profitable business for the recalcitrant party would have to pay for the animals feed and its keep within the lords close or sheriffs pound (Cam 1963, 13). Bishopstone was an important manor within the Bishop of Chichester's Sussex estate as it is also the manor to which the bishop's heriots and distrained cattle were driven:

> Roger de Haremere-shall drive the heriots to Busshopeston, and not elsewhere. And if there is need to drive distrained (cattle) to *Busshopeston* he and the *bedell*, according to his share, shall drive them, and shall carry writs to *Bysshopeston,* Robertsbridge, *Bexle* and Erlington if needed and they shall; be the couriers of the Bishop and the steward as far as *Riperefeud* if need be. Also, if there is any need of distraining at *Tyresersh* or *Rakkele* on the Bishop's fee, they shall fetch the distrained (cattle) there and drive them to *Busshopeston*. (*Cust. Chi.* 1925, 98)

It is also mentioned in 'The Chartulary of the High Church of Chichester' as being stocked with 27 oxen, 15 cows and a bull (*Chi. Chart.* 1942, 224), a herd that presumably could have incorporated heriot or distrained cattle or would have at least shared pasture with such.

The impounding of distrained cattle was a source of conflict in later medieval Sussex, for a John Cok was recorded in the court rolls of the Rape of Lewes (*Rec. Lew.* 1940, 53, 56) as having illegally recovered a bullock from the under bailiff as well as breaching the pound of the Countess during the year 1356–57. Breaking into several pastures for the purpose of grazing cattle was also a problem; Thomas Tilby and Philip atte Nalrette are named in a court case for having broken the close of the Bishop of Chichester at Wisborough (*Chi. Chart.* 1942, 258–59). Carrying swords, bows and arrows they, with horses, oxen, cows, pigs and sheep, entered '*Hodefoldeswode*' and '*Hoke*'. The animals trod down and consumed £10 worth of herbage; however, the pair claimed that they had common rights to these pastures. Though likely to have been hyperbole and not based on actual events, if Thomas and Philip's claim was just, they were not the only people of medieval Sussex to have their rights to pasture impinged on by a bishop. The rector and chaplain of the church of Slindon complained in 1176 that the Archbishop of Canterbury's servants were infringing the church's rights in wood and pasture (CCA-DCc-ChAnt/S/354).

Perhaps the most dramatic and obvious crime related to the cattle economy of the later medieval period was cattle rustling. Two brothers, Thomas and William Maufe, stole four oxen and a cow and detained them 'against the peace' at Firle (*Rec. Lew.* 1940, 30), and a rather troublesome William Winkpirie is recorded as having seized an ox whose ownership was in dispute (*Rec. Lew.* 1940, 26). This William was no stranger to the Barony Court and was a freeholder on a manor, Trubwick, which is known to be linked to cattle farming (Margetts 2017; Chapter 9). That such losses and conflicts of interest were part of the rich social aspect of the cattle economy of Sussex helps highlight the all-pervasive nature of livestock husbandry to those involved in pastoralism.

3.9 Movement

From the early medieval period and possibly before, Sussex, like much of the wider South-East, incorporated systems of transhumance and droving as a key component in the pastoral economy (Du Boulay 1961; Witney 1976; Everitt 1986; Brandon and Short 1990; Brandon 2010). The county's profusion of surviving drove roads is testament to the importance of this practice during the medieval period. Tangible indicators also remain of a parent and outlier relationship between primary settlements on the more favourable soils and subordinate, originally seasonal settlements within areas of poorer soils such as the Weald (Brandon 2010). The pannage of swine has often dominated historical accounts of the wider region's system of transhumance and in Sussex this bias is particularly acute. It is likely, however, that seasonal grazing of cattle was taking place within the early medieval Weald and western downs of Sussex as much as it was in the wooded regions of the neighbouring county of Kent (for cattle and seasonal wood-pasture in Kent, see Witney 1976; 1990; Everitt 1986).

That it was worth moving stock over 20 or 30 miles (Du Boulay 1961, 80–81; Everitt 1986, 54) is indicative of the value placed on woodland pasture (Chatwin and Gardiner 2005, 47); however, the old systems of seasonal grazing (firstly as common for the entire kingdom, later as folk-dens and later still as manorial dens) was all but over by the Norman Conquest (Witney 1976, 77). Indeed, during the 10th and 11th centuries these pastures had largely evolved into fully-fledged farms involved in cultivation as well as stock (Brandon and Short 1990, 49). During the later medieval period the ancient droveways were not, however, as one may suppose empty of the lowing of cattle for they were still utilised for the movement of livestock for reasons beyond simple drifting between pasture.

The law of distraint has already been mentioned in detail above, but it shall be revisited here for it was an important reason behind the movement of large quantities of cattle in later medieval times. Borgh of Uckfield, for example, is mentioned in the *Custumals of the Sussex Manors of the Archbishop of Canterbury* (*Cust. Cant.* 1958, 78) as being responsible for driving the distraints taken in the beadlery of Framfield to a place in the same beadlery where the driving of distraints as well as heriots is reasonably well recorded, and is also found in the Wealden areas of Wadhurst (*Cust. Cant.* 1958, 35) and Crowborough. In the latter, Borgh of Grenherst was responsible for driving the distraints entrusted to him by the beadle which had been taken from tenants between '*Gromenebregg*' (Groombridge) and '*Crouberge*' (Crowborough; *Cust. Cant.* 1958, 62).

This obligation to drive heriots and distraints seems to have been connected to the possession of '*Droflond*' for both Borgh of Grenherst and Beniot de Bukelyng (*Cust. Cant.* 1958, 35) were holders of such. These holdings probably originated as squatter settlements encroaching on the wide margins of old droves. It is probable that this obligation was some kind of levy upon those granted the right to intake land from the highway. Beniot de Bukelyng was mentioned along with two other '*Drofmen*' (Drofmannis) (*ibid.*). At Malling, people termed '*bermanni*' who were responsible for taking animals into the Weald (as well as carrying goods and guarding thieves) were also recorded (*Cust. Cant.* 1958, 113). Such references may in part be indicative of a phase of impersonal transhumance when people were paid or obliged to drive the livestock of others to grazing grounds or enclosures. A similar phase of comparative activity is known from Dartmoor, which shares many similarities with the Weald (Fox 2012). This is not to say that people were not still involved in personal transhumance in later medieval Sussex. Yardlanders from Amberley recorded in a custumal (*Cust. Chi.* 1925, 54) were allowed to common all their beasts from Candlemas (2 February) to Holy Rood Day (14 September) in the wood of '*Pubhurst*' in the Weald (Pephurst near Drungewick). This spring and summer grazing allowance was possibly deliberately exclusive of both the autumn pannage and autumn and winter deer-hunting seasons.

Moving cattle on the hoof was important in later medieval England to introduce new genes to the herd (Trow-Smith 1957, 109–10) and to take animals to the growing phenomena of the livestock market (*ibid.*, 99). Livestock drives could sometimes be huge affairs, such as the immense example undertaken by John le Barber from the Wash to Cowick, London in 1323 (TNA E 101/379/2). In Sussex things were no different as the county also acted as a supplier of meat for the London market. Robert de la Wode was required to drive pigs from Dorking (Surrey) to London as well as distrained animals to Ferring or Amberley (*Cust. Chi.* 1925, 77). That Dorking may have acted as a hub and market for livestock from the Sussex estate of the Bishop of Chichester is also reflected in the Custumal of Ferring (*Cust. Chi.* 1925, 74) where Richard de Hangleton was recorded as being required to drive beasts to Dorking at his own cost and from Dorking to London at the cost of the lord. Other such hub settlements must have existed on alternative drove routes to the capital.

3.10 Conclusion

What is immediately apparent during a documentary and historical search of Sussex is that cattle were, at least in the later medieval period, a ubiquitous element in the pastoral economy. From the coast to the High Weald cattle were present as both a meat and arable commodity. Although sheep are perhaps more often referred to in the texts, they were more regionally restricted in terms of areas in which they were kept. In the High Weald, for instance, cattle were the main sort of livestock; sheep were only pastured in areas where there was access to river valleys or wetlands (Gardiner 1999, 38). These wet, poorly drained pastures could, however, be problematic to the keeping of sheep. The animals are prone to disease on freshwater pasture, being more susceptible to foot rot and liver fluke. The intermediate host of the liver fluke found in sheep (*Fasciola hepatica*) is often carried by the freshwater slum species of snail *Lymaea truncatula* (French 1996, 653). This fact was not lost on medieval husbandmen, as the *Seneschaucie* records:

at Michaelmas, let all the sheep be drafted out; for although sheep are sound at Easter and in May and before Lammas, afterwards they can, between the two feasts of our Lady, by bad keeping, eat the web of the rime and the little white snails, from which they will sicken and die. (Oschinsky 1971, 284–85)

The unsuitability of the Weald for sheep pasture is reflected in their distribution in the early 14th century (Pelham 1934), while in contrast huge numbers of cattle were known to be pastured during the 13th century in the Wealden Ashdown Forest (Penn 1984, 115).

Cattle were an important part of the primarily arable economy of the Sussex Coastal Plain. The animals were kept as working oxen as well as for their secondary products, which perhaps most importantly included dung. That the landscape and arable systems of this area were designed to accommodate these much-needed cattle is reflected in grazing set aside for the livestock. In return for the use of oxen for draught the cattle economy received the benefit of surplus grain, which facilitated reasonably intensive husbandry. As far as the production of oxen can be tied to arable areas the production of dairy cows can be linked to wetland and upland. Marshland pasture was likely utilised for dairy around Rye and riverine pasture was home to manors with large amounts of cows at the foot of the downs (Amberley), on the Adur where it bisects the Greensand Ridge (Stretham) and in the Low Weald (Drungewick). The South Downs may have also been utilised for dairying where important evidence of commoning has been encountered.

Where beef cattle were raised is more problematic, river pasture at Stretham has been linked with such, although it is likely that cattle for the table were kept, to a greater or lesser extent, throughout medieval Sussex. When we consider the location of beef herds in detail, however, it is clear that the Weald may be the most likely location for herds of any size. The *pay* was characterised by the most extensive form of pasture-woodland, and although many cattle glades would have largely been unsuited to the production of dairy (Everitt 1986, 163; Witney 1990, 26) they had good access to markets and were unsuited to any other livestock apart from pigs and goats.

Suggestions as to the location of specific aspects of the cattle economy of Sussex are somewhat hampered by discrepancies in the degree to which particular *pays* were recorded. While the Coastal Plain and downland are reasonably well served it is evident that the Greensand Ridge and Weald are not. There is also a noticeable lack of early medieval documentary evidence that is directly applicable to the analysis of the cattle economy. Though suggestions as to the likely later medieval pastoral economy may be made from documentary evidence alone, this must not be done with any definite confidence. This is especially true when we consider the sources of documentary evidence themselves. As stated above, the records are heavily skewed towards seigneurial aspects, although glimpses of peasants and their role in the cattle economy is achievable through texts such as custumals. If the lordly economy is better represented, this is also heavily biased towards ecclesiastical records rather than lay. The estates of the Archbishop of Canterbury and the Bishop of Chichester are the best represented; however, Battle Abbey's Cellarers' Rolls also hold important information.

In terms of quantities of cattle kept by later medieval manors, the best records come from the estate of the Bishop of Chichester. Here the numbers of cattle surely reflect the existence of specialised cattle ranches or vaccaries intended to produce the animals themselves as well as secondary products such as dairy and manure. Trow-Smith's (1957, 94) analysis of the Pipe Rolls record cash receipts for rents of vaccaries in the Royal Forest of Windsor, at Odiham and in the New Forest. Within these vaccaries, which exploited thin woodland with underscrub, the normal breeding unit was judged to be one bull to ten cows. In the Wyresdale vaccaries, Lancashire, each stock keeper was responsible for one bull and between 21 and 44 cows. In Blackburnshire the number of cows was even higher (40 to one or two bulls; Winchester 2010, 114–15). That vaccaries were present in Sussex is clear from the Bishop of Chichester's records. Most of the manors recorded as keeping cattle (*Chi. Chart.* 1942, 223–24) had herds comprising 20 or more cows, although three manors – Stretham, Drungewick and Bexhill – had numbers of cows to bulls comparable with the upland vaccaries of Blackburnshire (40, 30 and 30 respectively).

The three vaccaries highlighted above were the minimum number on just one Sussex estate. Other examples must have existed on baronial and ecclesiastical land. Such are the gaps in the documentary record that the ability to analyse the cattle economy of Sussex in general and the presence of vaccaries in particular is unachievable through documentary evidence alone. Indeed, this fact may have led to the situation discussed in the beginning of this chapter where cattle have largely been overlooked in favour of sheep, which are more perceptible in both the documentary record and the pastoral identity of the county.

CHAPTER 4

Place-name indicators

4.1 Introduction

> Tawstock was pretty certainly the *stoc* belonging to Tawton, the cattle-farm or dairy-farm belonging to that great manor … Ekwall observes that the *stocs* are very old; they had received their names by an early period. Indeed, Tawstock must have grown into a permanent settlement and achieved independent status before the middle of the tenth century when the boundaries of the hundreds were drawn. (Hoskins 1952, 303)

A search of documentary records for the cattle economy of Sussex concluded that this component of medieval animal husbandry has been largely neglected in past studies (see Chapter 3). It has also been shown that cattle were farmed in specialised establishments known as vaccaries and that the practice of summering, often associated with upland regions, may have been a feature of downland and wetland exploitation within the region. That there were limitations in this documentary record was also realised. It is therefore important to look beyond a singular, historical approach, in order to facilitate a truly multi-disciplinary study. The place-names of the region clearly reflect a pastoral model of settlement in which livestock regimes dominated, and close examination of this toponymic evidence may shed further light on the extent and character of the medieval cattle economy.

While place-names add to the regional variation of landscape character and have been shown to reflect topographical features and forms, they may also act as indicators of past farming practices (Gelling 1984). As such their study remains an important contributor to historic landscape analysis. This said, they must not be used without some caution. Since the publication of many of the English Place-Name Society volumes, areas of original research have become outdated. For example, *ingas* names were once thought of as reflecting the earliest folk-names of a wave of conquering Anglo-Saxons; however, work during the 1960s showed that they derive from a later phase of settlement activity (Dodgson 1966). This said, the volumes produced by the Place-Name Society remain the authority for those wishing to study the toponymy of a region, though this should not be conducted without reference to more up-to-date work such as that by Watts (2004).

4.2 Methodology

A study of place-names linked to the medieval cattle economy of the South-East will by no means provide a comprehensive list of all the settlements or places linked to cattle farming, nor will it alone provide the key to understanding how and where this aspect of agriculture was undertaken. What it should facilitate, however, is a further contribution to a multi-disciplinary landscape analysis. It will complement additional techniques such as documentary and cartographic research in order to provide as holistic an approach as possible. To achieve such a method, certain parameters must be imposed on the gathering of place-name data. This part of the study will only be concerned with place-names that were considered important during the medieval period. Minor names, such as field-names, although still valuable, will be considered later, during an in-depth analysis of a portion of the study area (Chapter 6) as well as case studies resulting from the author's own fieldwork (Chapter 9).

In conducting analysis of place-names it is essential to examine the data with reference to time factors. To be sure that the place-names examined are medieval in origin, and considered valuable nomenclature at the time, it is proposed to restrict our examination firstly to place-names on record by 1348. By further highlighting which of these names were on record by 1086 it will be possible, as past writers have suggested (*e.g.* Dodgson 1978), to reveal two sets of names; those in existence by 1086 reflecting the earliest manorial sites and those by 1348 as evidence of places that had gradually emerged into independence by the late 13th century and entered the record by the Black Death. An additional, third tier of names will also be incorporated in this study, being those on record by 1450. This group will obviously be medieval in origin, and will fit neatly with the timescale of this project as a whole. They also hold the potential to illustrate the developed economy and are recorded during years that have been shown to display important changes in cattle consumption and husbandry practice (Grant 1988; Sykes 2009).

The place-name volumes of Sussex (*P.N.Sx* 1929; 1930) and Surrey (*P.N.Sr* 1934) remain ideal for this purpose, although no such volume yet exists for Kent. The volume for Sussex was ground-breaking in its time as the results were based upon a more extensive search of documentary material and Ordnance Survey mapping, including more minor and field-names than any of the earlier Place-Name Society volumes had achieved (*P.N.Sx* 1929, xiii–xxv; Mansion 1931). The same can be said of the volume for Surrey, though it must be remembered that no printed volume could hope to contain an exhaustive list of all the place-names of a county. The problems inherent in the fact that some of the ideas noted in these volumes have now been superseded have already been noted; however, further difficulties also exist. Many place-names contain elements that have multiple meanings, some may be applicable to the cattle economy, and some may not. For instance, the element *wic* has been variously interpreted as 'a dwelling, a building or collection of buildings for special purposes, a farm, a dairy farm', and it seems that the specialised purposes could include manufacture and coastal trade (see Hodges 1982, 47–86; Coates 1999) as well as farming (*P.N.E.* 1956b, 257–63; Coates 1999). It is a German loan word from the Latin for vicus with all its settlement connotations; indeed, in the laws of Kent London appears as *Lundenwic*, and the king's reeve there was known as a *wic-gerefa* (Finberg 1972a, 424). There also seems to be some association between early medieval *wic* names and Roman sites (*ibid.*). In addition to ambiguity in meaning, certain elements are difficult to distinguish from each other. For example, the root meaning of the element *stoc* is 'standing place' (*P.N.E.* 1956b, 154) and this has been shown by Ekwall (1960, 443) to be specifically related to a place where cattle stood for milking in outlying pastures. Watts (2004, 577), however, interprets the element as meaning 'a secondary settlement, an outlying farmstead, a dairy farm'. The name does have other possible meanings, such as 'Christian holy place or monastery' (*P.N.E.* 1956b, 153; Gelling and Probert 2010, 81). It can also be easily confused with the element *stocc*, meaning 'a tree trunk' or 'a stump, a log of wood' (*P.N.E.* 1956b, 155–56). Therefore, all names that show the possibility of being related to medieval cattle farming will be highlighted, and where possible will be further examined on the strength of other evidence.

Before analysis of place-names linked to the cattle economy can be undertaken it is worth pausing to further illustrate what is hoped to be achieved by this toponymic study as well as to consider what the place-name indicators of cattle might be. Firstly, it is perhaps most obvious to take names that include Old or Middle English words for cattle as a starting point. These names may not only indicate the geographical locations where cattle were important enough to have places named after them, but could also help illustrate types of pasture or enclosure that may have been linked to their husbandry. Though it is arguable whether the inclusion of an animal element within a place-name indicates that a given species was a common or rare occurrence in a particular district (see Hallam 1988b, 23), this author holds the increasingly accepted view that they signify their customary occurrence and the following analysis is based on that assumption. Supportive of this view was Everitt (1986, 170), who noted that Kentish cattle names, when connected to elements indicating pasture or enclosure, show that cattle stations of some kind existed during the early medieval period. The identification of such places where cattle farming was considered important enough that contemporaries named a locale after the practice is one of the key goals of this study. A further aim is an assessment of what else can be gleaned about the cattle economy on the strength of toponomy.

The following study is based on the English Place-Name Society volumes for Sussex and Surrey (*P.N.Sx* 1929; 1930; *P.N.Sr* 1934). Though two volumes on Kentish place-names have been produced by Wallenberg (1931; 1934), the works are rather antiquated and some of the ideas have been superseded. Similarly, Cullen's (1998) Ph.D. thesis, *The Place-Names of the Lathes of St Augustine and Shipway, Kent*, does not cover the whole of the county and its examination has therefore been omitted. Kent is marked as 'No Data' on the chapter illustrations.

4.3 Place-name indicators

In order to achieve the objectives outlined above it is envisaged that a hierarchy of place-name indicators should be proposed. As has already been suggested, cattle names should form the starting point. This can then be followed by names that indicate cattle establishments. Vaccaries and dairies are perhaps the most obvious of these, although seasonal settlements linked to the system of transhumance generally should also be considered. This is because cattle as well as pigs, which are more often associated with seasonal pasturing within the South-East, were part of the early medieval transhumance system.

'*Vacherie*' (*P.N.E.* 1956b, 229) place-names are the most recognisable of the names that indicate a cattle establishment, although names in '**stall**' and '**stoc**' are also good indicators (Everitt 1986, 165–68). Analysis of over 200 vaccary names from the upland Forests of northern England showed that the vast majority (72%) are topographical in nature, and a large number of these (44) include elements referring to woodland or woodland clearings (Winchester 2010, 116). Analysis of names like '*shaw*', '*hurst*' and '*leah*' in a wooded region like the South-East could never be suggested as an indicator of vaccaries themselves, although mapping of their distribution could aid understanding of where in the region these establishments might be located. *Leah* names in Surrey and Sussex are much more common than in Kent (*P.N.Sx* 1930) and in the former county they are distributed throughout, excepting a notable absence in the north-east along the Kentish border (*P.N.Sr* 1934).

Dairying may be indicated by the place-name **wic**, although this place-name element has a number of other possible meanings (see section 4.2 above). In its general sense this name means no more than a collection of buildings, but over time it came to denote buildings utilised for specialised purposes such as manufacture, trade and food production (including salt and fishing). The practice of treating it as a word to denote a specialised farm, especially a dairy one, became its principal usage, however, by the later medieval period (*P.N.E.* 1956b, 257–63; Finberg 1972a, 424; Coates 1999, 95). It is this fact that makes it most relevant to this study. Additional names indicating dairying activities include those linked to products of the industry such as butter, cheese and milk. The place-name element '**smeoru**' may also be linked to dairying (Fox 2008; 2012, 148–50). Another element that must be considered are '**maiden**' names. Fox (2012, 155–56) has shown these to be linked to both dairying and the practice of transhumance, which, as we have highlighted, was of such importance in the medieval pastoral history of the South-East.

This leaves those names that indicate the earliest medieval pastoral use of certain areas of the region such as the Weald and parts of the North and South Downs, as well as those place-names that denote detached seasonal pasture, linked to the system of transhumance. In the North of England, the evidence of vaccary place-names indicate that sometimes these establishments developed in areas that were previously put to a different pastoral use (Winchester 2010, 116). Scandinavian elements denoting summer pastures (*sǽtr* and *erg*) as well as temporary shielings (*skali/shele* 'a temporary hut, a shed') are present in the names of vaccaries at Burtersett, Ortner and Heggerscales (*ibid.*). Scandinavian elements will obviously be rare occurrences in the South-East, located far as it is from areas of greater Viking influence. This is certainly true for Surrey and Sussex where only a few Anglo-Scandinavian words are known (*P.N.Sr* 1934, xix; Dodgson 1978, 59), although the place-names of the region may include elements of Old and Middle English that have equivalent or similar meanings to those mentioned above.

The Old English elements **(ge)sell** ('a shed, a shelter for animals, a herdsman's hut'), **scydd/scedd** ('a hovel, a shed, a pig-sty') are common elements in both Kent and Sussex (*P.N.E.* 1956a; 1956b; but less so in Surrey, just three examples of *scydd* are recorded for that county, all of which are late or minor names; *P.N.Sr* 1934, 352) and the **stede** names of the Kentish downlands have been claimed by Everitt (1986, 20) to have originated as summer shielings in the Old English period. Perhaps the place-names of the South-East most synonymous with 'detached', seasonal pastoral use, however, are the 'dens' and 'folds' (**denn**, **fald/falod**; *P.N.E.* 1956b; Witney 1976; Everitt 1986; Brandon 2003, 46) and to a slightly lesser extent those in '**snoad**', of the Kent and Sussex Wealds (Witney 1976, 61–63; 1990, 22). The meaning of *denn* elements has been interpreted as 'a woodland pasture, especially for swine', although associated elements indicate that livestock apart from pigs (for example, the name Cowden present in both Kent and Sussex; *ibid.*, 129–30) were also a feature of these names. Cowden in Kent is of early origin as it is named in the *Txt. Roff.* 1720 as *Cudena* (Hasted 1797, 203) and its counterpart in Wartling parish, East Sussex, was on record by the late 13th century when it is named *Kudenn* (AD 1296; *P.N.Sx* 1930, 483). Such details are important for some vaccaries in the north of England may, on the evidence of place-names, have replaced use of forests for pannage (Winchester 2010, 116).

Each of the categories – cattle names, those indicating cattle establishments and those indicating summering or detached seasonal pasturing – will now be considered in turn. This will be accompanied by mapping of their distribution and then a wide-ranging discussion of the inferences that may be made about the nature of the medieval cattle economy of the South-East based upon the toponomy. This evidence will form a key part of this multi-disciplinary study that can be drawn together in a detailed analysis of a portion of the study area (Chapter 6). All interpretations will be checked against Watts (2004), which provides current thinking on the major names.

4.4 Cattle names

As suggested above, the most obvious toponymic indicators of the medieval cattle economy are those names that include Old or Middle English words for cattle. These include elements for bull (*fearr*, *bula* and *bule*), bullock (*bulluc*), oxen (*oxa*, *exna*), cow(s) (*cū*, *kyn(e)*), calves (calf, *cealf(a)*) and the generic for cattle (*hrīder*, *hrȳder*) (*P.N.E.* 1956a; 1956b). Important or major place-names that include cattle elements have been mapped for Surrey and Sussex according to the criteria set out above and are shown in Figure 4.1 and Table 4.1. The bold numbers provided in brackets after a place-name (*e.g.* Chaldon (1)) refer to its entry in the accompanying table and distribution maps.

What is immediately clear from the distribution map is that cattle names occur in all but one *pay* of the two counties (Romney Marsh being the exception). At first glance this does not seem to reflect staged processes of colonisation or changes in livestock choice for this general pattern is the norm for the entire medieval period. The only exceptions to this rule are that no cattle names are recorded on the North Downs of Surrey after 1086 and none are recorded prior to that date from the coastal marshes, South Downs or Coastal Plain of Sussex.

What is also apparent is the topographic nature of the contributing element in the majority of the place-names. Three of the 19 names include elements that indicate hilly, sloping or rising land, with the elements '*dūn*' ('a hill, an expanse of open hill-country'; *P.N.E.* 1956a, 138) and '*ōra*' ('a border, a margin, a bank, an edge'; *P.N.E* 1956b, 54) being represented once and twice respectively. Chaldon (1) meaning 'calves down', is possibly the earliest cattle place-name

FIGURE 4.1: Cattle place-names of Sussex and Surrey recorded prior to 1450 (drawn by the author)

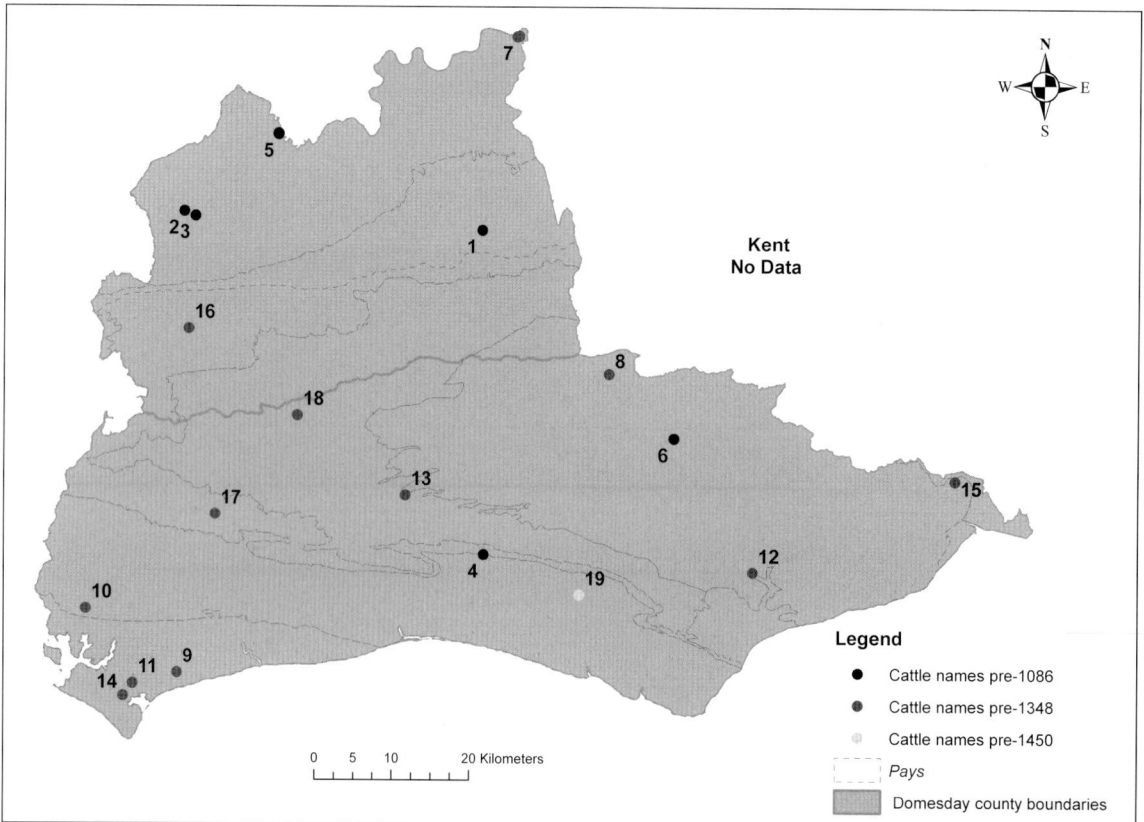

TABLE 4.1: Cattle place-names of Sussex and Surrey recorded prior to 1450

No.	Place-name	Element's 'meaning'	County	Date of first recording	Pays	References
1	Chaldon	*cealfa, dun* 'calves' down'	Surrey	675	North Downs	(*P.N.Sr* 1934, 42)
2	Cow Moor	*cu, mōr*	Surrey	675	Thames Basin	(*P.N.Sr* 1934, 145)
3	Cowshot Manor	*cu, scēat, huga* 'angle of land used for cow-pasturage'	Surrey	675	Thames Basin	(*P.N.Sr* 1934, 145)
4	Keymer	*cu, mere* 'cow's mere'	Sussex	1086	Greensand	(*P.N.Sx* 1930, 276)
5	Oxelak(e)	*lacu*, 'ox streamlet'	Surrey	675	Thames Basin	(*P.N.Sr* 1934, 107)
6	Rotherfield	*hrȳðera-feld* 'open land of the cattle'	Sussex	788	High Weald	(*P.N.Sx* 1930, 376–77)
7	Rotherhithe	*hrȳðer, hrȳð* 'place where cattle are either embarked or landed'	Surrey	1100–07	Thames Basin	(*P.N.Sr* 1934, 28)
8	Bolebrook	'bull brook'	Sussex	1249	High Weald	(*P.N.Sx* 1930, 366)
9	Chalcroft Barn	*cealf* 'calves' croft'	Sussex	1271	Sussex Coastal Plain	(*P.N.Sx* 1929, 91)
10	Chalcroft Copse	*cealf* 'calves' croft'	Sussex	1271	South Downs	(*P.N.Sx* 1929, 60)
11	Chalder Farm	*cealf*, ora 'calf-bank'	Sussex	1275	Sussex Coastal Plain	(*P.N.Sx* 1929, 85)
12	Cowden	*cu, den*	Sussex	1296	High Weald	(*P.N.Sx* 1930, 483)
13	Cowfold	*cu, falod*	Sussex	1255	Low Weald	(*P.N.Sx* 1929, 209)
14	Keynor	*cȳna-ora* 'cow's bank'	Sussex	1187	Sussex Coastal Plain	(*P.N.Sx* 1929, 86)
15	Oxenbridge	'oxen bridge'	Sussex	1279	High Weald	(*P.N.Sx* 1930, 528)
16	Oxenford Grange	*ex(e)na*	Surrey	1128	Greensand	(*P.N.Sr* 1934, 216)
17	Rotherbridge Farm	*hrȳðer, brycg* 'cattlebridge'	Sussex	1279	Greensand	(*P.N.Sx* 1929, 123)
18	Exfold	*ex(e)na, falod* 'oxen-enclosure'	Sussex	1327	South Downs	(*P.N.Sx* 1929, 157)
19	Oxteddle Bottom	*oxenaseten* 'seten of the oxen'	Sussex	14th century	Low Weald	(*P.N.Sx* 1930, 355)

recorded in either Sussex or Surrey as it is referred to as '*Chalvedune*' in a grant of lands by Frithuwald of Surrey to Chertsey Abbey in the late 7th or early 8th century (Sawyer 1181; *Cart. Sax.* 1885, charter 39). It must be remembered, however, that the dating of such early charters is always applied with some caution and Wormald (1985, 9, 25) and Dumville (1992, 51–53) should be consulted for discussion of this particular charter's dating and authenticity. *Dūn* names have been shown to be applied to low, fairly level hills with extensive summits (Gelling 1984, 140–58; Gelling and Cole 2000, 164–73), features that were favoured in the early medieval period for excellent dry pasture on which herdsmen and women could easily tend their charges (Banham and Faith 2014, 155–56). Chaldon has been utilised by Gelling (1984, 146) to be illustrative of high (*c.* 150 m) eminences for which *dūn* names are characteristic in Surrey.

The names Chalder (**11**) and Keynor (**14**) on the Sussex Coastal Plain are part of a corpus of *ōra* names that are a particular feature of the West Sussex coast (Gelling 1984, 179; Gelling and Cole 2000, 204). The name element is understood to mean 'bank' and the ridges occupied by both Keynor and Chalder would have acted as clear markers for seaborne travellers. Indeed, that places attached to *ōra* names acted as markers in the landscape seems to be a particular use of the word (*ibid.*, 203–05). These instances of cattle names related to elevated sites may be of more importance than the mere three of 19 instances may at first suggest. Plate 4.1 below shows the cattle names of Sussex and Surrey in relation to a relief model. What is apparent is that the vast majority of these sites are either on or close to uplands.

An equally, if not more significant, sub-set of cattle names is those linked to water. These are separated into those with direct associations, as in the name Oxlake (**5**), or indirectly in the form of crossing points such as Oxenbridge (**15**) and Oxenford (**16**). Cattle place-names are illustrated in relation to hydrology in Figure 4.2. Keymer (**4**) is one of the most interesting names belonging to the former category. It originates as a compound of the elements *cū* (cow) and *mere* ('pond, lake, pool') (*P.N.Sx* 1930, 276), the association suggesting a watering place for cattle. This place-name is located near the foot of the South Downs, on the ancient settled Spring-line; however, *mere* names do not appear to indicate the most immediately desirable settlement sites (Gelling 1984, 27). In the downs of Sussex such names have been associated with small man-made ponds fed by surface water (Gelling and Cole 2000, 22) and this type of pool could include those known as dew-ponds. Whether Sussex 'meres' were artificial in origin is, however, debatable. Few associated bodies of water have been investigated archaeologically and those on the downs occupy locations that may naturally hold water (as at Falmer).

Similar features that originated as stock-ponds are also located on the Kentish downland (Everitt 1986, 169) and are associated with the element *sol*, which, according to Smith (*P.N.E.* 1956b), initially meant 'mud, slough, a wallowing place' and only later 'a dirty pond'. Everitt (1986, 169) has suggested that *sol* names and the pools linked to them are associated with early vaccaries and

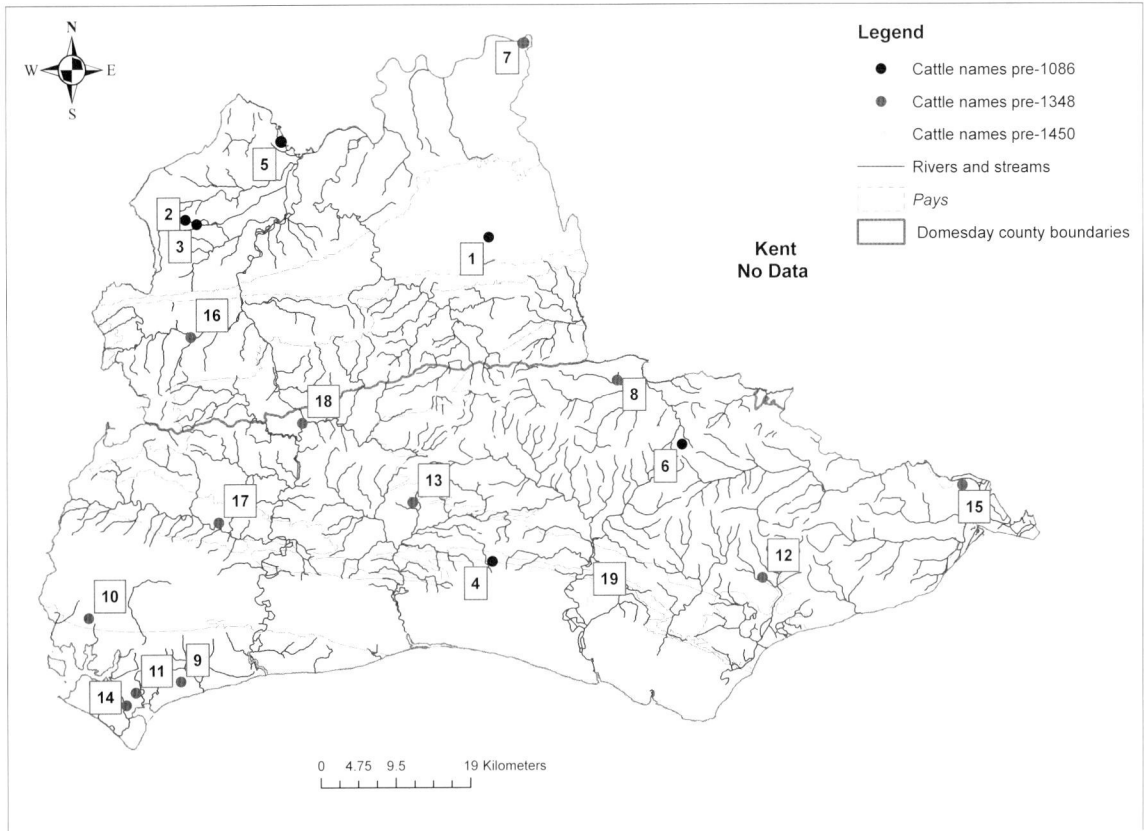

FIGURE 4.2: Cattle place-names of Sussex and Surrey recorded prior to 1450 in relation to hydrology (drawn by the author. Contains material covered by © Crown copyright and database rights 2019 Ordnance Survey, Educational Service Provider licence number v2.1)

downland dairying, with *mere* names bearing much the same significance. Thus the place-name Keymer may reflect the most explicit reference to the primary usage of these types of pool, an indicator of a type of downland or scarp foot dairying that was dependent on either naturally occurring bodies of water or features including or akin to so called dew-ponds. It is interesting to note that, while wild creatures are more often the first name element associated with *mere*, the only domestic animals associated with this topographic element are cattle (Gelling and Cole 2000, 26).

In similarity to cattle names being linked to watering places in areas of pasture, those associated with crossing points may be related to the movement of herds. As has been previously demonstrated, the movement of cattle was a hugely important part of the medieval cattle economy of the South-East. From the earliest days of the system of transhumance until the huge later medieval drives to market the network of drove roads utilised by herders would have needed to traverse watercourses. Oxenbridge (**15**) and Oxenford (**16**) are located close to the Rivers Wey in Surrey and Rother in East Sussex respectively. Both names are on record by the 13th century and the association of cattle with the nomenclature denoting these crossing points must surely be related to the movement of beef on the hoof within the Weald at this time. Rotherhithe (7) on the Thames may be recorded as early as the year 1100 and means 'place where cattle are either embarked or landed' (*P.N.Sr* 1934, 28). Surely this, too, indicates that places were named due to their association with the movement of cattle. Though this name may indicate where cattle were brought to the capital by ship or ferry, it would not be too far-fetched to claim that in the place-name Rotherhithe we have the location of where herds of cattle from the wider South-East were swum across the Thames to feed a burgeoning London.

The final place-name associated with water, crossing points and cattle, Rotherbridge (17) in West Sussex, is worthy of close inspection for this location maybe illustrative of wider patterns in the cattle economy of the South-East. The place-name is from the Old English *hryder* and *brycg*, effectively meaning 'cattle bridge', and although the location of the farm in which the name is preserved is not recorded until the late 13th

FIGURE 4.3: Rotherbridge and Hunger Lane as shown on the OS 1st Edition 1:2500, 1875 (with labelling by the author)

century (AD 1279), this was the original meeting place of the Domesday hundred, which shares its name (*P.N.Sx* 1929, 99, 123). The crossing point and the nearby farm are evocative locations for they are approached by a long distance droveway that survives nearby as a deeply sunken holloway (Plate 4.2).

This feature which is first named 'Hungers Lane' on the OS 1st Edition (1875; Figure 4.3) is traceable both on the ground and via cartographic evidence for some distance. The routeway also forms both a parish and hundred boundary and must date to at least the late 11th century. Rotherbridge is therefore important for it neatly demonstrates how early medieval cattle movement imprinted the landscape with infrastructure related to the practice of transhumance and also fixed places in both the administrative and communal landscapes of medieval society; as such, pastoral practice is fundamental in the development of the South-East.

Enclosures are a feature of the medieval landscape and, unsurprisingly, some are associated with cattle names. The element croft is represented by two similar place-names, Chalcraft Barn (**9**) and Chalcroft Copse (**10**) (*P.N.Sx* 1929, 60, 91) located on the Sussex Coastal Plain and dip-slope of the South Downs respectively. Croft in Old English has the meaning of a small enclosed field and is often combined with words indicating the nature of the livestock kept or crops grown. In these examples the croft was used for calves (*P.N.E.* 1956a, 113). Such names may be indicative of cattle's place in organised medieval field-scapes and small-scale settlements; however, the other two enclosure names, Cowshot (**3**) and Oxteddle (**19**), may be related to quite different landscape types.

Cowshot (**3**) is named '*Cuscetes hagen*' in a 7th-century charter of Frithuwald (Sawyer 1165; *Cart. Sax. 1885*, charter 34) that, according to Wormald (1985, 9), may be largely authentic. The name element *hagen* or *hægen* means 'an enclosure' and is part of a number of related words pertaining to enclosures fences and hedges (*hæg, haga, hagga, hege, hegn*; *P.N.E.* 1956a, 214–21). The association of a cattle name with such an element may be of some importance for it is known from the north of England that vaccaries were often surrounded by an enclosure known as a '*haya*' (Winchester 2003, 114). This could be formed of a bank (often probably hedged) and ditch, or, in stone using areas, vaccary walls (Atkin 1985). Such an enclosure has been encountered in Sussex at *The Hayworth* and has been directly related to a *heg, hege* or *haga* name as well as a vaccary site (Margetts 2017; Chapter 9). *Hægen* and *(ge)hæg* names in Kent have been connected to pastoral purposes and vaccaries specifically, and the county is an area where, according to Everitt (1986, 142), the word does not have its additional connotation as a hunting enclosure. Indeed, by basing some toponymic work on Wallenberg (1934) he was able to cite Oxenden Wood in Chelsfield, Oxenhill Shaw in Otford and the parish of Oxney near Deal as examples of Kentish downland ox pastures whose place-names are formed by a compound of *oxa* and *(ge)haeg* (Everitt 1986, 165).

Cowshot Manor, it seems, comprised an enclosure in a landscape of open pasture for it is connected with the nearby cattle name of Cow Moor (**2**), which is mentioned in the same 7th-century charter (Sawyer 1165; *Cart. Sax. 1885*, charter 34). Cow Moor incorporates the element *mōr*, which was interpreted by Mawer and Stenton (*P.N.Sr* 1934, 145) to mean 'marshy ground'; however, the place-name lies in an area of free-draining sandy soils of the Thames Basin, an area that retains reasonably extensive heathland to this day. It is more likely therefore that the element *mōr* in this context had the meaning of 'barren waste-land' (*P.N.E.* 1956b, 42). Cowshot Manor can clearly be seen on the map below (Figure 4.4) within an arc-shaped enclosure surrounded by open heath beyond.

An additional cattle name that was likely to have been located in open pasture is Oxteddle Bottom (**19**). The place-name enters the written record in the 14th century and means '*seten* of the oxen' (*P.N.Sx* 1930, 355). *Seten* in Old English means 'plantation' or similar, but it has the cognate *(ge)set* which means

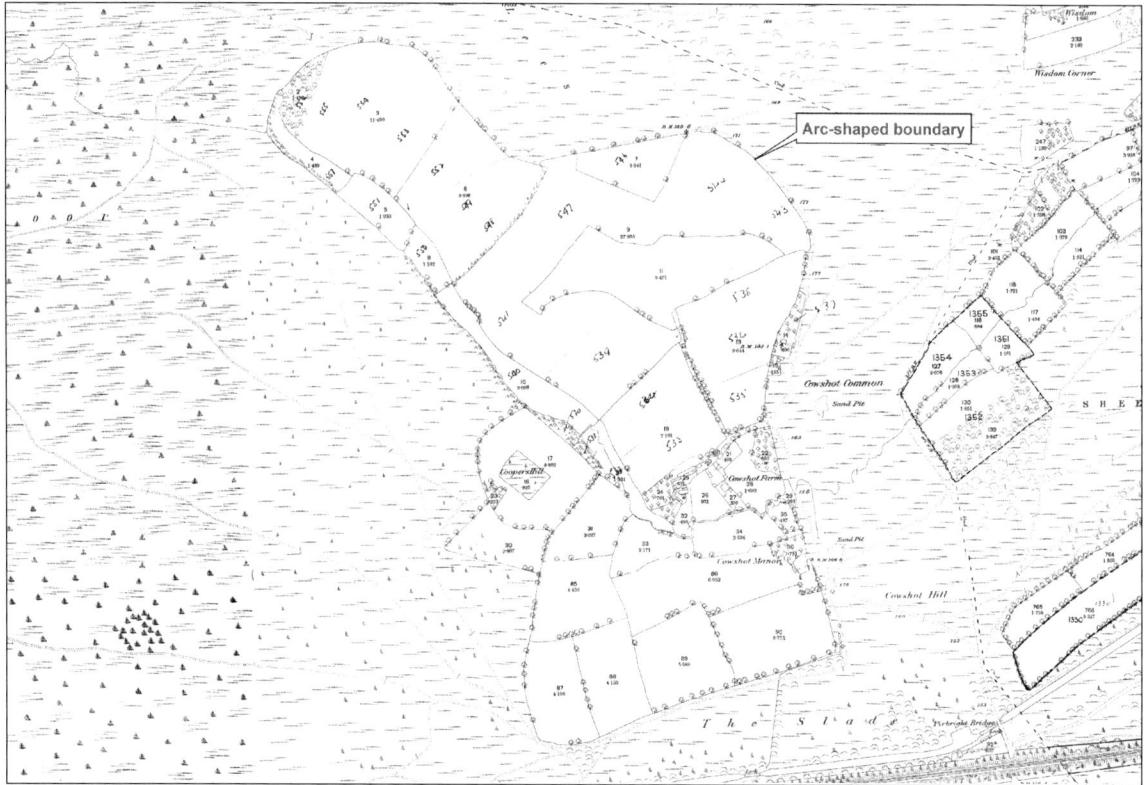

Arc-shaped boundary

'a dwelling, a camp, a place for animals, a stable, a fold' (*P.N.E.* 1956b, 120–21). The word *(ge)set* can sometimes appear as *seota* (*ibid.*), which is a common place-name in pre-Conquest charters of Romney Marsh. Here the name likely refers to lowland pasture equivalent of the Wealden 'dens' (Rippon 2000, 165). Oxteddle Bottom is located on the downs above South Malling and it is likely that the nearby rectangular earthwork known as *The Bible* is in fact the medieval *Oxenesetene*. The earthwork is more fully explored in Chapter 7; it is shown in the photograph below (Figure 4.5) as well as on a modern Ordnance Survey map (Figure 4.6).

If Oxteddle, from its association with the element *seota*, had some seasonal function in similarity to the Wealden dens it is not alone in the corpus of cattle names. Cowden (**12**), Cowfold (**13**) and Exfold (**18**) are all located in the Sussex Weald, and are associated with the elements *denn* and *fald/falod*, which have been briefly mentioned above. *Denn* is a common place-name in the Kentish Weald and it is perhaps unsurprising that Cowden has a namesake near Sevenoaks mentioned as '*Cudena*' in the *Txt. Roff.* 1720. It is thought that most dens originated for swine pannage and are often described as such in pre-Conquest records; however, Kentish *denn* names prefixed with cattle elements (Cowden and Oxenden, for example) suggest other livestock played a role in the origins of these early medieval woodland pastures (Everitt 1986, 123).

FIGURE 4.4: Cowshot Manor as shown on the OS 1st Edition 1:2500, 1871 (with labelling by the author)

FIGURE 4.5 (*opposite above*): 'Bible Bottom' with the earthwork known as 'The Bible', but actually 'The Oxteddle' situated centre left. The Ouse Valley can be seen in the background (source: the author)

FIGURE 4.6 (*opposite below*): 'The Bible' earthwork as shown on the modern Ordnance Survey 1:25000 © Crown copyright and database rights 2020 Ordnance Survey

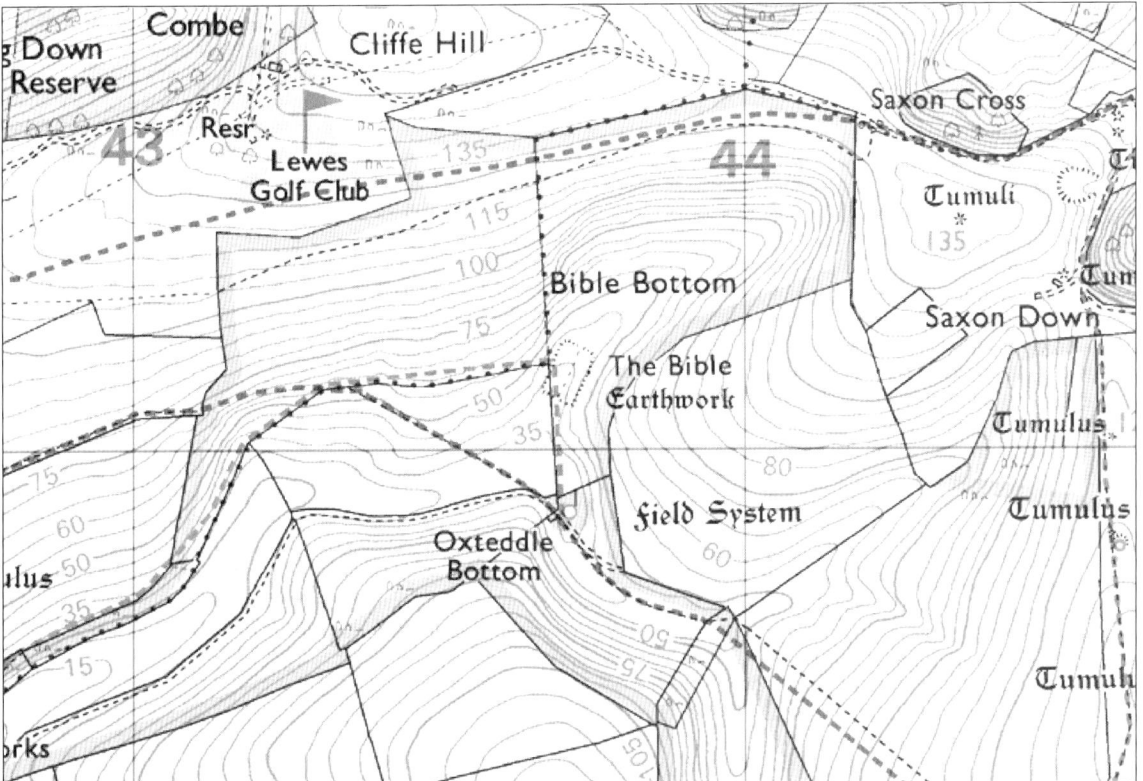

In the Sussex and Surrey Wealds *denn* names are uncommon, although it seems that equivalent land-use is indicated here in the abundance of names in fold, from *fald/falod* (Brandon 2003, 45–46). The names Cowfold (*cū* and *falod*) and Exfold (*ex(e)na and falod* meaning 'oxen-enclosure'; *P.N.Sx* 1929, 157, 209) show a similar pattern for the folds of Surrey and Sussex to that realised by Everitt for the *denns* of Kent.

4.5 Establishment names

'*Vacherie*', Old French and Middle English place-names indicating 'a vaccary, a dairy farm' (*P.N.E.* 1956b, 229) are perhaps one of the most recognisable indications of medieval cattle establishments. Such names seem to be rare occurrences nationally; however, the two examples listed by Smith (*P.N.E.* 1956b) (Vachery, Surrey (1) and Chelwood Vetchery, Sussex; *ibid.*) are both within the study area. The first record of Vachery House is *la Vacherie* in 1245 according to the Place-Name Society Volume (*P.N.Sr* 1934, 232), although an earlier dated feoffment (10 February 1244; SHC: G85/22/1) also exists.

FIGURE 4.7:
Establishment place-names of Sussex and Surrey recorded prior to 1450 (drawn by the author)

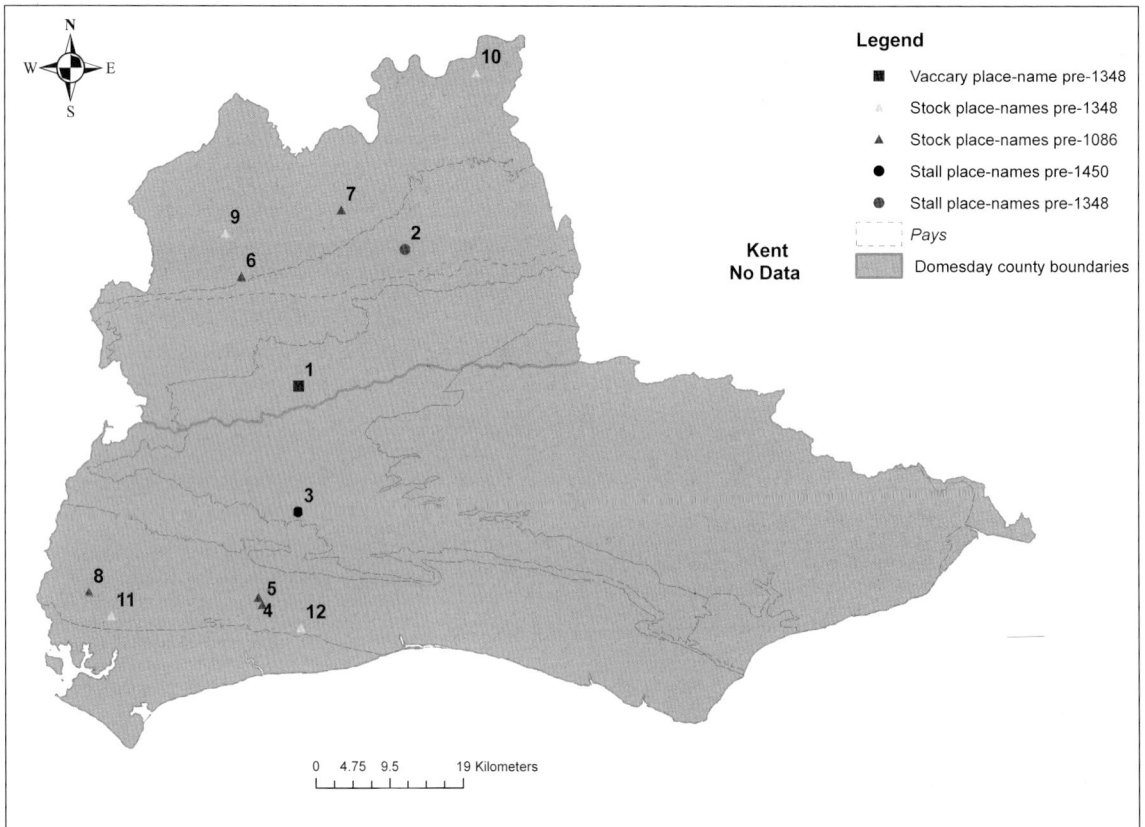

TABLE 4.2: Establishment place-names of Sussex and Surrey recorded prior to 1450

No.	Place-name	Element's 'meaning'	County	Date of first recording	Sub-type	References
1	Vachery House	'cow-farm' 'cowhouse'	Surrey	1244	Vaccary	(*P.N.Sr* 1934, 232)
2	Costal Wood	*cot(e)*, *steall*	Surrey	1327	Stall	(*P.N.Sr* 1934, 77)
3	Stallhouse Farm	*steall* 'cattle stall'	Sussex	1420	Stall	(*P.N.Sx* 1929, 154)
4	North Stoke	*stoc(c)*	Sussex	1086	Stock	(*P.N.Sx* 1929, 173; Watts 2004, 579)
5	South Stoke	*stoc*	Sussex	1086	Stock	(*P.N.Sx* 1929, 142; Watts 2004, 579)
6	Stoke	*stoc(c)*	Surrey	1086	Stock	(*P.N.Sr* 1934, 151)
7	Stoke D'Abernon	*stoc(c)*	Surrey	1086	Stock	(*P.N.Sr* 1934, 95)
8	Stoughton	*stocc*, *tun*	Sussex	1086	Stock	(*P.N.Sx* 1929, 54)
9	Crastock Farm	*stoc(c)* 'crow *stoc(c)*'	Surrey	1178	Stock	(*P.N.Sr* 1934, 157)
10	Stockwell	*stocc*, *wielle* 'well or spring by the stump or stock'	Surrey	1197	Stock	(*P.N.Sr* 1934, 24)
11	West Stoke	*stoc*	Sussex	1205	Stock	(*P.N.Sx* 1929, 61)
12	Barnstake Copse	*bern*, *stocc*	Sussex	1340	Stock	(*P.N.Sx* 1929, 249)

Names incorporating '***stall/steall***' are rare occurrences in Sussex and Surrey prior to 1450, with a search of the relevant place-name society volumes (*P.N.Sx* 1929; 1930; *P.N.Sr* 1934) returning only two results; Costal Wood in Surrey (**2**) and Stallhouse Farm in Sussex (**3**), both of which are late to enter the written record. In the South-East most early instances of these names come from North Kent where Everitt (1986, 142, 165–68) has viewed downland examples as being indicative (although not exclusively so) of woodland vaccaries. These cattle pastures may have been characteristic of the downland economy before, and for a time after, the Norman Conquest (*ibid.*; Witney 1990, 26). Everitt (1986, 168) cited a number of places including Stalisfield above Charing, Mystole in Chartham, Dunstall in Shoreham and Dunstall in Lenham as certain cattle establishments or dairy farms. His inclusion of Tunstall near Milton in this group of names can be commended in the light of the documentary evidence associated with the manor of Milton Regis explored previously (see sections 3.5 and 3.7) and the fact that 'tunstall' names have been seen by other scholars as being used to specifically denote vaccaries (*P.N.Y.* 1961, 125; Winchester 2010, 116). Indeed, Smith's (*P.N.Y.* 1961, 125) example of Saltonstall was actually recorded as a functioning vaccaria during the year 1315 when one Adam Attetownend was found guilty of keeping 11 sheep over the winter on the vaccary's hay (*WCR III*, 72). Additionally, of the seven vaccaries named in a 16th-century document referring to the possessions of the Earls of Warrene and Surrey in the medieval jurisdiction or liberty of Sowerbyshire, three were tunstall names (Cromptonstall, Oversaltonstall and Nethersaltonstall; Baildon 1906, xxix).

The correspondence of *stall/steall* names with vaccary sites may not always be straightforward, as other meanings such as 'homestall' are also possible. This confusion is compounded by the prevalence of minor settlements known as 'forstals' in Kent and East Sussex (Everitt 1986, 168). Within Kent, 'forstal' is virtually confined to the pastoral areas of the county, particularly to the Weald and the downs. While it may have latterly taken the connotation of a farm-green, it seems to have originally indicated a stall or standing place in front of a farmhouse, possibly one where cows were brought to be milked (*ibid.*, 168–69). Beerforstal in Elham was taken by Everitt to mean either a 'pasture forstal' or a 'stall in front of a byre or cattle shed'. Likewise, he took Mersham Forstal, in an area of riverine pasture, to denote a subordinate dairy farm (*ibid.*, 168). Though these variations in the meaning of stall names exist there can be little doubt that Stallhouse Farm (3) in the Sussex Weald is a potential vaccary site as its name means 'cattle stall' (*P.N.Sx* 1929, 154). Similarly, Costal (2) highlights the link between the element *stall/steall* with medieval rural buildings, as here the first element is *cot(e)* (*P.N.Sr* 1934, 77), meaning 'a cottage, a hut, a shelter, a den' (*P.N.E.* 1956a, 108). *Cote* has been connected with dairying in a marshland context (Rippon 2000, 205) and has featured as an element in the vaccary names of the northern Forests (Winchester 2010, 116).

To turn to '**stoc**' names the potential difficulties in separating the original derivation from the element '*stocc*' as well as its alternative meanings, apart from a standing place for cattle, have already been explored. It seems that such places may have been equivalent to the seasonal shieling settlements of the north, for in a southern English context, low-lying, well-watered standing places for cattle were termed '*stoc*'. These were used by herdsmen during the summer who drove their cattle from a parent *vill*. Often, therefore, the pastures came to be named as the *stoc* of a particular original settlement, as in Calstock (Cornwall) as the *stoc* of Callington, Plymstock (Devon) as the *stoc* of Plympton, and Basingstoke (Hampshire) as the *stoc* of Basing (Finberg 1972a, 425). It is likely that such *stoc* names originated as parts of wider estates and only later would they became outlying dairy or cattle farms (Everitt 1986, 73).

Though no clear parent settlements are indicated by the names of the 'stocks' of Sussex and Surrey, they do seem to be of early derivation as the majority are of clear pre-Conquest origin (numbers 4–8). The inclusion of the element *tūn* in Stoughton (8) may be of some note due to the element's village connotations (*P.N.E.* 1956b, 188–98) and its synonymy with the 'original lands' on the edge of the downs (Dodgson 1978, 62). Of the Kentish 'stocks' the most prominent group is to be found in the area near Milton Regis. These include Woodstock, Pitstock, Bistock, Pistock and Stockbury (Everitt 1986, 168). Milton Regis has access to the rich marshland pastures of north Kent and it seems that wetland pastures were also related to the 'stocks' of Surrey and Sussex. For the former county, Stoke (**6**) near Guildford, Stoke D'Abernon (**7**) and Crastock (**9**) all lie reasonably close to the River Wey, River Mole and Hoe Stream respectively, whereas Stockwell (**10**) illustrates another connection of these names with types of water. For Sussex, the locations of North and South Stoke (**4** and **5**) are the clearest 'stock' names associated with water, due to their close proximity of the River Arun. It is access to downland pastures, however, that may be of greatest significance for this type of place-name. The majority, six of the ten, 'stock' names encountered lie on the North and South Downs; the remainder are in the Thames Basin. This is important as vaccaries, in part indicated by *stoc* names, seem to have been a particular feature of the Kentish downland economy (Everitt 1986; Witney 1990, 26). If the 'stock' names on the Sussex downland are in fact derived from *stoc* and not *stocc*, as may in some instances be the case, it could be claimed that cattle's place in the medieval economy of the South Downs, especially the wooded western part, shares huge similarities with the North Downs of Kent.

The establishment names described above appear to be distributed within the western portion of the study area. They noticeably avoid the High Weald; however, this may be a product of a small sample size. An alternative explanation for this dearth of instances may be caused by the relatively late date that High Wealden place-names enter the record (*i.e.* generally not being recorded until the increase of documentation of the 12th and 13th centuries). It must be noted that the name of Chelwood Vetchery, which was highlighted above, was not recorded until 1546 when it was named *the Vatcherie* (*P.N.Sx* 1930, 350). The most widespread establishment names comprise those in 'stoc', although these were only found in the Thames Basin and South Downs. These *pays* were in contrast to those where names in *stall/steall* and *vacherie* can be found, which were limited to the wooded areas of the Low Weald and North Downs.

4.6 *Wic*

Analysis of the distribution of major Sussex and Surrey '**wic**' place-names entering the historical record by 1450 (Plate 4.3 and Table 4.3) shows on first glance little apparent patterning in occurrence. This seeming randomness is a feature of the place-names distribution that has not been lost on past authors (Dodgson 1978, 62); however, when analysed in relation to time factor a certain trend is discernible. The seven *wic* names on record by 1086 are fairly evenly distributed through the different *pay* of the two counties, although they are noticeably absent from the Greensand Ridge, North Downs, Pevensey Levels and Romney Marsh. What is clear from the 12th, 13th and early 14th centuries, however, is the explosion in recorded *wic* sites, particularly in the Weald, but also on the Greensand Ridge, which was neglected previously. This may in part be a product of source material availability, that is the upsurge in documentation coinciding with the increase in recorded instances. Of this profusion of Wealden, *wic* names, a concentration is located in the north-western Sussex

Weald and across the border in Surrey. This is an important area in medieval settlement studies and will be returned to later.

This vast increase in *wic* names during the 12th and 13th centuries may be of some significance for it is this period that is witness to the creation of the specialised cattle ranches or vaccaries that thus far have been largely seen as a feature of marginal upland areas. Vaccaries performed a variety of functions: as producers of beef stock (*herd wicks*), as breeding stations for the oxen that would provide the plough teams necessary to work arable lands and as dairies (producing milk and cheese) (Winchester 2010, 115). Of course, as has already been highlighted, *wic* names may not always be associated with the farming of cattle, although the link between one of these major place-names, Trubweek (**32**), with an excavated vaccary site (Margetts 2017; Chapter 9) and Drungewick (**11**), a vaccary already shown through documentary evidence (see Chapter 3), intensifies the need to look at these place-names as potential indicators of cattle stations. This is especially important for it has been almost four decades since Everitt claimed that the *wic* names of Sheldwich near Faversham and Boyke near Elham were likely vaccary sites (Everitt 1986, 168).

The association of *wic* names with sheep dairying is well known from the South-East and has been perfectly illustrated by Rippon (2000, 205) in the context of Romney Marsh. What he found during this study is that some of the *wic* names indicated the pasturing of cattle instead of sheep (*ibid.*). Sheep and goats are evident in the nomenclature of Surrey and Sussex with the names Gatwick (**13**), Gotwick (**15**) and Shopwyke (**29**) indicating goat dairies in the Weald and a sheep dairy on the Sussex Coastal Plain. Goats are more suited to a wooded Wealden environment than sheep, who suffer from foot rot on wet clays, while goats can take full advantage of rough grazing and browse. Such names must obviously be discounted from potential indicators of the cattle economy of the South-East, and perhaps the suitability of particular environments of the region's separate *pays* should be taken into account when judging the livestock kept at a particular location. It is interesting to note that the *wic* names of the South Downs are restricted to the eastern, less well-wooded downland that has been traditionally associated with sheep pasture; although it has been shown in Chapter 3 that cattle, too, were a feature of the medieval eastern downs.

The place-name Smithwick (**8**) may be an indicator of *wic* names associated with manufacture and industry, rather than any dairying or vaccary connotations, though it could be postulated that the name may come from a family or other root meaning. It must also be highlighted that the large quantities of *wic* names in the Weald, well known for its medieval and later ironworks, could potentially be associated with industrial activities rather than cattle farming. Other names hinting at alternative connotations to dairying have also been encountered. Terwick (**30**) or 'dung farm' (*P.N.Sx* 1929, 42) on the Sussex Greensand must be associated with the need to improve these poor soils. Seigneurial 'dung hills' (*mixen*) have been fully explored from a documentary perspective and the fact that dung can be associated with a *wic* place-name element further illustrates the paramount importance

TABLE 4.3: *Wic* place-names of Sussex and Surrey recorded prior to 1450

No.	Place-name	Element's 'meaning'	County	Date of first recording	References
1	Hazelwick Farm	*hæsel, wic*	Sussex	947	(*P.N.Sx* 1930, 281–82)
2	Hollick Farm	*?hēale wic*	Surrey	889	(*P.N.Sr* 1934, 110)
3	Lydwick	*hliþ, wic*	Sussex	956	(*P.N.Sx* 1929, 160)
4	Southwick	*wic* 'south wic'	Sussex	1073	(*P.N.Sx* 1929, 248)
5	Strudgwick Wood	*strod, wic*	Sussex	956	(*P.N.Sx* 1929, 107)
6	Whyke (Rumboldswhyke)	*Regenbeald, wic*	Sussex	1086	(*P.N.Sx* 1929, 13–14)
7	Wyke	*wic*	Surrey	1086	(*P.N.Sr* 1934, 136–37)
8	Smithwick	'smiths farm'	Sussex	1091–1125	(*P.N.Sx* 1930, 322)
9	Aldwick	*eald, wic*	Sussex	1235	(*P.N.Sx* 1929, 93)
10	Barpham Week	*Wic*	Sussex	1255	(*P.N.Sx* 1929, 165)
11	Drungewick	*wic, ing* 'Farm of the people of Dēora'	Sussex	1279	(*P.N.Sx* 1930, 131)
12	Endlewick	*Wic*	Sussex	1279	(*P.N.Sx* 1930, 413)
13	Gatwick	'Goat farm'	Surrey	1241	(*P.N.Sr* 1934, 288)
14	Goddenwick Farm	*Godinga-wic* 'wic of Goda's people'	Sussex	1261	(*P.N.Sx* 1930, 341)
15	Gotwick Farm	*gat, wic* 'goats farm'	Sussex	1279	(*P.N.Sx* 1930, 328)
16	Greatwick Farm	*grafet, wic*	Sussex	1288	(*P.N.Sx* 1929, 210)
17	Holywych	*halig, wic*	Sussex	1229	(*P.N.Sx* 1930, 367)
18	Howick Farm	*hoh, wic* 'dairy-farm at the foot of the hill'	Sussex	1166	(*P.N.Sx* 1929, 157)
19	Howicks	*hoh, wic* 'farm on the spur of land'	Surrey	1241	(*P.N.Sr* 1934, 236)
20	Lynwick House	*lind, wic* 'lime- tree wic'	Sussex	1279	(*P.N.Sx* 1929, 157)
21	Markwich Farm	*Mearc, wic* 'farm on the boundary'	Surrey	1282	(*P.N.Sr* 1934, 243)
22	Newick Farm	*niwe, wic*	Sussex	1121	(*P.N.Sx* 1930, 466)
23	Northwick	*norþ, wic*	Sussex	1121	(*P.N.Sx* 1930, 432)
24	Orleswick	'wic of one Ordlaf'	Sussex	1121	(*P.N.Sx* 1930, 325)
25	Rudgwick	*hrycg, wic* ' the wic on the ridge'	Sussex	1210	(*P.N.Sx* 1929, 156)
26	Runwick House	*?hruna, wic* 'farm by the treestump'	Surrey	1222	(*P.N.Sr* 1934, 173)
27	Rutwick	*Ruh, wic* 'rough'	Surrey	1263	(*P.N.Sr* 1934, 231)
28	Sedgewick Castle	*secg, wic* 'farm by the sedge'	Sussex	1222	(*P.N.Sx* 1929, 231–32)
29	Shopwyke	*sceap, wic* 'Sheep-farm'	Sussex	1187	(*P.N.Sx* 1929, 76)
30	Terwick	*tord, wic* 'dung farm'	Sussex	1271	(*P.N.Sx* 1929, 42)
31	Thornwick	*þorn, wic*	Sussex	1269	(*P.N.Sx* 1929, 162)
32	Trubweek	*Trub(b)a, wic*	Sussex	1166	(*P.N.Sx* 1930, 269)
33	Upwick	*uppe, wic*	Sussex	1296	(*P.N.Sx* 1930, 434)
34	Wick	*Wic*	Sussex	1261	(*P.N.Sx* 1929, 171)
35	Wick Wood	*Wic*	Sussex	1286	(*P.N.Sx* 1929, 34)
36	Dudwick	'Dudda's wic or dairy farm'	Surrey	1332	(*P.N.Sr* 1934, 88)
37	Slaughterwicks Barn	*sloughtre, wic* 'sloe-tree farm'	Surrey	1332	(*P.N.Sr* 1934, 288–89)
38	Newick	*niwe, wic*	Sussex	1364	(*P.N.Sx* 1930, 316)

manure played in medieval crop and pasture husbandry and may even indicate a farm specialising in manure (Cullen and Jones 2012, 98). It is interesting to note that stalled animals are far more likely to have been cattle as their tendency to poach (break the turf with hooves) the ground in winter is well known.

Of the corpus of names, those containing topographical elements are the most numerous, with nine examples out of a total of 38. Of these, five – Lydwick (3), Barpham Week (10), Howick Farm (18), Howicks (19) and Rudgwick (25) – are associated with 'upland' in the form of ridges, hills and slopes. Of these, all (apart from Barpham Week, which is on the South Downs) are located in the concentration of *wic* names on the Surrey–Sussex border. Of the topographic names, only a single example, Strudgwick (5) or 'farm in the marshy place' (*P.N.Sx* 1929, 107), can be said to be associated with 'wetland'. Names associated with trees are the next most commonly occurring category, with Hazelwick (1), Holywych (17), Lynwick (20), Thornwick (31) and Slaughterwicks Barn (37) all indicating different species, while Runwick (26) is included for it may essentially mean 'farm by the tree stump' (*P.N.Sr* 1934, 173). As one would expect, most of these are located in the Weald, although Runwick and Thornwick are near the foot of the North Downs and on the ridge of the South Downs respectively.

Personal names also make up a number of instances. Goddenwick Farm (14), Orleswick (24), Trubweek (32) and Dudwick (36) are all associated with Old English forenames and probably indicate the early appropriation of detached seasonal pastures by freemen, lords or families. The only exception to this is Trubweek, the nomenclature of which was never certainly defined by Mawer and Stenton (*P.N.Sx* 1930, 269), though they felt it may derive from an amalgamation of a personal name *Trubba* (a possible pet form of *Trumbeorht* or *Trumbeald*) and *wic*. An alternative explanation for this place-name has been ventured by Warne (2009, 18), who interpreted the first element *Trubba* as possibly being derived from the Latin *troppus* for flock or herd, thus forming 'herd-wick' or similar (Margetts 2017; Chapter 9). Prior to appropriation by individuals, seasonal pastures would have been utilised by communities and have been termed 'folk dens' (Witney 1976; Everitt 1986). Drungewick's (11) place-name is a clear indication of these earlier communal pastures associated with a *wic* name element. The combination of *wic* with an *ing* element gives it the meaning of 'farm of the people of *Dēora*' (*P.N.Sx* 1930, 131). This is significant, for *Dēora*'s people are also associated with Durrington on the Sussex coast (Glover 1975, 49) and as such Drungewick can be viewed as the outlying dairy farm for this parent settlement (Durrington) in the south (Hudson 1980, 83).

Alternative place-names associated with dairying seem to be rare occurrences in Surrey and Sussex, although minor names indicating the practice are yet to be analysed. Only a single major name, Somerley (1), exists prior to 1450 within the two counties. The place is located on the Manhood Peninsula around two miles from the cattle name, Keynor, and two and a half miles from Chalder. Somerley effectively means a 'clearing used in summer' (*P.N.Sx* 1929, 89) and surely reflects seasonal pastoral use of this area during the early medieval period, a time when the peninsula was characterised by woodland commons (Brandon 1978, 8). The lack of major names associated with dairying may not be true for Kent. Fox (2012, 149) has highlighted the place-name of Smarden as potentially indicating butter-making in a wood-pasture environment and Everitt (1986, 31, 122) gives the names Milkstead, Somerden and Summerlees as evidence of dairying and old, Wealden, summer pastures.

In comparison to establishment names, *wic* place-names appear to occupy those parts of the South Downs where *stoc* names do not exist (*i.e.* the eastern South Downs). The *wic* names of the Low Weald cluster around the single instance of *vacherie*, whereas those of the Thames Basin appear to be interspersed with the *stoc* names that also occur in that area.

4.7 'Shieling' names

Names incorporating '*scydd*', '*stead*' and '*gesell*' are habitative in nature and are associated with seasonal pasturing connected to the system of transhumance. It was determined to categorise these as shieling names as, though the term specifically relates to seasonal settlements, in the north of the country these southern Old English words share similar origins and associations. *Gesell* and *scydd* in particular may be related to buildings associated with out pasturing, transhumance, pannage and summering. They may be interpreted as signifying generally similar herdsmen's huts to those found on the moors of the south-west (Fox 2012), the north of England and the Scottish borders (Winchester 2000, 90–93), the Welsh uplands (Sambrook 2006) and the mountains of Ireland (Gardiner 2012a).

Major **(ge)sell** names recorded before 1450 are entirely restricted to the Sussex High Weald. The names include elements that indicate the buildings' timber construction, *bēam* in Bemzells (**3**) (*P.N.Sx* 1930, 480) and *bred* in Breadsell (**4**) (*P.N.Sx* 1930, 496) as well as an association with trees in Buxshalls (**1**) and with status in Drigsell, which means 'lord's hut' or similar (*P.N.Sx* 1930, 458). All are located within a mile of headwaters of rivers and major streams, perhaps demonstrating the need of the early pastoralists to be close to water. *Scydd* names, however, are associated with the Sussex Low Weald, perhaps indicating localised nomenclature for 'shieling' sites between the two *pays*. They do, however, share similarities with the *gesell* names in that they too are located close to river sources; in this case Limbo Farm/*Palshuddes* with the Rother (**5**), Bowshots (**6**) with the Arun and Gunshot (**7**) with the Adur.

As already mentioned, Everitt (1986, 20) has equated the numerous *stede* place-names of the North Downs as summer shielings of the early medieval period; this is in an area where vaccaries and sheep-farms were the dominant pastoral establishments in contrast to the swine dens more often associated with the Weald (*ibid.*, 126). That these shielings extended into the North Downs of Surrey is indicated by major place-names on record by 1086. Banstead (**8**), Chipsted (**10**) and Sanderstead (**13**) are all located on the North Downs of

TABLE 4.4: 'Shieling' place-names of Sussex and Surrey recorded prior to 1450

No.	Place-name	Place-name	County	Date of first recording	Sub-type	References
1	Buxshalls	*boc, sele* 'buildings by the beechtree'	Sussex	765	Gesell	(*P.N.Sx* 1930, 340–41)
2	Drigsell	*dryhten, geselle* 'lord's hut, buildings or the like'	Sussex	1086	Gesell	(*P.N.Sx* 1930, 458)
3	Bemzells	*beam, sele* 'house by (some prominent) tree'	Sussex	1296	Gesell	(*P.N.Sx* 1930, 480)
4	Breadsell Farm	'building made of planks or boards'	Sussex	1189–99	Gesell	(*P.N.Sx* 1930, 496)
5	Limbo Farm/ *Palshuddes*	*Ingas, scydd* 'sheds or swine-cotes belonging to the people of Poling'	Sussex	898	Scydd	(*P.N.Sx* 1929, 117–18)
6	Bowshots Farm	*burh, scydd*	Sussex	1296	Scydd	(*P.N.Sx* 1929, 185)
7	Gunshot Common	*Guma, scydd* 'Guma's shed or swine-cot'	Sussex	1279	Scydd	(*P.N.Sx* 1929, 132–33)
8	Banstead	*stede* 'place where beans are cultivated'	Surrey	675	Stead	(*P.N.Sr* 1934, 68–69)
9	Binsted	'Bean stede'	Sussex	1086	Stead	(*P.N.Sx* 1929, 138)
10	Chipstead	*ceap, stede* 'place where a market existed'	Surrey	675	Stead	(*P.N.Sr* 1934, 290)
11	Elsted	*ellen, stede* 'elder-tree place'	Sussex	1086	Stead	(*P.N.Sx* 1929, 34)
12	Oxted	*ac, stede* 'place of oak trees'	Surrey	1086	Stead	(*P.N.Sr* 1934, 332–33)
13	Sanderstead	*sanden, stede* 'sandy place'	Surrey	880	Stead	(*P.N.Sr* 1934, 53–54)
14	Walkingstead	*stede*	Surrey	970	Stead	(*P.N.Sr* 1934, 320)
15	Alderstead Farm	*stede* 'probably alder place'	Surrey	1225	Stead	(*P.N.Sr* 1934, 301)
16	Bedlested	*byden, stede*	Surrey	1235	Stead	(*P.N.Sr* 1934, 314)
17	Bursted	*beorg, stede*	Surrey	1255	Stead	(*P.N.Sr* 1934, 332–33)
18	Buxted	*boc, stede* 'place of beech-trees'	Sussex	1199	Stead	(*P.N.Sx* 1930, 389)
19	Crockstead	'place where crocks or pots were made'	Sussex	1268	Stead	(*P.N.Sx* 1930, 393)
20	Elstead	*ellen-stede* 'place of the elder-trees'	Surrey	1128	Stead	(*P.N.Sr* 1934, 167)
21	Grinstead (East)	'green place'	Sussex	1271	Stead	(*P.N.Sx* 1930, 331)
22	Grinstead (West)	*grene, stede* 'green place'	Sussex	1230	Stead	(*P.N.Sx* 1929, 184–85)
23	Haxted	*heah, stede* 'high place'	Surrey	1235	Stead	(*P.N.Sr* 1934, 329)
24	Hickstead	*stede* 'high (or highest) place'	Sussex	1279	Stead	(*P.N.Sx* 1930, 279–80)
25	Munstead	*stede*	Surrey	12th c	Stead	(*P.N.Sr* 1934, 198–9)
26	Polsted Manor	*pol, stede* 'place by the pool'	Surrey	1160–70	Stead	(*P.N.Sr* 1934, 194)
27	Lusted	*lufu, stede* 'place of love'	Surrey	1402	Stead	(*P.N.Sr* 1934, 337)

TABLE 4.5: 'Den', 'Fold' and 'Snoad' place-names of Sussex and Surrey recorded prior to 1450

No.	Place-name	Element's 'meaning'	County	Date of first recording	Sub-type	References
1	Hendon	*heah, denn* 'at the high swine- pasture'	Sussex	1086	Denn	(*P.N.Sx* 1930, 440)
2	Iden	*iw, denn* 'yew- tree swine- pasture'	Sussex	1086	Denn	(*P.N.Sx* 1930, 530)
3	Playden	*denn* 'Plega's swine-pasture'	Sussex	1086	Denn	(*P.N.Sx* 1930, 533)
4	Brambleden	*Den*	Sussex	1100	Denn	(*P.N.Sx* 1929, 247)
5	Birchden	*biercen, denn* 'swine-pasture overgrown with birches'	Sussex	1203	Denn	(*P.N.Sx* 1930, 370)
6	Collendean	*Cufela, denn* 'Cufela's denn or swine pasture'	Surrey	1223	Denn	(*P.N.Sr* 1934, 293)
7	Cowden	*cu, denn*	Sussex	1296	Denn	(*P.N.Sx* 1930, 483)
8	Danehill	*Den*	Sussex	1279	Denn	(*P.N.Sx* 1930, 335)
9	Gosdenheath	*gos, den*	Sussex	1249	Denn	(*P.N.Sx* 1929, 98)
10	Hammerden	*Den*	Sussex	1279	Denn	(*P.N.Sx* 1930, 452)
11	Haselden	*denn* 'hazel swine-pasture'	Sussex	1200–05	Denn	(*P.N.Sx* 1930, 474)
12	Lullenden Farm	*denn, ing* 'swine pasture of Lulla or of his people'	Surrey	1296	Denn	(*P.N.Sr* 1934, 329)
13	Maplesden	'denn of the maple-tree'	Sussex	1190	Denn	(*P.N.Sx* 1930, 453)
14	Painshill Farm (formerly Dunhurst)	*denn, hyrst*	Surrey	1235	Denn	(*P.N.Sr* 1934, 227)
15	Puttenden Farm	*Puda, denn* 'Puda's swine pasture'	Surrey	1198	Denn	(*P.N.Sr* 1934, 330)
16	Ringden Wood	*hring, denn*	Sussex	1271	Denn	(*P.N.Sx* 1930, 453)
17	Rounden	*ruh, denn* 'at the rough swine pasture'	Sussex	1197	Denn	(*P.N.Sx* 1930, 472)
18	Rumsden Farm	*rum, denn* 'spacious swine-pasture'	Sussex	1295	Denn	(*P.N.Sx* 1930, 379)
19	Thorndean Farm	*denn* 'thorny woodland pasture'	Sussex	1288	Denn	(*P.N.Sx* 1930, 265)
20	Stockenden Farm	*denn* 'stony swine pasture'	Surrey	1312	Denn	(*P.N.Sr* 1934, 325)
21	Danegate	*dun or den*	Sussex	1428	Denn	(*P.N.Sx* 1930, 377)
22	Riseden	*hris, denn* 'swine-pasture overgrown with brushwood'	Sussex	1438	Denn	(*P.N.Sx* 1930, 387)
23	Pitfold House	*pytt, fal(o)d* 'fold in the pit or hollow'	Surrey	909	Fold	(*P.N.Sr* 1934, 183)
24	Alfold	*fal(o)d* 'the old fold'	Surrey	1227	Fold	(*P.N.Sr* 1934, 222)
25	Barfold Farm	*burh, falod*	Sussex	1300	Fold	(*P.N.Sx* 1929, 111)
26	Barkfold	*falod* 'Beadeca's fold'	Sussex	1279	Fold	(*P.N.Sx* 1929, 103)
27	Barnsfold	*bern, falod*	Sussex	1279	Fold	(*P.N.Sx* 1929, 156)

(Continued)

TABLE 4.5: 'Den', 'Fold' and 'Snoad' place-names of Sussex and Surrey recorded prior to 1450 *(Continued)*

No.	Place-name	Element's 'meaning'	County	Date of first recording	Sub-type	References
28	Buckfold Farm	*boc, falod* 'beechtree fold'	Sussex	1273	Fold	(*P.N.Sx* 1929, 115)
29	Burningfold Hall	*ingas, fal(o)d* 'fold of Brūn's people'	Surrey	1177	Fold	(*P.N.Sr* 1934, 235)
30	Canfold Farm	*fal(o)d*	Surrey	1298	Fold	(*P.N.Sr* 1934, 230)
31	Cherfold	*cirice, fal(o)d* 'church fold'	Surrey	1298	Fold	(*P.N.Sr* 1934, 188)
32	Chiddingfold	'fold (or open land) of the dwellers in the hollow'	Surrey	1130	Fold	(*P.N.Sr* 1934, 186–87)
33	Cotterfold	'fold of the cottars'	Surrey	1199	Fold	(*P.N.Sr* 1934, 188)
34	Cowfold	*Falod*	Sussex	1255	Fold	(*P.N.Sx* 1929, 209)
35	Darwell Furnace Farm	*deor, fald* 'deer-fold'	Sussex	1294	Fold	(*P.N.Sx* 1930, 475)
36	Dunsfold	*falod* 'Dunt's fold'	Surrey	1241	Fold	(*P.N.Sr* 1934, 234–35)
37	Durfold	*deor, fal(o)d* 'animal enclosure'	Surrey	1295	Fold	(*P.N.Sr* 1934, 235)
38	Fishfold Farm	*fisc, fal(o)d*	Surrey	1241	Fold	(*P.N.Sr* 1934, 260)
39	Frithfold Farm	*fryhÞ, falod* 'wood fold'	Sussex	1280	Fold	(*P.N.Sx* 1929, 104)
40	Henfold	*henne, falod* 'hen fold'	Surrey	1250	Fold	(*P.N.Sr* 1934, 265)
41	Ifold House	*Eg*	Sussex	1296	Fold	(*P.N.Sx* 1929, 106)
42	Kingsfold	*Falod*	Sussex	1279	Fold	(*P.N.Sx* 1929, 149)
43	Linfold	*lind* 'lime-tree'	Sussex	1239	Fold	(*P.N.Sx* 1929, 106)
44	Petsalls Copse	*pytt, falod* 'fold of or in the pit or hollow'	Sussex	1280	Fold	(*P.N.Sx* 1929, 118)
45	Pollingfold Farm	*ing, fal(o)d* 'fold of the people of Poll(a)'	Surrey	1279	Fold	(*P.N.Sr* 1934, 240)
46	Ramsfold Farm	*Falod*	Sussex	1279	Fold	(*P.N.Sx* 1929, 112)
47	Redfold	*Falod*	Sussex	1296	Fold	(*P.N.Sx* 1929, 154)
48	Slinfold	*slind* 'fold on the slind or slope'	Sussex	1165	Fold	(*P.N.Sx* 1929, 159)
49	Stovoldshill Farm	*stan, fal(o)d* 'stone fold'	Surrey	1229	Fold	(*P.N.Sr* 1934, 243–44)
50	Temple Farm/ Temple Elfande	*ellen, fal(o)d* 'elder-tree fold'	Surrey	1235	Fold	(*P.N.Sr* 1934, 266–67)
51	Upper Ifold	*eg, fal(o)d* 'fold by or on the well-watered land'	Surrey	1241	Fold	(*P.N.Sr* 1934, 236)
52	Crawfold Farm	*crawe, falod*	Sussex	1310	Fold	(*P.N.Sx* 1929, 103)
53	Orfold Farm	*ofer, falod* 'fold by the bank'	Sussex	1338	Fold	(*P.N.Sx* 1929, 134)
54	Snathurst Wood	*snad, hyrst*	Sussex	1422	Snoad	(*P.N.Sx* 1930, 515)

Surrey and similar origins for Elsted (**11**) may be suggested for it lies in the area of the wooded western downs of Sussex. As well as these downland examples, two early recorded *stede* names are located on the Surrey Greensand (Oxted (**12**) and Walkingstead (**14**)) and a single example (Binstead (**9**)) is known from the Sussex Coastal Plain. By the 13th century, 'steads' (from *stede*) seem to have expanded into the Weald with nine examples located in the High and Low Wealds jointly. It must be remembered, however, that this may simply reflect the generally later date that Wealden names entered the documentary record.

The associated nomenclature may indicate that pastoralism was not the only use to which 'steads' were put. Horticultural practice is signified by the names Banstead (**8**) and Binstead (**9**), which include the element '*bēan*'. This possibly accounts for the latter's siting on the agricultural soils of the Coastal Plain. Industry, too, seems to feature as a component of these names. Fulling may be indicated by the place-name Walkingstead (**14**) (*P.N.Sr* 1934, 320) and potting by Crockstead (**19**) (*P.N.Sx* 1930, 393). Chipstead (**10**) is a 'place where a market existed' (*P.N.Sr* 1934, 290) and could be interpreted as the location of a summer fair. All such non-pastoral indicators should obviously be excluded as potential indicators of the cattle economy of the South-East.

As a group, 'shieling' names appear to be spread throughout the *pays* of the South-East, although they noticeably avoid the Pevensey Levels and Romney Marsh, as well as the Thames Basin. Single examples exist on the South Downs and Sussex Coastal Plain, but here Binstead (**9**) has been dismissed as being unrelated to the cattle economy. A noted cluster is evident on the North Downs and adjacent Greensand Ridge on the Kentish border. This may be interpreted as an extension of land-use and nomenclature from the adjoining county. In relation to cattle names, 'shieling' names appear to share a rough correlation, although this may be a product of the former's scattered distribution. Apart from Gunshot Common (**7**), no 'shieling' names existed within the concentration of *wics* and nor was there a close correlation with elements indicating potential cattle establishments.

4.8 *Denns*, folds and snoads

The Old English place-names most synonymous with the South-East are the **denns** of the Weald. Much work has been penned on the importance of these names, and the seasonal pastures that they represent, to both the development of medieval settlement and society in the region. That *denn* place-names could have been associated with the pasturing of cattle, as well as the swine that they are more often associated with, has already been indicated in the introduction to this chapter and it seems certain that, in some areas of Kent at least, wood pasture for cattle, sheep and goats may have been more important than the right of pannage (Everitt 1986, 31). Indeed, the pasturing of cattle on wooded commons, folk dens and several pastures may have been key to the clearance and colonisation of certain areas such as the North Downs. This is a factor that shows the Domesday evidence for medieval pastoralism to be deceptive, for it is overwhelmingly concerned with the record of pannage rights (*ibid.*).

In the Weald of Surrey and Sussex *denn* place-names are, in comparison to the large numbers from Kent, uncommon. Of a systematic search of the relevant Place-Name Society volumes (*P.N.Sx* 1929; 1930; *P.N.Sr* 1934) only 22 enter the record by 1450 and two of these are situated on the Sussex coast and the Greensand Ridge (Brambleden (**4**) and Gosdenheath (**9**) respectively). On the face of it, 20 Wealden examples seems a lot; however, when we consider that over 500 have been recorded from Kent (although these are not restricted by time factor), the numbers are insignificant.

In addition to cattle, as represented by the place-name Cowden (**7**), geese are also represented as an associated form of livestock (**9**). The remainder of the names are largely related to trees, woodland and other vegetation, although the iron industry, which is also a feature of Wealden exploitation, is represented in the name Hammerden (**10**). The lack of *denn* names in the two counties may suggest that pastoral management of these areas evolved along different lines to that of Kent; however, Brandon (2003, 46) felt this to be incorrect as an identical system of parent settlement and detached seasonal outlier was in evidence in this area and was represent by place-names incorporating 'fold'. That the 'dens' of Surrey and Sussex also fulfilled this outlier role is demonstrated by the name Lullenden (**12**) in Surrey, which contains the element *ing* and thus means 'Swine pasture of Lulla or of his people' (*P.N.Sr* 1934, 329). Personal names recorded in Playden (**3**), Collendean (**6**) and Puttenden (**15**) may have similar connotations, although this could be interpreted as early appropriation by individuals of once communal pastures. Playden is of further note due to its close proximity to the cattle name Oxenbridge, a juxtaposition it shares with the place-name Iden (**2**).

The *'fald/falod'* names of the region are largely located on the clay-lands of the north-western Sussex Weald and adjoining parts of Surrey. This distribution was not lost on the writers of the Place-Name Society volumes (*P.N.Sx* 1930, 550) and it seems that this concentration of names denotes similar outlying pastures to the Kentish 'dens' (Brandon 1974, 72); indeed, the number of still traceable droveways that link these detached 'folds' to their parent settlements is still a noticeable feature of the landscape of Sussex (*ibid.*, 74). As has been noted previously, this area of the two counties is also home to a multitude of names with a *wic* place-name element, and it is possible that the two may share some symbiosis in medieval pastoral land-use.

That fold names were associated with early medieval communal use of the Wealden forest is reflected in the names Burningfold (**29**) and Chiddingfold (**32**), which both contain the Old English *ing* element (*P.N.Sr* 1934, 186–87, 235) and it seems that individuals (Barkfold (**26**), Canfold (**30**)) and even kings (Kingsfold (**42**)) were keen to claim these Wealden pastures. The use of 'folds' extended to lower sections of society, too, as evidenced by the place-name Cotterfold (**33**), which means 'fold of the cottars' (*P.N.Sr* 1934, 188), and even to ecclesiastics as shown by Cherfold (**31**) and Temple Farm/Temple Elfande (**50**).

The latter is especially interesting as this farm was held by the Knights Templar, although the name may have originated as '*Ella's* fold' or perhaps 'elder-tree fold' (*P.N.Sr* 1934, 266–67). Of the remaining names the profusion of woodland, tree, hill or slope and water-related elements associated with this category simply reinforce the findings of all the searches attempted above. That is to say, all of these categories of place-name seem to place import on these particular topographic elements. Of 'fold' names related to animals, Cowfold (**34**) is the only one associated with cattle but deer (Darwell Furnace Farm (**35**)), 'wild beasts' (Durfold (**37**)), chickens (Henfold (**40**)), sheep (Ramsfold (**46**)) and even fish (Fishfold (**38**)) also feature.

Only a single **'*snoad*'** name was encountered within Sussex and Surrey, that being Snathurst Wood (**54**) in the eastern Sussex Weald. A '*snoad*' was an area severed from the common use of the forest and denotes a contrasting type to the 'dens'. Indeed, names incorporating *snoad* seem to be of earlier derivation from a time before 'dens' were appropriated or had become manorial, a time when the only parts of the forest that were outside of common usage were the parts owned by the early Saxon kings (Witney 1976, 61–63).

The distribution of *fald/falod* names versus those in *denn* is distinctive and, whilst they may represent similar outlying pastures (Brandon 1974, 72), the sharp boundary between east and west is worthy of further comment. Gardiner (1995, 63) has seen the lack of *denn* names in Sussex as being unlikely to be the product of survival or of local usage, it being dubious that dialect would be contained by administrative borders. It is more likely that a lack of names in *denn* represented an absence of swine pastures in the eastern Sussex Weald versus neighbouring parts of Kent (*ibid.*). *Fald/falod* was interpreted by Smith (*P.N.E.* 1956a, 164) as 'a fold, a small enclosure for animals', and its occurrence in western Sussex in preference to *denn* could indicate these locations were put to an alternative pastoral use. Certainly, they appear to correlate with the concentration of *wic* names noted above and they are fringed by a number of cattle and establishment names including Vachery and Stallhouse Farm. They appear to show little correlation with any of the other explored elements.

4.9 Conclusion

This study of place-names that may be connected to the medieval cattle economy has succeeded in highlighting a number of common themes. That cattle were a ubiquitous element in the pastoral and, indeed, arable usage of all the various *pays* of the region has been proven by analysis of names that include some cattle-related element. This is a conclusion from the toponymy that is shared with the results of the earlier documentary study of the region. This again highlights the lack of attention this side of the pastoral economy of the South-East has received. The place-name data has shown that specialised cattle establishments certainly existed within the region, as borne out by the identification of '*vacherie*' names which are a rare occurrence nationally

(*P.N.E.* 1956a, 229; only gives the two examples cited here). Names containing stall are also strong candidates for vaccary sites and their existence on the North Downs of eastern Surrey seems to be an extension of this land-use from the neighbouring county of Kent.

Topographic analysis together with in-depth scrutiny of the contributory name elements have shown that potential indicators of the cattle economy often share a number of important aspects as to their siting and nomenclature. Elevated sites seem to have some kind of importance, as do woodland and water. The latter connotation is strengthened when the entire corpus of names are plotted against the hydrology of the two counties (Figure 4.8). This shows the vast majority to be sited close to the headwaters of both major rivers and their tributaries. The need for a ready water supply is an obvious consideration when choosing the location of a stock establishment, although infrastructure also seems to play a role, as illustrated by the number of crossing points alluded to within the cattle-name category. Access to droveways would have been important for both moving cattle to and from market but also between pasture and parent and subordinate settlement.

As well as indications that strengthen the chosen place-name categories' association with the cattle economy, it was also found that there were a number

FIGURE 4.8: The entire corpus of place-names plotted against the hydrology of Sussex and Surrey (drawn by the author. Contains material covered by © Crown copyright and database rights 2019 Ordnance Survey, Educational Service Provider licence number v2.1)

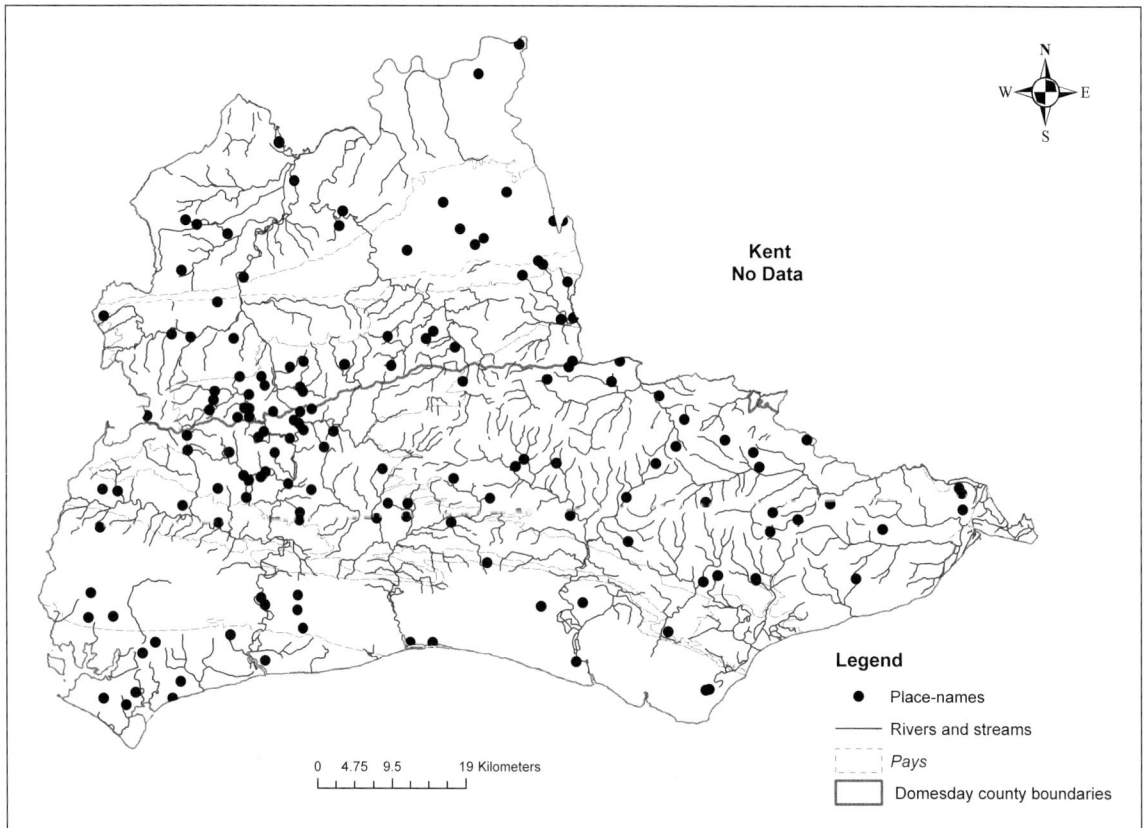

Kent
No Data

Legend
● Place-names
— Rivers and streams
Pays
Domesday county boundaries

0   4.75   9.5   19 Kilometers

of instances that detracted from any connection. The most notable of these are elements indicating that animals apart from cattle were important to the different place-name types. Sheep and goats were the most frequent occurrence, although non-domestic animals, namely deer, also existed. Industry, including fulling, potting and iron-working, featured and it may be that, similarly to the cattle economy, such tasks were carried out on a seasonal basis until the later medieval period.

In the light of this toponymic exploration of the cattle economy of the South-East it may be suggested that during the medieval period there were certain areas in which this form of livestock husbandry flourished. A plot of the entire corpus (Plate 4.6) bears out a reoccurring theme, which is a concentration of names in the north-western Sussex Low Weald and across the border in Surrey. Though at first glance other cattle landscapes beyond this 'heartland' are difficult to discern, this is simply due to the profusion of potential name indicators throughout the two counties. When time factor is taken into consideration these landscapes may be easier to reveal. By highlighting place-name indicators recorded by 1086 it is easier to distinguish where cattle economies may have been sited (Figure 4.9).

The heathlands of the Thames Basin were clearly of some importance for the pasturing of cattle during the early medieval period and the same is true

FIGURE 4.9: Potential indicators recorded prior to 1086 (drawn by the author)

for the wooded North Downs of Surrey and the western downs of Sussex. The eastern South Downs also show some potential as cattle-grazing grounds at this time, and it may be that cattle featured here as well as sheep prior to the later medieval period. When names recorded by 1348 are added (Figure 4.10) the so-called heartland mentioned above becomes more apparent; however, it is also noticeable that the Sussex Coastal Plain and in particular the Manhood Peninsula show increasing potential. Names on the High Weald are fairly numerous, but in places thinly scattered, while small nuclei exist at certain points, most notably to the north of Rye, which may have been able to take advantage of nearby rich pasturage on Romney Marsh.

FIGURE 4.10: Potential indicators recorded prior to 1348 (drawn by the author)

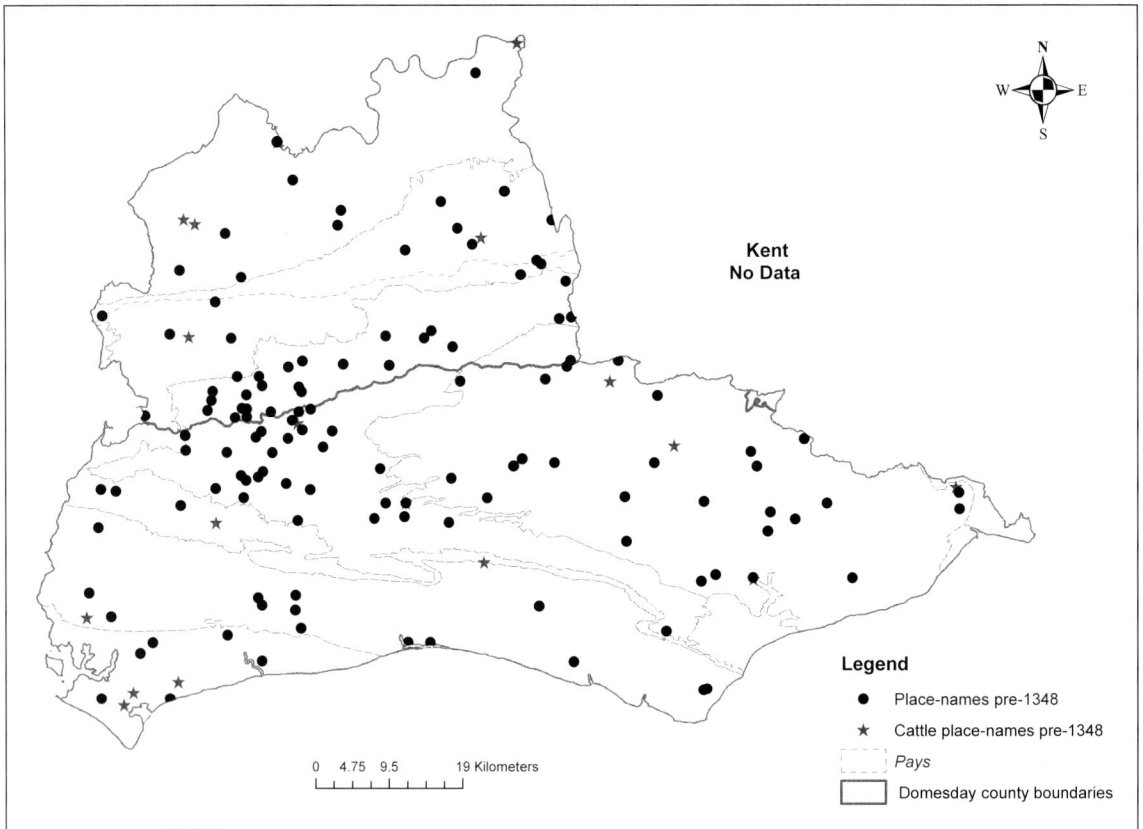

CHAPTER 5

Roads, commons, forest and chase

5.1 Introduction

> The priory accused them of unjustly obstructing a way beside their land in 'Baldyneland' in Preston vill by erecting ditches. The priory perpetrated a writ of novel disseisin. They grant the priory free right of driving beasts through their land. This droveway is 3 ells wide and 33 rods 3 feet long. Lying with the priory's land called 'Southdonne' to east and their land called 'Baldyneland' to west. (CCA-DCc-ChAnt/C/266)

Exploration of both documentary and place-name evidence has shown that droveways were important for the movement of cattle as well as other livestock during the medieval period. These routeways linked parent settlements with seasonal pastures as well as common and areas of Forest and Chase. The latter, subject to specific legal status, are well known to be utilised as elite hunting grounds, although their importance for grazing at both demesne and leased level has only recently been explored at any depth (Winchester 2010; Fox 2012). From the time of the early seasonal herders until the later drives to market, roads were important for both society and the medieval economy. Such routeways were, however, just one element in a medieval infrastructure that existed to serve myriad different (and often competing) needs. As will be shown, they were intimately tied to areas of common and often possessed areas of roadside waste of varying size and morphology. Within this category were a specific type known as 'greens'. Such locations were important not only for providing watering places for stock engaged in transhumance but also as areas for rest and sometimes overnight stay (Fox 2012, 201–04).

The fact that roads and particularly droveways were of fundamental importance to the historic landscape and rural development in the South-East has already been touched upon in the introduction (Chapter 1). It has been noted that routeways were necessary for the early medieval method of resource exploitation. A pattern of landholding emerged that was best suited to the management of the region's banded resources. This was often via a system of parent and outlying seasonal settlements. The road system is one of the most obvious ways in which the early arrangement of landholding has influenced the historic landscape of the South-East (Everitt 1986, 35). Study of the patterns of old droveways in Kent, Sussex and Surrey has shown that they clearly reflect the system of parent and outlier linked via transhumance (Brandon 1974, 73–74; Witney 1976, 132–39; Blair 1991, 6, 14–15). Due to the Weald's broadly elliptical shape, roads have tended to radiate from the central high ground towards the region's circumference (Witney 1976; Brandon 2003, 46). These droveways, and the patterns of landholding they reflect, trend roughly north–south in Surrey and parts of west Kent, before a south-west/north-east axis becomes dominant further east. A north–south direction prevailed in central Sussex, before a south-west/north-east axis becomes the norm in the west (see Figure 5.1 below).

The origin of the droveways is still poorly understood. Apart from some county-based mapping there has been no modern detailed study of these patterns of communication in order to help elucidate their origins and development (Chatwin and Gardiner 2005, 32). Witney (1976, 128–32) saw the droveways of Kent as largely belonging to early medieval, 'Jutish' land-use of the Wealden interior. These routeways were not entirely new, however, and they filled gaps within a pre-existing, looser arrangement of Roman 'iron ways'. The claim that droveways are largely of early medieval origin but may be built on preceding (prehistoric and/or Roman) elements has been further developed by Everitt (1986) in Kent, Brandon (1974, 72–75; 2003, 47) and Bell (2020, 239) in Sussex, and Blair (1991, 6) in Surrey. The equation of these routeways with medieval usage has largely rested upon the circumstantial evidence of their suitability for resource exploitation by multiple estates as well as the fact that they are used for early medieval tenurial boundaries. Seasonal pastoralism as a

FIGURE 5.1: Simplified mapping of territorial links and droves of the South-East showing the dominant pattern around the circumference of the Weald (drawn by the author after Brandon 1974, fig. 5; Witney 1976, fig. 14; Blair 1991, 6, fig. 5)

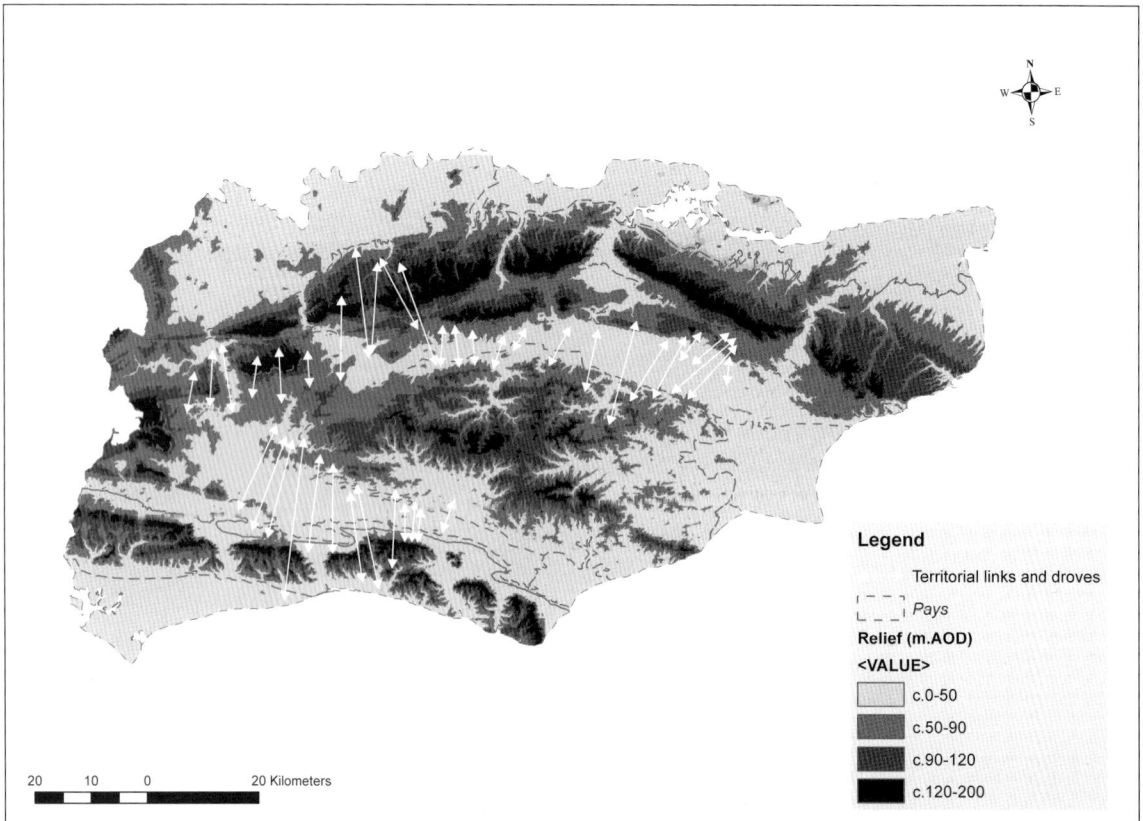

Legend

Territorial links and droves

Pays

Relief (m.AOD)

<VALUE>

c.0-50

c.50-90

c.90-120

c.120-200

20   10   0   20 Kilometers

component of these systems is recorded within evidence such as Anglo-Saxon Charters as well as place-names, but this only provides a *terminus ante quem* for their use.

The study of medieval routeways has been slow to gain popularity within the disciplines of either landscape history or archaeology (Fox 2012, 192). This is likely due to the difficulties in their study that are explored within the following discussion of methodology. This is not to say that useful work has not been completed. As well as the Kentish examples mentioned above (Witney 1976; Everitt 1986), exploration of droveways has also taken place in Leicestershire, Dartmoor and the Forest of Arden (Fox 1989; 2012; Hooke 1998). In addition to this work, examination of so-called co-axial landscapes often shows that parallel droveways or 'resource linkage routes' often existed alongside 'watershed boundaries' (Williamson 2013) as elements within extensive, apparently planned landscapes (*e.g.* Williamson 1987). Potential evidence of such a landscape has been highlighted within the western Sussex Weald through the efforts of Chatwin and Gardiner (2005). This showed that a roughly parallel set of routeways separated by loosely co-axial field-systems was in place by at least the 10th century, although no firm conclusions as to the landscape's origins could be drawn.

The lack of a detailed chronology and the rather speculative assumption that the majority of the South-East's droveways are of early medieval origin has not been tested through excavation, scientific dating, regional scale analysis or comparisons with other similar patterns around the country or the continent. Nor has the road system been examined in comparison to underlying variables that may have had an effect on their siting or direction such as geology, topography and hydrology. The role played by environmental factors has only recently re-emerged as important in respect to landscape evolution. Authors such as Williamson (2013) are beginning to realise the fundamental influence that such variables had on the shaping of the landscape, perhaps with more importance placed on these than any social determinism. Over the last two decades he has begun to view landscapes such as the *Scole-Dickleburgh Field-System* as the result of a long process of adaptation and change rather than any single planned event (Williamson 1987; 2013, 106). It will be an important element of the following work that environmental variables, which have not been considered in any detail previously, will be fully explored here. This analysis will be aided by examination of a recently excavated droveway (Margetts 2018a) and an open mind as to the true origins of the medieval road network of the South-East.

5.2 Methodology

Before exploring the methodology utilised to map and examine the history of roads, commons, Forests and Chase, it is important to pause and reflect upon the various hindrances facing the gathering of data and the archaeological recognition of these features. Perhaps the greatest problem with investigating an early road network is that, unless the area being traversed was characterised by agricultural fields (whether open or enclosed), roads were often not definite physical entities with well-defined limits. Rather they comprised rights of way or easements created through customary usage leading from one settlement or resource to the next (Hindle 2012, 6). This is particularly true of the medieval period where only if the route was much frequented would it become a physical track with legal attachments and status (*ibid.*). By contrast, if a routeway lost importance or fell out of use its physical trace could diminish or even disappear. These factors can cause problems in not only locating a routeway but also in discovering its origins. If use of a roadway persists, its original surface will often be truncated by later activity or buried under a new road (*ibid.*). Any remains that do survive are often comprised of roadside ditches that are found to have been re-cut or periodically cleaned of sediment. If deposits related to the surface itself are encountered these are often not constructed of inherently datable material or are found to have been re-worked by traffic and subject to erosion. Such taphonomic processes serve to remove or limit the usefulness of any associated dating assemblage. Despite these problems, which can have a great effect on attempts at surveying and excavation, ancient roads can sometimes be traced in the 'richest historical record we possess', the landscape itself (Hoskins 1955, 14).

In order to both illustrate the South-East's medieval road network and to subsequently highlight the resource-linkage routes and long-distance droveways utilised by herders and stock farmers, a staged process has been devised. Firstly, a well-defined boundary comprising the transect study area outlined in Chapter 1 was imposed upon the wider South-East (Figure 5.2). The use of this nested study area was necessary for the task would be too great (for this author at least!) to plot the entire system of the South-East. It is hoped, however, that this work may form the foundation for future mapping.

In order to begin the process, it must first be recognised that prior to the medieval period there was already a road system in place. Thousands of years of prehistoric movement had created both long-distance and shorter-length routeways, and while the former tended to persist, especially in upland landscapes, the latter have largely disappeared and are only recoverable through archaeological survey and excavation. It is arguably the Roman road system that left the greatest legacy inherited by the medieval network, and therefore the plotting of this period's major roads (*Stage 1*) provides the basis for the mapping of later systems. This was done with reference to Ordnance Survey mapping as well as Margary's *Roman Ways in the Weald* (1948), which is still regarded as the key text on the Romano-British road network of the South-East (Figure 5.3). This was followed by plotting the bounded roads shown on the OS 1st Edition (1:2500, Sussex and Surrey, 1863–94; *Stage 2*; Figure 5.4). The completion of this stage showed that, along with roads related to the expansion of post-medieval towns, this map also incorporated turnpike roads and a noticeable gap in data

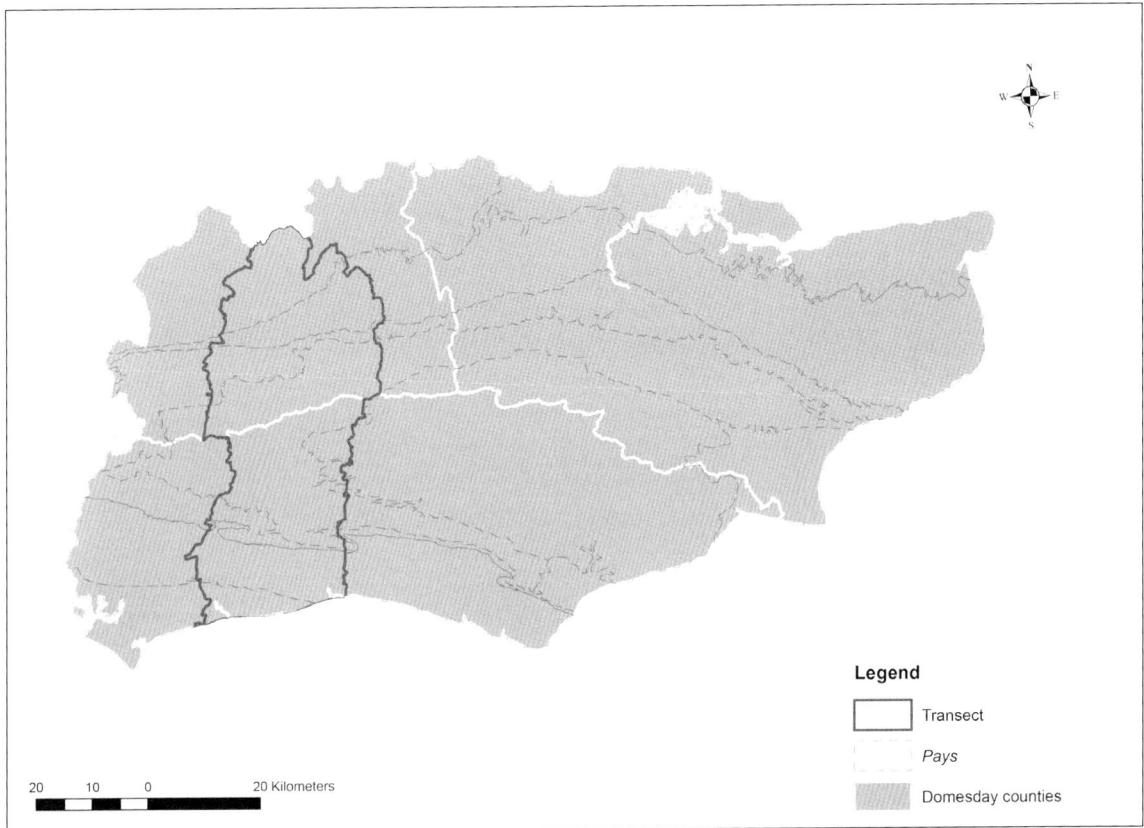

FIGURE 5.2: Main study area showing location of transect (drawn by the author)

on the South Downs. Gaps also existed on the North Downs, although these were less marked. This is largely due to the unbounded nature of routeways in the open downland; here tracks did exist, although they were usually not edged by ditches or any other physical barrier.

In order to map the preceding medieval road system of the transect study area it was determined that a retrogressive approach was followed. This methodology largely related to the use of landscape stratigraphy. This method of examining the countryside's evolution has been utilised previously for the mapping of routeways and associated field-systems. Williamson's work on the *Scole-Dickleburgh System* (1987) in particular utilised such a technique. This technique is not without criticism, and whilst some of this is perhaps unfounded (see Hinton 1997; Williamson 1998) it should not be employed without caution. Environmental factors such as hydrology, topography and geology should always be taken into account. This helps to avoid superficial judgements regarding patterns and apparent phasing (2013, 106).

In accordance with this methodology, the next step (*Stage 3*) involved the removal of turnpike roads, other roads of clear post-medieval origin and short stretches of routeway that were of only very localised use (such as short dead-end

FIGURE 5.3 *(left)*: Roman roads within the transect study area overlain on topography (drawn by the author. Contains material covered by © Crown copyright and database rights 2019 Ordnance Survey, Educational Service Provider licence number v2.1)

FIGURE 5.4 *(right)*: Bounded roads as shown on OS 1st Edition 1:2500, 1863–94 (drawn by the author)

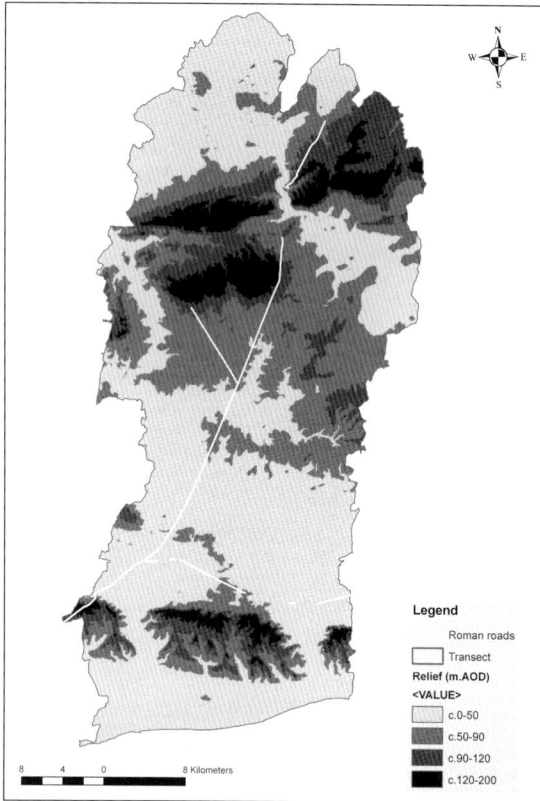

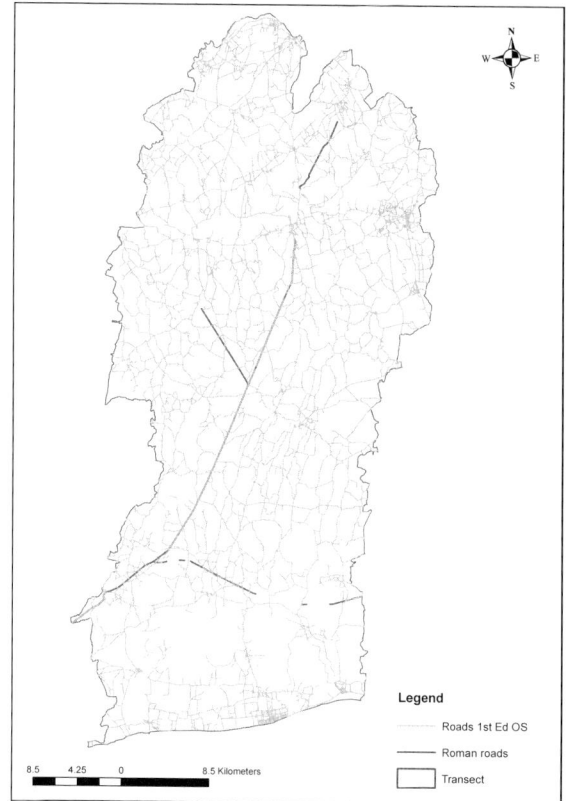

roads leading to farms). In the case of the latter care was taken not to remove examples that may have once been part of the long-distance networks. This was achieved by consideration of the surroundings as shown on historic cartography. If a suspected lost routeway could be traced (for example, in collinear field boundaries between two separate surviving lengths of road) the short length of surviving road was not deleted (Figure 5.5). In the case of turnpike roads their forerunners could sometimes be of medieval origin; however, the act of turnpiking them (or sections of them) would have served to resurface and straighten their course, thus making the cartographic record an unreliable reflection of the medieval network (at least at face value). It was determined, however, that once analysis was complete, medieval or earlier sections could be retraced through historic landscape analysis. Often the previous course of a turnpiked medieval road would survive as an adjacent green lane or footpath (Figure 5.6). Occasionally they would survive 'fossilised' within the boundaries of narrow fields. Turnpike roads were identified with reference to Margary (1950) and Fuller (1953) as well as 'Yeakell and Gardner's map of Sussex' (1778–83). The results can be found in Figure 5.7.

A fourth phase of mapping was completed (*Stage 4*) which involved reference to the Surrey and Sussex tithe maps, most of which date to the late 1830s and

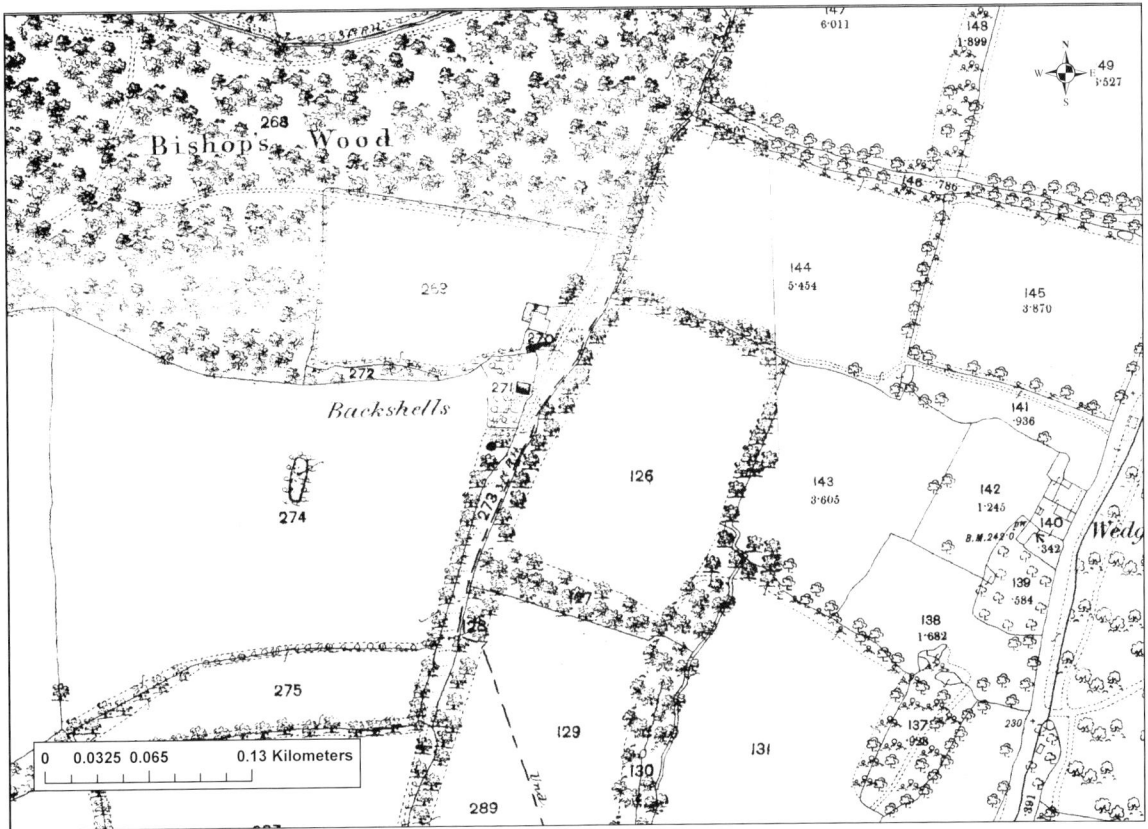

FIGURE 5.5: The small stretch of green lane (labelled 273) next to 'Backshells' near Barns Green, West Sussex, is collinear with field boundaries and footpaths. It is likely that the portion of green lane was once part of a 'lost road' parallel to the extant routeway to the east (OS 1st Edition 1:2500, 1876, with labelling by the author)

1840s, as well as late 18th-century cartography (Rocque's Map of Surrey, 1768; Yeakell and Gardner's map of Sussex, 1778–83; Gardner and Gream 1795). This stage involved the addition of a few lengths of routeway that had not survived into the 19th century as well as completion of the downland areas that were not fully mapped at *Stage 2* due to the largely unbounded nature of the roads in these areas. Confirmation of these routes by 18th-century cartography strengthened the case for their longevity and medieval or pre-medieval origins. They were mapped and the results can be seen in Figure 5.8. This stage is thought to largely reflect the transect study area's network as it would have appeared in the late medieval period.

These routeways would have been the result of a long period of change begun in prehistory. As such it can never be claimed that a network can be recreated in its entirety. Roads are not always static, they can shift as old routes close down, repairs are made, new routes open up and obstacles materialise. It was thus determined to add one further layer of evidence exploring the potential of the historic landscape to provide even earlier evidence of lost routeways (*Stage 5*; Figure 5.9). Of course, such evidence can, without the benefit of archaeological dating, only ever be hypothetical, although historic landscape analysis can be utilised to recreate the line of early roads (Rippon

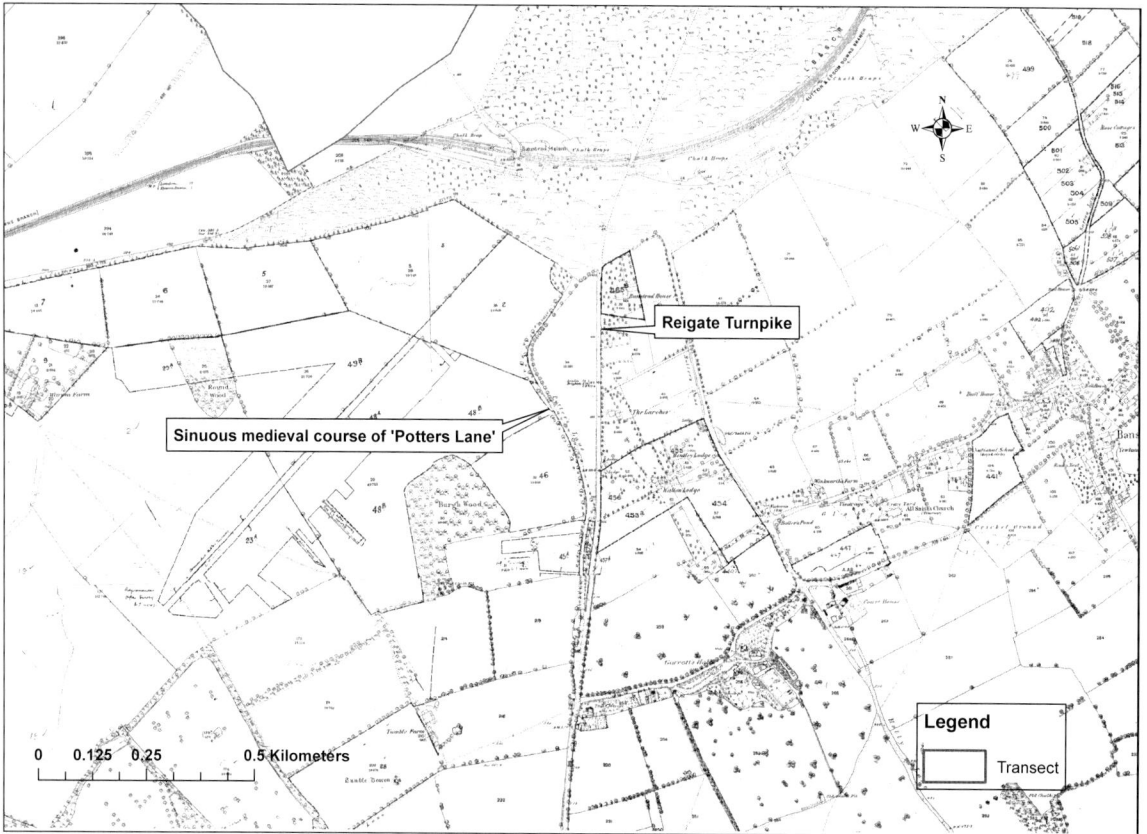

Reigate Turnpike

Sinuous medieval course of 'Potters Lane'

Legend

Transect

0   0.125   0.25   0.5 Kilometers

2004, 34, 134–42). These lost roads were added where the presence of narrow elongated fields either side of a long-distance field boundary or later turnpiked road indicated their presence. Former droveways which were later turnpiked were also easily distinguished. This was due to their inherent broadness (a minimum width of 10–12 m), high bordering hedgebanks and wide verges (Brandon 1974, 74–75).

Where north–south field boundaries extended from the scarp foot of the South Downs these were mapped as part of the 'lost road' dataset. These occasionally corresponded with parish boundaries or the earthworks of redundant holloways known locally as *bostals* or *borstals* (from *beorg-steall*, 'pathway up a steep hill': *P.N.E.* 1956a, 42). In areas of the Weald where long-distance field boundaries, wide shaws and green lanes exist, these often correspond with manorial, parochial and hundredal boundaries. These have been shown by Chatwin and Gardiner (2005) to reflect potential droveways or routes associated with co-axial field-systems. They also often linked road lines that survived into the cartographic record and incorporated ponds for the watering of stock (Figure 5.10).

FIGURE 5.6: The Reigate Turnpike heading south from Banstead Downs, Surrey. The medieval course of the road can be seen to the left. Note that the earlier line of the road is re-joined to the south (OS 1st Edition 1:2500, 1868, with labelling by the author)

Legend
······· Roads minus post-medieval
——— Roman roads
□ Transect

Legend
······· Roads following tithe and 18th century
——— Roman roads
□ Transect

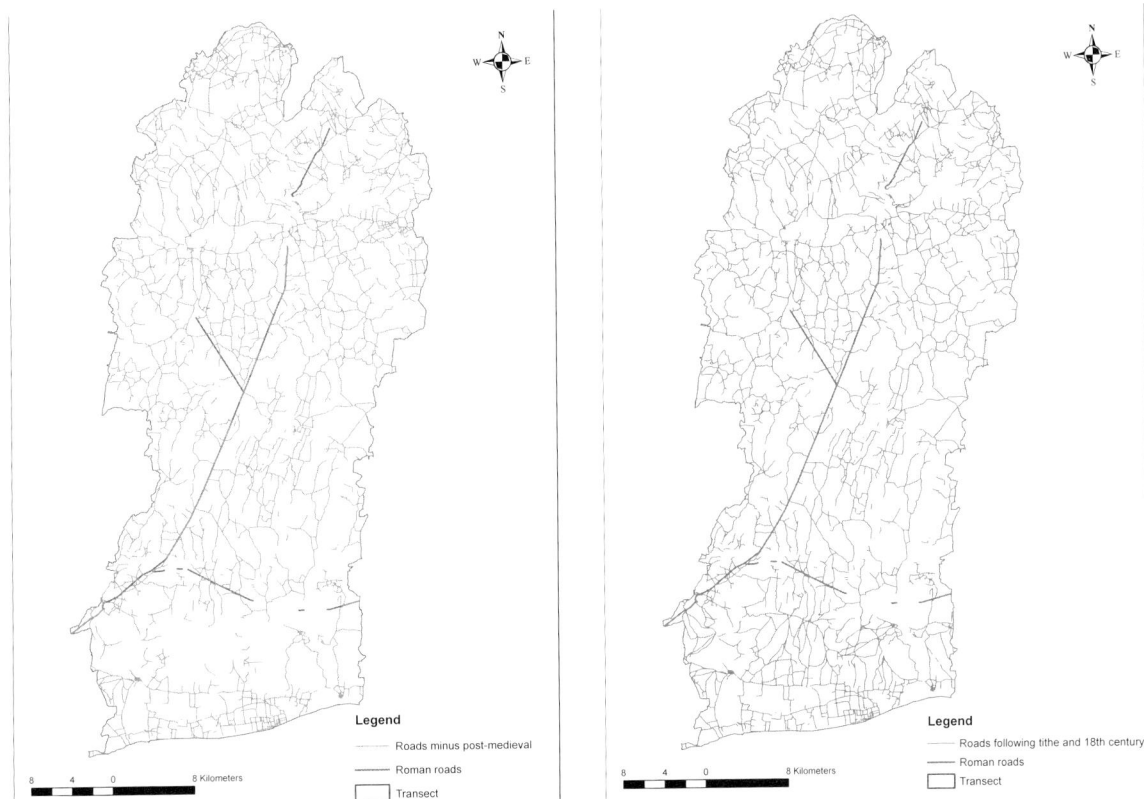

FIGURE 5.7 *(left)*: Stage 3: Road network after removal of turnpikes and other post-medieval routes (drawn by the author)

FIGURE 5.8 *(right)*: Stage 4: Road network following tithe and 18th-century mapping (drawn by the author)

Upon completion of the road network, the next task was to map the commons. These two elements of the historic landscape are intimately tied (see Figure 5.6, for example) and the waste status of many roads and roadsides in the medieval period illustrates that such areas of land can best be seen as elongated areas of common. It should be remembered, however, that all commons were owned by someone and were not open to use by all. This rested upon manorial and other rights. In contrast, roads were often under the jurisdiction of the king as well as manorial lords, although obligations to maintain particular sections often rested with those who lived nearby. All named commons as shown on the 18th-century cartography listed above, the tithe apportionments and OS 1st Edition were mapped excluding roadside waste except for named greens (*Stage 6*; Figures 5.11 and 5.12). At this point the mapped areas of common are thought to have been smaller than their medieval forebears and often subject to early (non-Parliamentary) and later (Parliamentary) enclosure. A phase of historic landscape analysis was therefore considered which would help to clarify the previous extent of those commons that survived into the cartographic record or that had been lost through enclosure. After careful contemplation this was deemed to be a considerable task that ran the risk of confusion of areas of enclosed former 'open field' with the commons themselves. The analysis was therefore not undertaken.

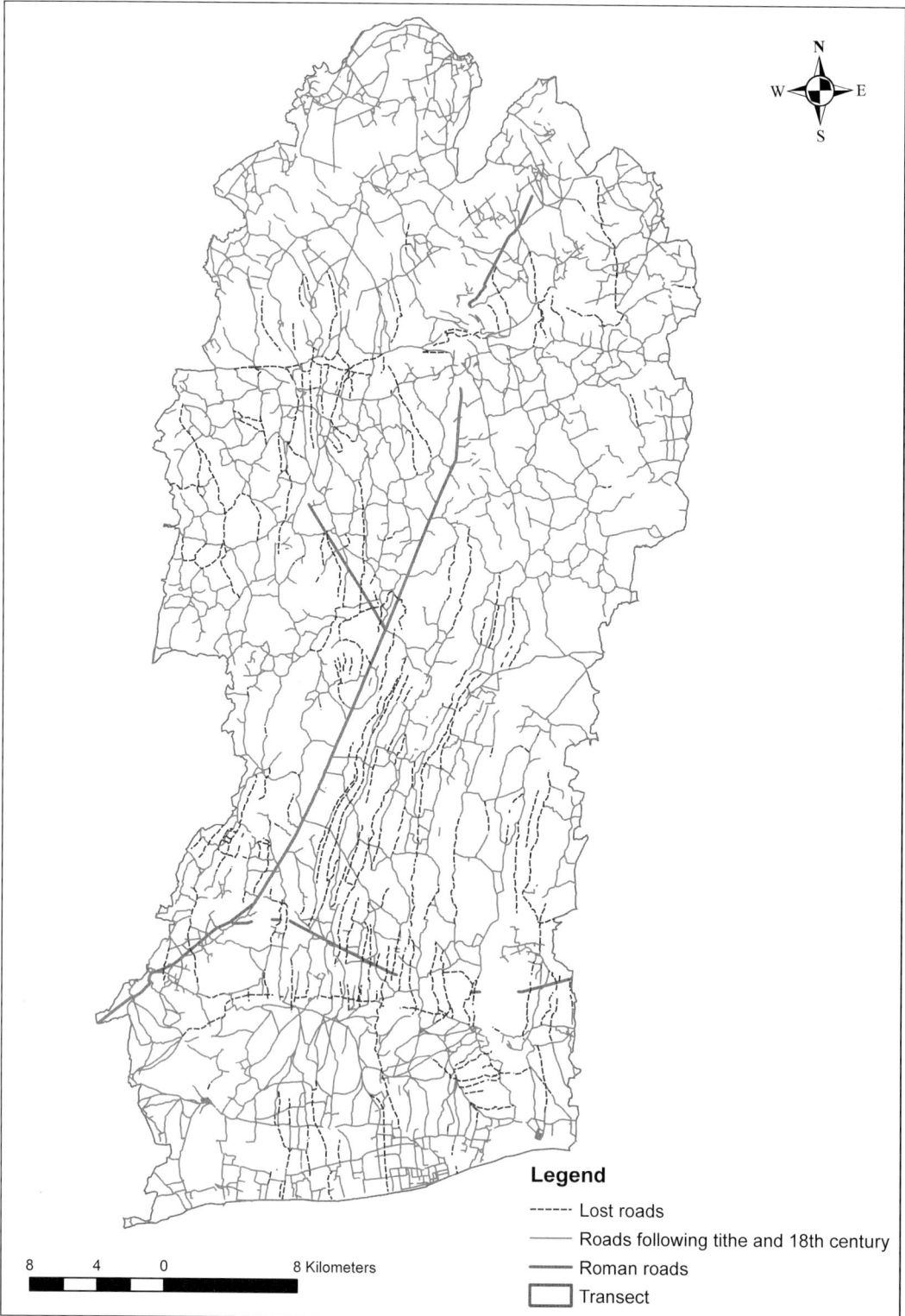

Legend

----- Lost roads
——— Roads following tithe and 18th century
——— Roman roads
☐ Transect

8   4   0   8 Kilometers

FIGURE 5.9: Stage 5: The potential medieval road system of the transect study area showing 'lost' hypothetical routeways (drawn by the author)

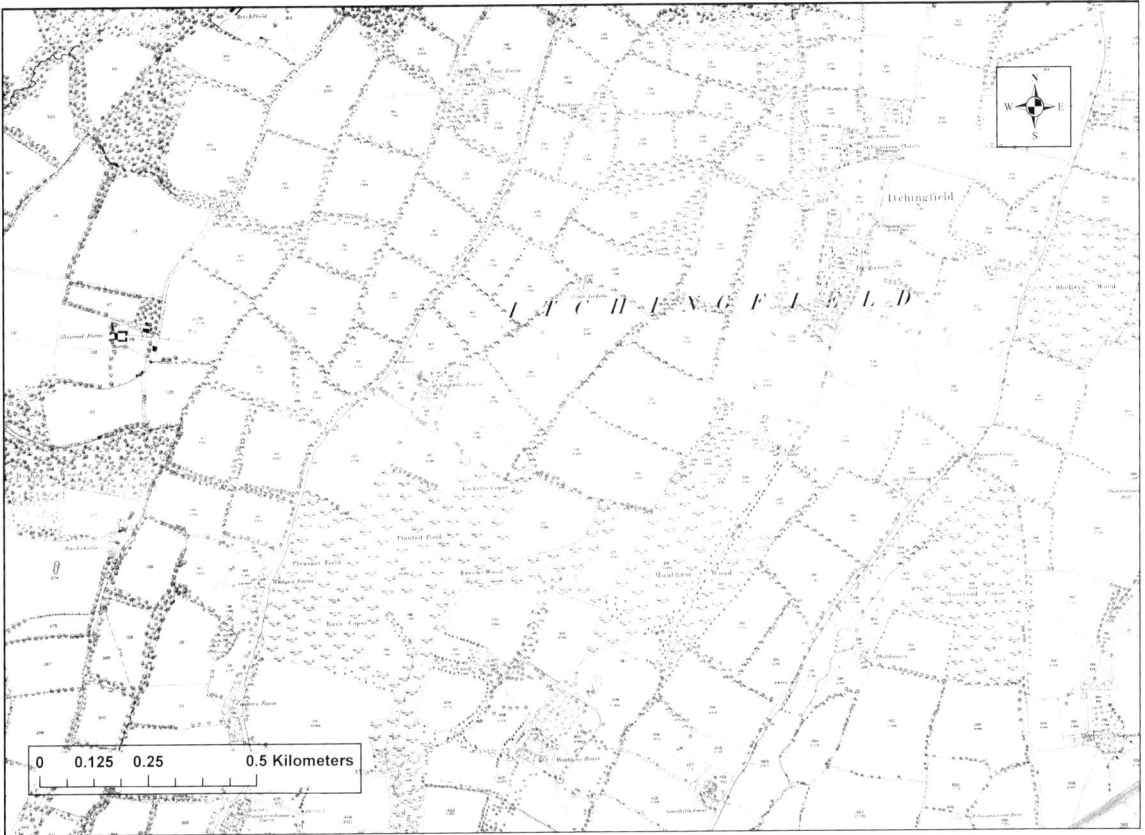

FIGURE 5.10: The loosely co-axial landscape of the Sussex Low Weald. The axial elements comprise droveways and long-distance field boundaries (OS 1st Edition 1:2500, 1876, with labelling by the author)

The ultimate stage of mapping comprised the planning of areas of Forest and Chase. As mentioned above, these have been associated with the pasturing of livestock and it was deemed important that their locations were known. Mapping followed Langton and Jones (2010, fig. 1), which comprised 'Forests and Chases of England and Wales at their fullest, but not necessarily contemporary extents' (*Stage 7*; Figures 5.13 and 5.14).

5.3 Results

The results of this map regression and historic landscape study are discussed below within the context of both the topography and *pays* of the transect study area (Figure 5.15, Plates 5.1 and 5.2). This shows some clear differences in the form of routeway layouts and the presence of commons, 'Forest' and waste, which may be related to underlying variables. What follows is an in-depth analysis of these differences which will also take into account both geology and hydrology in relation to specific patterns, road morphology, distance and dating. It was clear during both the retrogressive analysis and the process of mapping itself that a number of specific *Character Areas* existed within the region. In all,

FIGURE 5.11 *(left)*: The commons and waste of the transect study area, excluding roadside waste (drawn by the author)

FIGURE 5.12 *(right)*: The commons and waste of the transect study area in relation to the medieval road system (drawn by the author)

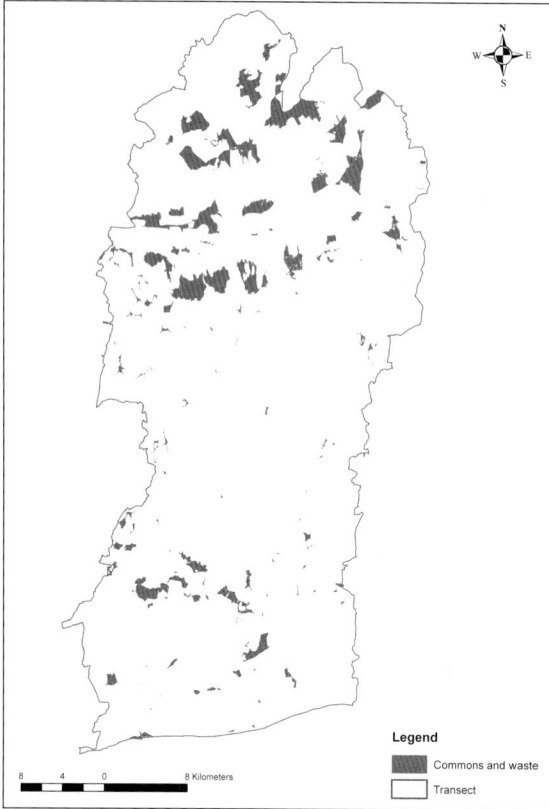

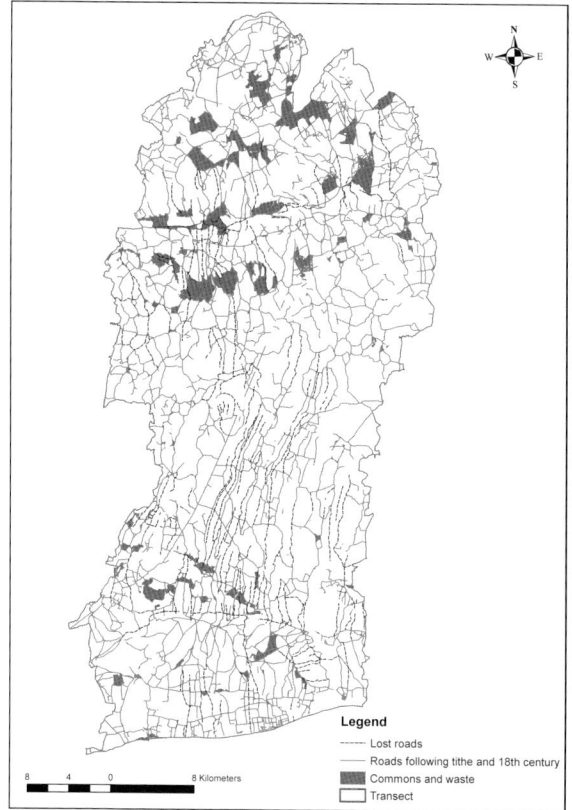

nine distinctive zones were apparent within the transect study area and these are discussed below. This will be undertaken from south to north. The first area to receive discussion is located on the West Sussex Coastal Plain.

Character Area 1: The West Sussex Coastal Plain

Here, in this area of low topography, between the coast and the foot of the South Downs, a rectilinear pattern of roads predominates. Clear north–south routes reach up the dip-slope of the downs and southwards towards the coast. The seaborne routes may have once led to medieval villages now long lost to the sea through coastal erosion (Brandon 1974, 116); however, the routeways often pass close to, or through, places whose names include the '*ingas*' element associated with early folk territories of the South Saxon kingdom. The geology here is raised beach deposits, or terrace gravels, overlain by loessic brickearth. These rich agricultural soils were one of the few areas in the South-East to extensively farm via the open-field method (Chapter 1). This system may have had some bearing on the medieval road network, however, earlier origins can also be suggested. Margary (1948, 205–07) proposed that a similar pattern of boundaries located at Chalvington and Ripe in East Sussex was the result of planning according to Roman land units or *centuriation*. While this has never

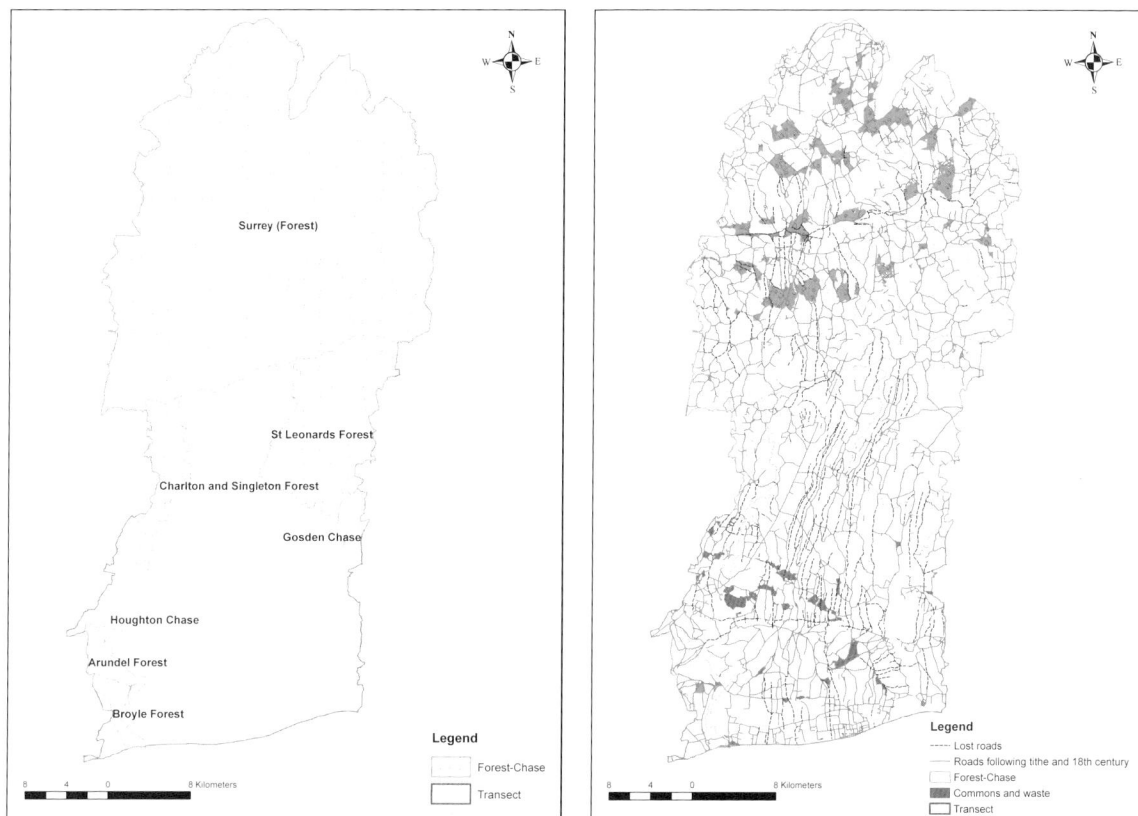

FIGURE 5.13 *(left)*: The Forests and Chases of the transect study area (drawn by the author after Langton and Jones 2010, fig. 1)

FIGURE 5.14 *(right)*: The Forests and Chases of the transect study area in relation to the medieval road system, commons and waste (drawn by the author)

been proven, recent large-scale excavations to the west of transect study area may indicate an even earlier, Late Iron Age–Early Romano-British date for this rectilinear layout.

Such rectilinear landscapes may be reasonably characteristic of the Coastal Plain where they later formed the basis for the historic as well as the modern road pattern (*ibid.*). The rectilinear arrangement encountered within the transect study area is only broken by the presence of the Arun and Adur estuaries; it is also noticeable, however, that it is traversed by two long-distance east–west routeways. The southerly of these splits at Sompting from the more northerly, which roughly corresponds with the modern-day A27. Each has been proposed as Roman in origin (Margary 1947; Shields 2005, 143, 146; Carpenter *et al.* 2016, 67–72) and the A27 was likely an important communication link during the medieval period (Shields 2005, 143).

Within this area of the Coastal Plain, commons and waste were sparse and generally small in size. One of the largest is Stonefield Common in the parish of Littlehampton with neighbouring waste in the parish of Climping. Common pasture for cattle is recorded at Atherington in the 14th century (1334; *Cal. Close* 1333–37, 194–95) the demesne of which was managed by the bailiff of Séez Abbey (AD 1378: TNA E 106/11/2). Atherington Farm lies a little to the west of the commons. These grazing areas occupy a coastal location at the mouth of the Arun estuary. The geology here is windblown sand, however, it is assumed to have been stable during the medieval period with grassland and scrub species such as sea buckthorn, blackthorn and gorse being prevalent. The other large common is Tortington, which occupied at least a quarter of the parish of the same name. This was apparently heathland by 1468 (ACM, M 828) and during the earlier part of the same century the demesne farm of Tortington Manor was recorded as being able to support two farm horses, one bull, 18 oxen, 24 cows and 300 sheep (Clough 1969. 146; cf. ACM, M 316). Further, smaller, coastal commons occurred in the parishes of Goring and Heene, while tiny inland areas of common and waste occur at roadsides and as portions of open field. Like Tortington, two areas of common, Ecclesden and Clapham, lie close to the dip-slope of the South Downs. These occupy London Clay and the sandy geology of the Reading Beds. By contrast, the Coastal Plain's better agricultural soils are largely devoid of this land-use type.

The Forest of Broyle occupied land around Chichester and was disforested in 1227 (Calendar of Charter Rolls, Henry III 4 February). At this time Henry III granted the then Bishop of Chichester (Ralph II) the 'broyles' (from Old English *broile*, 'a park, an enclosed park for deer or other game'; *P.N.E.* 1956a, 52) of Chichester, namely, the 'broyle' called the King's Broyle and the 'broyle' called Deepmarsh, with 'licence to disafforest, assart, cultivate and inclose them with ditches' (Salzman 1935, 81). Prior to its dissolution the Broyle probably lay beyond the transect study area, however, this generally wooded land was surrounded by the 'Free Chase' belonging to the 12th- and 13th-century lords of adjoining manors. These included Savary de Bohun, Geoffrey Falconer, the Archbishop of Canterbury and the Abbot of Séez (Salzman 1935, 80). Tortington Priory existed within a parish of the same name and the church was obtained from the Abbey of Séez (Page 1973, 82; Hudson 1997, 214). It is likely, therefore, that an area of Chase extended into Tortington parish. It is also possible that *The Broyle* was once a much more extensive Forest and could have occupied the extreme western end of the transect study area. The generally rectilinear pattern of local roads is much more irregular in this district, especially in the vicinity of Tortington Common. It is clear from their direction that access to this area was required by neighbouring parishes.

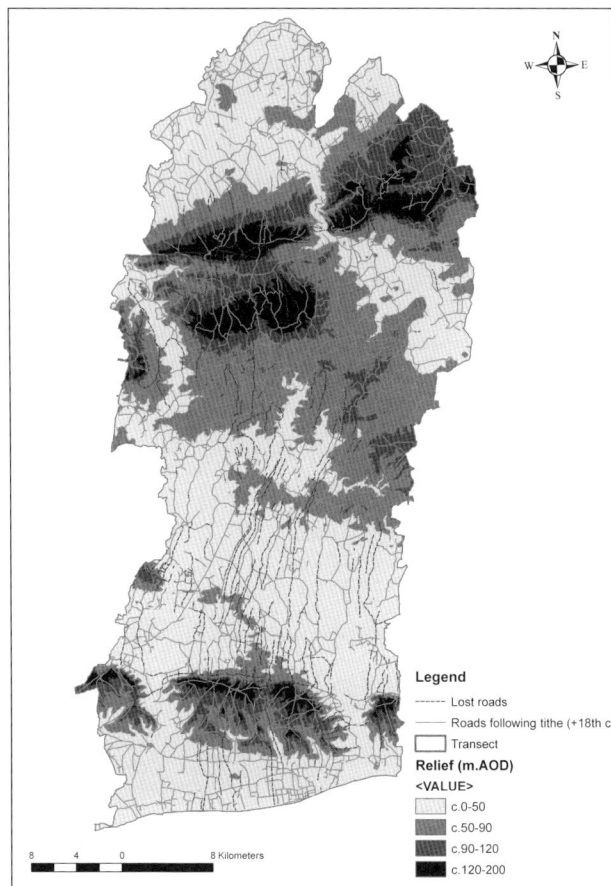

Legend
- - - - - Lost roads
——— Roads following tithe (+18th c)
▢ Transect
Relief (m.AOD)
<VALUE>
c.0-50
c.50-90
c.90-120
c.120-200

8 4 0 8 Kilometers

FIGURE 5.15: The medieval road system of the transect study area in relation to topography (drawn by the author. Contains material covered by © Crown copyright and database rights 2019 Ordnance Survey, Educational Service Provider licence number v2.1)

The only place-name discussed in Chapter 4 that exists within *Character Area 1* is *Wick*. The settlement that bears this name lies astride a north–south routeway. On both the tithe map and the OS 1st Edition this is a neatly bounded road with little waste, bordered by enclosed strips characteristic of both former open field and the landscape of much of the West Sussex Coastal Plain. Apart from the documentary evidence discussed above the only references to cattle explored within Chapter 3 were at the Bishop of Chichester's manor of Ferring (see section 3.4). Here, both peasants and demesne herds were recorded as well as distrained beasts (*Cust. Chi.* 1925, 73, 77; *Chi. Chart.* 1942, 223–24). All were likely pastured within 'open' fields. This is in contrast to animals to the west of the Arun, which would have had access to more extensive areas of pasture, woodland and heath.

Within the locality the hundred boundaries invariably encompass the Coastal Plain but also reach up to incorporate parts of the South Downs (see below). Most of the parishes are either of irregular shape and respect hydrological features and roads or are of 'interlocking type' characteristic of division of existing field patterns between two territories (see Winchester 2000, 59–60). As such they tend to follow pre-existing enclosures or headlands in open fields (*ibid.*, 60).

Character Area 2: *The South Downs*

Move a little further to the north and the picture is very different. Here, on the South Downs, the road system has been highly influenced by the area's distinctive topography. Routeways follow coombes as well as ridgetops and have combined to create an irregular web-like pattern of roads. Where these routes enter the river valleys they are clearly influenced by restricted crossing points. Geology does not seem to have had much bearing on road location; however, as with the Coastal Plain a number of clear long-distance routes are evident. Some of these stretch up from the Coastal Plain heading for the Weald, while others cross in a roughly east–west direction. An example of the latter, the South Downs Way, corresponds with the top of the scarp and may be prehistoric in origin. Another east–west route traces a more circuitous course from the Saxon settlement of Steyning in the east to the Alfredian burh (at Burpham) and later Norman town of Arundel in the west. Many of the long distance north–south routes correspond with hundred and parish boundaries, although the marked topography may have had an equally influential role on their siting.

In the case of the parish boundaries there is an example reminiscent of what Winchester (2000, 61) termed 'converging boundaries'. Such patterns are often seen where an area of common has been divided between communities. Therefore, the presence of a large area of unenclosed downland, East Tenantry Down, in Findon parish, is undoubtedly a survival of a once even larger common pasture. It is known that Findon Manor held extensive common land in this area prior to inclosure in 1856 (Mark Gardiner, pers. comm.) and the area that survived to be mapped by the Ordnance Survey is the minimum, but by no means the full medieval or even post-medieval extent. Whilst only four parishes, Findon, Steyning, Bramber and Sompting, converge on the same general area, the parishes of Bramber, Botolphs, Coombes and Lancing share a linear north-westerly course to part of their boundaries. This has been interpreted as the location of a track that only partially survived into the cartographic record. It clearly originated as an ancient droveway heading for the centre of the common.

There are other indications, however, that this common was once much bigger. Adjoining Tenantry Down can be traced the elliptical shape preserved within the field-boundary pattern that once comprised Findon Park. This was obviously created through enclosure of the downland and the park was in existence by at least 1229. This is known due to a surviving record that the Abbot of Fécamp unsuccessfully claimed the right to hunt here (Hudson 1980, 21). This therefore implies that the large common was even earlier than the 13th century in origin. Another example of convergence can be seen a little way to the west at the junction of the parishes of East and West Angmering, Burpham and Storrington. At the point at which these administrative boundaries meet (which was marked by a thornbush in the 19th century) two detached portions of the parishes of Angmering and Clapham exist. This remote location in the midst of the downs may have been the setting for medieval dairying, as close by two significant place-names have survived. These are Thornwick and Barpham Week, discussed in Chapter 4. A record of such places in combination with converging boundaries and parochial detachments indicates the likely presence of seasonal grazing areas and/or specialised settlements. These surely existed within a larger expanse of unenclosed pasture, utilised by multiple communities.

These seasonal places, which later became more permanent settlements or farms, were not associated with the long-distance movement of stock. This is due to the close proximity of the parent communities. The detached portion of Angmering is associated with Thornwick whereas the detached part of Clapham is associated with Lee Farm (*La Leye*, 1289; *P.N.Sx* 1929, 195). This is from the place-name element *lēah* which in this instance may mean 'a clearing in a wood' (*P.N.E.* 1956b, 18–22), but such names were also initially used to describe extensive woodlands used as wood-pasture (Hooke 2008). The presence of Angmering Park close to the south may also indicate that the wider area was wooded in the medieval period. This is likely due to the large deposit of Clay-with-Flints in that area. A strip of common woodland named Tenantry Coppice survived here in the 19th century.

The remaining commons within *Character Area 2* comprise small areas of waste, a further piece of 'tenantry down' (meaning where tenants of a manor had common rights) in Findon parish (West Tenantry Down) and some common downland on the edge of the Adur Valley. This relates to 'Sheep Tenantry Down' and 'Cokeham Tenantry Down' in Sompting. The latter is reached via roads named Boundstone Lane and Halewick Lane on the 19th-century mapping.

Halewick is recorded by the mid-17th century and possibly as early as 1273 (*P.N.Sx* 1929, 202). There is a record of dairy cows in the area during the reign of Edward III (Vanderzee 1807, 351) and perhaps they were sometimes pastured on Cokeham Down.

Apart from the '*Wick*' place-names mentioned above, the only other instances of potential cattle-related toponymy discussed in Chapter 4 comprise names in '*stoc*'. These include Barnstake Copse, which lies in the 16th-century combined parish of Angmering close to the south of the parochial detachments mentioned above, as well as North and South Stoke in the Arun Valley. These occupy distinctive meanders but do not appear to be associated with any common.

Part of Arundel Forest extended within the transect study area. Strictly speaking, this was 'Free Chase' belonging to the Earls of Arundel (TNA SC 6/1019/22, rot. 1). At one time there was also an area of Chase in the vicinity of the parish of Houghton. This is proven by a 17th-century record of a dispute between the bishopric of Chichester and one James Butler of Amberley. This relates to the cutting of wood in 'Houghton Chase' (WSRO Add. MSS 11,247). The extents of this area can only be guessed at, but it probably corresponds with 'Houghton Forest' marked on the 19th-century mapping. A detached portion of Bury parish, 'Langham Wood', exists within this area. This was entered via 'Wapelgate Corner'. Such '*wapple*-gate's' often lead onto '*wapple*-ways' (*P.N.Sx* 1929, 129). 'Wapple' is derived from the Old English *werpels*, 'a path', which survived in the local Sussex dialect to mean 'a bridle-path, a cart-track, a track in the common field' (*ibid.*; *P.N.E.* 1956b, 255–56).

Character Area 3: The South Downs scarp and the 'Sussex Spring-line'

Where the north–south routeways descend the scarp slope they have given rise to distinctive holloways or *bostals*, the depth of which surely corresponds with great antiquity (Plate 5.3; Brandon 1998, 17). At the foot of the scarp, along the Spring-line, a denser more regular pattern of routeways establishes itself. Here, tracks extend from the downland crossing a conspicuously regular distribution of rural settlement along the southern edge of the Lower Greensand (Brandon 1974, 71). An east–west route links these evenly distributed Spring-line villages, although it is the density and regularity of the north–south routes that are the most striking.

This road pattern is mirrored in a group of strip-like parishes that occupy the central portion of this Character Area. It is clear that the roughly north–south roads, which originated as droveways for the seasonal movement of stock (Brandon 1974, 72–74), may have had some bearing on the layout of these parishes. It is also probable that this arrangement of administrative boundaries is related to resource procurement (Topley 1873, 45; Brandon 1974, 71) and may be a legacy of much earlier multiple estates. Just one of these resources comprised common grazing land, an asset that is well represented in this Character Area. Common exists on the Gault Clay at Washington and Wiston and there is a detached part of Ashington parish in the locality. This was likely intended to provide access to both the clay and the scarp slope where wooded hangers and large chalk quarries exist. The vast majority of the common grazing was situated on the Lower Greensand, however, where light, acidic and easily exhaustible soils give rise to large areas of heath. The presence of this habitat is likely due to prehistoric clearance and farming, as has been demonstrated for the Bronze Age at Iping Common, a little to the west of the transect study area (Keef, Wymer and Dimbleby 1965).

Apart from the Greensand heaths another extensive area of pasture exists within the Arun Valley. At Amberley the common fields were well associated with cattle, as has been illustrated by the documentary evidence in Chapter 3, but this area was also home to extensive marshland grazings. These were in the form of Amberley Wild Brooks, Waltham Common and to a lesser extent Greatham Common. These wetlands and riverside meadows represent a considerable expanse of unenclosed pasture and were open to commoners as well as the Bishop of Chichester, who kept large numbers of cattle in the parish (see section 3.5). The habitat that characterised this area of the Arun Valley probably once existed at both North and South Stoke described above, although the cartographic evidence indicates that these areas were drained and reclaimed at an earlier date.

No land designated as Forest or Chase is known to have extended into this area and no cattle place-names exist. Parochial detachments were few in number and concentrated in the central portion of the Character Area.

Character Area 4: The southern Low Weald

The orderly ground plan of roads within *Character Area 3* sets the precedent for the aligned pattern of roads and tracks that extend from the Greensand into the Low Weald. These were well studied by Chatwin and Gardiner (2005). It was clear to those authors that the north-east–south-west routes show a remarkably similar direction to that followed by the Roman road of Stane Street (*ibid.*, 38). The aligned, long-distance trackways are characteristic of the usage of the woodland by remote estates (*ibid.*, 44), and where they have survived to be recorded on early cartographic sources they are uniformly wide with significant verges or accompanying roadside waste. Lost routeways suggested through the process of historic landscape analysis often correspond with this alignment of roads and survive as long-distance boundaries or green lanes (Figures 5.16 and 5.17). In this area, both routes that have endured into the historic mapping and those that have been hypothetically suggested often form features followed by parochial and hundredal boundaries. The general course of this closely spaced pattern of roughly parallel routeways was astutely observed by Brandon (1974, 74) to be aided by the physical nature of this area of the Weald. Although gently rolling with low consecutive east–west ridges, this part of Sussex, with its largely uniform clay geology, would have been an obliging environment in which so-called planned landscapes could develop (Figure 5.18).

FIGURE 5.16: Boar Lane near Shipley, West Sussex. A green lane as it appears today, bordered by ancient hedgerows, woodland and banks (source: the author)

There are noticeably few commons within this area, especially within the large portion occupied by the closely spaced pattern of parallel boundaries and roads. Where they do exist they usually comprise large areas of roadside waste and greens. The latter places were important elements of medieval droveway infrastructure in Devon, where they provided a resting place for people and animals engaged in transhumance (Fox 2012, 201–04). The examples within this Character Area are closely associated with roads, generally triangular in shape, and are provided with watering places in the form of ponds or springs. The rough grassland habitats that characterise many of them today probably also existed during the medieval period. A reasonably large common, 'Jolesfield Common', does, however, exist to the north of Partridge Green in the parish of West Grinstead. This may be a fairly atypical example from this Character Area in that it is located close to the River Adur. This is an area where the close alignment of routeways appears to be broken by the hydrology and the need for crossing points. The routeway that runs into the western side of Jolesfield Common mirrors the line of the river beyond its floodplain. As such it occupies the local watershed.

The parishes in this area are generally large and irregular but their outlines follow routeways, land-division and hydrology. The hundred boundaries do the same. This indicates that the loosely co-axial landscape division that exists

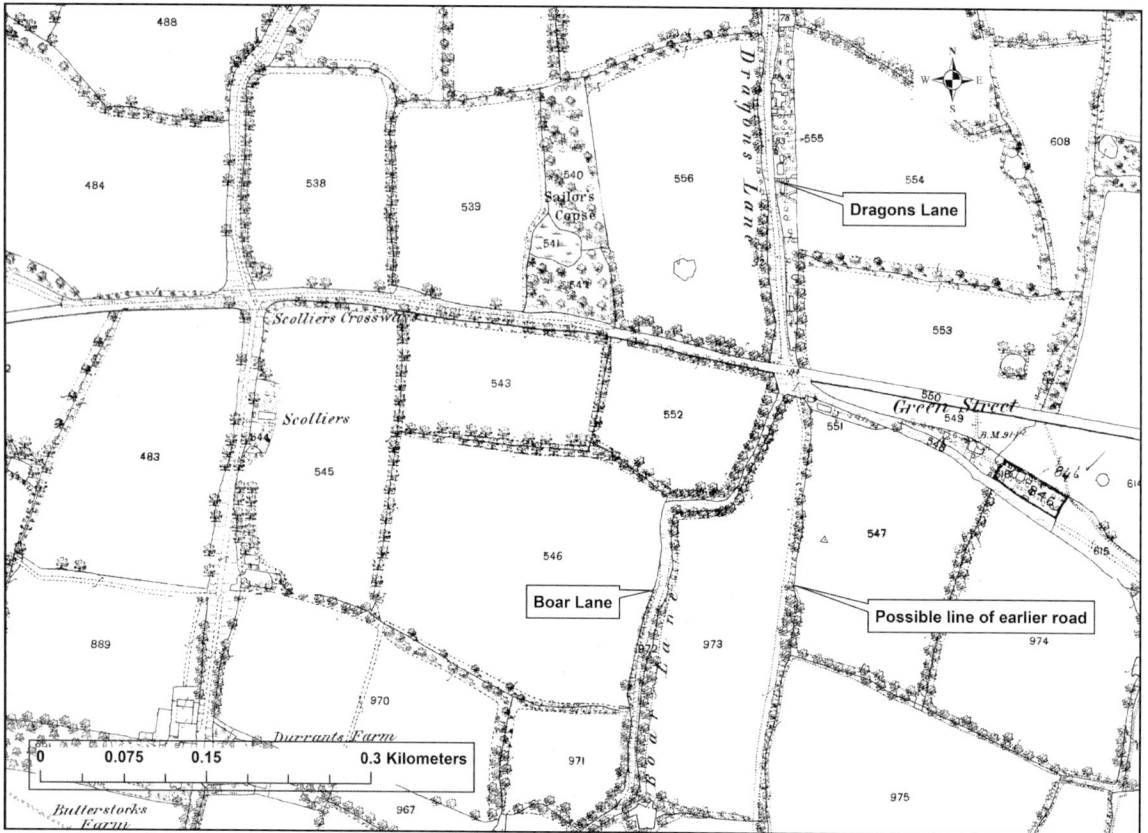

FIGURE 5.17: OS 1st Edition mapping (1:2500, 1875) of Boar Lane where it meets a later turnpiked road. This is typical of the arrangement of parallel routeways that exist in the area south of Horsham. Note that the line of an earlier routeway may be preserved in a long-distance boundary extending from the junction of Dragons Lane and the later turnpike (with labelling by the author)

within the area, and appears to fill the intervening spaces between parallel routeways, not only precedes the creation of the parishes but also the hundreds, which themselves are of early date. Despite this, so-called strip parishes did not emerge in the likeness of the scarp foot and the Greensand discussed above and this is probably due to the area's poor agricultural soils and historically dispersed settlement pattern.

There was little documentary evidence encountered for cattle within the southern Low Weald, although place-names possibly connected with their pasturing exist. These include Cowfold and Greatwick, which are obviously associated with the same north–south droveway making for Lower Beeding on the High Weald and linking it with Upper Beeding in the downland section of the Adur Valley (Plate 5.4). The 'upper' and 'lower' elements of these place-names likely refer to the varying status of the two settlements, not to their geographical locations; 'Lower' Beeding is on higher ground than Upper (*P.N.Sx* 1929, 205). Of the other place-names, Redfold and Stallhouse Farm exist within a network of irregular routeways that is at odds to the aligned pattern dominating the wider area. This divergence can be explained upon examination of the tithe and OS 1st Edition for Pulborough. The area occupied by these

FIGURE 5.18: The flat, well-wooded aspect of the Low Weald near Cowfold (West Sussex) with the chalk escarpment of the South Downs in the background (source: the author)

names is labelled as North Heath on the cartographic record. The field-scape here is one of rectilinear straight-sided fields characteristic of Parliamentary or, in this case, probably pre-Parliamentary Enclosure. This is obviously an area once occupied by an extensive area of common with which the place-names were associated. Lydwick and Slinfold are sited on the edge of a large sub-oval circuit of routeways that at one time surely corresponded with the bounds of Slinfold Park. Kingsfold exists in Billingshurst and is close to the Roman road of Stane Street, as are North Heath, Lydwick and Slinfold. This name has the obvious connotation of the '*falod*' of the king (*P.N.Sx* 1929, 149) and surely corresponds with an important seasonal pasture belonging to the South Saxon royal line. Sedgewick Castle occupies a detached portion of Broadwater, the elongated shape of which respects the parallel routeways in this area. Known as 'Little Broadwater' (Hudson 1987, 97, 101), it comprises one of a small number of parochial detachments further discussed below.

The Bishop of Chichester had a Chase called Gosden which extended into this area from the borders of St Leonard's Forest (see below; Hudson 1987, 171). This was mentioned in 1256 when it occupied about two-thirds of Cowfold parish from its boundary in the east to Mockford in the west and Parkgate on the centre of the northern boundary (*ibid.*). An outlying bailiwick of St Leonard's was known at Knepp during the late 15th century (Hudson 1987, 13) where there was an earlier park and castle probably built by the de Braoses as a hunting seat (Hudson 1986, 111).

Character Area 5: The High Weald

The closely parallel strips of land, with their accompanying boundaries and roads within *Character Areas 3 and 4*, extend onto and across the periphery of the High Weald. Other examples that occur within this area are more notable through their sparseness. Some of the few, such as the Ashdown Forest–Horsham Ridgeway, are likely of great antiquity and follow ridge tops rather than the deeply incised valleys and *ghylls* (Margary 1948, 264). Where routeways climb from the Weald Clay onto the sandstone geologies, deep holloways are formed (Plate 5.5). These are contrasted by the straight, well-defined and durable tracks that traverse the High Wealden plateaus.

This area possesses a few small commons such as Manning's Heath and Monks Common in Nuthurst parish. These are intimately related to the various droveways that head for the High Wealden interior and the core of St Leonard's Forest. This area was strictly 'Free Chase' belonging to the Barons de Braose and only entered Crown possession during times of wardship or forfeiture (Hudson 1987, 13–14). The 'Forest' was named as *'de foresta Sancti Leonardi'* in AD 1208 (Hall 1903, 60), which is also the year of its first recording. By the late 15th century it had been divided into a number of bailiwicks that included Sedgewick mentioned above. At this time it was surrounded by a pale and the names of its bailiwicks indicate that it extended over the parishes of Lower Beeding, Horsham, Crawley, Ifield, Rusper and parts of Cowfold (Hudson 1987, 13). The 'Forest' has been shown to be associated with cattle through 13th-century documentary evidence (Chapter 3, section 3.3) and many manors probably held grazing rights there.

Parochial detachments exist around the fringe of the High Weald and St Leonard's Forest. These include a detached part of Nuthurst as well as Sedgewick in the south and a detached portion of Sullington at Broadbridge Heath in the west. During the Middle Ages (from *c.* 1100 and the formation of parishes; see Adams 1999, 40) Lower Beeding was once a single parish with Upper Beeding, which is located within the Lower Adur Valley. During the later medieval period (AD 1279) it was known as 'Nether Beeding' (Hudson 1987, 7). These two disparate parts of the same parish were severed in the 17th century and Lower Beeding was subsequently divided during the 19th century, resulting in the creation of Bewbush tithing (*ibid.*). The authors of the VCH (1987, 7) felt that the parochial link between 'Upper' and 'Lower' Beeding came about due to the fact that the tithes of the Forest were granted to Sele Priory (AD 1235; Salzman 1923, 10). This priory is located in Upper Beeding. To the present author, however, this link is wholly more ancient. Not only do the parish names indicate a connection, both being derived from the '*ing*' element for 'the people of *Bēada*' (*P.N.Sx* 1929, 205), but also the areas were once components of two divided portions of the same Domesday Hundred

(Burghbeach; Haselgrove 1978, 214). Beeding was first mentioned in the late
9th-century will of King Alfred (Sawyer 1507) and was once part of a royal
estate (Haselgrove 1978, 214). Edward the Confessor held it prior to William
de Braose at Domesday. At this time it was recorded as having woodland for
70 pigs – 20 pigs from tribute (Domesday 13, 1). Surely the area later occupied
by Lower Beeding parish relates to a late survival of an extensive Wealden
folk common and royal outland? This would be consistent with the process of
Wealden development seen in Kent (Jolliffe 1933; Witney 1976, 31–55; Everitt
1986) and perhaps the earliest form of 'Lower Beeding' was something akin to
the '*limen-waro-wealde*' attached to the royal settlement of Lyminge in the east
of that county. As well as its poor soils, status as part of a royal estate may have
ensured some longevity to this large area of early common and warranted its
adoption as Norman hunting 'Forest'.

Of the other detachments mentioned above, Nuthurst does not lie far from
its parent parish. This is an interesting area for the vicinity is also the nexus
of a number of hundred boundaries. These are located upon the south-facing
slopes of a projecting ridge of Tunbridge Wells Sand near the headwaters
of the River Arun. A small common, really an area of roadside waste, exists
here, which is named Maplehurst Common. The probable home farm of the
Nuthurst detachment is High Hurst; however, this settlement did not enter
the documentary record until the 16th century (*P.N.Sx* 1929, 232). Recorded
earlier is the adjacent farm of Woldringfold (AD 1327; *P.N.Sx* 1929, 211), which
is associated with the '*ing*' element. Though a minor place-name it has potential
cattle associations as it includes the *falod* element (Chapter 4).

Sedgewick has already been mentioned as part of a parochial detachment
of Broadwater on the Coastal Plain and bailiwick of St Leonard's Forest.
The detachment was surrounded by Nuthurst parish described above and its
place-name has been highlighted for its potential cattle-related connotations
(Chapter 4). The western boundary of the detachment is named as Broadwater
Lane and it is possible to link the parent with its outlier via the postulated
medieval road network. This is not, however, by a particularly direct route. The
least circuitous course leads to Steyning, which is the chief settlement of the
hundred. The woodland that yielded 20 swine for Broadwater at Domesday (13, 30)
was presumably at Sedgewick (Hudson 1987, 101).

The detached outlier of Sullington, Broadbridge Manor possessed an area of
common at Broadbridge Heath. This was directly related to a droveway named
Wickhurst Lane on the OS 1st Edition (1875–76; Margetts 2018a, 159). This
routeway and its name have survived into the modern day. Over 40 hectares of
the local landscape were recently subjected to archaeological mitigation, which
resulted in approximately 14 hectares of excavation (Margetts 2018a, 1). Elements
of this work will be utilised as a case study (Chapter 9), however, the course of
Wickhurst Lane was exposed to detailed excavation and it is worth pausing to
briefly outline the results here. Few or no other Wealden droveways have been
explored to this degree and as such this represents an important contribution to

our understanding of the South-East. The remains comprised a holloway that deviated from the modern line of 'Old Wickhurst Lane', as well as droveside ditches that followed its course. A pond, some adjacent animal pens and a stone causeway were also encountered. The latter crossed an area of low-lying, wet ground and comprised an undated deposit of large sandstone blocks directly beneath the current road surface. Approximately 15 m to the north-west, a ditch, which shared Wickhurst Green's orientation, was interpreted as an early boundary of the routeway. The only datable finds comprised two sherds of relatively un-abraded post-Conquest Roman sandy wares (AD later 1st century). It was a stretch of holloway, however, which produced the majority of the dating evidence. Here, the earliest recognisable features consisted of a thick deposit of livestock poaching as well as an erosion gully. The finds produced included a mixed assemblage of pottery that is likely due to the re-worked nature of the deposits. The earliest material comprised a few fragments of Roman tegula and there were a number of intrusive post-medieval sherds. In the main the pottery ranged from the late 11th to the early 14th centuries. The only stratigraphic relationship, apart from later post-medieval activity, comprised a small group of ditches interpreted as animal pens. These were dated to the mid-11th to late 12th century by ceramics, and although they appeared to be 'cut' by the holloway the relationship is not thought to be reliable. The pens could have easily been affected by the latest use of the holloway, which obviously enjoyed some longevity.

The course of this droveway can be traced on the OS 1st Edition and clearly links the parent settlement of Sullington with its outlier at Broadbridge (Plate 5.6). It likely dates from at least the 7th or 8th centuries as this is a suggested period of seasonal transhumance between parent settlements and detached outliers. It could be as early as the 1st century AD, however, as it shared a common orientation with land division of this date and incorporated contemporary 'residual' finds (Margetts 2018a; 2018b). The lack of medieval material earlier than the 11th century can probably be explained by the complete unsuitability of pottery vessels for those engaged in transhumance. Horn, leather and wooden containers are more likely to have been used in the Weald as they are lighter and less prone to breakage (*ibid.*, 149).

Character Area 6: The north-western Low Weald

As Chatwin and Gardiner noted (2005, 37–38), there is a change in alignment both at the county boundary, where roads from Surrey estates met those coming from Sussex, and to the west of Stane Street, where roads seem more reflective of the Farley Heath spur than Stane Street itself. In these areas, beyond the loosely co-axial landscape evident in much of the Sussex Low Weald, a more irregular pattern predominates. These contrasting arrangements may reflect varied histories of woodland exploitation. Whereas the aligned, long-distance trackways may be characteristic of the usage of the woodland by remote estates, an irregular system may suggest a more complex development linked to local needs (*ibid.*, 44). The role of topography may also be a significant factor. The area in the vicinity of, and a short distance beyond, the Sussex–Surrey border is more undulating in nature than the low relief found in the neighbouring *Character Area 4*. Such factors may have influenced how early medieval communities utilised their environments and in turn affected the landscapes they created (*ibid.*, 47). A further element worthy of note is that, once lost roads had been mapped, it seems that rather than being totally devoid of equidistant routeways, the irregular road network of the Surrey Low Weald and west of Stane Street actually once possessed limited areas where strip arrangements of parallel boundaries and tracks existed. These are located north of Fittleworth in an area known as 'The Mens' (from *ge-mænnes* meaning 'common land, a common holding'; *P.N.E.* 1956a, 33; Gardiner 1984, 78) and in a restricted area to the east of Cranleigh.

A contributing factor to the varied orientations and density of roads within the Low Weald may be suggested once hydrology is overlain on the mapped network (Plate 5.7). This shows that within *Character Area 4* streams and rivers are generally aligned perpendicularly or parallel to the road network. The streams in the remainder of the Low Weald are more varied in their orientation, perhaps, in part, accounting for the irregular nature of these routeways. This area is far better served with commons and greens than *Character Area 4*. In the absence of a closely parallel framework of tracks and an associated co-axial field-system the parish and hundred boundaries almost exclusively follow watercourses. The only exception occurs in the north-east of the Character Area, where the line of Stane Street has been used as a boundary and in the east near Slinfold where droveways and the arc-shape of a possible park pale have been followed. Langton and Jones (2010, fig. 1) have mapped the 'Forest' (strictly 'Chase') of Charlton and Singleton as extending into this Character Area and as covering the Sussex parishes of Wisborough Green and Stopham. During Henry II's reign the whole of the county of Surrey, or at least the royal demesne within it, was declared 'Forest' (Blair 1991, 9). By 1191, however, Richard I had disafforested all but the north-western quarter (*ibid.*). At one time, therefore, the legal writ of a royal Forest likely extended into at least part of this Character Area.

A concentration of place-names potentially associated with cattle was highlighted within this area (Chapter 4). It was also a district where cattle were documented, notably on the Bishop of Chichester's manor of Drungewick (see sections 3.5 and 3.10). A route cannot easily be traced between the location of this manor and its supposed early folk centre at Durrington. If one did exist it was not via a direct route and would have involved crossing the South Downs in a north-westerly manner before striking out north across the Weald. Parochial detachments abound within the Surrey portion of this Character Area, with clusters noted in the east and west.

Character Area 7: The Surrey Hills

A further limited arrangement of parallel routeways is encountered a little way to the north within the Surrey Greensand. This stretches towards the

North Downs scarp and is surrounded by an irregular network of roads that are similar in nature to those within *Character Area 6* to the south. It is clear, however, that these examples form much tighter clusters of sub-oval or polygonal intervening spaces between roads. Once the network in this area is compared with topography it soon becomes clear that the Surrey Hills and their associated relief are responsible. Where holloways ascend these hills the depths are dramatic and, although most of these routes are on a rough north–south orientation, a clear east–west example runs along the foot of the Tillingbourne Valley between the Greensand and the downs.

The commons here are vast, wooded and heathy, blanketing the summits of this range of hills. Smaller examples exist within the surrounding valleys and include a rare area of marsh adjacent to the River Tillingbourne at Gomshall. No 'cattle place-names' exist within this Character Area.

Character Area 8: The North Downs

The road network of the North Downs of Surrey has many similarities to that found on its sister escarpment in Sussex. The roughly north–south routes, like those on the South Downs, largely follow dry valleys and ridgeways. The frequency of roads in this area is, however, noticeably sparser than that found within *Character Area 2*. A further comparison can be made in that long-distance routeways exist both on the scarp side and along the base of the dip-slope. The former of these includes the route known as the Pilgrim's Way. The existence of this track as a continuous North Downs path now seems dubious and its role as a medieval pilgrim's route linking Winchester with the shrine of Thomas Becket at Canterbury is still keenly debated (Blair 1991, 6; Bright 2010; 2012). It does seem probable, however, that both the main ridgeway and the line along the scarp-slope terrace may well approximate to ancient routes (Margary 1948, 259–62; Blair 1991, 6). The latter of these is often claimed to be sited so as to avoid the wet valley bottom but also the Clay-with-Flints head deposit at the top of the ridge (Margary 1948, 260). Further north, a curving long-distance track connects the villages along the base of the dip-slope (Blair 1991, 6). This early routeway may be seen as performing a similar function to that which links the settlements along the Sussex Spring-line.

This area is again well provisioned with large commons similar to the Surrey Hills; however, due to the underlying Chalk and Clay-with-Flints geology they are of slightly different character. Like the North Downs of Kent this was an area of secondary settlement of a largely wooded and pastoral nature (Everitt 1986; Blair 1991, 44–46). During the medieval period the commons were likely dominated by wood-pasture but also large tracts of downland and scrub. A royal pasture existed at Kingswood, which was attached to Ewell Manor. This enjoyed some longevity, although by the 12th century its use as a wood-pasture was in decline and it would later be assigned for assarted clearance (Blair 1991, 49). The 'Kingswood' likely occupied much, if not all, of the Ewell parochial detachment. Banstead Manor also had access to an early downland pasture known as '*Suthmeresfelda*' or Summerfield in a late Saxon charter (Sawyer 420). This area has been equated with Canon's Farm in Banstead parish (Dodgson and Khaliq 1970, 39) and almost certainly reflects an area of early seasonal grazing.

The pattern of the parish boundaries displays the area's history of secondary settlement in that they are usually of the strip form with downland at one end of the parish and occasional areas of convergence. This system seems to have been adequate for resource procurement from the neighbouring districts; as a result, detachments are few and small in size. A notable exception from this rule is provided by the detached portion of Ewell associated with the 'Kingswood'. Only a single place-name with potential cattle associations was encountered within this Character Area, 'Costal Wood' in the parish of Walton on the Hill (see section 4.5).

Character Area 9: The Thames Basin

The final zone to receive investigation comprises the area of low topography between the North Downs and the Thames known as the Thames Basin. This land of heavy London Clays and barren heaths of the Bagshot Series extends beyond the thin fertile strip of Thanet and Reading Beds at the base of the downland. Within the basin roads are few in number and irregular in plan. This pattern of roads, some of which may have originated as droveways leading to Thameside pastures, is difficult to explain. An area of low topography alongside a major river seems eminently suitable for the development of regular planned landscapes; however, when hydrology is taken into account the presence of three tributaries of the Thames serve to disrupt this landscape's cohesion. Rather than being able to pursue a symmetrical pattern of tracks that extend perpendicularly to the downland, as was the case on the Sussex Spring-line, the roads have to account for river lines and crossing points. They tend to follow watersheds as they wind their way into the interior of the basin.

The area has a profusion of large commons and one of these, Ockham Common, seems to be related to an area of converging parish boundaries. Two place-names recorded in Chapter 4 exist, close to the course of the River Mole. These are Dudwick and Stoke D'Abernon. The parish and hundred boundaries seem to follow routeways and watercourses with equal merit.

5.4 Conclusion

What has been revealed through this systematic analysis of the road network, as well as commons, Forests and Chase, is that routeways often developed over a long period of time and were significantly influenced by environmental factors such as geology, hydrology and topography. The varied landscapes of the South-East gave rise to distinctive physical routeways formed in contrasting ways. This may have been largely due to the movement of animals; however, this was only one (albeit perhaps the most significant) of a myriad ways in which the road network was exploited. In areas of rising ground with underlying geologies prone to erosion, deep holloways developed. By contrast, in areas of lower relief where heavy soils inclined to waterlogging existed, wide but relatively straight routes often evolved. These were habitually bounded by hedgebanks and extensive areas of roadside waste. Droveway functions were discernible by associated names, facilities (such as watering places, greens and pounds) as well as stock funnels and links with common.

While flat topography seems to have been conducive to the organisation of routeways, hydrology appears to have played a disruptive role. The preferred way for roads to develop looks to have been in straight alignments along dry valleys or ridgetops, where A–B could be traversed in the shortest and easiest way possible. The effect of rivers and streams was troublesome to this pattern in that roads often had to take the nearest parallel watershed or strike out for fording places or areas of drier ground. There may, however, be an additional, more complex factor at play. Roads might have actually been deliberately sited to allow access to rich riverine pastures, remote downland valleys or extensive areas of wood-pasture or heath.

The second most striking outcome of this work has been the degree to which arrangements of roads were contrasted between different geographical areas. In a relatively short distance road networks could change from regular patterns of parallel routes bounding strip-like areas of loosely co-axial fields, to irregular, more roughly organised patterns that bounded polygonal or sub-oval intervening spaces. These were often filled with assart-like fields that look to have developed in a more organic way. This is not to say that parallel areas did not occur beyond their primary zone, or that irregular patterns did not exist in areas dominated by parallel roads. Indeed, both types of road pattern were found to a greater or lesser extent in all the various *pays* of the transect study area. This is not a phenomena that is restricted to the South-East. Regular co-axial landscapes can often fade imperceptibly into areas of more irregular fields whose boundaries display a degree of rough parallelism (Warner 1996, 48–51). These irregular areas are often located in more complex topography, where major tributary watercourses run at angles to the main valley and large areas of woodland and heavy soils exist (Williamson 2013, 100).

Local choices in land-use as well as varied systems of land management and resource exploitation may partially account for these dramatic contrasts found within the transect study area. The regular pattern of parallel roads encountered within much of the Low Weald, the scarp foot of the South Downs and parts of the Coastal Plain may be reflective of a degree of planning or at least the negotiation of boundaries between communities; as such, it may to some degree be analogous with the systematic organisation known in early medieval arable areas (Hooke 1987; 1988, 138–40). It superficially appears, therefore, that there has been a systematic and large-scale division of the landscape connected to the region's banded resources and their exploitation. This pattern could be the result of early medieval multiple estates, although earlier, Roman or prehistoric origins are also possible. Such landscapes are most often associated with the intensively studied co-axial field-systems that have been identified in a number of areas of England (Williamson 2013, 93–98). The Sussex example shares a common element with many of these in that the major linear axes appear to consist of roads, tracks and long-distance field boundaries.

The most obvious parallels can be found in the south Essex claylands that in the past were regarded as a single planned landscape, possibly the result of a Roman Imperial estate (Rodwell 1978, 90–93). It is no longer thought that regularity necessarily reflects planned origins, however, and more gradual modes of development, influenced by environmental factors, provide a more favoured explanation (Williamson 2013, 106). A number of scenarios for the evolution of the southern Essex examples have been suggested by *The Fields of Britannia* project (Rippon, Smart and Pears 2015, 160–64, fig. 4.14) and similar suggestions can be made for the regular arrangement found in Sussex. It appears that this aspect of the landscape could have evolved in a number of ways but was significantly influenced by environmental factors, especially topography and hydrology. Like many co-axial landscapes (see Williamson 2008, 131–32; 2013, 94–103) the Sussex system appears to run perpendicular to topographical and geological boundaries found across the Coastal Plain, South Downs, Greensand and Weald. Essentially it appears that the regular network should be regarded as Rippon, Smart and Pears (2015, 164) have viewed southern Essex; that is, as a number of separate landscapes with different histories that must be studied in the context of a region with diverse natural resources. The parallel routeways of Sussex probably developed as a result of specific social and economic contexts that were heavily influenced by environment. They acted as the axial elements of field-systems that were laid out at the same time as the droveways or more likely filled the intervening spaces over a long period of time and were constantly subject to adaptation and change.

If this regular area reflects the exploitation of the region's banded resources and a partially systematic approach by communities and/or authorities to the landscape, what does the more irregular area reflect and how did it develop? It has been postulated that the differences found within these two contrasting road systems owes much to hydrology and topography; however, it is also possible that differences in land-use approach also played a role. The irregular area is roughly analogous with the 'fold area' of the north-western Weald identified by Chatwin and Gardiner (2005). This well-wooded country possessed a higher number of commons than its more regular Low Wealden counterpart and potential cattle-related place-names were prevalent. It may be that this area developed in some way differently to its south-easterly neighbour via different forms of woodland exploitation (*ibid.*).

Such contrasts may also exist due to differences in temporal origins and degree of survival within the historic landscape. It is still open to debate at which point the system of transhumance and the roads that developed to serve it originated. Prehistoric, Roman or medieval roots have all been ventured and debated and it is clear that the issue is complex and difficult to resolve (Everitt 1986, 39; Chatwin and Gardiner 2005; Margetts 2018a). What is certain, however, is that by the late medieval period the road system owed its formation to many phases of human history, both fluid evolution through customary usage and planned boundaries through negotiated agreement. What had arisen is a road network that comprised elements of different antiquity that only survived through persistence in use. We can be sure that the network was utilised in the early medieval period for the movement of stock within a system of multiple estates; however, the difficulty really lies in distinguishing the origin of components and how they reflect local patterns of land-use.

In similarity to the road system, areas of commons, Forest and Chase were intimately tied to environmental factors. They largely existed in areas of poorer agricultural soils but this was not exclusively the case. *Character Area 4*, which encompassed some of the worst arable land in the entire South-East, was almost devoid of common. In contrast to its marginal connotations common was also situated close to areas of so-called primary settlement such as the Sussex Spring-line. This is testament to the importance placed on grazing by medieval communities, although in the earlier part of the period it also appears to have been necessary or desirable to move cattle 15 km and more to seasonal pastures.

Commons, Forests and Chase existed in areas of higher topography where irregular patterns of routeway dominated. These may relate to alternative modes of land-use to the axial systems of the Low Weald claylands. The latter potentially marks an intervening area between zones utilised for seasonal and specialised grazings. Such locations may be indicated by potential cattle related place-names that often existed within or fringed areas of Forest or Chase. This was not exclusively the case and a north-east–south-west sequence of place-names appears to be associated with the line of Stane Street. Road networks will never be capable of illuminating the cattle economy in isolation, they can merely provide the links between other avenues of enquiry. The results of this chapter may, however, imply that areas characterised by an irregular pattern of roads, rising topography, access to commons as well as extensive grazing provided by Forest and Chase may be the most likely locations in which cattle-related elements could exist.

CHAPTER 6

Oval enclosures and medieval parks

....

6.1 Introduction

> If … any beast breaks hedges and wanders at large within, since its owner will not
> or cannot keep it under control, he who finds it on his cornland shall take it and
> kill it. The owner [of the beast] shall take its hide and flesh and suffer the loss of
> the remainder. (*Laws of Ine 42.1*; Attenborough 1922, 51)

Such was the cost to the negligent stockmen of 7th-century Wessex that
preventing cattle from straying must have been of paramount importance
to their husbandry choices. The concept of enclosure and its significance
to medieval livestock, and agriculture in general, has already been touched
upon in Chapter 1. What follows is a more detailed analysis of the types of
enclosure in which medieval cattle were kept and their place within the region's
landscape. From the exploration of documentary and place-name evidence
we have seen that some of the more marginal landscapes of the South-East
were home to cattle enclosures and pastures throughout the medieval period.
From the '*hridra leah*' of Kent to the '*Cuscetes hagen*' of Surrey (section 4.4)
these were important elements of the early medieval landscape. The idea that
the construction and maintenance of enclosure boundaries was in some way
separate to the 'open' nature of much early pasturing is a mistaken belief for,
as will become clear in this and the following chapter, even open landscapes
required some form of enclosure to facilitate effective livestock husbandry. Over
the course of the medieval period the increasing need to fence agricultural land
in a response to population and grazing pressure becomes apparent and this
will be demonstrated by the form of 12th- and 13th-century vaccaries and the
grazing of domestic and feral cattle in parks.

Before we embark upon this detailed exploration it is first prudent to
examine the various traditions of enclosure throughout the *pays* of the South-
East. Understanding the regionally dominant forms of land division will aid
both recognition and contextualisation of cattle enclosures. As discussed in
Chapters 1–3, the most arable-dominated districts of medieval South-East
England comprised the West Sussex coast and parts of the North Kent Plain.
In these areas open fields existed, although they differed significantly from
the *Midlands system*. These were not the co-operative communities of the
nucleated model, but large populations of cottagers and free tenants who
worked yardlands, crofts and yokes. Nevertheless, coastal Sussex was also
often characterised by significant areas of demesne where bodies of dependant
cultivators were grouped into extensive honours and ecclesiastical lordships.

In this area, demesne land was only occasionally separated by a physical boundary from the common fields of the servile tenantry (see section 3.3). More often, the large rectilinear blocks (Chapter 5) were only divided by temporary boundaries for folding or sowing purposes.

Within the arable districts of east Kent, the enclosure of farmland differed from that of the Sussex Coastal Plain due to the dominance of partible inheritance or Gavelkind. This effectively ensured that with the passing of each generation further sub-division of land was necessary, leading to a countryside comprised of blocks of small enclosures (Brandon and Short 1990, 58). This model was also suited to parts of the Kentish Weald where from the 11th century manorial *denns* were broken up and there was widespread granting of land rights. This led to a countryside of small holdings won from the waste. Across the border in Sussex a similar pattern predominated where small assarted fields held in severalty were the norm. A variant on assarting forms a great swath of loosely co-axial fields, bordered by hedgerows or narrow *shaws*. This stretches from Stane Street in the west to the River Adur in the east (Chapter 5). The co-axial landscape forms the boundary between zones dominated by both aggregate and cohesive assarts (Bannister 2014; Plate 6.1). Whilst the former comprise irregular fields created through piecemeal enclosure without any apparent planning, the latter tend to be regularly patterned and formed in a systematic manner. The cohesive area may be a legacy of the former extent of the Low Weald co-axial system.

Of the South-East's more marginal landscapes, that is the Weald, and parts of the downland, a particularly interesting sub-set of enclosures can be discerned. These become apparent following a glance at many OS 1st Edition maps and are notable for their distinction from the more widespread methods of enclosure and land division outlined above. These features, which Roberts and Wrathmell (2002, 152–55) have termed 'loop form' or 'ring-fenced enclosures', are a reasonably common phenomenon of Britain's historic landscape. They are characterised by distinctive curving or oval boundaries and appear to have been established in unenclosed landscapes as early intake from the waste. The fact that these and similar oval-shaped enclosures appear to pre-date development of the surrounding landscape indicates their early origins and they have been noted as elements of wooded (English 1997; Chatwin and Gardiner 2005), upland (Fleming and Ralph 1982; Atkin 1985) and wetland (Rippon 2000; 2002; Costen 2011, 106) areas across the British Isles. Past research on these landscape components is further explored within the methodology section below.

Interestingly, these oval enclosures appear to be largely absent from the South-East's other marginal areas of the Pevensey Levels and Romney Marsh (save a possible example at Snave cited in Rippon 2002, 65). Here the dynamism of the landscape is encapsulated in a move from the open, early medieval saltmarsh, to 12th- and 13th-century wet meadows divided by ditches. These were replaced by arable fields and livestock pasture during the late medieval period (Brandon 1974, 111–13; Eddison 1995; Eddison and Green 1988; Barber and Priestley-Bell 2008). The dominant forms of land division within these areas today comprise informal enclosure relating to inning fields that owe much to post-medieval 're-reclamation' of land lost to the sea during the catastrophic floods of the 13th–16th centuries.

In contrast to the neighbouring parts of the Weald, the Greensand contained fewer assart fields during the medieval period. It was moreover characterised by extensive heaths and commons as well as open fields and closes held in severalty (Brandon and Short 1990, 174–75). A similar pattern is apparent within the Thames Basin, although this area also benefited from significant expanses of riverine meadow. On the North and South Downs areas of aggregate assart and managed woodland predominated and show a strong correlation to superficial geological deposits of Clay-with-Flints. Open fields also existed and often extended onto parts of the scarp from the downland foot or were located on the more favourable dip-slopes. Most extensive, however, would have been the open landscapes of common pasture and sheepwalk that epitomise the eastern South Downs. Such classic downland habitat may have once been more widely found on the Kentish part of the sister escarpment to the north.

6.2 A historiography of oval cattle enclosures and parks, and a methodology for their exploration

Oval enclosures

The inherent morphology of these enclosures is perfectly suited to their early function as intakes within newly colonised landscapes. An oval is the most economic approach to the bounding of such land and is also suited to medieval deer parks, which often adopted this form because it provides the shortest length of boundary per area enclosed. This helps reduce the cost of initial construction as well as subsequent maintenance, demonstrating that an oval or sub-oval shape is a natural response to the bounding of land. As a consequence, oval enclosures originated in multiple periods and for a multitude of different reasons. Nevertheless, past studies have shown that some may be particularly relevant to the livestock economy and this may have been one of their major uses.

The uplands of Dartmoor, a landscape now better known for the medieval pasturing of cattle (Fox 2012), have been demonstrated to be particularly rich in oval enclosures. These were first demonstrated by Fleming and Ralph (1982) who showed that 'lobe'-shaped intakes existed on Holne Moor prior to the 11th century. Defined by stock-proof corn ditches, similar to park pales but with the ditch on the outside to prevent animals entering from the open moor, the enclosures measure around 12 hectares (30 acres). They appear to have been created primarily to facilitate pre-Conquest cultivation and colonisation of upland, often incorporating evidence of ridge ploughing within their interiors. A clear association with lanes (locally named 'strolls') shows that, as well as cultivation, management of (probably dairy) cattle was also a key consideration of their layout (*ibid.*, 134). Faith (2006) would later expand this work, demonstrating that equivalent enclosures existed on Dartmoor's edge. She saw these 'worthys' as early ring-fenced farms. A later collaboration with Fleming (2012) identified the pear-shaped *Walkhampton Enclosure*, an early medieval royal inland that at one time may have acted as a horse stud. This enclosure, 7 km south-east of Tavistock on the western fringes of Dartmoor, dwarfed the lobe shaped enclosures occupying *c.* 175 hectares (432 acres) of land.

Away from the South-West, other upland landscapes where oval enclosures have been recognised include those in Leyland Hundred, Lancashire. Here, Atkin (1985, 173–75) showed the existence of paired ovals with a larger pastoral unit with stock funnels acting as a vaccary and a smaller oval that contained field divisions intended for arable, pasture and convertible land. It is clear that the ovals acted as self-contained units (Atkin 1993) and they seem to have been deliberately sited so that a watercourse runs through their centre.

Oval enclosures as early medieval infields were first explored by Rippon in wetland landscapes (1996; 1997a; 1997b). These oval enclosures, defined by a bank with an internal ditch, were important landscape features within the early colonisation of these areas, often representing primary elements within the historic landscape (Rippon 2000; 2002). Within wetlands boundaries tend to survive once they are created and Rippon has shown that the Severn Estuary marshes were colonised through the construction of a series of small, oval-shaped 'ring dikes', which may initially have only afforded protection from flooding during the summer months. Puxton in North Somerset represents one of the few oval enclosures to have received systematic archaeological investigation showing probable human and animal occupation through soil chemistry, earthwork survey, excavation and artefactual evidence (Rippon 1997b; 2006). The type of oval epitomised by Puxton may well relate to an early medieval infield comprising permanently manured and cultivated land around, or immediately adjacent to, an associated settlement. The infield would have operated in partnership with a less intensively utilised outfield beyond the immediate vicinity of the settlement zone (Rippon 2002, 54–55). The oval infields of the Severn Estuary appear to typically measure *c.* 5–19 hectares (12–47 acres) in size, with an average of 13 hectares (32 acres) (*ibid.*, 60).

More variable in extent are the 'arc-shaped' or sub-oval boundaries of the western Weald (English 1997; Chatwin and Gardiner 2005; Margetts 2018a). These showed that early intakes of oval shape also existed within wooded contexts and could measure from *c.* 9–60 hectares (22 to around 150 acres), with the majority being over 40 hectares (100 acres) (*ibid.*, 36). Chatwin and Gardiner found this category of enclosure to often be surrounded by roads and tracks aligned in a similar direction, to bear a resemblance to, but have no evidence of being, medieval parks and to often become tenurially distinct by the late medieval period (*ibid.*). They were shown to have a distribution that correlates with that of the Anglo-Saxon *fald/falod* names of the region, which occur largely in the north-western Sussex Weald and across the border with Surrey (see Chapter 4; Figure 6.1). Thus they may be linked to the early, seasonal, pastoral origins of Wealden colonisation.

There is also an area to the south of St Leonard's Forest in which fold place-names exist. Here, an arc-shaped or oval enclosure has been investigated archaeologically (Margetts 2017; Chapter 9). The holdings of Hayworth and Bolnore, components of the manor of Trubwick, conform to the double oval pattern described by Atkin (1985; 1993; Figure 6.2) and appear to have originated as early seasonal pastures that developed into a later medieval vaccary or specialised cattle farm (Margetts 2017; Chapter 9). Enclosures appear to have been the defining landscape feature of a vaccary and examples in the north of England often have at least one stock funnel or driftway allowing livestock to move between the oval and an area of open pasture (Winchester 2000, 69, 115; Newman 2006, 124–25). The ovals contained buildings and areas of grassland, hay meadow and woodland, which were surrounded by a '*haya*' (a Middle English form of *haga* 'a hedge, an enclosure'; *P.N.E.* 1956a, 221; Winchester 2003, 33). This was often formed of a bank and ditch, or in stone using areas vaccary walls. The purpose of these enclosures was to accommodate the cattle over winter as well as to protect winter fodder in the form of hay and browse. The areas of open grazing were intended as summer pasture and would be situated on poorer upland landscapes often comprising areas of Forest and Chase (Winchester 2010).

FIGURE 6.1: 'Fold' place-names recorded prior to AD 1450 within the Domesday counties of Surrey and Sussex (drawn by the author)

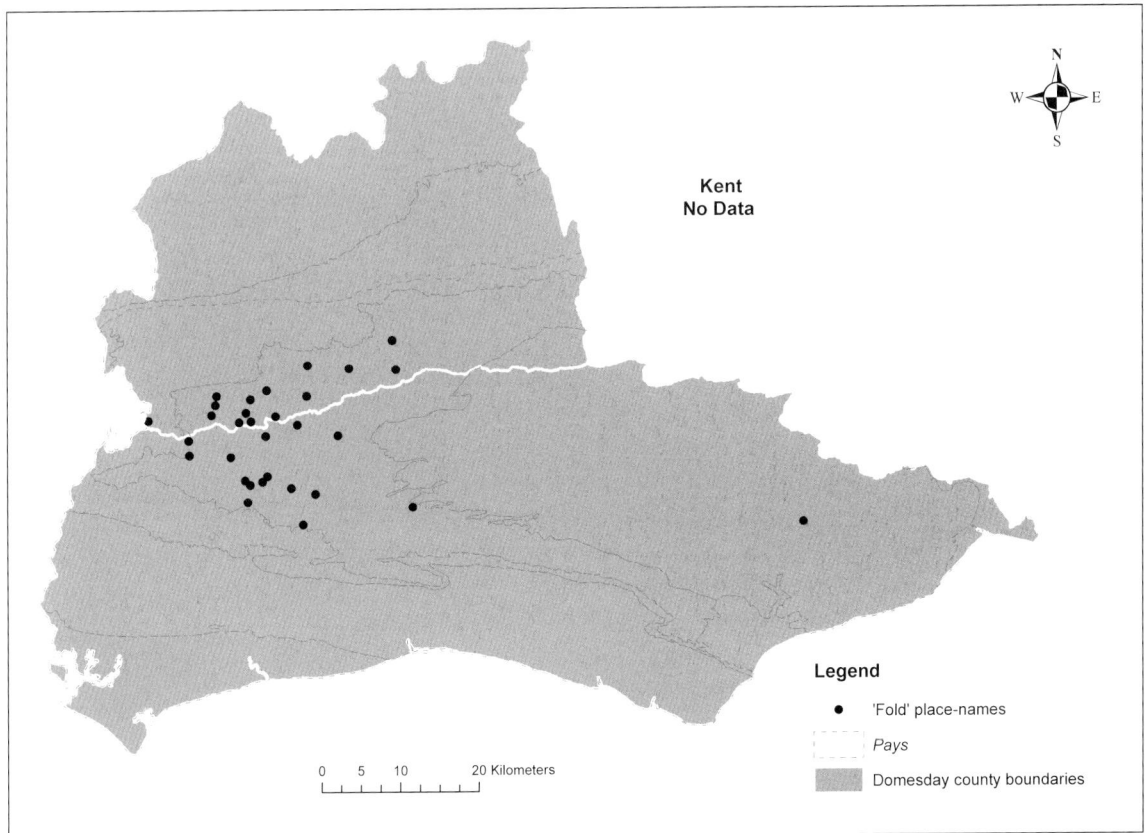

Kent
No Data

Legend

● 'Fold' place-names

⋯⋯ *Pays*

Domesday county boundaries

0   5   10   20 Kilometers

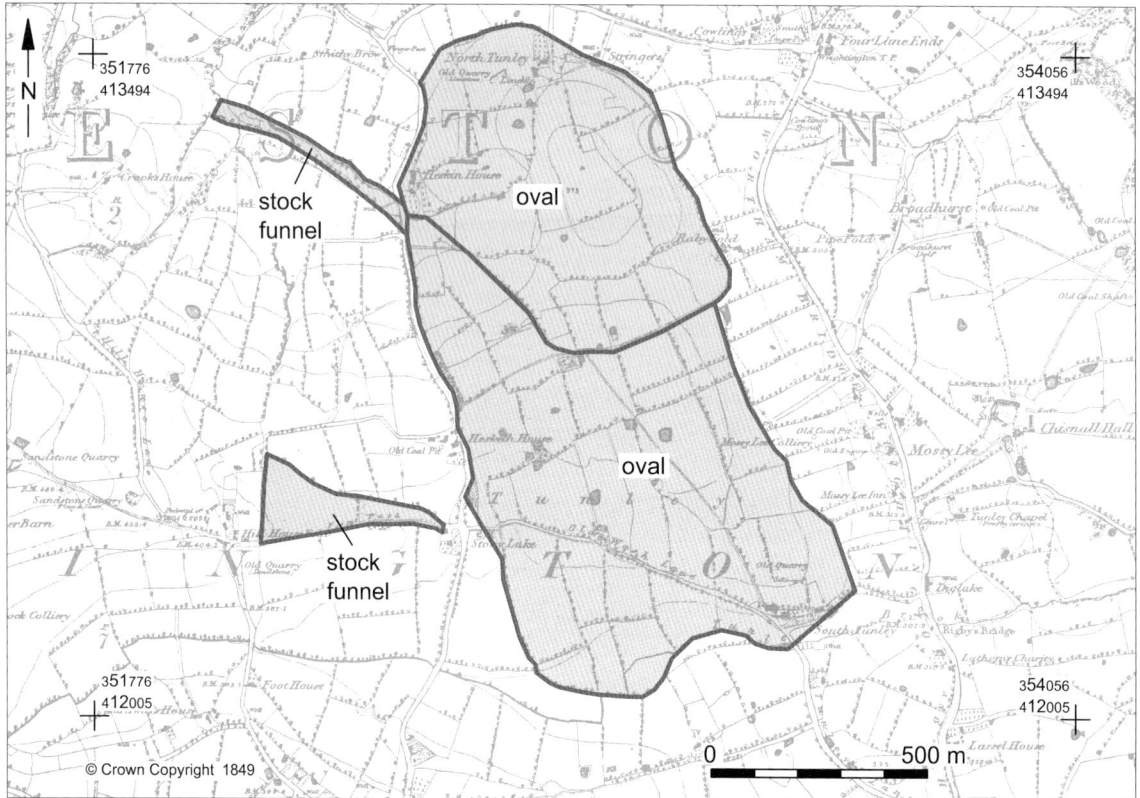

FIGURE 6.2: An example of the 'double oval' field pattern: from Tunley, Lancashire (after Atkin 1985, fig 12.2; Drawing by F. Griffin. © Archaeology South-East, UCL)

Two probable vaccary sites were identified within Chapter 4 due to their associated place-names. *The Vachery* or the 'Manor of Shere Vachery' is located close to the Sussex–Surrey border and is within the bounds of the transect study area. It is worth pausing to highlight some of the elements of the associated historic landscape as indicated by the OS 1st Edition as these are also associated with oval-shaped enclosures (see Figure 6.3 below).

It is clear from Figure 6.3 that the areas on the eastern and western sides of the map show woodland and irregular piecemeal enclosure or assarts. Also prominent are long arc-shaped boundaries which surround a field-scape of slightly more regular form. To the south of this area are the relict feature of a medieval moated site and a tributary of the River Arun named Cobbler's Brook. A feeder stream to this brook would have flowed on a north-east–south-west orientation prior to its damming for the creation of a mid-16th-century hammer pond (Straker 1941). The Vachery was recorded in 1245 when Henry III granted bucks to John son of Geoffrey to stock his park (*parcum*) of *Vacherie* (*Cal. Close, 29 Hen. III. m. 15*), although the fact that it already bore a vaccary place-name in 1244 (SHC: G85/22/1) indicates it possibly originated as an enclosure for cattle. Of course, the association of a vaccary place-name with an oval enclosure is not definitive evidence that the two elements were necessarily linked; however, the similar site of Chelwood Vetchery on the Ashdown Forest is once again

FIGURE 6.3: 'The Vachery' within its historic landscape setting as surviving and shown on the OS 1st Edition 1:2500, 1871, and Esri satellite imagery. The possible extent of the oval enclosure is shown (drawn by the author)

dominated by an oval boundary Figure 6.4. This separates the enclosure from the open forest beyond and is bordered to the south by a watercourse (Mill Brook) and has two streams crossing the enclosure on a north-east–south-west orientation.

The fact that these two sites, which are very likely to have been the locations of medieval vaccaries, display the oval form associated with such establishments in Lancashire and elsewhere indicates that further vaccary farms may have been of similar morphology within the wider South-East. Though it is important not to over-emphasise the potential link between vaccary sites and oval boundaries, enclosures appear to be the defining feature of a vaccary. It is the alliance with other forms of evidence, however, which has the greatest potential to highlight the geographical locations of these specialised farms. Oval enclosures of early type may be shown to comprise a number of different landscape criteria shown on historic cartography (tithe and OS 1st Edition). These include:

1. distinctive curving field boundaries, of the sort which are a feature of the Low Weald (see Chatwin and Gardiner 2005)
2. historic roads and trackways (often equipped with stock funnels) respecting or following the boundaries
3. fields within the boundaries that bear no relation to those outside them (*i.e.* the oval being enclosed prior to/or less likely after the formation of the local field pattern)
4. being respected or followed by historic administrative boundaries not related to river lines (county, rapal, hundredal, parish)
5. making use of watercourses as part of the defining circuit but never being defined solely by them

Mapping of oval enclosures or arc-shaped boundaries was carried out for the transect study area in order to aid a survey of potential vaccary sites and exploration of seasonal pastures. At this stage care was taken not to include features that had at one time functioned as a park (see mapping parks with possible cattle origins below). A thorough search of the appropriate Victoria County History volumes as well as Cantor's (1983) gazetteer and *Parks and Forests of Sussex* (Smith Ellis 1885) was undertaken for each locale in order to exclude examples with possible park-related origins. This work was carried out over a wider geographical area than that of Chatwin and Gardiner's (2005), but followed the same principles in that the examples showed 'no evidence, either documentary or through place-names, that any of the holdings … ever functioned as a park' (*ibid.*, 37).

The landscape criteria outlined above allowed a confidence rating to be given for each enclosure: 4 = Certain, 3 = Probable, 2 = Possible, 1 = Tentative. It was determined that sites would need to fulfil at least two of the above criteria to be included; however, a second dataset would be created comprising tentative oval enclosures associated with locations recorded within the place-names chapter (Chapter 4). These two datasets will be considered separately below.

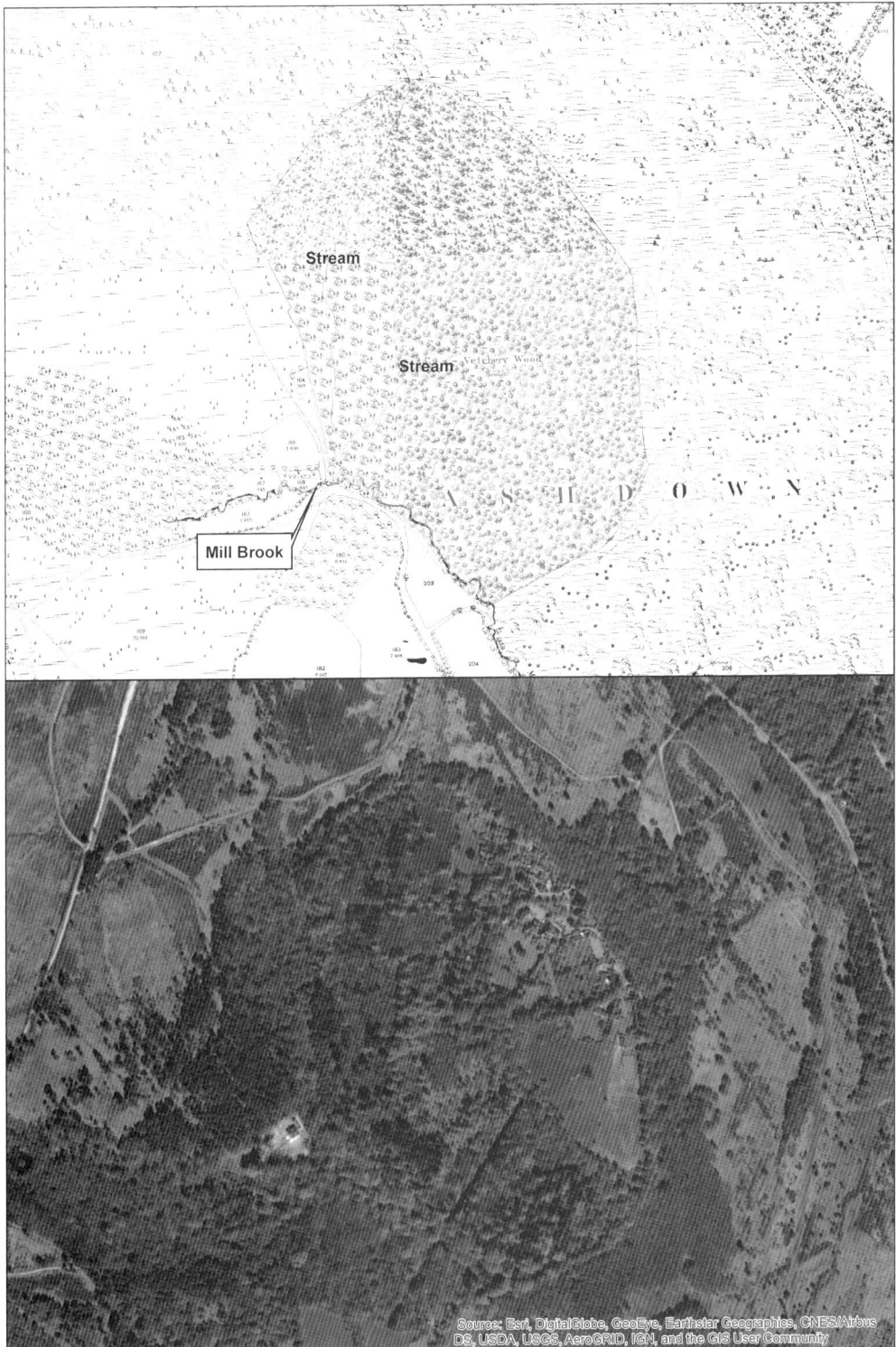

FIGURE 6.4: 'Chelwood Vetchery' as surviving and shown on the OS 1st Edition 1:2500, 1874, 1874–75 and Esri satellite imagery. The possible extent of the oval enclosure is shown (drawn by the author)

Cattle in parks

As has been learnt from our exploration of medieval documents relating to Sussex (Chapter 3), cattle were often pastured within parks, landscape features that also comprise oval enclosures sometimes of significant extent. Cumulatively, the South-East's medieval parks comprised hundreds of hectares of land encompassing various resources, not least amongst which were huge tracts of potential grazing (Figure 6.5). The records explored show that permission to turn animals out within these enclosures would rest on whether the cattle belonged to the owner of the park in question; others could, however, graze their livestock by way of manorial rights or the payment of an agistment fee. This is not a picture that is restricted to Sussex or even the wider South-East. National studies have shown that grazing, and even arable agriculture and industry, took place within medieval parks and this has led to debate as to whether the motivations behind park creation was ever really leisure and status or economic concerns (Mileson 2009, 45). Indeed, it seems that medieval parks could sometimes focus on activities other than hunting. Economic interests could surround the production of timber, horse breeding or specialised cattle pasturing (*ibid.*). Whilst differences between authors who emphasise the economic importance of parks (*e.g.* Cantor 1982; Rackham 1990, 153–58) and those who see such activities as subsidiary to hunting and display

FIGURE 6.5: One of Britain's oldest breeds of cattle, longhorns, grazing in the medieval park on the Knepp Castle Estate. The animals are part of a successful rewilding project (source: the author)

(Richardson 2007; Mileson 2009) persist, this study will focus upon the use of parks for cattle while acknowledging their primary importance was for the hunting and keeping of deer.

In certain locations (*e.g.* Essex: Britnell 1977, 109) it has been claimed that the high point of park creation in the 12th and 13th centuries was a seigneurial response to the control of pasture rights. Medieval parks could provide secure and easily manageable pastoral reserves that would safeguard lords' income through agistment fees while protecting valuable grazing during a period of population growth and land pressure. Compartmentalisation of these establishments has therefore occasionally been seen as an effort to facilitate effective economic exploitation to help alleviate the costs of devoting precious acreages to the management of deer (Mileson 2009, 59, 64). Parks provided secure locations for the effective grazing of cattle and as pounds for the keeping of strays and heriot beasts. Such activity is well documented from the South-East, with one example provided by the obligation of the widow Herburga recorded in the Custumal of Selsey. She was to go with 'the bedell of the hundred, or the bedell of the manor, to take and drive distrained [animals] to the park' (*Cust. Chi.* 1925, 20).

Concerns surrounding the use of parks for activity other than hunting has been cited for larger examples, the significant size of which helped facilitate alternative economic activity (Mileson 2009, 65). That smaller parks, established by lesser lords (not always legally) were compartmentalised for similar reasons may have been demonstrated in Sussex by excavated evidence at Broadbridge Heath (Margetts 2018a). Here the persistence of earlier field boundaries through a period of imparkment into the post-medieval agricultural landscape has been confirmed (see Chapter 9). It is the parks of the north of England and parts of the Midlands, however, which show the most recognisable evidence of these enclosed spaces being used to facilitate effective livestock husbandry. In these areas parks appear to have been increasingly utilised for the pasturing of large numbers of livestock during the 14th and earlier 15th centuries (Stamper 1988, 146; Pollard 1990, 204; Moorhouse 2003, 329, 332, 334). Records occasionally show that these establishments were directly converted into stock farms. This was the case in Richard Neville the Earl of Warwick's lordship of Middleham, where six parks were turned over to livestock farms in the later 15th century (Pollard 1990, 62). In Yorkshire more generally, the rearing of cattle expanded in the 15th century and parks became increasingly used as grazing grounds for cattle (Pollard 1990, 202–06). In this area they appear to have had a direct association with external vaccaries, a situation that occurred in the manor of Wakefield and around Middleham (Moorhouse 2007, 114).

One final, often forgotten aspect of cattle and parks is that the species could sometimes comprise a beast of the chase. Perhaps the most famous herd to have been kept in parks are the feral Chillingham Cattle of the Tankerville estate in Northumberland. These proud beasts have upright horns, freckles on the face and neck, and their muzzles and ears are coloured red (Porter 2001, 8; Plate 6.2).

The park in which they are kept has effectively enclosed an entire ecosystem and could be considered as a relic of the medieval practice of imparking, which sometimes included the deliberate or accidental enclosing of wild, domestic or semi-domestic grazing animals (Rotherham 2007, 85–86). The fact that these animals are white and have red ears evokes a theme discussed by medievalists and scholars of Celtic literature, which has shown that red-eared white animals have been associated by some cultures with fairies and other supernatural beings (Hemming 2002). The Chillingham herd is genetically distinct, a situation that is most likely a product of their long enclosure (*ibid.*, 73). Studies have shown that emparkment of these originally feral or domestic cattle occurred sometime between the 13th and 17th centuries (*ibid.*, 75).

Despite the possibility that cattle could have been deliberately imparked to provide a medieval hunting opportunity, this is difficult to substantiate on documentary grounds. Nevertheless, in areas of medieval forest 'wild bulls' were certainly considered as a beast of the chase (Jones 2010, 57). Hunting of cattle has a long history in both Britain and the near continent. The Frankish kings are known to have hunted the wild bull or aurochs and the value placed on these animals is suggested by a 6th-century record of King Gunthram who had his chamberlain stoned for killing an auroch in the forest of Vosges (*Hist. Franc.* x, x). In Britain 'wild bulls' were present on Enfield Chase (Darby 1936, 32) as well as on the 14th-century Wyresdale Forest where the keeper did not answer for 'bulls and cows with their woodland issues … because they remain to be taken at the king's will' (Cunliffe Shaw 1956, 17).

The above discussion and documentary chapter (Chapter 3) has shown that medieval deer parks were important elements of the contemporary pastoral economy. Mapping of oval enclosures also demonstrated that a number of medieval parks may have originated in areas already associated with cattle or seasonal pasturing activity. The park known as *Vachery* (Shere Vachery) is the clearest evidence of this, although documentary records also shows that some of the South-East's early medieval 'dens' were later converted into parks – for example, the 1285 record of the Abbott of Battle's conversion of the *denn* of Angley into a deer park (Witney 1990, 37). Excavation has also demonstrated that some medieval parks may have utilised pre-existing oval enclosures (Margetts 2018a; Chapter 9), an important revelation, as extant oval enclosures and the seasonal pastures they sometimes served may have had some influence over later choices and distribution of land-use. It was therefore determined that the relevance of medieval deer parks to the cattle economy of the South-East needed to be explored in more detail. In addition to a general historiography, it was decided to discuss those parks that lay within manors shown to be strongly associated with cattle during the documentary search conducted for Chapter 3. This approach restricts in-depth exploration to the Sussex portion of the South-East.

In order to explore medieval parks whose origins may have lain in seaso nal pastures, it was additionally resolved to explore Sussex parks with place-names discussed in Chapter 4. This would be based on the reasonably up-to-date list of parks provided by Gardiner (1999b, 39). The examination would comprise a cursory investigation followed by more detailed desk-based landscape study of parks that lay inside the transect study area.

6.3 Results

Oval enclosures and arc-shaped boundaries

Twenty oval enclosures were included for the transect study area with a confidence rating of two and above (Table 6.1). These ranged in size from 7 to 140 hectares, with an average of 49 hectares. The oval enclosures and their associated confidence rating are shown on Figure 6.6. Tentatively identified sites (those with a score of one) are discussed separately below. Only one example of a double oval was encountered, Whitenwick and Clothalls. Although others may have existed, the rigorous – perhaps overly cautious – nature of the methodology often meant that the definition of a second oval was not justifiable. Over 60% of the mapped enclosures utilised rivers or streams as part of their boundary circuit; 85% were within 300 m of running water and only the downland example of Langham Wood was more than a kilometre away from a significant watercourse (Plate 6.3; see section 7.4 for the importance of water for cattle). Cartographic evidence also showed that by the 19th century field boundaries, routeways and shaws were employed to define these enclosures, which were often of sub-circular or oval shape. Semi-circles or truncated ovals were also sometimes found. The influence of hydrology and topography on the siting of the enclosures was assessed with reference to modern OS mapping. These environmental factors were judged to have had an influence on the siting of enclosure boundaries if part of the defining circuit followed breaks in slope (ridges or valleys) or watercourses. Only 25% were judged to be influenced by both topographic and hydrological factors (Lydwick, Strood, Lickfold and Rye Farm). Thirty per cent were judged to have been influenced by topographic factors and 60% by hydrology.

In terms of distribution throughout the various *pays* of the transect study area, oval enclosures were encountered within the North and South Downs, the Greensand, the Low Weald and the Thames Basin. They were noticeably absent from the West Sussex Coastal Plain and the High Weald. The greatest concentration was in the Low Weald close to the Sussex–Surrey border, an area that previous chapters have shown has strong potential to be associated with medieval cattle pasturing. This Low Wealden bias means that oval enclosures are most often located on a mixture of clay and sandstone geologies; however, as a group across the various *pays* the strongest correlation appears to be with deposits of alluvium and river terrace gravels, geological units that often border the enclosures. The majority were found at an elevation of under 50 m OD with four found between 50 m and 100 m OD; two were at elevations over 100 m OD. The example of Hazel Hall, Surrey was the highest with an elevation of

TABLE 6.1: Oval enclosures of the transect study area based on rigorous cartographic evidence (Confidence 2–4). For tentatively identified sites (Confidence 1), see Table 6.2

Name	Name meaning/elements	Date of first recording	Oval recorded previously?	County	Pay	Main geology	Size ha	Distance from significant watercourse	Influenced by topography	Influenced by hydrology	Confidence
Rutwick	rough wick *rub, wic*	1263	No	Surrey	Low Weald	Weald Clay	140	0 m	No	No	3
Lydwick	slope wick *hlip, wic*	956	Chatwin and Gardiner 2005	Sussex	Low Weald	Weald Clay	16	400 m	Yes	Yes	3
Hazel Hall	Hazel wood *holt*	1241	No	Surrey	Greensand	Lower Greensand	16	25 m	Yes	No	3
Clemsfold	Climpe's fold *falod*	1285	Chatwin and Gardiner 2005	Sussex	Low Weald	Terrace Gravels	22	0 m	No	Yes	3
Strood	Pers. Name	1279	Chatwin and Gardiner 2005	Sussex	Low Weald	Horsham Stone	23	445 m	Yes	Yes	3
Rye Farm	at ther ee *æt, ēg*	1560	No	Sussex	Low Weald	Terrace Gravels	24	245 m	Yes	Yes	2
Rumbeams Farm	large tree *rum, beam*	1428	English 1997	Surrey	Low Weald	Weald Clay	27	65 m	No	No	3
Langham Wood	long enclosure *lang, ham(m)*	1420	No	Sussex	South Downs	Chalk	35	1.75 km	Yes	No	4
Tickfold	Ticca's fold *falod*	1551	Chatwin and Gardiner 2005	Sussex	Low Weald	Weald Clay	44	530 m	No	Yes	2
Leigh	forest clearing, pasture *leah*	1184	No	Surrey	Low Weald	Weald Clay	52	100 m	No	No	2
Hale/Pephurst Wood	Pers. Name/'Tybba's hyrst'	1256/1303	Chatwin and Gardiner 2005	Sussex	Low Weald	Weald Clay	53	295 m	No	No	2
Caplins	look-out place *cape, land*	?	Chatwin and Gardiner 2005	Sussex	Low Weald	Weald Clay	57	0 m	No	No	3
Howick	wick/farm by the heel or spur of land *hōh, wic*	1166	Chatwin and Gardiner 2005	Sussex	Low Weald	Weald Clay	62	0 m	No	Yes	3
Rowfold	rough fold *rub, falod*	1566	Chatwin and Gardiner 2005	Sussex	Low Weald	Weald Clay	62	0 m	No	Yes	4
Park Farm	Self-explanatory	?1777	Chatwin and Gardiner 2005	Sussex	Low Weald	Weald Clay	7	30 m	No	Yes	2
Lickfold	herb, leek fold *leac, falod/falod*	1509	No	Sussex	Greensand	Alluvium	76	0 m	Yes	Yes	4
Little Bookham	Beech enclosure *boc, ham(m)*	1086	No	Surrey	Thames Basin	London Clay	8	130 m	No	No	2
Watersfield	Open land of or by the water or stream '*feld*	1226	No	Sussex	Greensand	Alluvium	86	0 m	No	Yes	2
Clothalls	Pers. Name or 'nook of land where the burdock grows' *clate, healh*	1271	No	Sussex	Low Weald	Weald Clay	86	0 m	No	Yes	4
Whitenwick	Hwita's *wic'*	1539	No	Sussex	Low Weald	Weald Clay	90	0 m	No	Yes	4

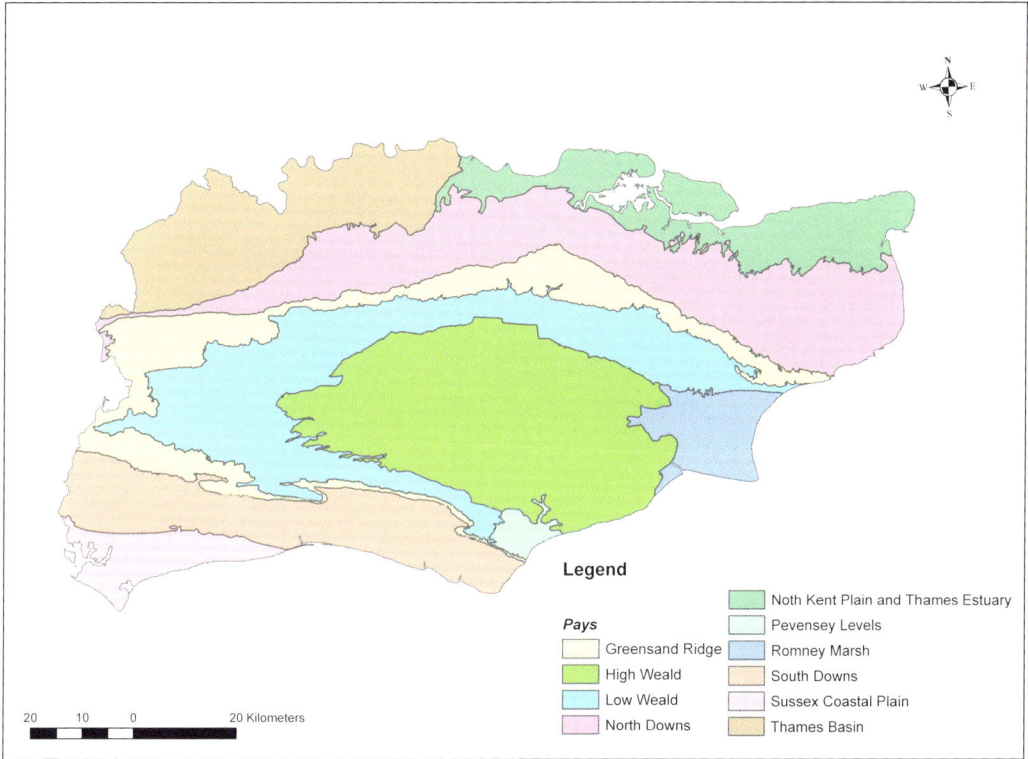

Legend

Pays

Greensand Ridge
High Weald
Low Weald
North Downs

Noth Kent Plain and Thames Estuary
Pevensey Levels
Romney Marsh
South Downs
Sussex Coastal Plain
Thames Basin

20 10 0   20 Kilometers

PLATE 1.1: The *pays* of the South-East (drawn by the author)

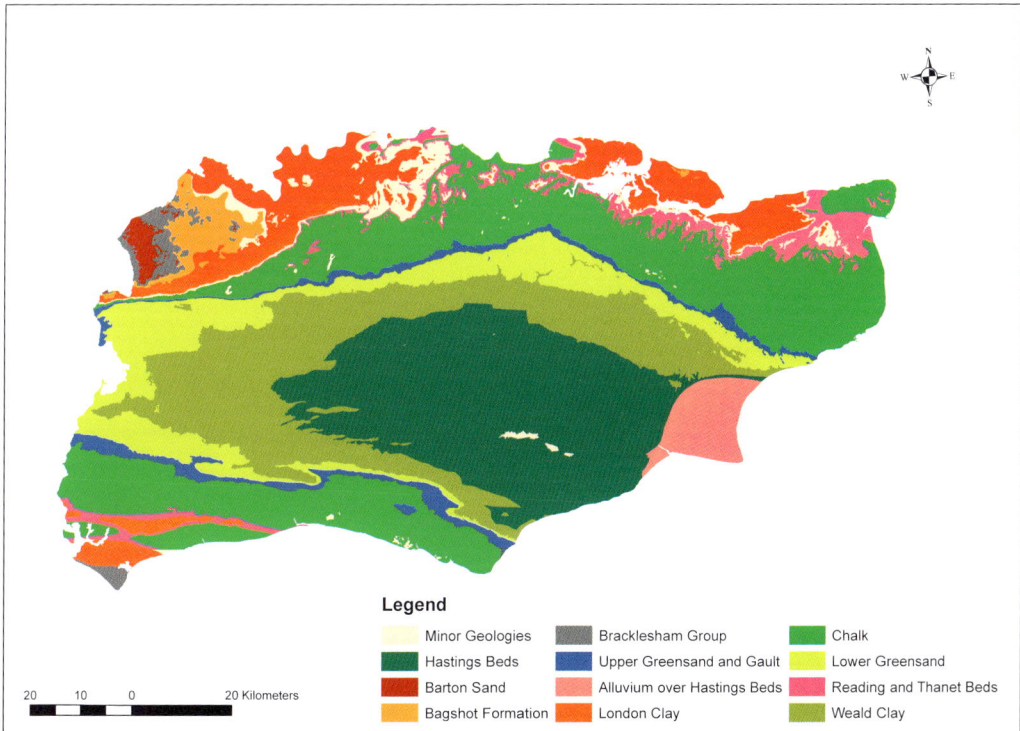

Legend

Minor Geologies
Hastings Beds
Barton Sand
Bagshot Formation

Bracklesham Group
Upper Greensand and Gault
Alluvium over Hastings Beds
London Clay

Chalk
Lower Greensand
Reading and Thanet Beds
Weald Clay

20 10 0   20 Kilometers

PLATE 1.2: A simplified geological map of the South-East, showing major geological units (after Geological Map Data BGS © UKRI 2019; drawn by the author)

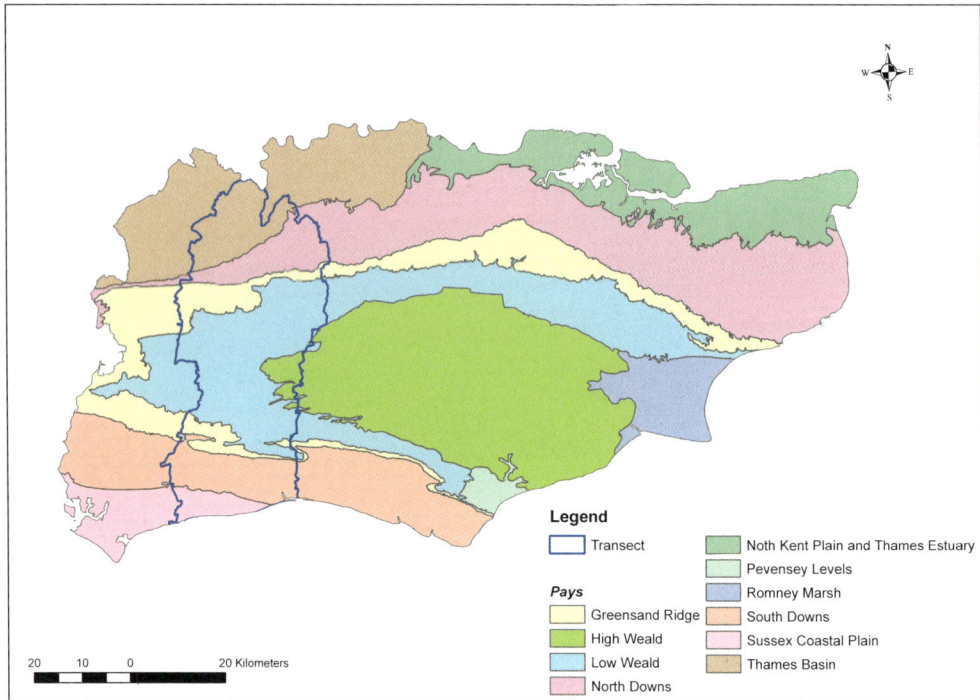

PLATE I.3: The transect study area in relation to the *pays* of the wider study area, the South-East (drawn by the author)

PLATE 3.1: Looking across the open flats of the modern Pevensey Levels towards the South Downs ('NCA124 Pevensey Levels' by naturalengland is licensed with CC BY-NC-ND 2.0)

PLATE 3.2: English White cattle grazing on the South Downs near Lewes (source: the author)

PLATE 3.3: Longhorn cattle grazing within the medieval parkland landscape at Knepp Castle, West Sussex (source: the author)

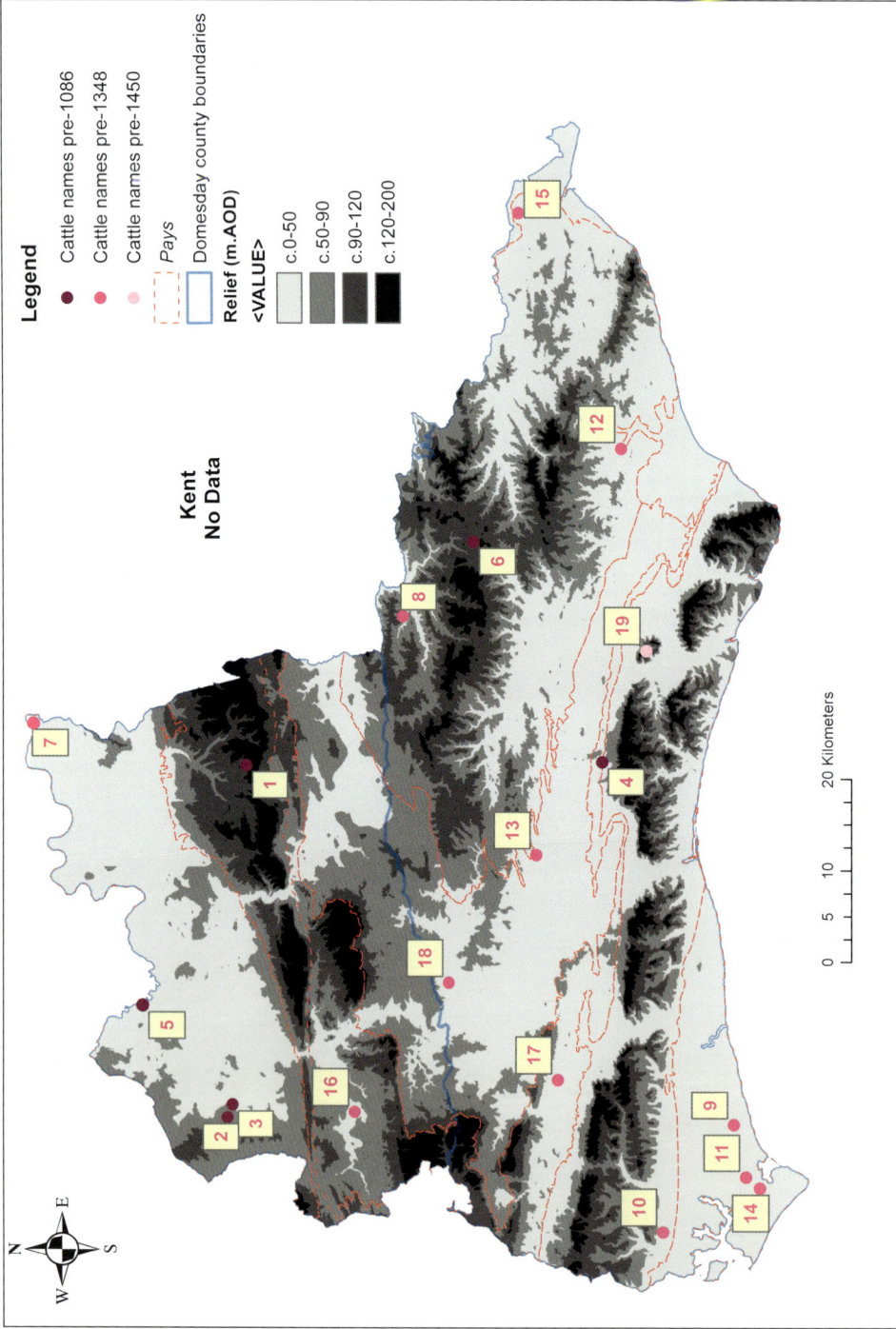

PLATE 4.1: Cattle place-names of Sussex and Surrey recorded prior to 1450 in relation to relief (drawn by the author. Contains material covered by © Crown copyright and database rights 2019 Ordnance Survey, Educational Service Provider licence number v2.1)

PLATE 4.2: The author and his dog on 'Hunger Lane' north of Rotherbridge Farm (source: the author)

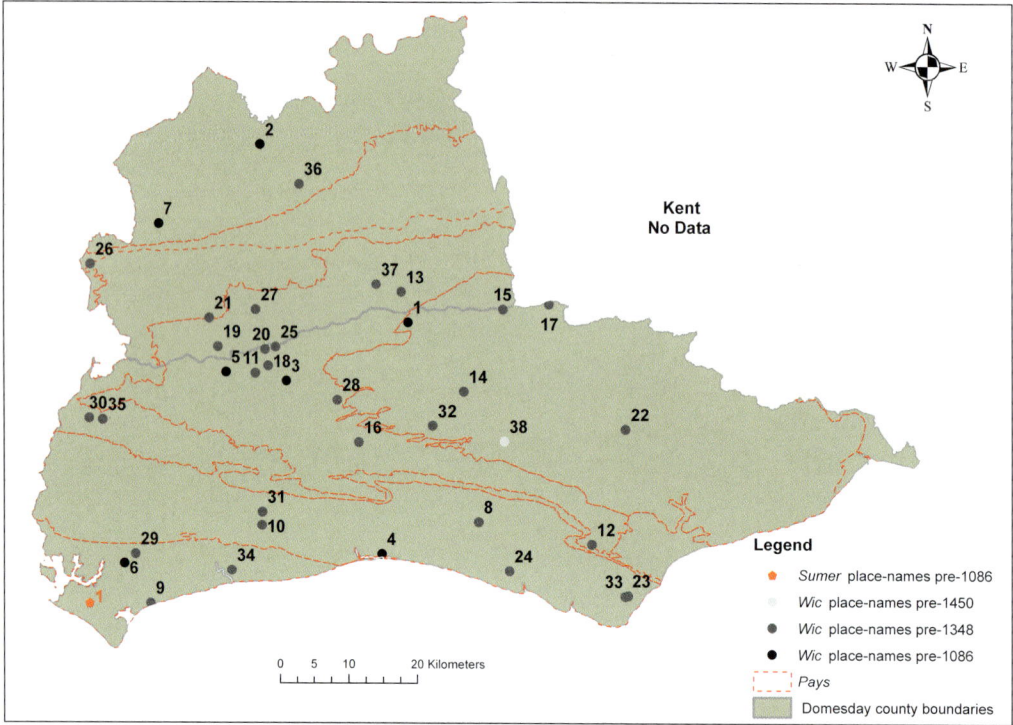

PLATE 4.3: *Wic* place-names of Sussex and Surrey recorded prior to 1450 (drawn by the author)

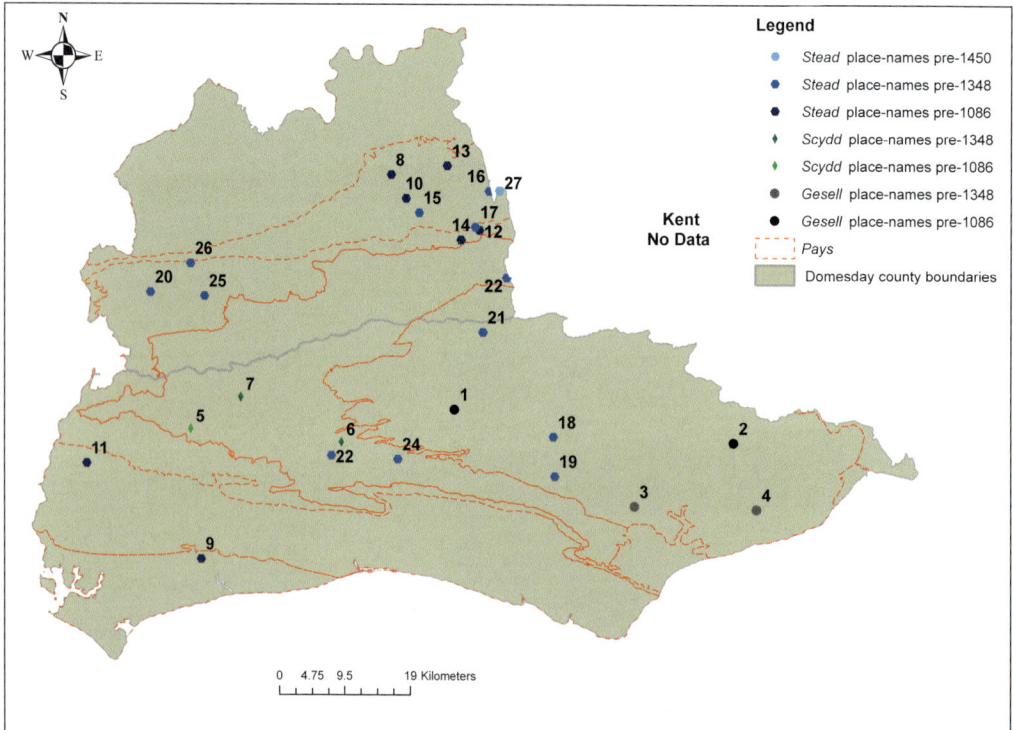

PLATE 4.4: 'Shieling' place-names of Sussex and Surrey recorded prior to 1450 (drawn by the author)

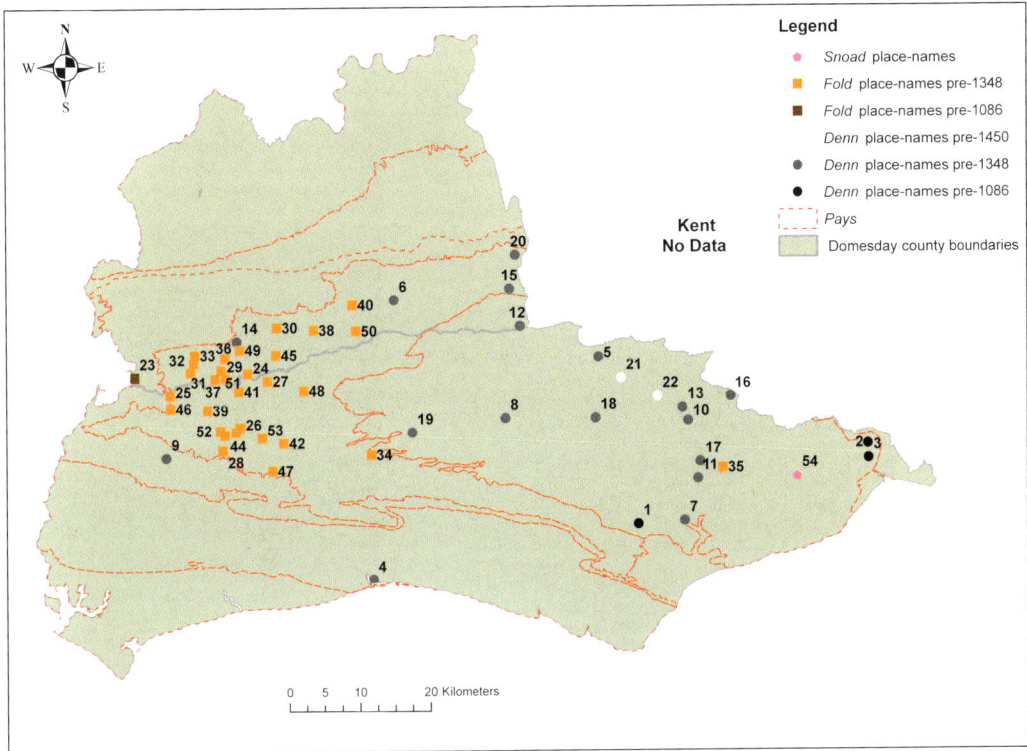

PLATE 4.5: 'Den', 'Fold' and 'Snoad' place-names of Sussex and Surrey recorded prior to 1450 (drawn by the author)

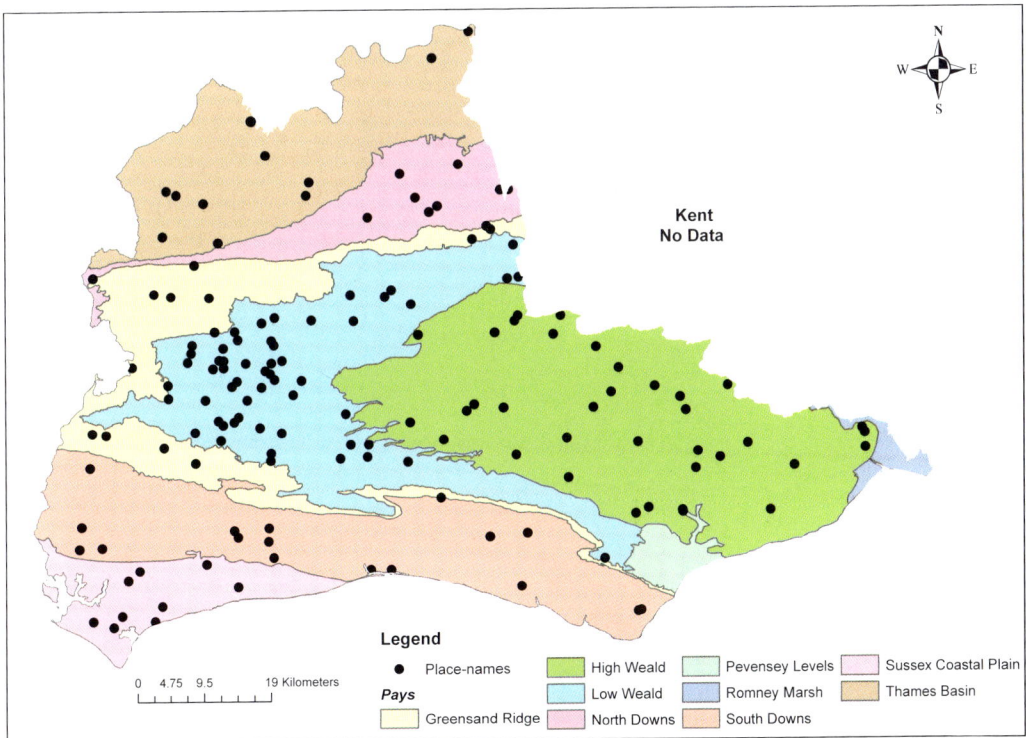

PLATE 4.6: The entire corpus of place-names plotted against the *pays* of Sussex and Surrey (drawn by the author)

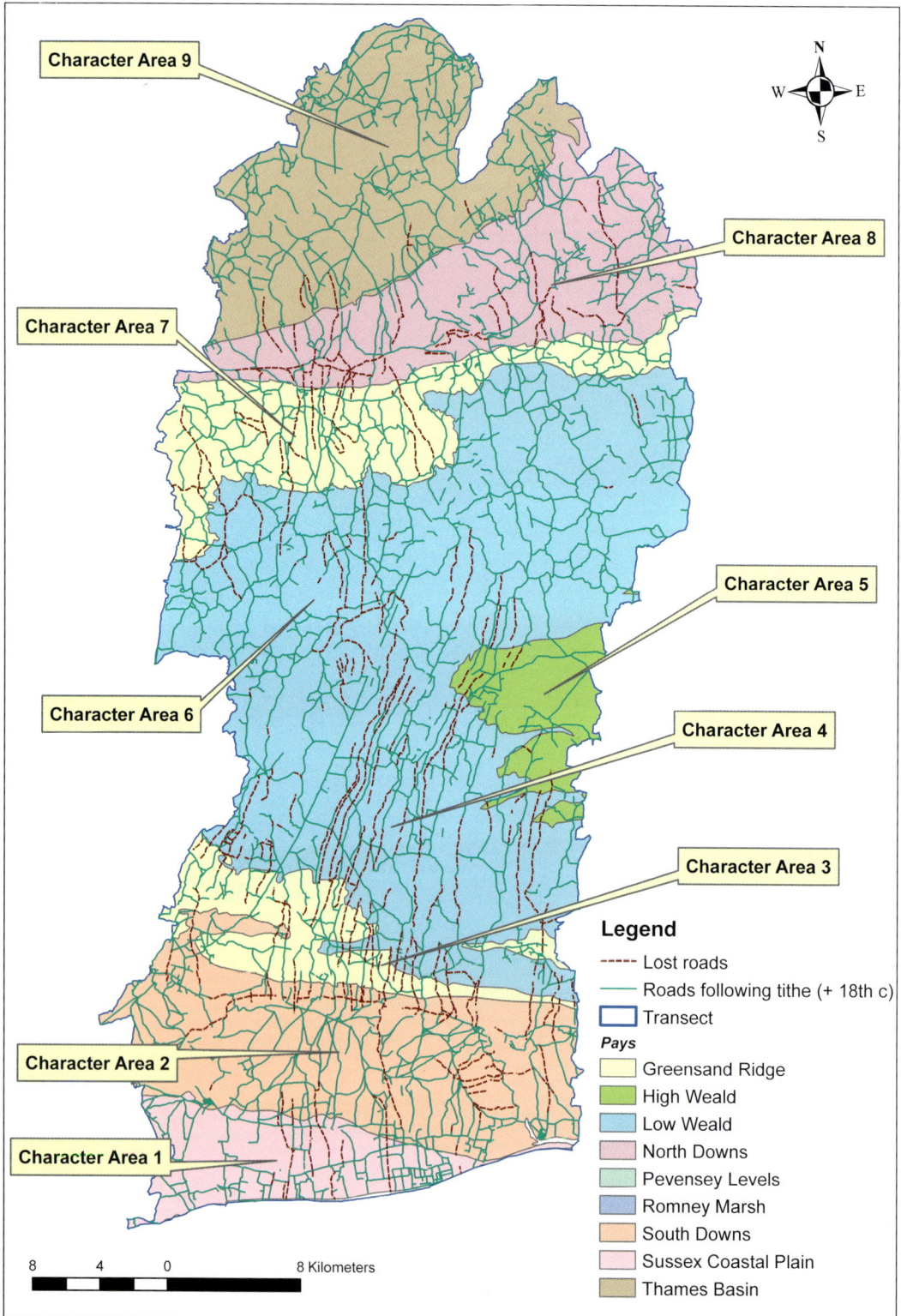

Legend

--- Lost roads
— Roads following tithe (+ 18th c)
☐ Transect
Pays
☐ Greensand Ridge
☐ High Weald
☐ Low Weald
☐ North Downs
☐ Pevensey Levels
☐ Romney Marsh
☐ South Downs
☐ Sussex Coastal Plain
☐ Thames Basin

Character Area 9
Character Area 8
Character Area 7
Character Area 5
Character Area 6
Character Area 4
Character Area 3
Character Area 2
Character Area 1

8 4 0 8 Kilometers

PLATE 5.1: The medieval road system in relation to the *pays* of the transect study area (drawn by the author)

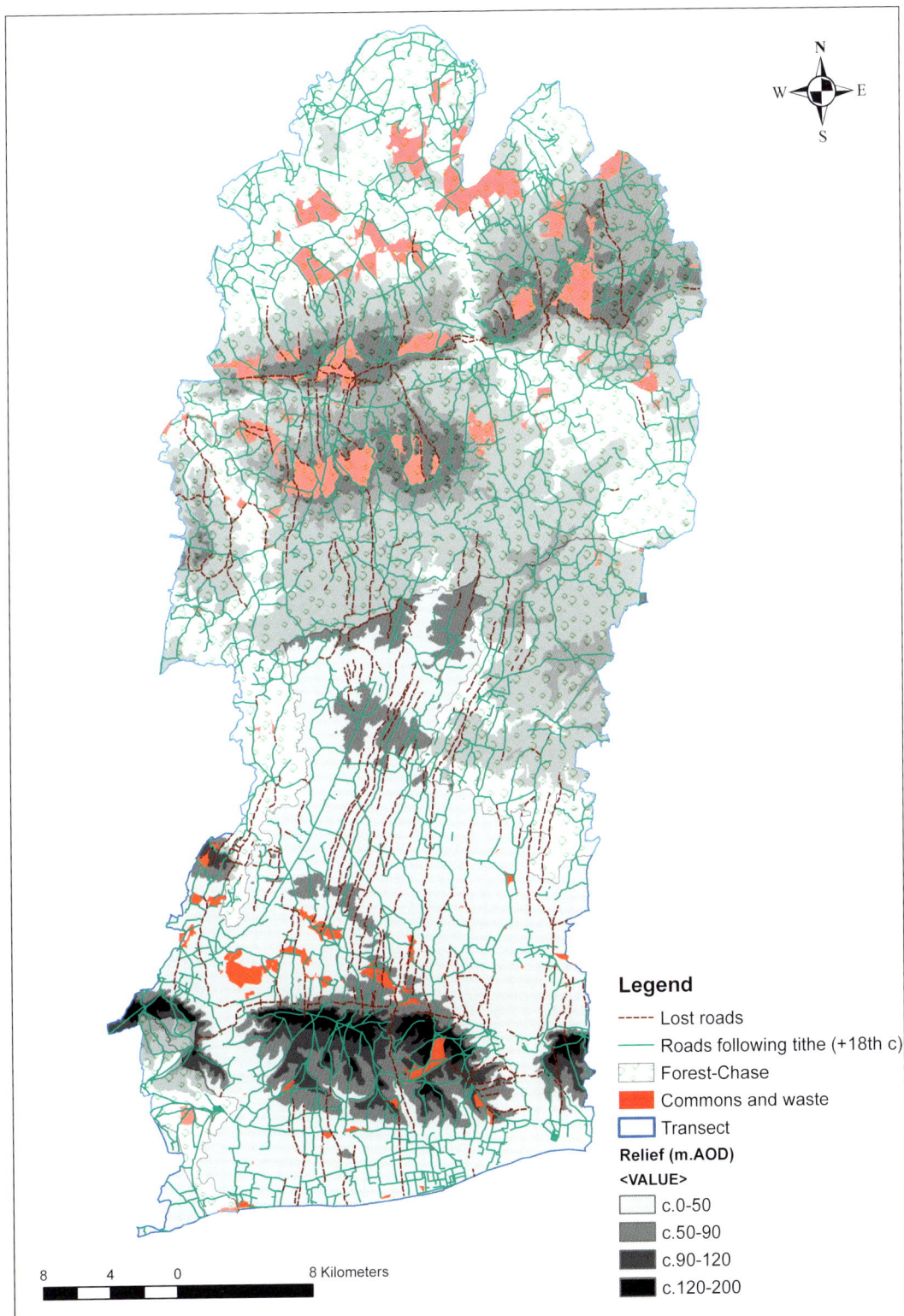

PLATE 5.2: The medieval road system of the transect study area in relation to topography, Forests, Chase, commons and waste (drawn by the author, Forest and Chase after Langton and Jones 2010, fig. 1)

Legend

- - - - - Lost roads
───── Roads following tithe (+18th c)
Forest-Chase
Commons and waste
Transect

Relief (m.AOD)
<VALUE>
c.0-50
c.50-90
c.90-120
c.120-200

8 4 0   8 Kilometers

PLATE 5.3: A deep holloway or *bostal* descending the scarp face of the South Downs. Evidence of our bovine quarry can be seen in the foreground (source: the author)

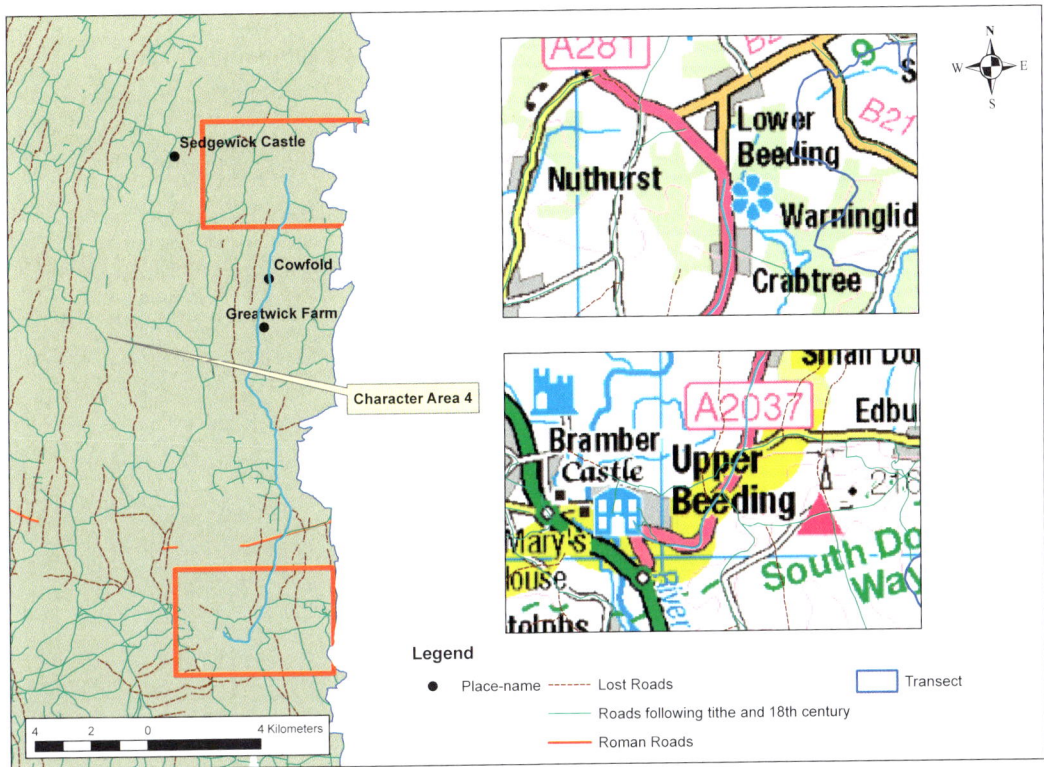

PLATE 5.4: Droveway (highlighted) linking Upper and Lower Beeding as well as the place-names Cowfold and Greatwick (drawn by the author. Includes Modern OS 1:250000) © Crown copyright and database rights 2020 Ordnance Survey

PLATE 5.5: A holloway cutting sandstone geology at Picts Hill near Cowfold on the very edge of the High Weald (source: the author)

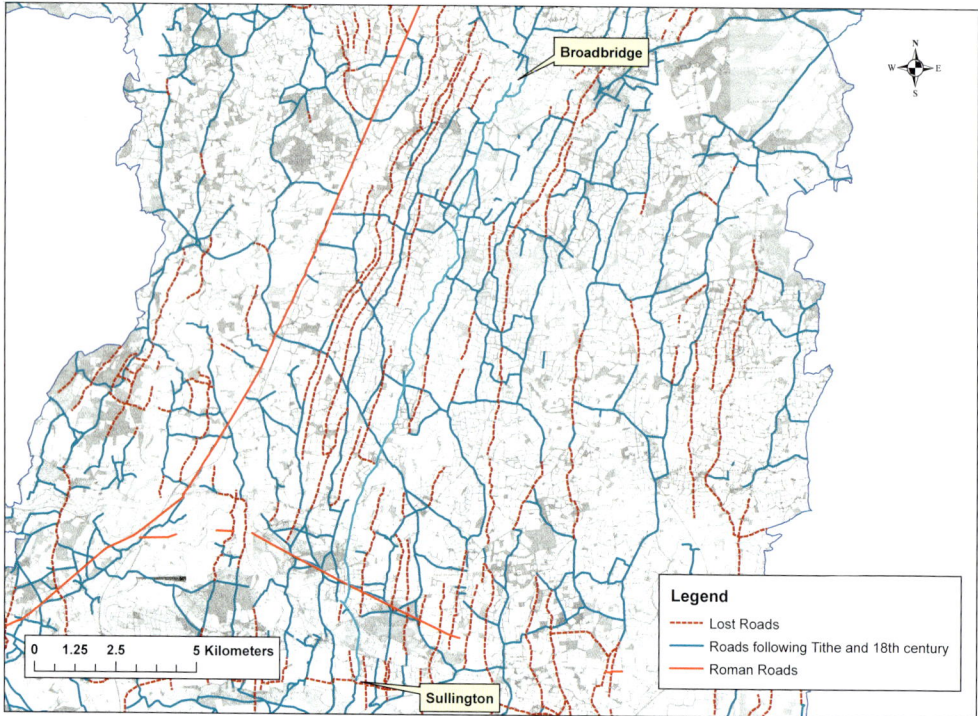

PLATE 5.6: The course of Wickhurst Lane (highlighted) linking the parent manor of Sullington with its Wealden outlier Broadbridge (drawn by the author)

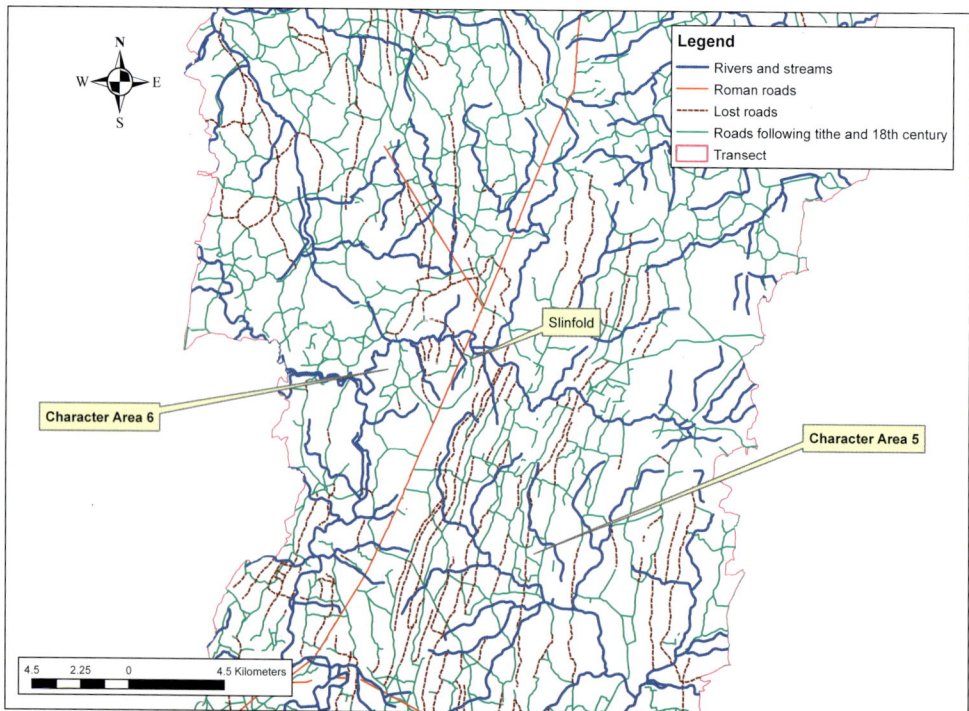

PLATE 5.7: The medieval road network of the Low Weald in relation to hydrology (drawn by the author. Contains material covered by © Crown copyright and database rights 2019 Ordnance Survey, Educational Service Provider licence number v2.1)

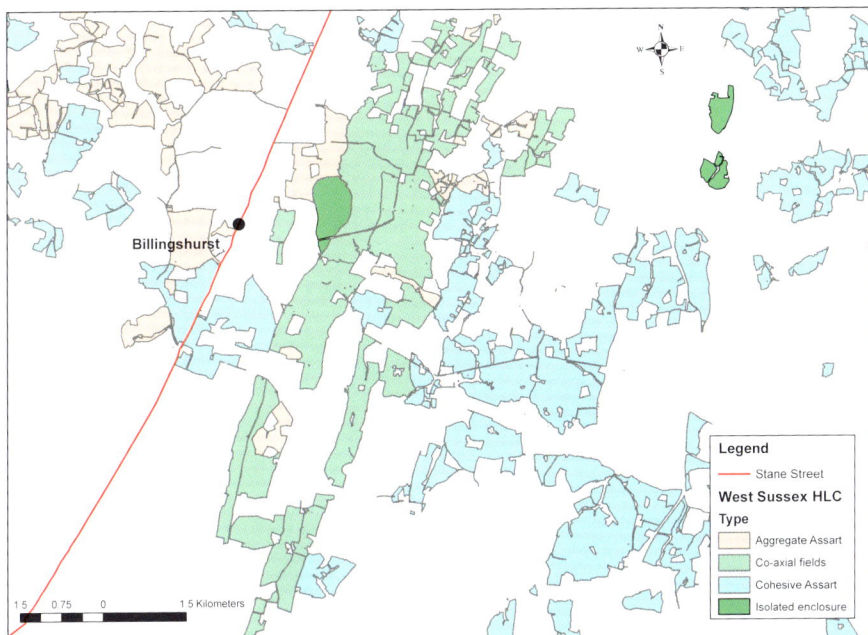

PLATE 6.1: Elements of the West Sussex Historic Landscape Characterisation (Bannister 2014) showing areas of aggregate and cohesive assarts surrounding the Sussex Low Weald co-axial system near Billingshurst. Isolated sub-oval enclosures are also features of the local landscape (drawn by the author. Data copyright © West Sussex County Council, Historic England)

PLATE 6.2: A Chillingham bull (Image courtesy of Rick Waddington)

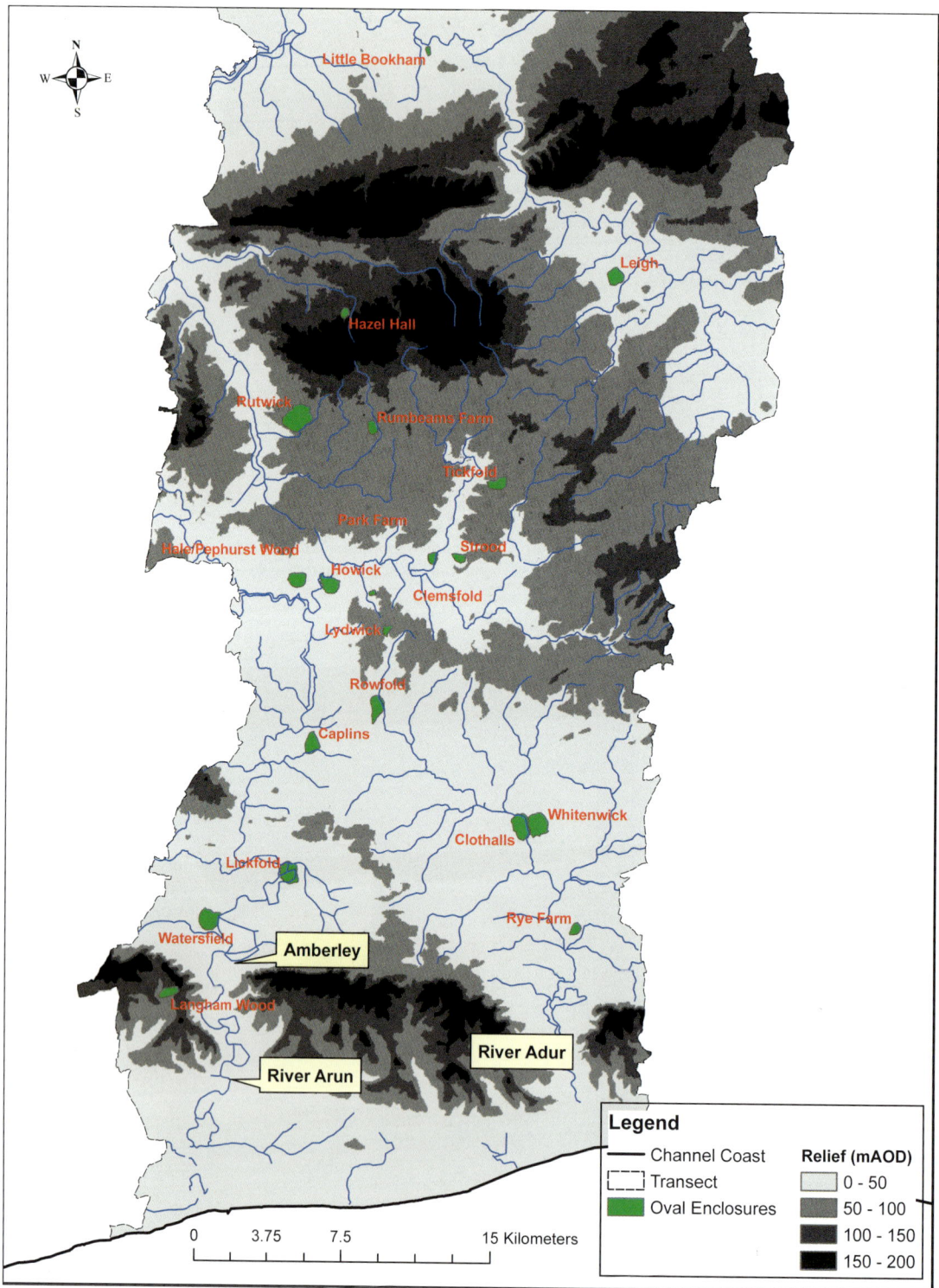

PLATE 6.3: Mapped oval enclosures of the transect study area with a confidence rating of 2–4 in relation to hydrology (drawn by the author. Contains material covered by © Crown copyright and database rights 2019 Ordnance Survey, Educational Service Provider licence number v2.1)

PLATE 7.1: Sussex cattle grazing on Summer Down in July (source: the author)

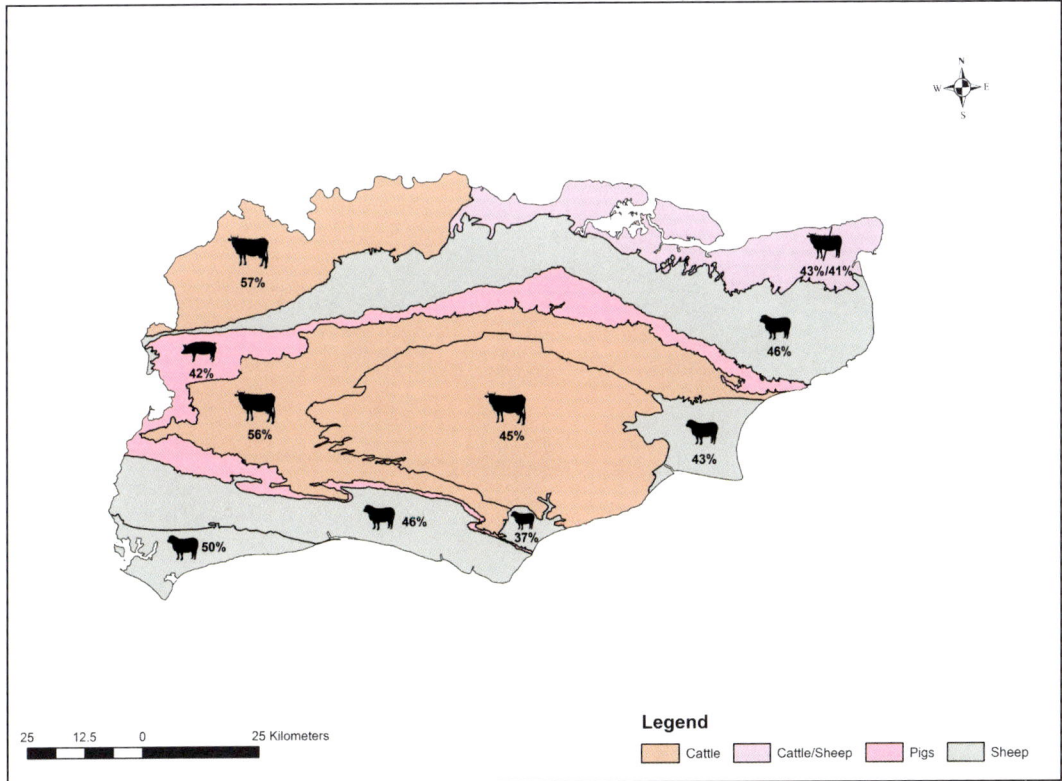

PLATE 8.1: An indication of the dominant domesticates of the different *pays* of the South-East during the middle medieval period

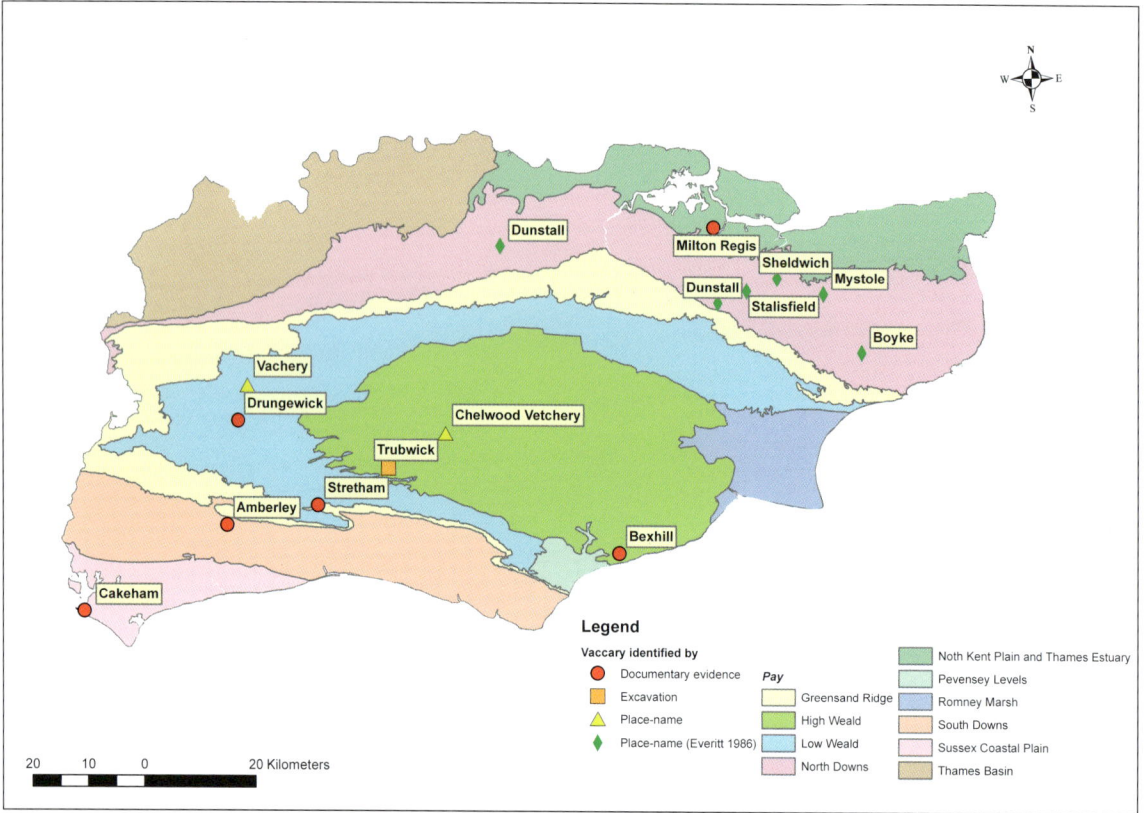

PLATE 10.1: Highlighted vaccaries and the *pays* of the South-East. The vaccary sites are distinguished by their primary means of identification (with a confidence scale of red = confidently identified, green = tentatively identified/identified by others)

PLATE 11.1: Cattle grazing in woodlands is a fairly common occurrence in modern cattle husbandry practice (source: the author)

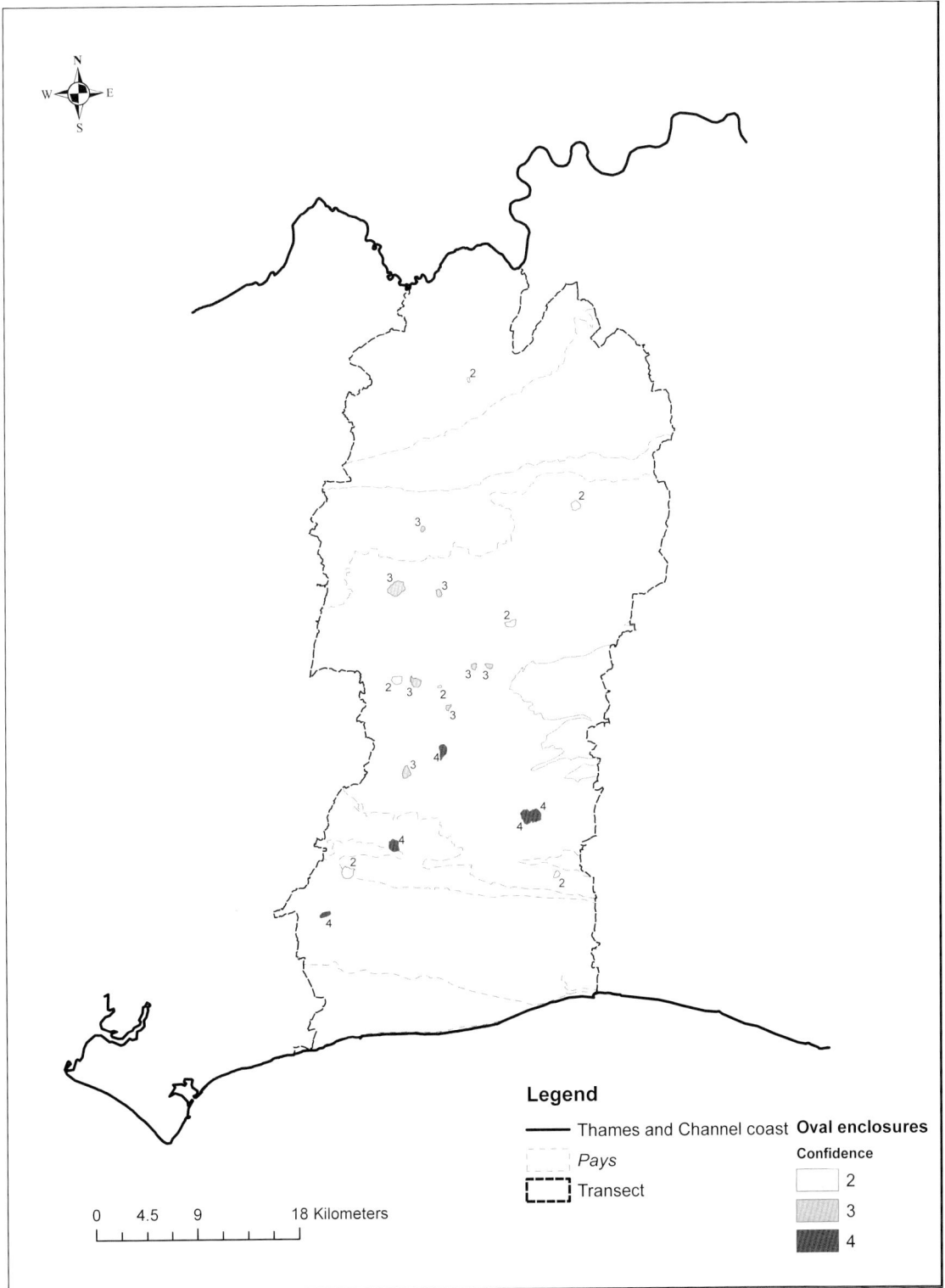

FIGURE 6.6: Mapped oval enclosures of the transect study area with a confidence rating of 2–4 (drawn by the author)

c. 140 m OD. All apart from one example (Lickfold on the banks of the Arun) were located on the slopes of rising land.

The distribution of oval enclosures in relation to the historic road system of the South-East shows some correlation with the line of Stane Street and the Farley Heath Spur. Oval enclosures appear to spread along the line of these Roman roads and in one case (Lickfold) an oval is bisected by the Greensand Way. This trend may be circumstantial, although it is also possible that these long-established routes were utilised as droveways during the medieval period. There is another explanation, however, which is concerned with the origins of these enclosures. Some may owe their inception to the Romano-British or even Iron Age periods, and the apparent correlation between the transect study area's Roman road system could be understood in this regard. Whatever their origins, oval enclosures appear to be an element of those landscapes that have an irregular pattern to their routeway layout. Though they can be found in the aligned pattern of roads and tracks of the southern Low Weald, they appear to be located on the edge of this zone (Figure 6.7). The exception is the double oval of Whitenwick and Clothalls. Upon closer inspection, however, these twin enclosures appear to be more intimately tied to riparian pastures on the banks of the River Arun than they are to the cohesively assarted landscape beyond. It is possible, therefore, that the oval enclosures may be associated with medieval land-use outside the area of strip manors and small several closes associated with *Character Area 4* discussed within Chapter 5.

Half of the oval enclosures had a proximate relationship with areas of common mapped during Chapter 5. This may be slightly misleading, however, as the commons were plotted from those which survived into the 19th century. Therefore, it is possible that there may have once been a more extensive relationship between the two datasets. Thirteen of the 20 oval enclosures existed outside areas of Forests and Chase; however, Figure 6.8 shows that as a group they were proximate to these zones. This may be a reflection of the size of the area at one time or another designated as elite hunting preserves, but may be more reflective of the earlier medieval history of these landscapes. Certainly, the majority of oval enclosures were situated in areas that during part of the early medieval period were considered largely intercommonable. The Forest and Chase of the post-Conquest South-East can partly be considered a legacy of these earlier landscapes.

Forests and Chase were not the only administrative areas to be explored. Of the two Rapes of Sussex within the transect study area, Arundel proved to have more oval enclosures than Bramber and differences in distribution were also noted in terms of the Domesday hundreds. Between the North and South Downs most hundreds possessed at least one oval enclosure and of these many appeared to occupy locations on, or close to, Domesday hundred boundaries. One interesting example, Hale/Pephurst Wood, was bisected by the boundary between Bury and Easewrithe Hundreds therefore indicating a possible

FIGURE 6.7: Mapped oval enclosures of the transect study area with a confidence rating of 2–4 in relation to historic roads (drawn by the author)

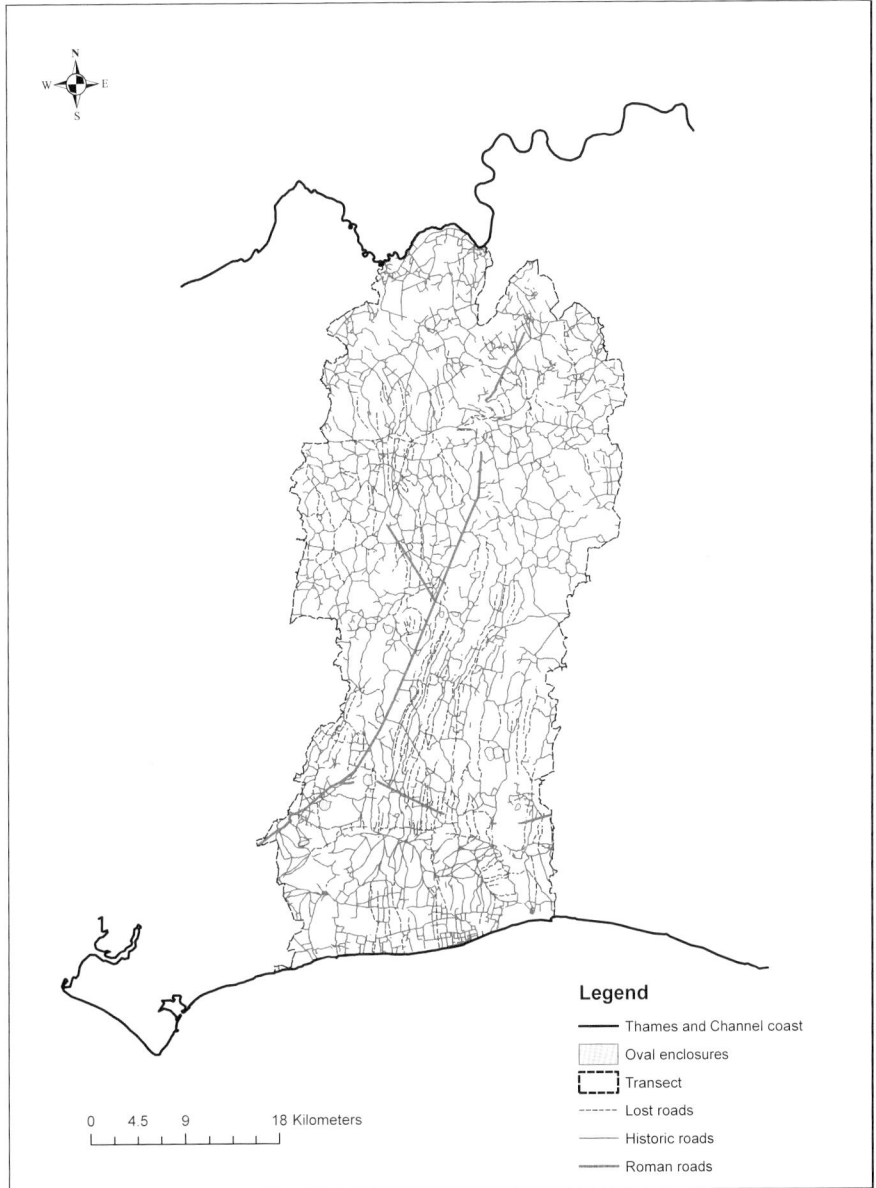

FIGURE 6.7: Mapped oval enclosures of the transect study area with a confidence rating of 2–4 in relation to historic roads (drawn by the author)

pre-10th-century date. It was certainly utilised as a seasonal pasture for both 'beasts' and pigs by the later medieval period, as is demonstrated by the *Custumal of Amberle* (Amberley; *Cust. Chi.* 1925, 54). A similar pattern was discerned for the Watersfield oval that straddles the converging historic parish boundaries of Bury, Coldwaltham, Greatham and Amberley. This may indicate its early origins as part of Greatham Common and the Amberley Wild Brooks. The associated field pattern would suggest that this area at one time comprised

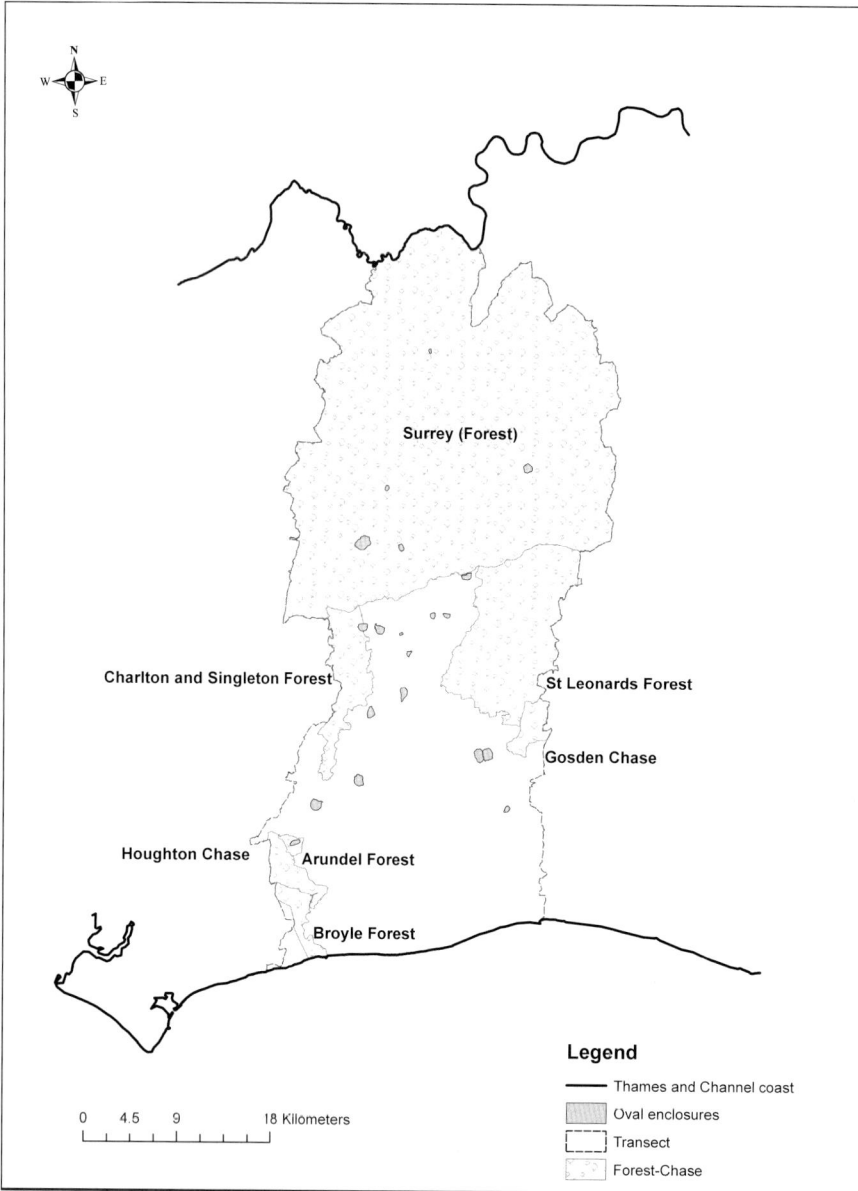

FIGURE 6.8: Mapped oval enclosures of the transect study area with a confidence rating of 2–4 in relation to areas at one time designated as medieval Forest and Chase (drawn by the author after Langton and Jones 2010, fig. 1)

open fields, which would possibly accord well with its *feld* place-name element. The pattern of ovals being close to the boundaries of hundreds was even more pronounced for historic parishes. This indicates that oval enclosures may be a feature of what Everitt termed 'parish edge settlements' (1986, 144–45). These appear to have originated during the early medieval period as early intercommonable pasture or as isolated pasture-farms in an intercommonable countryside (*ibid.*). The fact that watercourses, which have also been shown to have a strong association with oval enclosures, often mark parish boundaries could also explain this apparent correlation.

The relationship between oval enclosures and locations recorded within Chapter 3 as being connected to the medieval cattle economy is marked. This has already been noted in relation to Hale/Pephurst Wood above, which together with Howick (both oval enclosures recorded by Chatwin and Gardiner 2005), lay close to the manorial centre of Drungewick; a location noted for its high number of cows (see section 3.5). Gelling was cited by Chatwin and Gardiner (*ibid.*, 37) as suggesting that Howick would have been named before AD 800, with the '*wic*' name element suggesting some kind of settlement here by this date. The enclosure is bounded on the west and north-west by the River Arun and on the south and east by an arc-shaped boundary. Though it was sometimes described as a manor, it never had any subordinate holdings, nor did it hold manorial courts (*ibid.*).

Also well documented for the keeping of cattle, the riverine meadows and pastures near Amberley on the River Arun were well provisioned with oval enclosures (Plate 6.3), an association that may be mirrored on the banks of the River Adur. The manor of Stretham (alias Henfield) belonged to the bishopric of Selsey at the time of the Conquest but by Domesday had passed to the Bishop of Chichester (Domesday 3,2). Stretham's manorial complex is centred around two moated sites on the banks of the river, one of which was subject to intermittent excavation from the 1950s to 1980s (Funnel 2009). This showed that the site was probably in use from the 13th century to the early/mid-15th century, when it was abandoned possibly as the result of documented flooding (*ibid.*). It was suggested that the moated sites may have been utilised as secure enclosures to protect the large manorial cattle herd from theft (*ibid.*, 92) and a small stratified 13th- to 14th-century bone assemblage was dominated by *Bos* (Bedwin 2009, 92).

The manorial complex is situated close to an oval enclosure in the area of Rye Farm (mentioned from 1560 and containing the place-name element *ēg* 'an island'; *P.N.Sx* 1929, 220; *P.N.E.* 1956a, 147); however, the oval is the least confidently identified example amongst the current dataset. It is clear that the form is partially the result of relief, the enclosure effectively forming a ring around an island in the marsh. The tithe map and apportionment shows a stock funnel leading from this enclosure onto the riverside meadows to the north of the moated sites. Field-names 'Cowfield', 'Herds Brook' and 'The Herds' within and on the edge of this enclosure confirm its historical association with cattle, whilst field-names derived from the element *wic* elsewhere within the parish possibly point to riverside dairying (Figure 6.9). Interestingly, Stretham Manor held land probably originating as outlying pastures in Cowfold parish to the north (Hudson 1987, 141).

The most striking associations between oval enclosures and strands of evidence explored in previous chapters are those associated with place-names. Overlie these two datasets and the association of potential cattle related place-names with oval enclosures is clear (Figure 6.10). The place-names appear to share a broad correspondence with the distribution of mapped oval enclosures, a trend that may not be unsurprising given the vaccary and seasonal pastoral

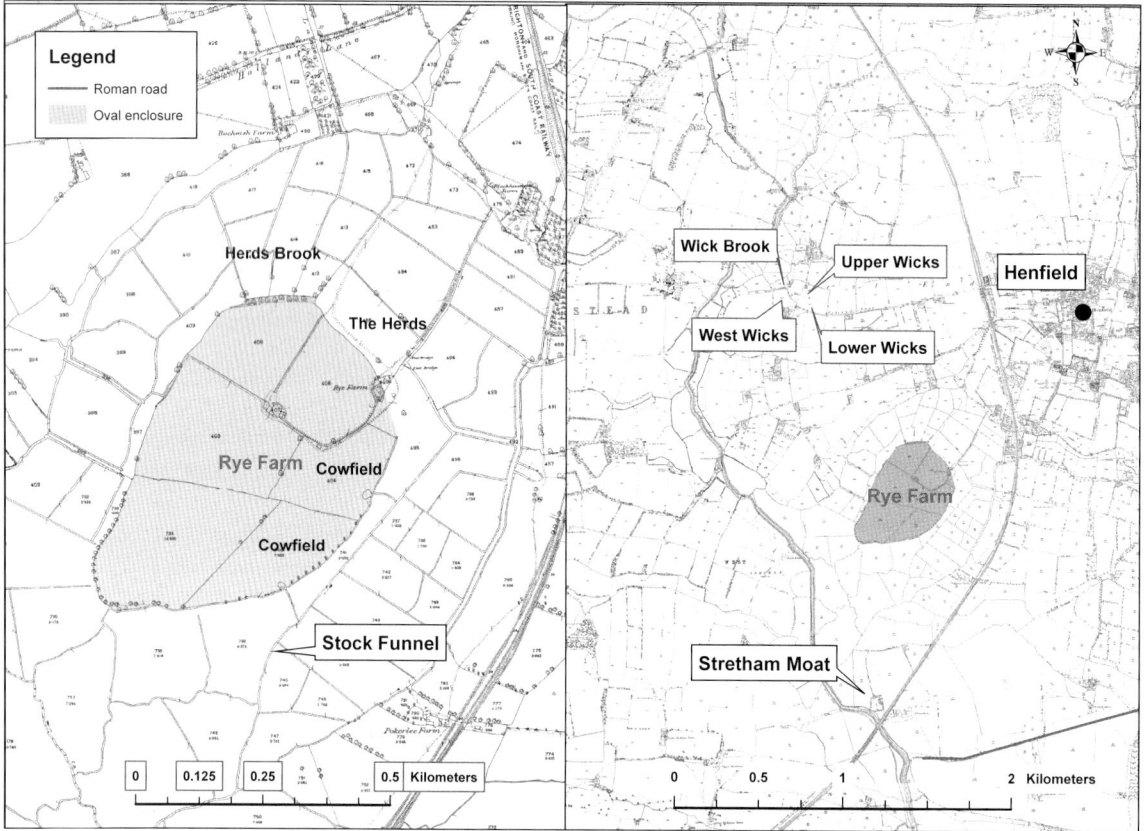

FIGURE 6.9: The Rye Farm Oval overlain on historic mapping (tithe 1844 and the OS 1st Edition 1:2500, 1878). Showing field-names and places mentioned in the text (drawn by the author)

connotations explored above. The so-called heartland (section 4.9) located in the north-western Low Weald is particularly rich in oval landscape elements a phenomenon already noted by Chatwin and Gardiner (2005). Though they associated this area with the 'fold' place-names of the region it is perhaps equally clear that the data presented here suggests an association between oval enclosures and potential toponymic indicators of the cattle economy. The element '*wic*' seems to be particularly relevant in this regard. Indeed, across the transect study area oval enclosures were directly related to place-names that included this element and where conclusive associations between oval enclosures and place-names explored within Chapter 4 occurred, all were related to a '*wic*' name element (Howick, Lydwick and Rutwick; Figure 6.11).

A second dataset was mapped illustrating tentative examples of oval enclosures (those with a rating of one) that had an association with place-names recorded in Chapter 4. These are shown in Figure 6.12 and Table 6.2. They are presented alongside the oval enclosures discussed above in Figure 6.13. These should in no way be considered as a rigorous dataset, although the examples superficially appear to reinforce the correspondence between '*fald/falod*' and '*wic*' place-names with oval enclosures. The dataset also illustrates the possibility that oval enclosures may have once been more extensive within the South-East

FIGURE 6.10: Mapped oval enclosures of the transect study area with a confidence rating of 2–4 in relation to potential cattle-related place-names (Chapter 4) (drawn by the author)

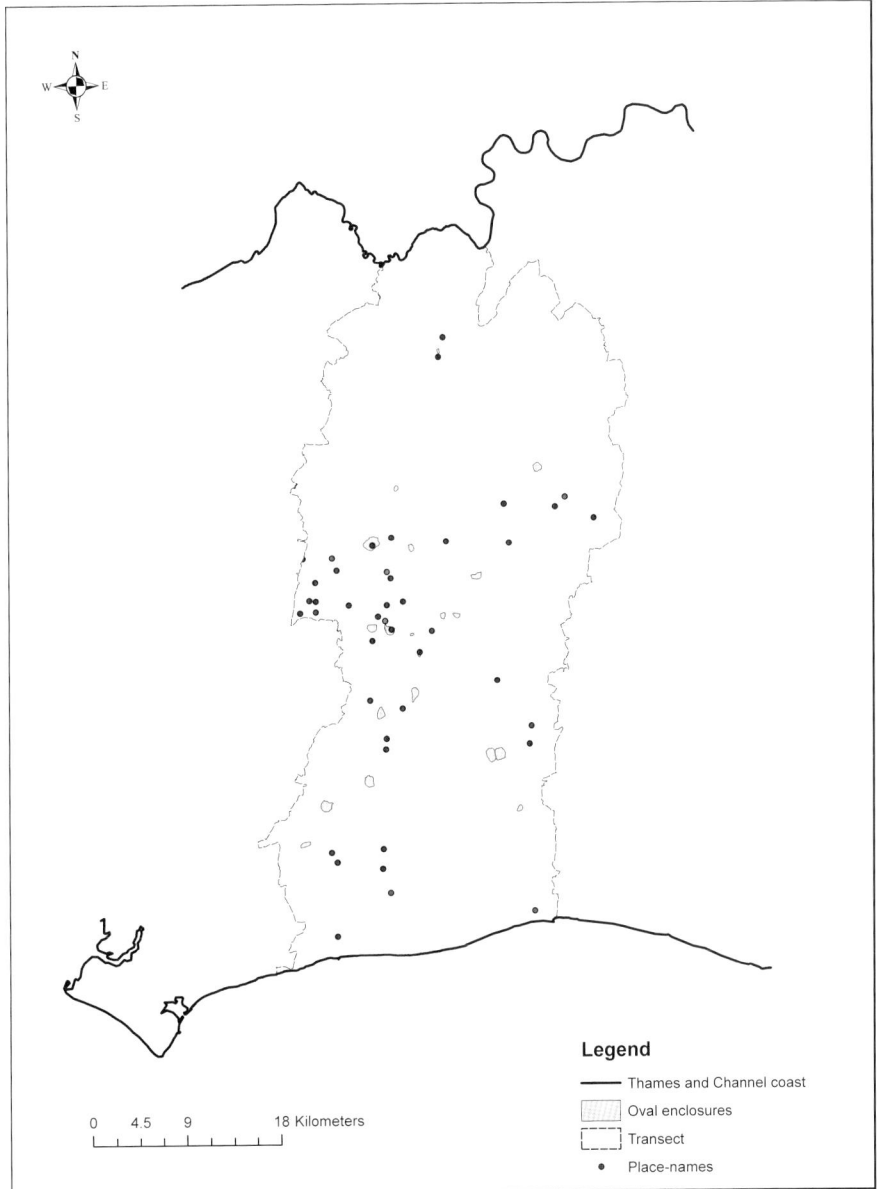

FIGURE 6.10: Mapped oval enclosures of the transect study area with a confidence rating of 2–4 in relation to potential cattle-related place-names (Chapter 4) (drawn by the author)

than analysis of 19th-century cartographic evidence can achieve. It is possible, therefore, that landscapes that no longer appeared to possess oval enclosures by the late post-medieval period could have once been more strongly associated with these features. Prior to modification of land management practice, such as the enclosure movement of the 18th century, the South-East may have been more extensively characterised by oval landscape enclosures. Romney Marsh and the Pevensey Levels, for instance, are particular candidates as post-medieval reclamation effectively swept away earlier field-systems, perhaps removing

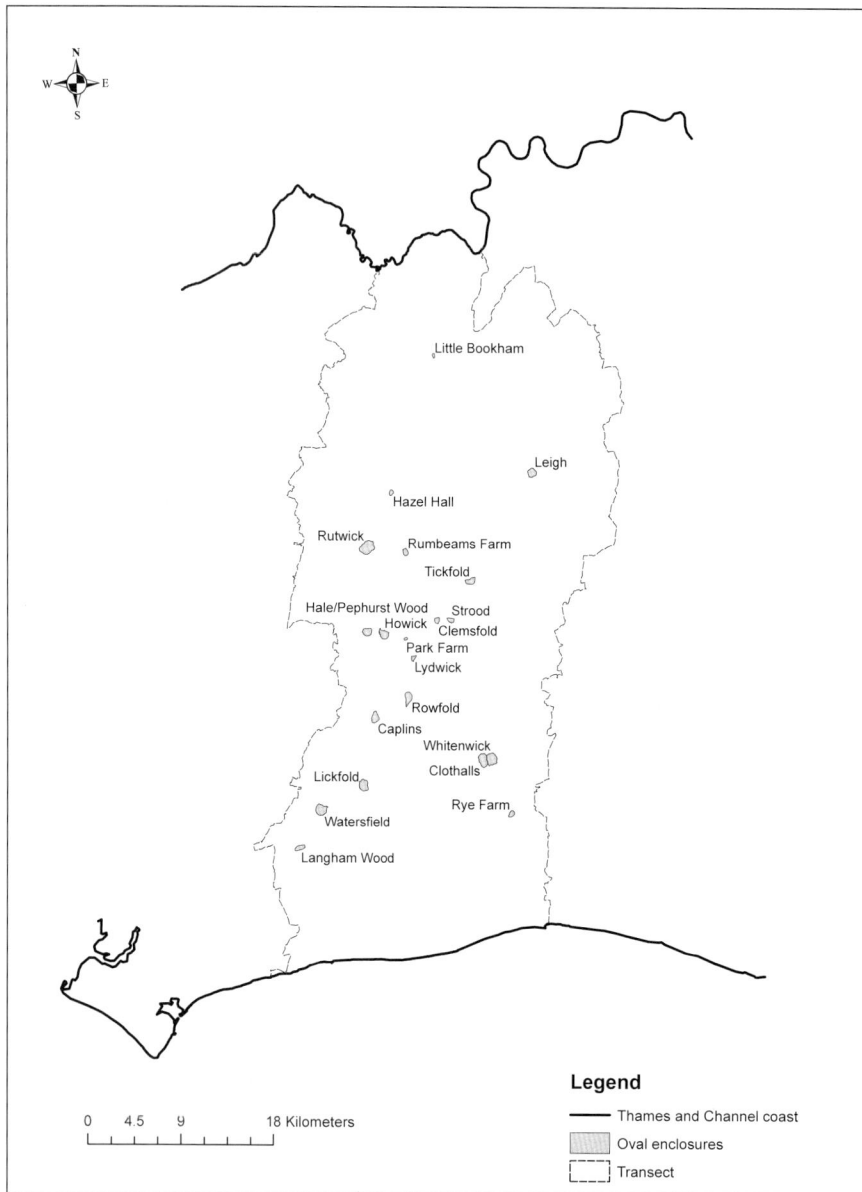

similar enclosures to those found in other historic wetlands (*e.g.* the Somerset Levels: Rippon 2000; 2002).

Parks

Perhaps encouraged by the area's predominantly wooded nature, the enclosure of medieval parks began early in Sussex with five examples recorded in Domesday (Brandon 1974, 104). Parks became established on the poorer soils of the Weald

FIGURE 6.12: Mapped
oval enclosures of the
transect study area with
a confidence rating of 1
(drawn by the author)

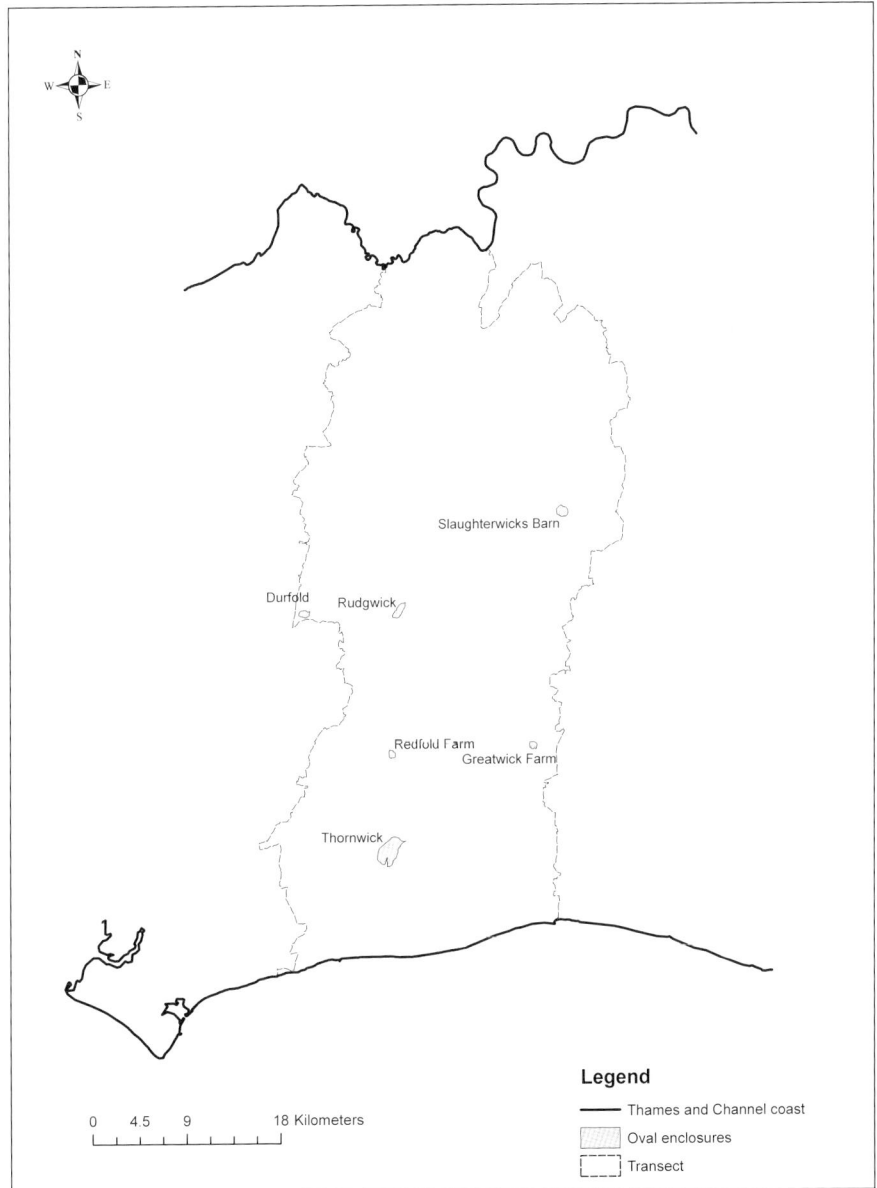

FIGURE 6.12: Mapped oval enclosures of the transect study area with a confidence rating of 1 (drawn by the author)

and the Clay-with-Flints of the South Downs but were noticeably fewer in the richer arable area of the Coastal Plain or the open landscape of the eastern South Downs (Gardiner 1999b, 38). As a mark of status, parks could belong to the greater lordships, such as the Honour of Arundel or the Archbishop of Canterbury, and by 1145 all the lords of the rapes held parks (Brandon 1974, 104). By the 13th century many lesser nobles were also beginning to hold these establishments, often, but not always, having obtained the right to empark by royal writ. The documentary

TABLE 6.2: Tentative examples of possible oval enclosures of the transect study area. Based on a search of place-names recorded in Chapter 4 (Confidence 1)

Name	Name meaning/ elements	Date of first recording	County	Pay	Main geology	Size	Distance from significant watercourse	Influenced by topography	Influenced by hydrology
Thornwick	thorn-tree wick *þorn, wic*	1269	Sussex	South Downs	Chalk	396 ha	730 m	Yes	No
Greatwick Farm	excavation trench, wick *grafet, wic*	1288	Sussex	Low Weald	Weald Clay	43 ha	250 m	No	Yes
Redfold Farm	cleared fold *ridde, falod*	1296	Sussex	Green-sand	Lower Greensand	39 ha	530 m	No	No
Rudgwick	the wick or farm by the ridge *hyrcg, wic*	1210	Sussex	Low Weald	Weald Clay	92 ha	105 m	No	No
Durfold	animal enclosure *deor, fal(o)d*	1295	Surrey	Low Weald	Weald Clay	54 ha	340 m	No	Yes
Slaughterwicks Barn	sloe-tree wick *slāh-trēo, wic*	1332	Surrey	Low Weald	Weald Clay	91 ha	0 m	Yes	No

section has already illustrated that the parks of Sussex could be considered important pastoral reserves, although as indicated above (section 6.2) their significance as livestock establishments as opposed to hunting preserves should not be overplayed. Nevertheless, parks proved beneficial to peasants short of grazing land and lords wishing to gain extra income. Four manors shown through documentary evidence to be strongly associated with the pasturing of cattle also possessed parks listed by Gardiner (1999b) and Cantor (1983). These were the Bishop of Chichester's manors of Cakeham, Aldingbourne, Stretham/Henfield and Selsey.

Cakeham is situated on the sands and clays of the Wittering Formation with superficial deposits of river terrace gravels and raised beach deposits nearby. It is located on the Manhood Peninsula at the western extremity of the Sussex Coastal Plain. This area is more wooded and of poorer agricultural quality than the remainder of the *pay* and was used for hunting by the Bishops of Chichester during the early 13th century (*Cal. Chart. R.* i, 31, 135, 179). The origin of Manhood is probably *mæne-wudu* meaning 'common-wood' (*P.N.Sx* 1929, 79) and the meeting place of the local hundred (which shares the peninsula's name) was at Somerley (named in Domesday and meaning 'clearing used in summer'; *P.N.Sx* 1929, 89). The earliest recording of a park at Cakeham appears to be in 1235 when 100 oaks were granted for its enclosure (*Cal. Close*, 1234–37, 113). It was suggested in Chapter 3 that the high number of oxen associated with Cakeham could have been related to the production of plough teams for the Coastal Plain's extensive arable. The location of the park is difficult to suggest,

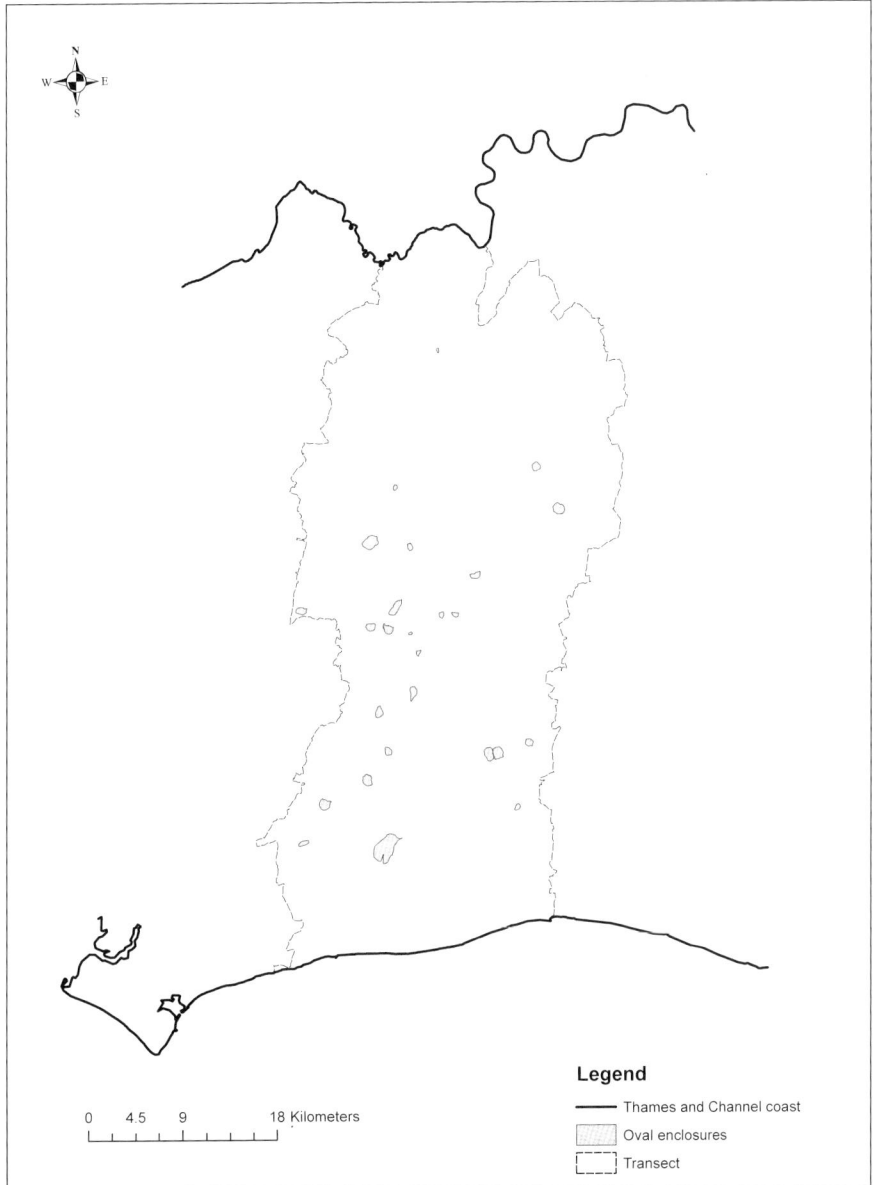

although the name 'Park Field' on the tithe apportionment (1848) indicates it lay to the west of the episcopal manor-house. Fields named 'Great Cow Leases' and 'Little Cow Leases' occupy the intervening space between the land parcel with the park name and the manorial centre. These are likely a corruption of Cow Leaze or Cow Leys, meaning 'land on which cows were kept' (Field 1972, 55).

A little way to the east of Cakeham is the parish of Selsey. Here the park was obviously utilised for the keeping of distrained beasts, as witnessed by the record of the widow Herburga's obligations mentioned above (section 6.2). Documents show the manor was reasonably well endowed with cattle with a minimum of 18 oxen, one bull and 24 cows kept; however, sheep seem to be similarly important (wethers 260, rams 10, ewes 250; *Chi. Chart.* 1942, 223). The park was most likely situated in the north-east of the parish where the names 'Park Barn' and 'Park Coppice' are named on the tithe apportionment (AD 1841). Also within the West Sussex Coastal Plain but beyond the Manhood Peninsula is Aldingbourne. This manor was in the possession of the Bishops of Chichester prior to the Conquest (Domesday 3,3) but the first documented mention of a park was in a letter written *c.* 1225 by the bishop's steward to Bishop Ralph de Nevill, asking him to provide dogs fit to catch foxes in the park of Aldingbourne (Blaauw 1850, 46–47; Salzman 1953, 135). The park was extensive in size and was possibly utilised for the pasturing of cattle. Oxen fattened for the bishop's larder were driven here (*Cust. Chi.* 1925, 114) possibly accounting for the high number of these beasts recorded on the manor in the Chichester Chartulary (36 oxen; *Chi. Chart.* 1942, 223–24).

Stretham Manor was recorded during Chapter 3 as possessing numbers of cows comparable to the vaccaries of the northern uplands (see section 3.10). These animals are more likely to have been linked to dairying on the River Adur, possibly associated with an oval enclosure (see Rye Farm above); however, the episcopal manor and its herds also had access to a park recorded by Gardiner as Stretham (1999b, 39). An alternative name for this manor is Henfield (Hudson 1987, 140) and Henfield Park, which has been noted previously for its record of agistment (Chapter 3), can be equated with that of Stretham. The enclosure lay to the north of the village as witnessed by 'park' field-names bordering the Chess Brook. Streamside pastures in this area were utilised for cattle (as they are today) because the manor of Wantley (the lands of which lay to the south and east of the park), which belonged to the de Braose lords of Bramber Rape, was recorded in the 13th century as providing pasture for the oxen of William son of Adam of Woolfly (*SRS* xl, 70).

In terms of parks listed by Gardiner (1999b, 39) and Cantor (1983) that have place-names containing elements indicative of early seasonal pastures, these appear to be in the minority. Of the 135 parks Gardiner mapped, only four have place-names discussed in Chapter 4. These are Buxted (Boxted 1199, 'place of beech trees'; *P.N.Sx* 1930, 389), Iden (Idene 1086, 'yew-tree swine pasture'; *P.N.Sx* 1930, 530), Ifold (Ifold 1296, fold [on the] 'well-watered land'; *P.N.Sx* 1929, 106) and Sedgewick (*Segwike* 1222, 'farm by the sedge'; *P.N.Sx* 1929, 231–32). Of these, only the latter exists within the transect study area.

Sedgewick

A park at Sedgewick is first recorded in 1248 (*SRS* ii, 121) when it was likely owned by the Sauvage family (Winbolt 1925). Its late medieval bounds can be gauged from a mid-17th-century parliamentary survey (Daniel-Tyssen 1873,

FIGURE 6.14: The possible bounds of Sedgewick Park in the 16th century prior to its disparkment recreated through cartographic analysis and examination of the parliamentary survey. The points represent places mentioned in the text and 'gate' field-names recorded on the Broadwater (1847) and Nuthurst (1845) tithe apportionments (drawn by the author. Contains OS 1st Edition 1:2500, 1875–76)

43–44) that records several farms it was divided into, as well as the lands it abutted upon its disparkment (in the 16th century, before 1573; *Cal. Pat.* 1572–75, 104). Figure 6.14 recreates the maximum possible bounds of the park based on cartographic analysis and the place-names recorded in this survey. If this late medieval extent is correct, it dwarfs the 400-acre park recorded in 1326, of which 300 acres was held of Fécamp Abbey (*Cal. Inq. p. m.* vi, 436). An earlier park can be proposed based on arc-shaped boundaries that occur on historic mapping (Figure 6.15). The earliest map available (and on which these boundaries appear) is Whitpain's map of Sedgewick Park (AD 1701; WSRO Add. MSS 29709; Figure 6.16). This establishment would measure 550 acres in extent, according better with the 14th-century document.

Sedgewick Park occupies high ground on sandstone and Weald Clay geologies. During the 15th century the park formed one of the bailiwicks of St Leonard's Forest (Hudson 1987, 98) and probably originated from 11th- or 12th-century forest hunting grounds of the Sauvages. It is possible that a moated hunting lodge preceded the 13th-century 'fortalice' which possessed concentric moats, a stone

FIGURE 6.15: The possible bounds of the earlier (late medieval) Sedgewick Park recreated through cartographic analysis. The points represent places mentioned in the parliamentary survey and 'gate' field-names recorded on the Broadwater (1847) and Nuthurst (1845) tithe apportionments (drawn by the author. Contains OS 1st Edition 1:2500, 1875–76)

curtain wall, gatehouse, keep and tower(s) (Winbolt 1925). Amongst the finds recovered during excavation were 'bones of oxen, sheep and deer antlers' as well as 28 bone 'draughtsmen … thought to be Saxon' in date (*ibid.*, 109–10). Whether or not the latter truly are of pre-Conquest date, the '*wic*' place-name associated with the site would certainly seem to indicate early medieval occupation, perhaps connected to the large pond in the area hence the '*secg*' element ('farm by the sedge', *P.N.Sx* 1929, 231–32). Sedgewick Castle has already been noted (Chapter 5) for occupying a detached portion of Broadwater parish named 'Little Broadwater' and it is likely that the woodland that yielded 20 swine for Broadwater Manor at Domesday was at Sedgewick (Domesday 13,30; Hudson 1980, 73).

Fécamp Abbey held other lands in the wider parish (Nuthurst) and in 1086 the Hamwood's ownership ('*Hamode*'; Figure 6.17) was disputed with William de Braose (Hudson 1987, 98). Woods at Rickfield lay in Nuthurst and the de Braoses contested the abbey's claim here, also saying that the abbey owned only the enclosure within them called Hamwood, though it could take heybote and housebote (wood allowed to tenants or commoners for repairing fences or houses respectively) in the rest (Hudson 1987, 98). Rickfield lay close to the late medieval extent of Sedgewick Park and can be traced through historic cartography (Figure 6.15). The lands described in the early 13th century

FIGURE 6.16: Whitpains map of Sedgewick Park (WSRO Add. MSS 29709; reproduced by kind permission of West Sussex Record Office)

provided pasture for game and apparently for cattle (Hudson 1987, 98; Figure 6.18). Tenants of Fécamp still practised transhumance to Nuthurst in 1228 when animals could be moved from Steyning to common pastures, '*communa pasture*' in the parish (*Cal. Pat.* 1225–32, 219) and it seems that pannage was still being undertaken in the area in the 15th century (Hudson 1987, 98). Nuthurst parish was reasonably well provisioned with common including Manning's Heath and Monks Common, which lay on the edge of Sedgewick Park (Figure 6.15). Extensive grazings in St Leonard's Forest may have been available where tithes of calves and cheese were recorded in the 13th century (Chapter 3).

6.4 Conclusion

This in-depth exploration of oval enclosures has shown that they are a reasonably widespread component of the historic landscape. On the whole they appear to pre-date the more extensive enclosure of the surrounding countryside and comprise areas distinct from the more characteristic land division (or lack thereof) that had, by the late medieval period, come to typify the areas in which they are found. It is possible therefore that many of the enclosures relate to a stage of colonisation when older intercommonable pastures were being appropriated either by estates or so-called folk groups. Oval enclosures are non-existent in areas that show a non-pastoral tradition of agriculture (*i.e.* the Sussex Coastal Plain); however, medieval parks such as those found at Cakeham and Aldingbourne appear to have provided important pastoral reserves in a *pay* better known for its arable agriculture. In the case of the former park, it is clear that the poorer soils of the Manhood Peninsula were chosen for such activity due to their wooded nature and unsuitability for cereal production. The land was far better utilised for producing venison and beef and the park may have helped yield the plough teams necessary for the Bishop of Chichester's corn land.

In the downland landscapes of Sussex and Surrey, oval enclosures are present but uncommon, and it is possible that this may be a product of survival and preservation rather than a former absence. This said, such enclosures appear

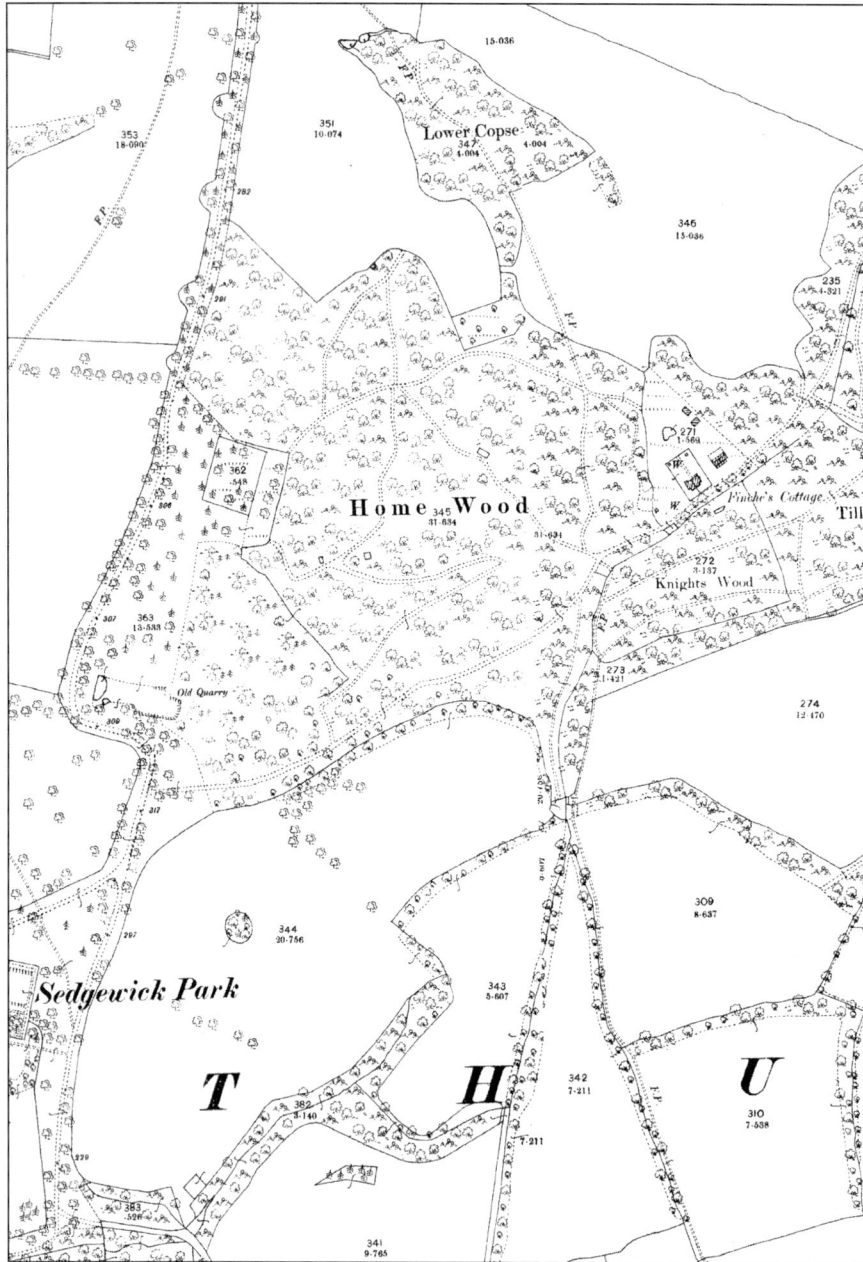

FIGURE 6.17: OS 1st Revision, 1897. Showing Home Wood, probably the 'Hamode' from 1086. The name possibly derived from OE *hamm*, 'enclosure, a meadow, a water-meadow'; P.N.E. 1956a, 229; or OE *hamol/hamel*, used chiefly in hill names, in the sense 'crooked, scarred, mutilated'; P.N.E. 1956a, 231. The linear quarries that exist here would account for the latter, although they do not appear on cartographic evidence until 1911. The straight NE–SW boundary between Home Wood and Knights Wood may be the 11th-century '*hagia*' mentioned in accounts.

moreover to be of a feature of traditionally wooded or heathy environments of areas such as the Weald or western South Downs where tree cover persisted due to geological cappings of Clay-with-Flints. The absence of oval enclosures from the High Weald, however, may be a product of the relatively reduced size of the examined *pay* within the transect study area.

Oval enclosures appear to be intimately tied to waterside locations either beyond or on the edge of tidal reaches, an association that appears to have

FIGURE 6.18: A view
across the Weald from
Sedgewick Park (source:
the author)

influenced both their siting and formation. The choice to be near areas with a ready water supply may account for the generally low-lying nature of many of the sites, although the vast majority occupied the slopes of rising land. Apart from the downland examples, these slopes are often south-facing, possibly a product of land appropriation prior to more widespread colonisation of the surrounding landscape. The areas in which oval enclosures are found are characterised by irregular routeway layouts rather than the regularly spaced roads that exist on these area's fringes. Such a situation may indicate that the ovals were the destination of droveways that characterise the surrounding zones. This would certainly bear out the place-name associations that show a broad correspondence with those elements which have seasonal connotations (*i.e. wic* and *fold/falod*), thus indicating that many of the ovals probably existed during the Old English period and were similar or equivalent to the Kentish *denns*. Indeed, the name Ringden (AD 1271, *hring, denn*: *P.N.Sx* 1930, 453; *hring* meaning 'a ring, a circle', used of something circular'; *P.N.E.* 1956a, 265), highlighted in Chapter 4, effectively suggests an oval form to *denn*-related landscape elements. Those containing the *wic* name element were most probably linked with dairying.

The exploration of parks was significant not in demonstrating an intensive usage of these enclosures for cattle, for those associated with related place-names and documented high numbers of cows were few, but for illustrating examples that could have originated as seasonal pastures. In the history of Sedgewick, we have evidence of a pre-existing seasonal pasture that only after the Conquest was converted into a hunting preserve. Nevertheless, despite the appropriation of the area by those at the elite end of society, the locale showed a marked persistence in transhumance rights for people lower down the social scale (the tenants of Fécamp Abbey). It can be claimed, therefore, that Sedgewick displays a process similar to that experienced by some of the 'dens' of Kent whereby earlier seasonal pastures were later converted into parks. It is tempting to suggest that pre-existing oval enclosures may have helped facilitate this move by providing an already ring-fenced area of land.

CHAPTER 7

Downland enclosures: 'valley entrenchments'

7.1 Introduction

Lhoup after calue cu.
Bulluc stertep, bucke uertep,
Murie sing cuccu!
(Sumer Is Icumen In; Harley MS 978, f. 11v)

During the documentary chapter (Chapter 3) we learnt of the *faldhriera* or *fal'd'reere*, bullocks pastured in enclosures, and their possible distinction from *feldhryer*, cattle grazing open land. Animals pastured within the latter context may have generally been free to roam, their owners taking advantage of common rights or other means of accessing large acreages of grazing land. Such animals may have spent most of their time being able to wander wherever they wished as long as they kept to the 'commons' and did not stray into the enclosed agricultural land beyond. There were, however, times of the year when the owners of cattle and other domesticates pastured in this manner needed to round up their stock. These occasions may have included the end of the summering season, matters of husbandry or the selection of animals for slaughter. Round ups would have required a pinfold or pound, an enclosure to which animals could be driven for collection.

Within the South-East, it is probable that wherever livestock were kept on open land, be it small village greens or great expanses of woodland or heath, pinfolds or pounds existed. Upon the rolling chalk downland of Sussex a form of pinfold occurs as a distinctive class of monument long known as 'valley entrenchments'. These largely undated enclosures have possible associations with the medieval pastoral economy, which makes them worthy of detailed exploration. This is despite their often enigmatic origins, potentially stronger association with sheep and rather patchy survival due to modern ploughing and erosion. As a site type, they represent a disparate group of poorly dated, ill-understood enclosures; however, this chapter will attempt to examine them in relation to the cattle economy.

7.2 A historiography of 'valley entrenchments' and a methodology for their exploration

The now rather antiquated term 'valley entrenchment' was influenced by the work of General Pitt-Rivers (1887) and was first coined in Sussex by Toms

(1907; 1912; 1913; 1924; 1926) working in the early years of the 20th century. He ascertained that features similar to those explored by Pitt-Rivers in Dorset and Wiltshire existed on the South Downs and occupied positions within the heads, sides and bottoms of valleys (Toms 1912, 42). The features comprise square or rectangular embanked enclosures, often with external ditches, and were once postulated to be the product of prehistoric settlement (Toms 1907; Allen 2005). Though few have been excavated, they are now thought to be related to medieval and later livestock husbandry (Bedwin 1983, 201; Barber, Gardiner and Rudling 2002, 135; Gardiner 2012b, 107).

The Bible is just one of these enclosures and in an earlier chapter (Chapter 4) has been reinterpreted as the *Oxseten* known from toponymy and cartography. The name of this example suggests that some of these features may be associated with medieval pasturing of cattle, an interpretation that is sometimes applied to this feature type during designation by Historic England. They may not, therefore, be solely concerned with late medieval and post-medieval sheep husbandry and it is likely that no single explanation of use can exist for this type of site (Barber, Gardiner and Rudling 2002, 140; Gardiner 2012b, 107). The potential of some of these features to be associated with the downland pasturing of cattle and the relation of examples such as Eastwick Barn and those near Thornwick Barn with the *wic* place-name element (Barber, Gardiner and Rudling 2002, 136; see also Curwen and Curwen 1923, 19) makes exploration of these enigmatic features prudent.

Known valley entrenchments of the South Downs were included via a search of the West and East Sussex HERs, the Archaeology Data Service (ADS) website and with reference to works on valley entrenchments in the area of Brighton by Toms (1912; 1913; 1924; 1926). Most examples are known from the open downland of East Sussex, although the author suspected that further examples exist within West Sussex that remain un-surveyed as they have been historically obscured by woodland. A thorough search of high-resolution LiDAR data made available to the author by the *Secrets of the High Woods* project (Carpenter *et al.* 2016; Manley 2016) was undertaken in order to plot any as yet unrecognised examples. Landscape analysis of valley entrenchments was then undertaken for each individual site and conclusions as to their role and function within the cattle economy of the South-East (if any) was given.

7.3 Results

The plotting of known valley entrenchments produced 22 results (there were two adjoining entrenchments at Chantry Bottom). Most were located in East Sussex and were previously recognised by Toms (1912; 1913; 1924; 1926). The West Sussex 'valley bottom' entrenchment of Bramshott Bottom was recognised by Bedwin (1983), having been previously excavated by Keef (*ibid.*). The Scheduled Monument on Saxon Down was brought to the attention of the author by Greg

Chuter (formerly ESCC) whose help is gratefully acknowledged. Two further possible valley entrenchments were plotted via analysis of the high-resolution LiDAR data made available to the author by the *Secrets of the High Woods* project (Carpenter *et al.* 2016; Manley 2016). The results are shown in Table 7.1 and Figure 7.1. Individual analyses of examples with the best evidence follow, although it must be reiterated that the group presents a rather poor dataset. The analyses are undertaken in alphabetical order.

2. Belle Tout (larger)

The larger of the two entrenchments at Belle Tout was described by Toms (1912, 44) as being similar to that at Oxteddle Bottom (5) in that it was designed not only to enclose the valley floor but parts of each side of the valley as well. It had an entrance on the east side (in line with the centre of the valley), but this was slightly disputed by Bradley (1970, 320) who found a break in the bank but not the internal ditch. Much of the enclosure has since been lost to cliff erosion, but excavation during 2016 managed to obtain OSL dates from this enclosure bank/ditch. The results, which range from the late medieval to earlier post-medieval period, are shown in Table 7.2.

3. Belle Tout (smaller)

Both this and the larger valley entrenchment discussed above (2) were built within a more extensive enclosure thought by Bradley (1971) to be an Iron Age promontory fort associated with cattle ranching (Figure 7.2). Cliff erosion has removed much of the purported Iron Age enclosure and destroyed the smaller valley entrenchment. Before its destruction it was recorded by Toms (1912) as a valley-side entrenchment with the lowest side adjoining the base of the Belle Tout dry valley. Both Toms (1912, 54) and Bradley (1970, 314) ascertained that the smaller entrenchment was earlier than its larger counterpart (2). The enclosure probably originated as a square earthwork with an external ditch. Both Bradley and Toms interpreted the Belle Tout valley entrenchments as stock enclosures and, whilst Toms ventured no specific date for the enclosures, Bradley (1970, 369) phased them to the Beaker period. This was largely on the basis that they bounded Early Bronze Age remains (including possible structures), although little contemporary material was retrieved from the entrenchments themselves. The large outer enclosure is now thought to be early medieval in origin rather than an Iron Age promontory fort as it was previously interpreted. Recent archaeological trenching has produced medieval OSL dates from the bank associated with the enclosure (Greg Chuter and Chris Greatorex, pers. comm.). The results of the OSL dating is provided in Table 7.3. Sample X7177 (AD 1296±70) was derived from a secondary ditch fill that also produced late Anglo-Saxon pottery, whereas sample X7178 (AD 526±110) was retrieved from the bank make-up, providing a very secure date for the construction of the monument.

TABLE 7.1: South Downs valley entrenchments

No.	Name	County	Dating evidence	Shape in plan
1	Ashcombe Bottom	East Sussex	Roman pottery	Sub-rectangular
2	Belle Tout (larger)	East Sussex	Later medieval to early post-medieval (OSL)	Sub-rectangular
3	Belle Tout (smaller)	East Sussex	Stratigraphy (later medieval or earlier)	Sub-rectangular
4	Bepton	West Sussex	None	Sub-square
5	The Bible/Oxteddle	East Sussex	Medieval place-name	Rectangular
6	Bramble Bottom	East Sussex	Stratigraphy (later medieval or earlier)	Square
7	Bramshott Bottom	West Sussex	Roman (excavated)	Square
8	Chantry Bottom Entrenchment	West Sussex	Roman and medieval pottery	Sub-square
9	The Denture	West Sussex	None	Sub-square
10	Eastwick Barn	East Sussex	Roman and medieval pottery	Sub-rectangular
11	Ewe Bottom	East Sussex	Stratigraphy (late prehistoric or later)	Rectangular
12	Falmer Hill	East Sussex	None	Linear
13	Faulkner's Bottom	East Sussex	None	Rectangular
14	Giant's Grave/Devil's Dyke	East Sussex	?Residual prehistoric flints	Rectangular
15	Home and Dencher Bottoms	East Sussex	None	Square
16	Home Bottom Spur	East Sussex	Stratigraphy (late prehistoric or later)	Rectangular
17	Houndean/Cuckoo Bottom	East Sussex	Prehistoric, Roman and medieval pottery	Sub-rectangular
18	Leap Bottom Entrenchment	West Sussex	Roman and medieval pottery	Sub-square
19	Newmarket Plantation	East Sussex	None	Sub-oval
20	Piddingworth	East Sussex	Early medieval place-name	Rectangular
21	Saxon Down	East Sussex	Medieval finds	Sub-rectangular
22	Swanborough Coombe	East Sussex	None	Square
23	Well Bottom	East Sussex	None	L-shaped

TABLE 7.1: (*Continued*)

Size	Distance from water	Nearby trackway?	Indications of cattle	Reference
300 m × 200 m	200 m	Yes	None	Toms 1926, 51–53
140 × 44 m +	1 km	Yes	None	Toms 1912
64 m × 36 m +	1 km	Yes	None	Toms 1912
175 m × 170 m	690 m	Yes	None	Carpenter *et al.* 2016
98 m × 62 m	155 m	Yes	Place-name	Toms 1924, 72
75 m × 65 m	270 m	Yes	Bone	Toms 1913
40 m × 40 m	380 m	Yes	Large numbers of cattle teeth	Bedwin 1983, 201
70 m × 55 m and 55 m × 35 m	1.30 km	Yes	None	Curwen and Curwen 1922; 1923
170 m × 140 m	1.20 km	Yes	None	Carpenter *et al.* 2016
125 m × 125 m	350 m	Yes	None	Toms 1924, 63–65; Barber, Gardiner and Rudling 2002
100 m × 100 m	270 m	Yes	None	Toms 1924, 67–68
850 m	100 m	Yes	None	Toms 1907
160 m × 110 m	1.20 km	Yes	None	Toms 1926, 46–51
44 m × 18 m	435 m	Yes	None	Toms 1924, 69–72
21 m × 21 m	420 m	Yes	None	Toms 1924, 63
60 m × 35 m	170 m	Yes	None	Toms 1924, 59
150 m × 150 m	390 m	Yes	None	Toms 1926, 55–57; Allen 2005
105 m × 65 m	1.40 km	Yes	None	Curwen and Curwen 1922; 1923
145 m × 105 m	20 m	Yes	None	Toms 1907; 1926, 60–61
110 m × 45 m	150 m	Yes	None	Toms 1926, 45
110 m × 90 m	0 m	Yes	None	NHLE: 1005568
145 m × 130 m	0 m	Yes	Used for cattle at time of recording	Toms 1926, 57–60
183 m × 107 m	0 m	Yes	None	Toms 1924, 68–69

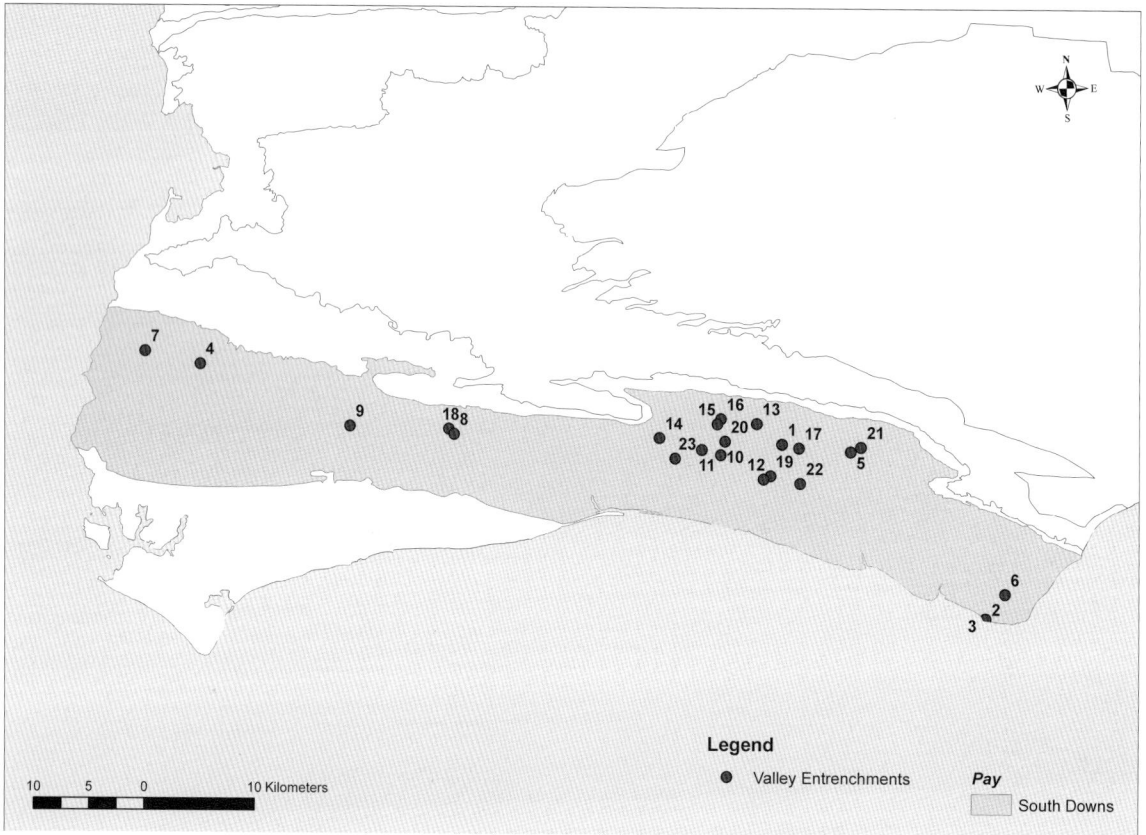

FIGURE 7.1: The distribution of South Downs valley entrenchments (drawn by the author)

Field code	Lab. code	Burial depth (cm)	Measured water content (%)	Palaeodose (Gy)	Dose rate (Gy/ka)	OSL age estimate (years before 2016)
BLG16-03	X7179	47	7.1	21.55±1.59	2.47±0.17	810±80
BLG16-04	X7180	32	7.9	8.56±0.75	2.68±0.14	370±30
BLG16-05	X7181	40	10	48.04±2.18	2.60±0.14	480±40

TABLE 7.2: Luminescence dating (valley entrenchment), Belle Tout, Birling Gap, East Sussex (courtesy of Greg Chuter and Chris Greatorex ESCC)

North-west of the site, two routeways, the modern Birling Gap Road previously named 'The Wish' (originally from Old English *wisc* meaning 'marshy meadow'; *P.N.Sx* 1930, 418; *P.N.E.* 1956b, 270) and an old holloway that led across the downs to the village of East Dean, exist. The nearest sources of fresh water are dew-ponds *c.* 1 km away at Hod Combe to the east and Cornish Farm to the north-east. Close to the site are Bulling Dean and Bullock Down named on the OS 1st Edition (Figures 7.3–7.4).

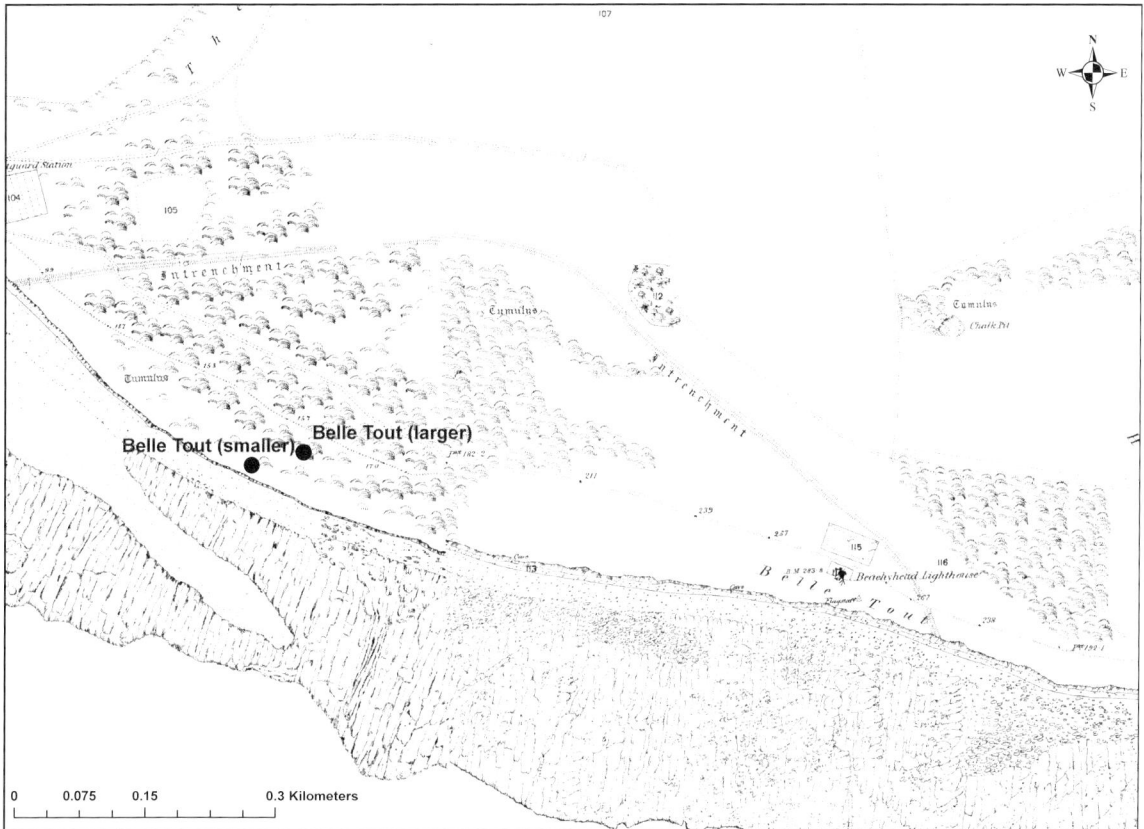

FIGURE 7.2: The Belle Tout entrenchments as shown on the OS 1st Edition 1:2500, 1875 (with labelling by the author)

TABLE 7.3: Luminescence dating (outer enclosure), Belle Tout, Birling Gap, East Sussex (courtesy of Greg Chuter and Chris Greatorex ESCC)

Field code	Lab. code	Burial depth (cm)	Measured water content (%)	Palaeodose (Gy)	Dose rate (Gy/ka)	OSL age estimate (years before 2016)
BLG16-01	X7177	56	13.7	48.18±2.23	1.08±0.06	720±70
BLG16-02	X7178	47	12.6	41.71±1.90	2.32±0.12	1490±110

5. *The Bible/Oxteddle*

The enclosure in Bible Bottom has been briefly introduced in a previous chapter (Chapter 4) where it was suggested that the rectangular earthwork known as 'The Bible' is in fact the medieval *Oxenesetene*. It was also suggested that an association with the place-name element *seota* may indicate a seasonal function to the enclosure. The Oxteddle was only briefly noted by Toms (1924, 72), who claimed that the 'Ox-Stall' was similar to the enclosure at Devil's Dyke (**14** below). He claimed that 'such three-sided structures were formally in use locally for the stalling of working oxen and for the winter housing

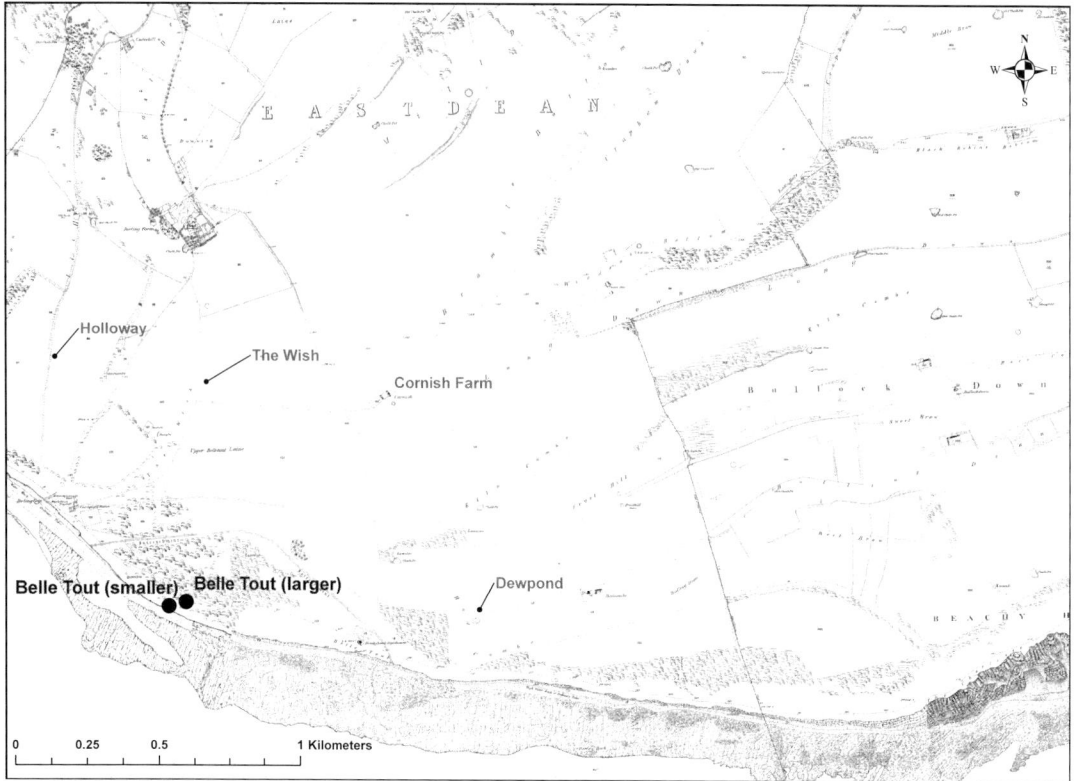

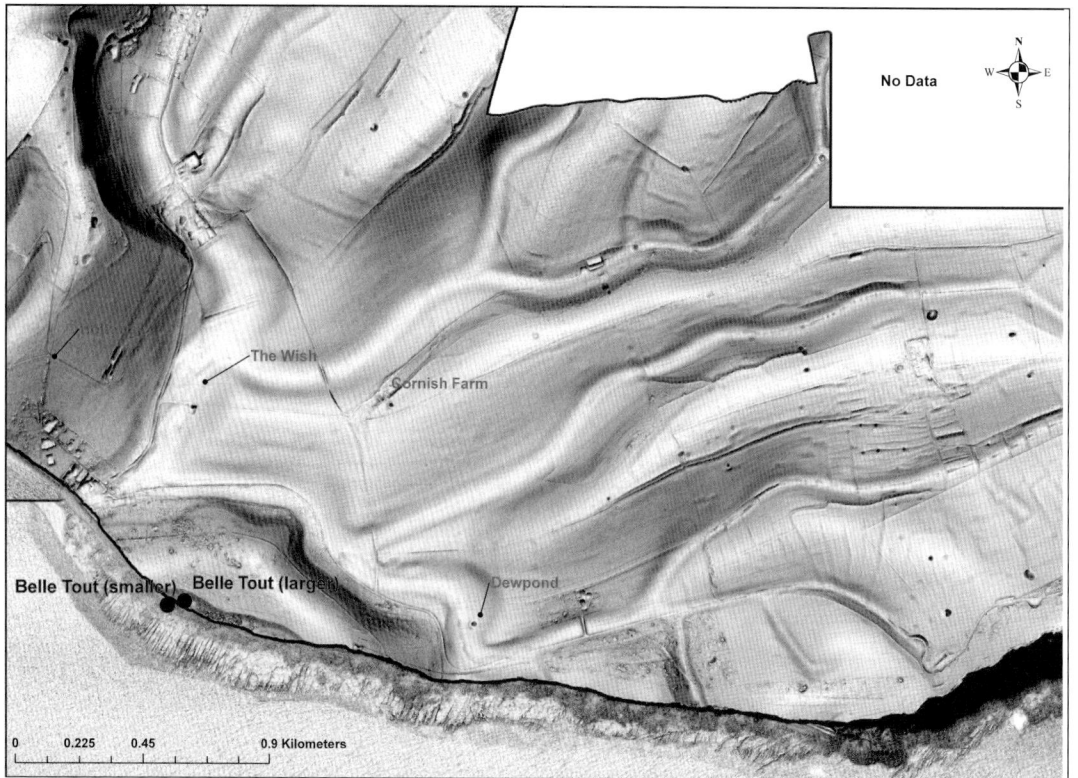

FIGURE 7.3 *(opposite above)*: The historic landscape in the vicinity of Belle Tout as shown on the OS 1st Edition 1:25000, 1875 (with labelling by the author)

FIGURE 7.4 *(opposite below)*: LiDAR Model: Sky-View Factor (SVF-A_R10_D16_A315) (drawn by the author. Contains public sector information licensed under the Open Government Licence v3.0)

of those which were being fattened for the market' (*ibid.*). The Historic England list entry for the monument records it as a medieval stock enclosure (NHLE: 1002285). It is orientated north-east to south-west and measures approximately 98 m by 62 m (Figure 4.6). The enclosure has traces of exterior ditches and internal banks that are broken centrally by a trackway or division aligned on the centre of the dry-valley. The coombe (a side valley of the Ouse Valley) forms a natural driveway for the corralling of stock into the enclosure. The nearest source of water is a dew-pond situated in a spur of the same valley some 155 m to the south (Figures 4.6 and 7.5). The enclosure is directly associated with a cattle-related place-name.

6. Bramble Bottom

The valley-side entrenchment in Bramble Bottom measures 75 m × 65 m. It was first surveyed by Toms (1913), who showed it to comprise a square enclosure surrounded by a low bank with an external ditch. Subsequent excavations in the south-western corner of the enclosure encountered a 13th-century flint-built building aligned with, but stratigraphically later than, the monument's bank (Musson 1955). The excavations produced a small but mixed assemblage of animal bone and marine shell that included fragments of ox, pig, sheep and domestic fowl (Jackson 1955, 169–70). The entrenchment is well placed to receive animals driven up the coombe from Bramble Bottom (Figure 7.6), the name of which was in existence by AD 1224, but may be much earlier as it contains a possible *ing*-derivative (*P.N.Sx* 1930, 418). The enclosure had an internal mound similar to those noted in the Ewe Bottom and Houndean entrenchments (Toms 1924, 68; Figure 7.7). The enclosure lies close to a borstal and track leading between Eastbourne and East Dean. The nearest source of water is a pond at Crapham Barn; however, a depression close to the south-west corner of the enclosure may relate to a former waterhole (Figure 7.7). Three '*wic*' place-names exist in the wider vicinity, Upwick and Northwick (Chapter 4; *c.* 2.50 km and 3 km away respectively) near Eastbourne, and Dunwick (*c.* 1.50 km away) near East Dean. A 'Summerdown' probably

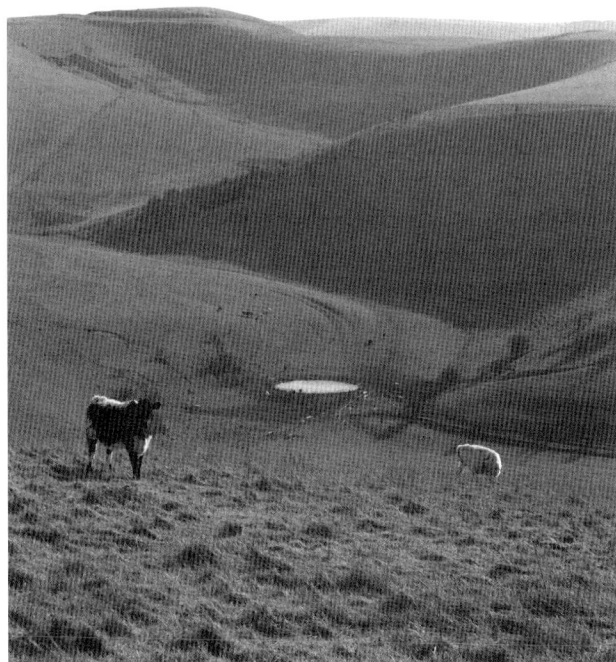

FIGURE 7.5: A winter's view across Oxteddle Bottom. The dew-pond can be seen as well as the Iron Age hillfort of Mount Caburn (back left; source: the author)

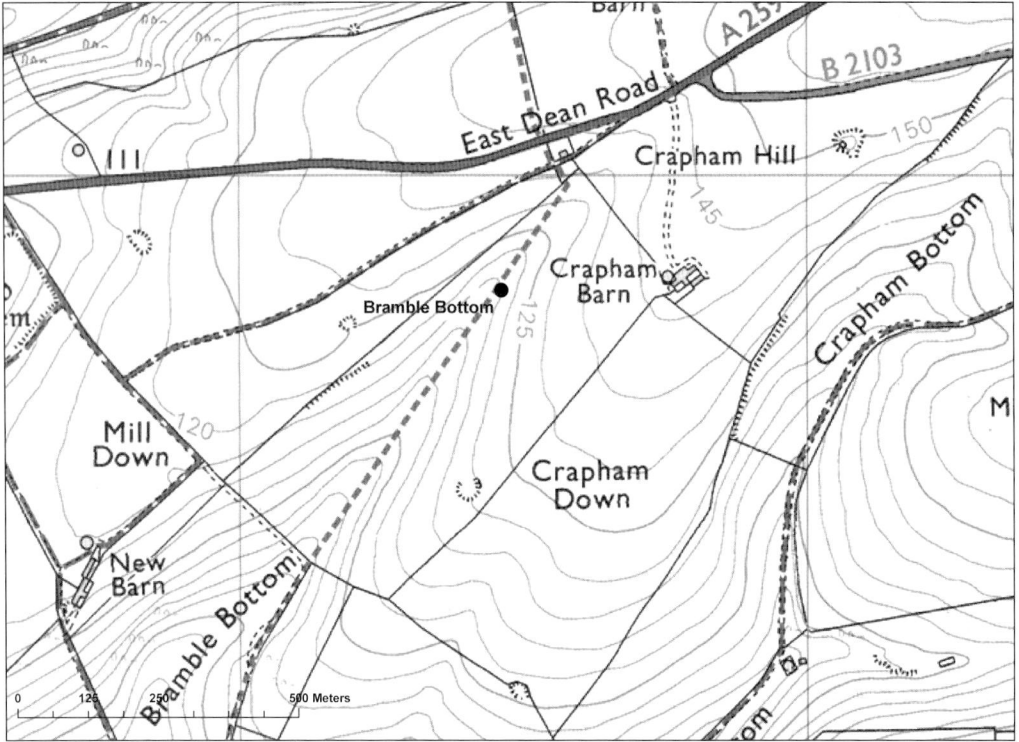

originated as a seasonal pasture 1.20 km to the north-west (first recorded in the 14th century; *P.N.Sx* 1930, 419).

7. Chantry Bottom entrenchments

These two adjoining valley entrenchments are situated close to the head of the valley and are roughly rectangular in shape with external ditches (Figure 7.8). The larger north-eastern enclosure measures *c.* 55 m in width by *c.* 70 m in length. The southern enclosure is the same width but just over half the length (Figure 7.9). The entrenchments were constructed in an area of earlier lynchets. Entrances to the enclosures exist on the northern, uphill side and in the south-eastern corners. The lynchets may have aided the herding of any animals up the dry-valley and into this southerly entrance. Though the Curwens (1923, 13) found a few sherds of Romano-British pottery in the enclosures, a larger group of late medieval sherds were retrieved from an area of hollows (quarrying?) to the west (Figure 7.9). Like the entrenchments in neighbouring Leap Bottom (18), the nearest source of water is at Lee Farm. The enclosures are close to Thornwick within the tentatively identified oval (see section 6.3). To the north, the South Downs escarpment is deeply incised by borstals turning into droveways as they head into the Weald to the north.

Chantry Bottom

Quarrying?

0   0.0475   0.095   0.19 Kilometers

8. *The Denture*

This rectilinear earthwork enclosure measures *c.* 170 m by *c.* 140 m. It is situated on a spur of land above the head of a dry valley known as 'the Denture' (from 'denshiring' or burn-beating, a method of improvement utilised in the breaking up of 'maiden down'; Brandon 1998, 99). The enclosure which was recorded as being of medieval or post-medieval origin by the Secrets of the Highwoods project (Carpenter *et al.* 2017) can be seen on LiDAR visualisations to adjoin a larger enclosure which in turn is attached to the oval enclosure of Langham Wood (see section 6.3). It appears to overlie field-systems of probable late prehistoric date (Figure 7.10). Though the enclosure is skirted by a holloway/trackway that follows the Denture, a north-westerly aligned routeway following valley bottoms appears to be more directly related to the enclosure itself (as well as the Langham Wood oval and its 'wapelgate'; for the meaning of this term, see section 5.3; Figure 7.10). The nearest source of water is a possible silted dew-pond in the north-west corner of the Langham Wood oval (Figure 7.10). The two enclosures that adjoin this 'valley head entrenchment' can be said to form the double oval pattern discussed elsewhere, although their contemporaneity cannot be proven (Chapters 2 and 9). The Denture enclosure is associated with

FIGURE 7.9: Chantry Bottom LiDAR Model: Sky-View Factor (SVF-A_R10_D16_A315) (drawn by the author using public sector information licensed under the Open Government Licence v3.0)

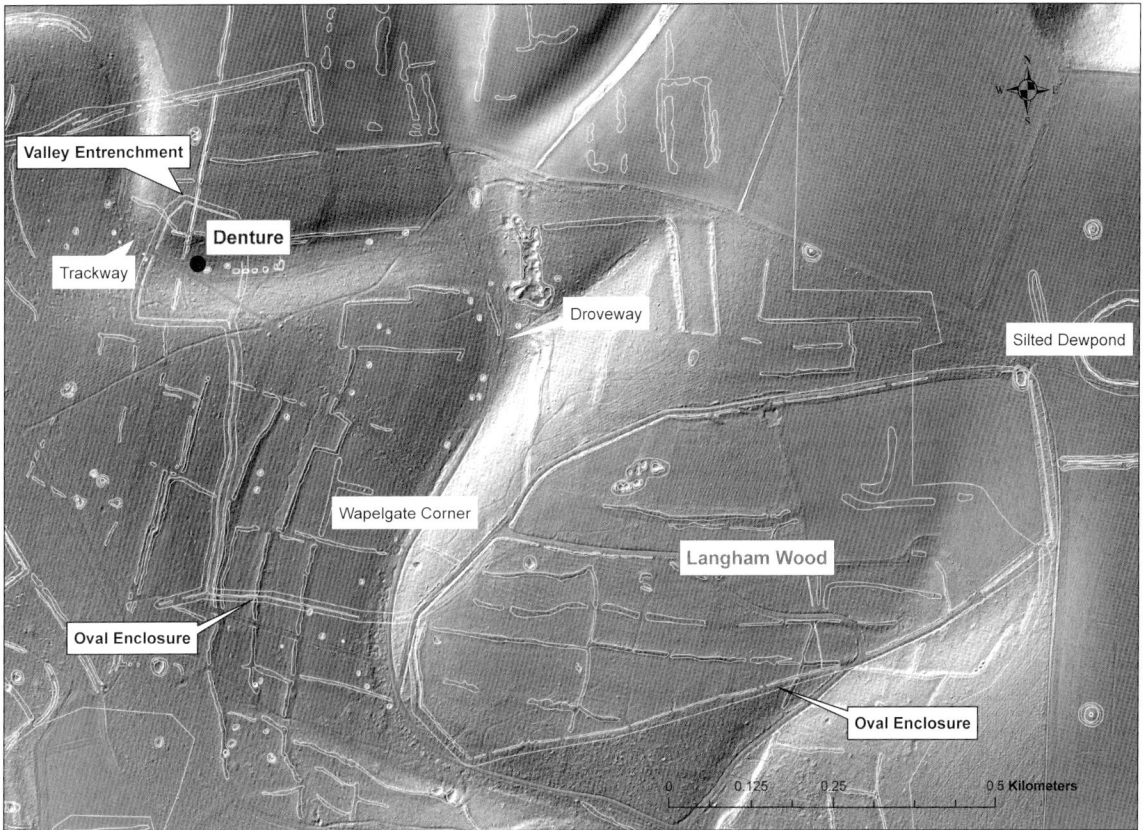

FIGURE 7.10: The Denture LiDAR Model: Hillshade overlain with the results of a National Mapping Programme associated with the Secrets of the High Woods project (Carpenter *et al.* 2016) (drawn by the author. Mapped features represented in the figure are © Historic England)

a droveway that heads towards the Wealden interior (particularly the area known as 'the Mens'). An early medieval date for this set of interrelated enclosures can be tentatively suggested. This is due to Langham Wood's association with Old English place-name elements (*lang* and *ham(m)* 'long enclosure'). Langham Wood's status as a detached portion of Bury parish may indicate that the set of enclosures were associated with seasonal pasturing on the downland.

9. Eastwick Barn

This enclosure is rectilinear in shape with a slight bank and external ditch (Toms 1924, 63). It is situated so as to straddle the valley and has been subject to excavation (Barber, Gardiner and Rudling 2002). The entrance is in the centre of the valley on the south-west side and is wide enough (3.8 m) for the driving of animals (*ibid.*, 139). This entrance is associated with a trackway between two lynchets. These are part of a wider field-system of late prehistoric–Roman origin that pre-dates the enclosure. Evidence of nearby (probably 13th-/14th-century) ridge-and-furrow is thought to post-date the enclosure (*ibid.*, 140). Only a single medieval sherd was recovered amongst an assemblage dominated by (?residual) Romano-British material. Though dating evidence was insubstantial,

Gardiner favoured a medieval origin for the enclosure on the basis of landscape stratigraphy and its comparison to similar enclosures (*ibid.*, 139–40). It was probably used for cattle and sheep and the association with the place-name element '*wic*' may have been significant (*ibid.*, 136). Prior to the 1930s the nearest source of water would have been the now destroyed pond east of Eastwick Barn (*c.* 350 m south-west of the enclosure). As well as Eastwick Barn (probably the home of Walter de *Estwyke* in the 13th century; *P.N.Sx* 1930, 294) the enclosure is close to Tegdown Hill, the name of which clearly relates to sheep. These lands formed part of the demesne of the manor of Patcham Court (Barber, Gardiner and Rudling 2002, 135).

12. *Falmer Hill*

This linear 'valley head entrenchment' is comprised of a bank up to 1 m high and external ditch up to 1.5 m deep and 2.7 m wide. It is situated at the head of Loose Bottom on the side of Falmer Hill. The enclosure has a break on the lower side, which Toms interpreted for the ingress and egress of people and cattle (Toms 1907, 19–20). Though it was undated, he felt the enclosure to be very similar to Bronze Age examples investigated by himself and Pitt-Rivers in

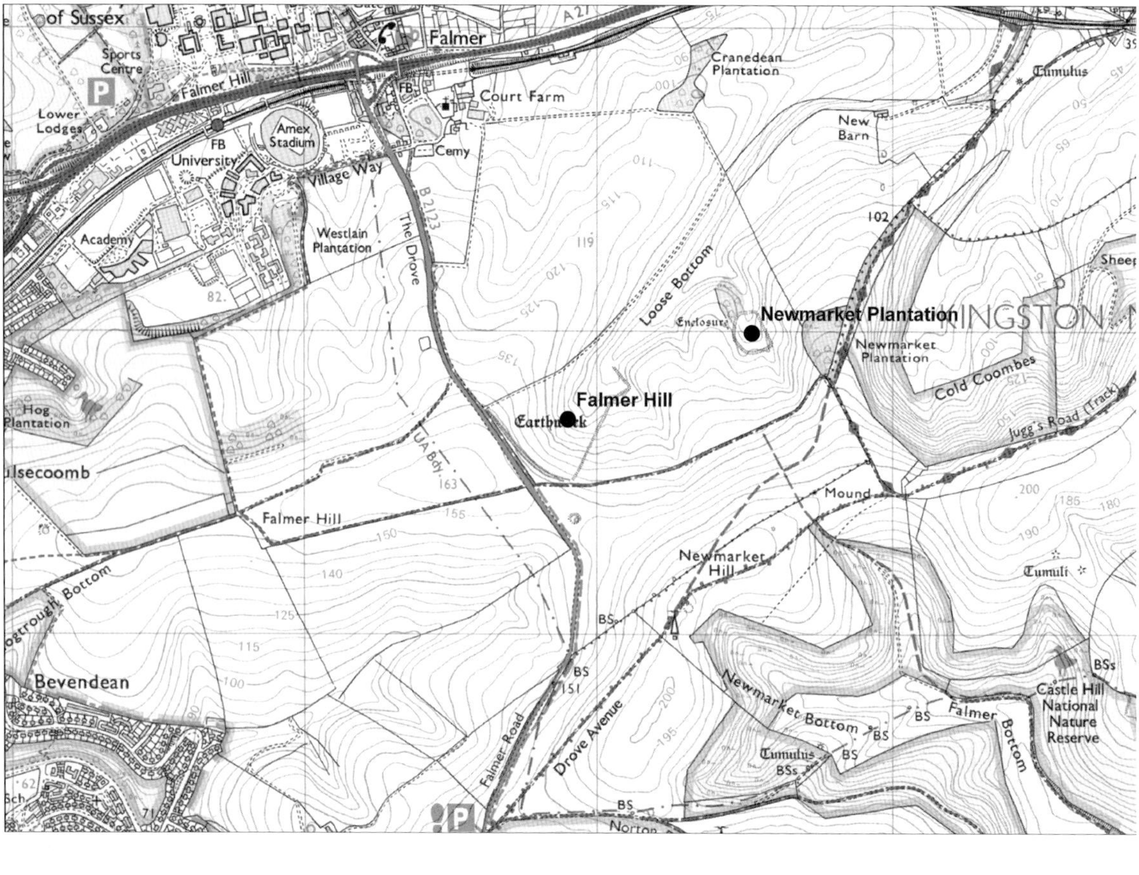

FIGURE 7.11: The location of the Falmer Hill and Newmarket Plantation entrenchments (Ordnance Survey mapping data 1:25000 © Crown copyright and database right 2007 with labelling by the author)

Wiltshire (*ibid.*). The Historic England list entry mentions that the monument has been documented as medieval in origin, probably used for corralling stock and associated with a nearby building (NHLE: 1002262). The source of this information is not given and remains unknown. The earthwork is close to the north–south route known as 'The Drove' (now the modern B2123; Figure 7.11). The nearest sources of water are dew-ponds on Falmer Hill (*c.* 100 m) or in Loose Bottom (*c.* 480 m north-east). There is also Falmer Pond to the north, probably the original 'dark mere' of the Old English place-name (*P.N.Sx* 1930, 308; for the significance of *mere* names to the cattle economy see 20 Piddingworth below). Another place-name of interest in the vicinity is Bullock Hill, around 1 km to the south-east.

13. Faulkner's Bottom

This rectangular valley-head entrenchment is reasonably well preserved lying under scrub. The enclosure is formed by a bank (3 m wide and 0.4 m high) and external ditch. It measures *c.* 160 m long by 110 m wide. When Toms recorded it in 1912 he noted lengths of surviving internal ditches on the northern, eastern and southern sides (Toms 1926, 49). Within the enclosure, which he interpreted

FIGURE 7.12: The location of the Faulkner's Bottom entrenchment (Ordnance Survey mapping data 1:25000 © Crown copyright and database right 2007 with labelling by the author)

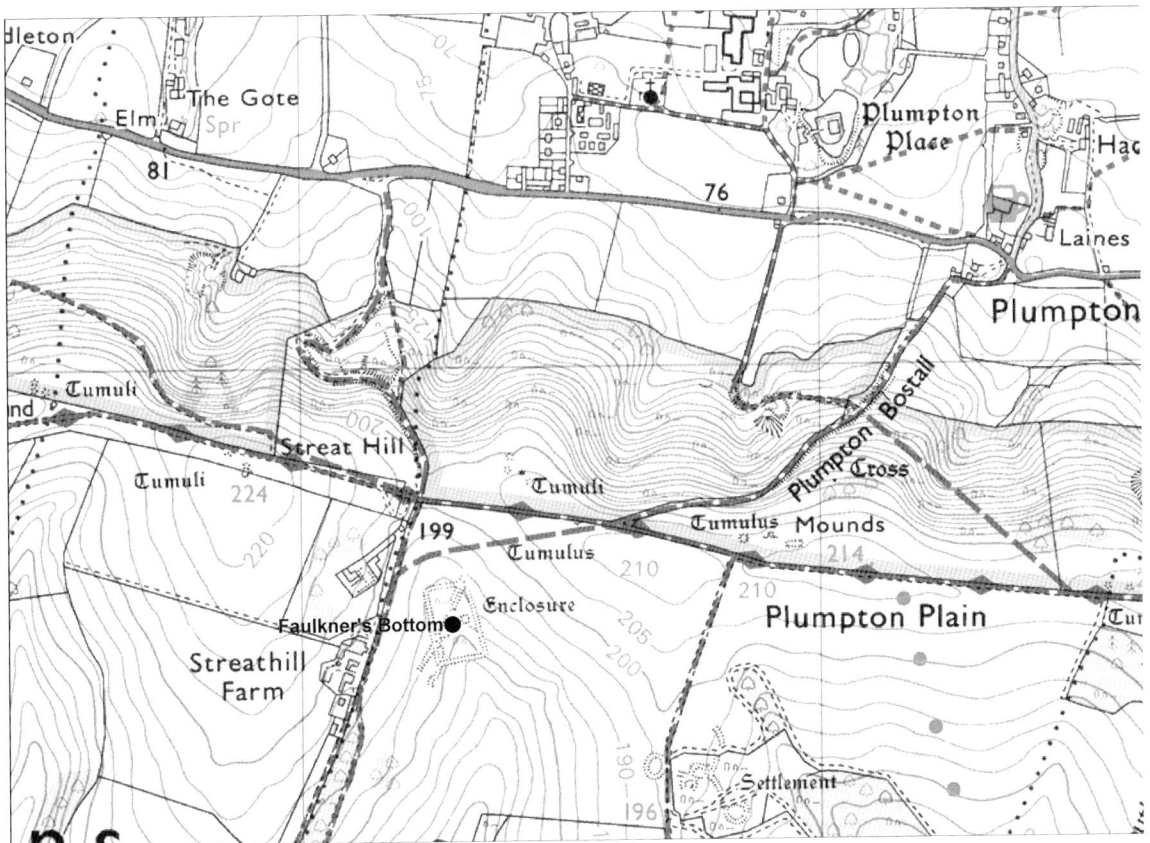

as a cattle-fold, were two square ditched features thought to be fodder ricks (*ibid.*, 47). The original entrance was on the southern side in line with the centre of the valley. The entrenchment overlies an earlier track and is close to 'Streat Bostall', a droveway heading into the Weald (Figure 7.12). The nearest sources of water are springs at the foot of the scarp or a dew-pond over 1.20 km to the south-west. This Scheduled Monument (NHLE: 1002312) is recorded in the Historic England list as a medieval or later livestock enclosure similar to the one in Bible Bottom near Lewes (see The Bible/Oxteddle 5 above). It is interesting to note that there is a Faulkner's Farm at Hartfield in the Weald. It is first named in 1199 and means '*Folcwine*'s wood' (*P.N.Sx* 1930, 367). There is a partially excavated deserted medieval settlement here that showed signs of operating a part dairy economy (Tebbutt 1981). Whether there is an ancient connection between the two places is unknown. Faulkner's Bottom is not recorded in the *Place-Names of Sussex* (*P.N.Sx* 1929; 1930).

14. Giant's Grave/Devil's Dyke

'The Giant's Grave' or 'The Grave of the Devil and his Wife' is a three-sided earthwork comprising banks with external ditches at the two ends. It is located near to a large Iron Age hillfort in the deepest, longest and widest dry chalk

FIGURE 7.13: Devil's Dyke looking south-west up the coombe. The entrenchment is in the centre foreground (source: the author)

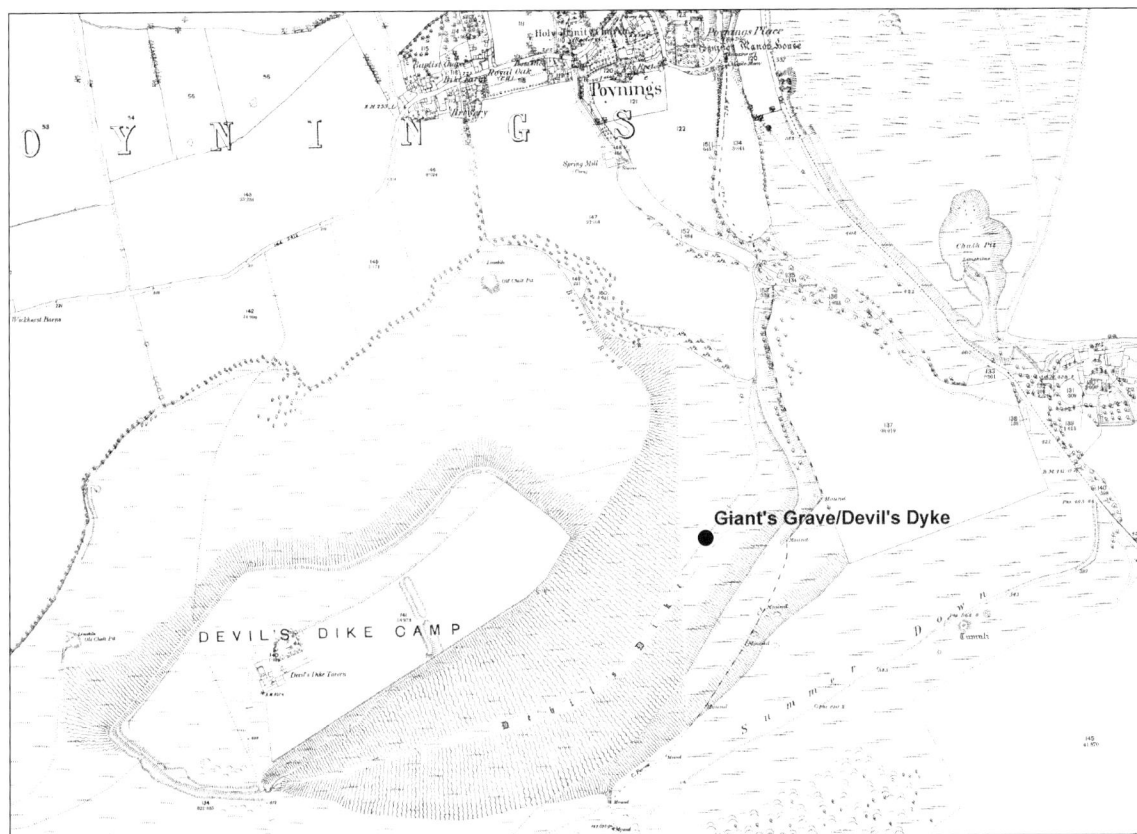

FIGURE 7.14: Devil's Dyke shown on the OS 1st Edition 1:2500, 1873 and 1874 (with labelling by the author)

coombe in Britain (Figure 7.13). It is likely that a ditch once existed on the long side but it has probably been masked by colluvium (Toms 1924, 69). The enclosure measures *c.* 44 m in length by *c.* 18 m in width. Excavation of the earthwork encountered prehistoric finds that Toms considered residual. The shallow depth, morphology and taphonomy of the earthwork led Toms to interpret it as a cattle enclosure similar to the 'Ox-stall' in Oxteddle Bottom near Lewes (Toms 1924, 71–72). The Historic England list entry for the monument describes it as a stock enclosure of a type used in the medieval and post-medieval periods for winter shelter and corralling of beasts ranging over open pasture (NHLE: 1014954). It is described as post-medieval in date but the reasons for classing it as such are not clear. The topographic situation of the enclosure, within the deep, steep-sided coombe, would make it ideally situated for driving animals down the valley into this corral. It would also be well placed for stock arriving at the South Downs scarp along a nearby droveway from the Weald. The name of the earthwork is clearly related to local folklore. The nearest sources of water are a spring fed millpond *c.* 435 m to the north or a dew-pond close to the head of the coombe (*c.* 610 m to the south-west). Place-names related to seasonal grazing of livestock include 'Summer Down' recorded on the OS 1st Edition (1873 and 1874; Figure 7.14 and Plate 7.1) and Wickhurst Barns

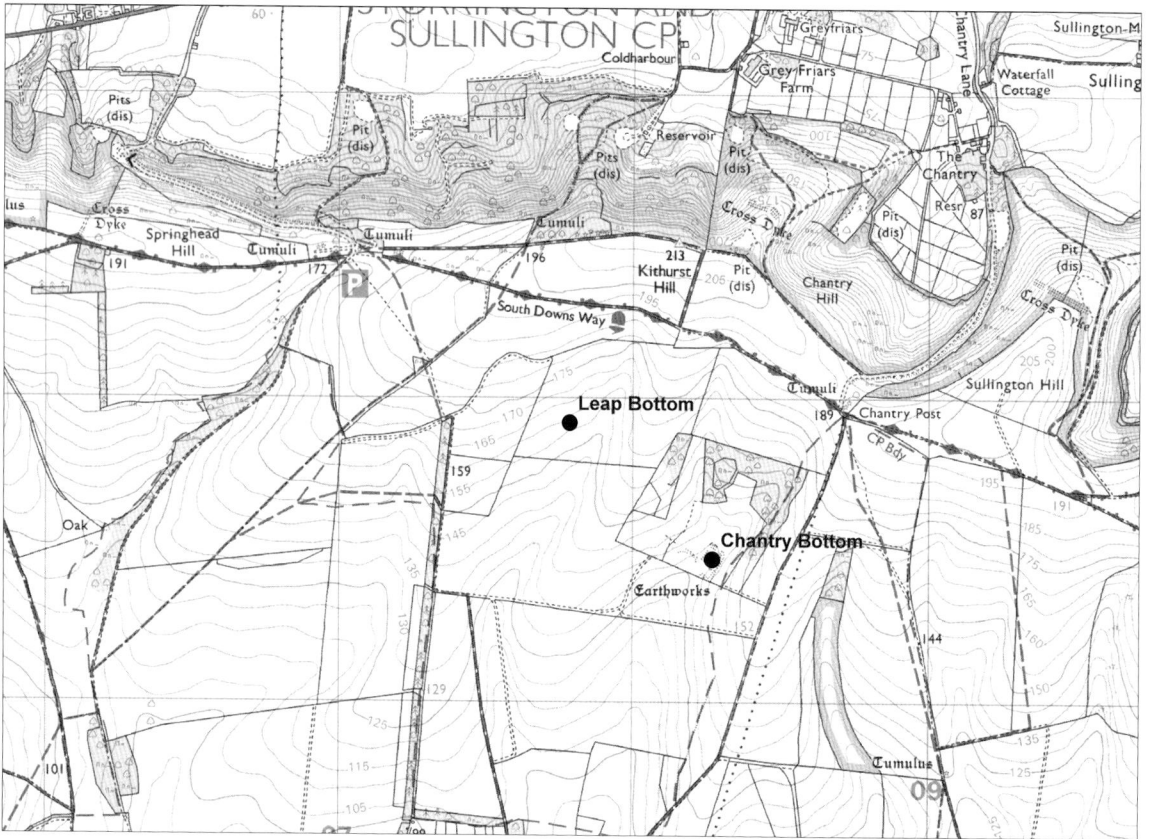

and associated fields recorded on the Poynings tithe map (1843). Wickhurst Barns was probably associated with local resident Bartholomew *Wyker* in the 13th century (*P.N.Sx* 1930, 287).

18. Leap Bottom entrenchments

These two valley entrenchments situated close to the head of Leap or Lepe Bottom are no longer visible due to ploughing (Figures 7.15). The southerly example is only just discernible with the benefit of LiDAR. The Curwen's (1923) recorded the upper, north-eastern enclosure as sub-oval in shape with an exterior ditch and no visible entrance. The lower, south-eastern entrenchment was rectangular with entrances in the northern and western corners. It made use of a massive lynchet as part of its western boundary (Curwen and Curwen 1923) and it is possible that the lynchets were also used as convenient barriers in the driving of animals up the dry-valley and into the enclosures. The nearest sources of water are an old farm pond at Lee Farm some 1.4 km to the south. The Curwen's recovered both Romano-British and medieval pottery from the enclosures (*ibid.*, 15).

FIGURE 7.15: The location of the Leap Bottom and Chantry Bottom entrenchments (Ordnance Survey mapping data 1:25000 © Crown copyright and database right 2007 with labelling by the author)

The entrenchments are to the west of those found in Chantry Bottom (7) and are *c.* 1.18 km from the location of the place-name Thornwick (see Chapter 4) within the bounds of the tentatively identified oval enclosure (see section 6.3). The name Leap Bottom is not recorded in the *Place-Names of Sussex* (*P.N.Sx* 1929; 1930), however, it possibly comes from the Old English *hlēp* meaning 'a leap, a jump, a leaping place', especially in names of 'a place than can be crossed by leaping' such as 'a chasm, a narrow defile, that part of a fence which some animals can leap over but which restrains others' (*P.N.E.* 1956a, 251). This suggestion awaits confirmation by a place-name scholar, but the connections may relate to the narrowness of the valley and the restraining of animals. It is important to note the custom of '*lep*' recorded near Eastbourne in Chapter 3. This was documented in a medieval custumal and was connected to the commoning of cattle and specifically their herding into a pinfold (Wilson 1961, 30–31). An alternative meaning for 'Lepe' in Sussex is 'half-a-bushel' of grain (*P.N.Sx* 1930, 441).

20. Piddingworth

The valley-side entrenchment at Piddingworth is situated in Stanmer Park close to the Ditchling Road. The interior of the enclosure is relatively flat, with some artificial levelling apparent in the south-west corner (Toms 1926, 45). The northern part is overlain by the remains of houses and farm buildings destroyed by Canadian artillery practice in WWII. The earthworks are reasonably pronounced. The nearest source of water is the dew-pond 150 m to the west. Piddingworth is first mentioned in the year 1200 (*Pidelingeworth*) but is of earlier origin as it means the 'enclosure of *Pydel*' or 'of *Pydel*'s people' (Pydel being a derivative of the Old English personal name *Puda*; *P.N.Sx* 1930, 302). Piddingworth's proximity to Stanmer is also of interest. Stanmer means 'stony pool' (*stan*, *mere*; *P.N.Sx* 1930, 302) and '*mere*' names on the North Downs have been seen by Everitt as bearing the same significance as those in '*sole*'. That is, they originated as stock-ponds and in many cases indicate early vaccaries associated with dairying (Everitt 1986, 169). Downland names in 'pool' and '*wæl*' may have similar connotations (*ibid.*). The entrenchment is recorded as medieval in origin on the HER, which also notes a probable medieval field-system to the west (HER: MES1278).

21. Swanborough Coombe

Clearly once a four-sided square enclosure measuring *c.* 130 m by *c.* 145 m, this valley-head entrenchment is situated on a deep holloway or borstal known as Breach Road (Figure 7.16). At the time it was recorded by Toms (1926, 59) it may have only recently been used as a cattle pound. It has banks with an external ditch and was equipped with a small pond close to the borstal and the probable original entrance. The associated holloway leads from the medieval Swanborough Manor in the Ouse Valley (Figure 7.16) which was the meeting place of the hundred that bears the same name (*P.N.Sx* 1930, 317).

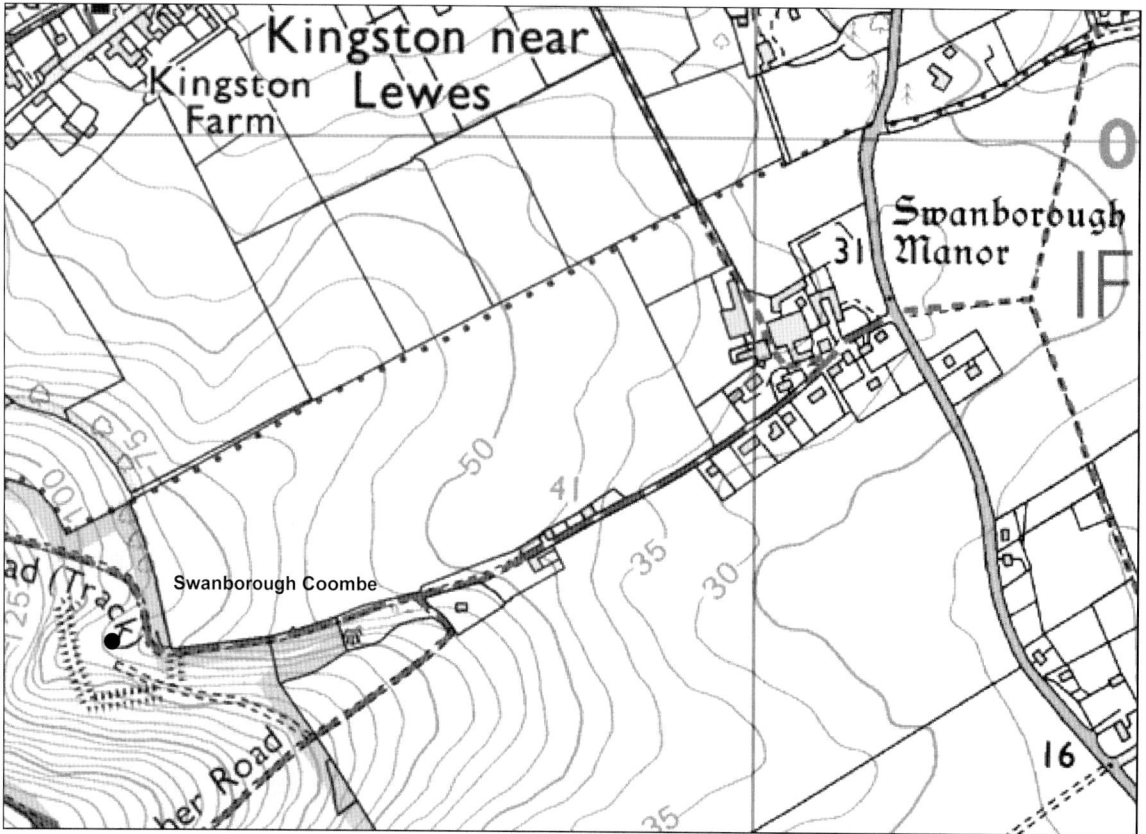

7.4 Discussion and conclusions

This chapter has shown that a distinctive class of rectilinear ditched and banked enclosure occupies valley locations within the South Downs. A glance at the distribution map (Figure 7.17) shows they often occupy positions close to the scarp slope facing the Weald, areas on the high downland or, more importantly, side valleys with access to floodplains (particularly that of the River Ouse near Lewes). A clear bias can be discerned between the number of valley entrenchments in the wooded landscapes of the western downs and the open landscape of the east. This is moreover the case when example 7 (Bramshott Bottom) is dismissed due to its interpretation as a Romano-British farmstead rather than a medieval pastoral enclosure. Upon initial examination this distribution would appear to reflect the relative density of later medieval wool production with its characteristic landscape of close-cropped sheep-walk and method of sheep-corn husbandry so beneficial to the downland farmer (see Brandon 1998, 64–70). Indeed, the enclosures, which may have acted as folds, areas of winter housing or even lambing sheds, could certainly have aided sheep husbandry in this iconic chalk landscape. Upon further examination, however, this revelation may not be so clear-cut. Of those downland parishes known

FIGURE 7.16: The location of the Swanborough Coombe entrenchment (Ordnance Survey mapping data 1:25000 © Crown copyright and database right 2007 with labelling by the author)

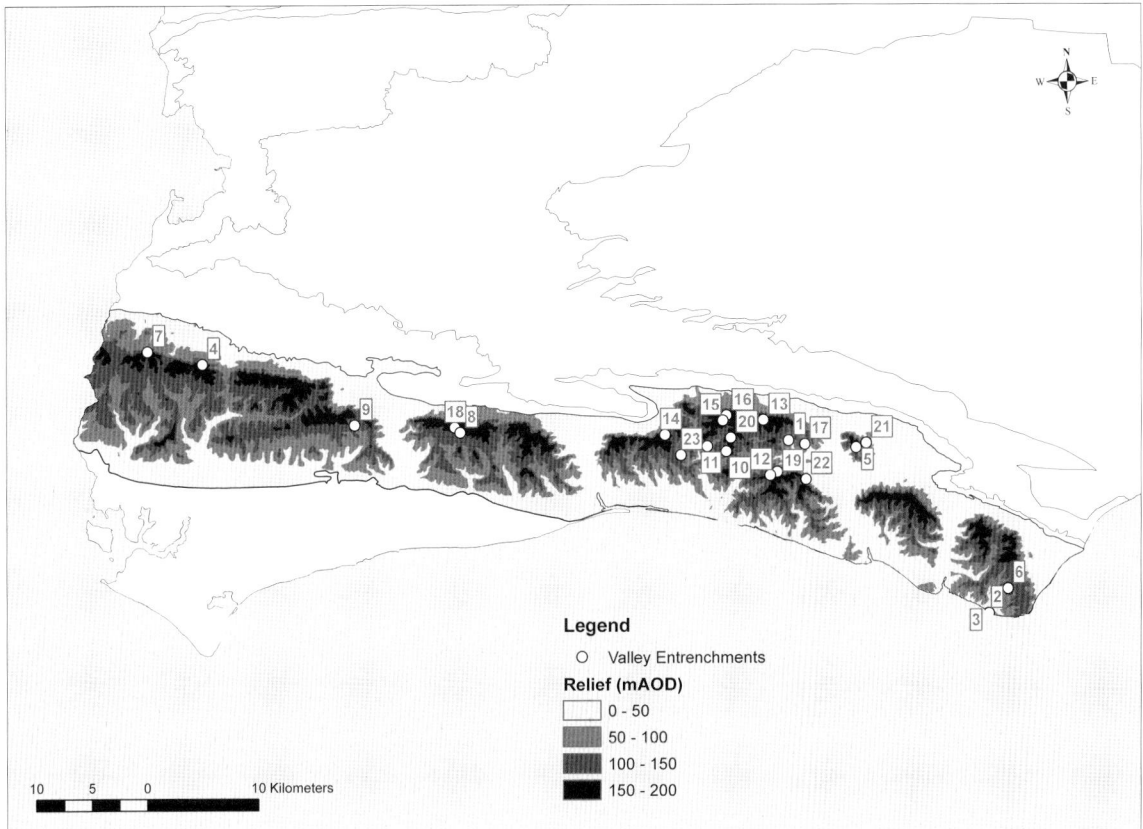

FIGURE 7.17: Distribution of South Downs valley entrenchments in relation to topography (drawn by the author)

for the largest later medieval sheep flocks, such as Findon, Pyecombe, Falmer, Piddinghoe, Alciston and Eastbourne (all of which possessed 2,000 or more adult sheep in 1340; Brandon 1998, fig. 46; see also Pelham 1934), only Falmer contained recognisable valley entrenchments (**12** and **19**). The suggestion that valley entrenchments may have been solely concerned with later medieval sheep pasturing may also be called into question when we consider the possible dates of the enclosures themselves.

It is true to say that this class of monument still requires a dedicated programme of excavation but, where evidence has been forthcoming, valley entrenchments appear to have been utilised during the medieval period with a certain number showing probable 7th- to 12th-century origins based on place-names, dating evidence and landscape stratigraphy. They have potential to date to the Romano-British period; however, survey of many has demonstrated that they overlie the lyncheted fields of late prehistoric and/or Romano-British date that occupy much of the downland. It is possible that the Roman pottery encountered at six of the 23 examples was derived residually from these earlier fields. This said, 1st-century occupation of the downland is also characterised by similarly sized square enclosures (*e.g.* Rewell Hill South-Western Site and Goblestubbs East Enclosure: Curwen and Curwen 1920; 1928) and at least one valley entrenchment, Bramshott Bottom (**7**), was of proven Roman date.

At Belle Tout the larger entrenchment has been reliably dated to the beginning of the 13th century ±80 years, although it should be noted that it post-dated the earlier, smaller entrenchment that surely belongs to the 12th century or earlier (**3**). At the nearby enclosure of Bramble Bottom (**6**) excavations have shown that the valley entrenchment was older than a 13th-century flint building (Musson 1955) and a similar situation is evident at Eastwick Barn (**10**). Here the enclosure probably dates to the 12th century or pre-Conquest period as it post-dated Roman features but pre-dated nearby ridge-and-furrow probably belonging to a later medieval phase of population expansion (Barber, Gardiner and Rudling 2002, 139–40). Three or four further enclosures indicate early medieval origins based upon Old English place-name evidence. The entrenchment at Piddingworth (**20**) surely relates to the enclosure of '*Pydel*' or 'of *Pydel*'s people', whereas the Oxteddle's (**5**) nomenclature not only indicates a pre-Conquest date for the enclosure but also some cattle-related function for its origins. The valley entrenchment of The Denture (**9**) was less certainly ascribed an early medieval date, on its association with the Old English or earlier oval enclosure of Langham Wood, and the same can be said for the example in Leap Bottom (**18**), the place-name associations of which require confirmation by a toponymic expert.

The explored valley entrenchments have an average size of 146 m × 81 m. They appear to be associated with droveways, particularly those north–south routes that link the Coastal Plain, the South Downs and the Weald. Whilst some of the examples, including Saxon Down (**21**) or Falmer Hill (**12**), are directly associated with these resource linkage routes, others such as Leap Bottom (**18**) simply exist in their vicinity. A further clear association between valley entrenchments and other topographic features was a close correspondence between the enclosures and dew-ponds, or, more rarely, draw wells. Water is a scarce commodity on the dry chalk downland, and if these features are contemporary and related to pastoralism (as seems probable) the ponds would have been necessary additions to any areas set aside for grazing. Indeed, that stock ponds would have been required for downland pasturing of livestock may be reflected in the '*mere*' names of the chalkland that Everitt has seen as indicating early vaccaries associated with dairying (1986, 169). The enclosures at Piddingworth (**20**), Falmer Hill (**12**) and Newmarket Plantation (**19**) are all located within 1.50 km of '*mere*' settlements. If cattle were pastured in any numbers on the downs water would have been of key consideration on the dry chalkland. The suitability of sheep as opposed to cattle is clearly reflected in modern guidelines for the daily water needs of various livestock types. Water advice for livestock farmers supplied by part of the UK government (DAERA 2017) is consistent with more detailed advice provided by Ontario's Ministry of Agriculture Food and Rural Affairs (OMAFRA 2017). Here it is stated that, during the cooler seasons of the year, sheep can require relatively little additional water beyond what they receive through forage. Indeed, unless sheep are lactating or being

Animal type	Weight range (kg)	Water requirement range[a] (L/day)	Average typical water use[b] (L/day)
Feeder lamb	27–50	3.6–5.2	4.4
Gestating meat ewe/ram	80	4.0–6.5	5.25
Lactating meat ewe plus unweaned offspring	80+	9.0–10.5	10
Gestating dairy ewe/ram	90	4.4–7.1	5.75
Lactating dairy ewe	90	9.4–11.4	10.4

TABLE 7.4: Water consumption by sheep (adapted from National Research Council 1985)

[a] A result of the animals' environment and management.
[b] Typical consumption over a year on a daily basis under average agricultural conditions in Ontario.

Dairy cattle type	Level of milk production (kg milk/day)	Water requirement range[a] (L/day)	Average typical water use[b] (L/day)
Dairy calves (1–4 months)	–	4.9–13.2	9
Dairy heifers (5–24 months)	–	14.4–36.3	25
Milking cows[c]	13.6	68–83	115
	22.7	87–102	115
	36.3	114–36	115
	45.5	132–55	115
Dry cows[d]	–	34–49	41

TABLE 7.5: Water consumption by dairy cattle (Adams 1995; NRAES 1998)

[a] A result of the animals' environment and management.
[b] Typical consumption over a year on a daily basis under average agricultural conditions in Ontario.
[c] The average milk production in 2006 for a Holstein dairy cow in Ontario was 33 kg/day.
[d] Approximately 15% of the milking-age cows present on a dairy farm could be considered 'dry'.

Beef cattle type	Weight range (kg)	Water requirement range[a] (L/day)	Average typical water use[b] (L/day)
Feedlot cattle: Backgrounder	181–364 (400–800 lb)	15–40	25
Feedlot cattle: Short keep	364–636 (800–1,400 lb)	27–55	41
Lactating cows with calves	–	43–67	55
Dry cows, bred heifers & bulls	–	22–54	38

TABLE 7.6: Water consumption by beef cattle (adapted from National Research Council 2000)

[a] A result of the animals' environment and management.
[b] Typical consumption over a year on a daily basis under average agricultural conditions in Ontario.

Swine type	Weight range (kg)	Water requirement range[a] (L/day)	Average typical water use[b] (L/day)
Weaner	7–22	1.0–3.2	2.0
Feeder pig	23–36	3.2–4.5	4.5
	36–70	4.5–7.3	4.5
	70–110	7.3–10	9
Gestating sow/boar	–	13.6–17.2	15
Lactating sow[c]	–	18.1–22.7	20

TABLE 7.7: Water consumption by swine (Froese and Small 2001)

[a] A result of the animals' environment and management.
[b] Typical consumption over a year on a daily basis under average agricultural conditions in Ontario.
[c] Includes unweaned piglets.

fed on dry food, their supplemental water requirements between 0°C and 21°C are almost non-existent (National Research Council 1985, 26; MSU 2016). The usual daily requirements of water consumption for modern major domesticates are set out in Tables 7.4–7.7.

It is clear from the evidence for modern livestock provided above that sheep and pigs require far less water than cattle. Dairy cattle are the most reliant on a ready water supply with fully grown cows requiring between 68 and 155 litres per day. A typical dew-pond contains over 273,000 litres (60,000 gallons) of water (Pugsley 1939, 44) and so it is possible that these artificial ponds would be capable of supporting small cattle herds, something confirmed by the chronicler of the English countryside White writing in the 18th century. Observing a dew-pond near his home at Selbourne, Hampshire, he wrote that it contained:

> perhaps not more than two or three hundred hogsheads [*c.* 85,921 litres] of water, yet it is never known to fail, though it affords drink to three hundred or four hundred sheep, and for at least twenty head of large cattle besides. (White 1836, 198)

Of course, medieval cattle were slightly different beasts to those of the modern period (being generally smaller; Albarella and Davis 1996; Albarella 1997; Sykes 2006; 2009), but not overwhelmingly so, and it would seem that water would be required close to valley entrenchments had they been designed for holding cows. Sheep, however, may have been able to glean much of their daily requirement from their diet. This would have been the case in all but the driest of summer months and for all sheep excluding those ewes intended for milk production. After discounting the Bepton enclosure, which showed no indication of being related to the cattle economy, all the remaining valley entrenchments (the adjoining Chantry Bottom entrenchments making 23 examples) were within 1.50 km of water. Up to four valley entrenchments were directly associated with water (17%) and a further 12 (52%) were within 500 m of a pond or well.

It seems that many valley entrenchments were intended as collection points for driven animals, as most are located in convenient coombs beneficial for the rounding up of stock pastured in an open landscape. Some even took advantage of pre-existing lynchets that must have been utilised to guide animals towards the enclosure entrances. Few, if any, valley entrenchments have been associated with contemporary buildings and their generally slight banks (probably originally topped by hedges) and external ditches appear more suited to the corralling of livestock than anything else. Even the effort of constructing slight banks and ditches may be at odds with the enclosure of sheep, which can be sufficiently contained by movable wattle fences. Nevertheless, if large numbers of sheep were being rounded up (as the size of some of the enclosures may indicate) more permanent and robust enclosures capable of being divided may have been required.

The provision of ditches and banks may be suggestive of the keeping of cattle, as the animals have a tendency to push against any fenced enclosure. Later medieval sheepfolds are more likely to have been located off the down so that their dung and feet could aid the Sussex method of sheep-corn husbandry (see Brandon 1998, 64–70). The presence of mounds and square ditched enclosures within some of the entrenchments have been interpreted as fodder ricks (*e.g.* at **13** Faulkner's Bottom; Toms 1926, 47) and the name of the Oxteddle Bottom enclosure (**5**) may indicate that as well as corrals these enigmatic monuments were used for the stalling of cattle.

Valley entrenchments were almost certainly intended to aid the earlier medieval seasonal pasturing of livestock and the similar morphology of many, such as the Giant's Grave/Devil's Dyke (**14**), Faulkner's Bottom (**13**), Swanborough Coombe (**22**), The Bible/Oxteddle (**5**) and those at Belle Tout (**2, 3**), would indicate they represent a phase of similar husbandry upon the southern downland. The instances given above are the most easily interpreted as cattle-related, but associations with place-names containing '*wic*' could possibly indicate a dairying connotation (whether that be for ewes or cows). That the enclosures could have been utilised during the early medieval period for the summer production of sheep's milk and cheese is a possibility, although the sites lacked running water. This function would explain their close proximity to dew-ponds and the apparent association with the place-name '*wic*'. Names indicating summering are also found close to some of the enclosures such as the 'summerdowns' near East Dean or Devil's Dyke and examples such as The Denture (**9**), the Belle Tout (**2, 3**), Leap Bottom (**18**) or Chantry Bottom (**8**) entrenchments are associated with oval or potential oval enclosures. The large outer enclosure at Belle Tout has been reliably dated to the early medieval period and could relate to the early appropriation of downland, either as common land or an area of seasonal pasture belonging to a specific community or folk-group. The example of Leap Bottom (**18**) within the tentatively identified Thornwick oval (see section 6.3) is also very interesting in this regard. It has been postulated that Leap may come from the Old English *hlēp* and the potential associations with the custom of '*lep*' recorded near Eastbourne are clear. The custumal to which this relates concerns the commoning of cattle and specifically their herding into a pinfold (Wilson 1961, 30–31). On the instruction of the reeve or beadle of the manor seasonally pastured cattle of the entire hundreds of Willingdon and Eastbourne may have been herded into the said pinfold. The large outer enclosure of Belle Tout and its associated valley entrenchments exist in the hundred of Willingdon and it is interesting to speculate that the larger enclosure (**2**) could have been capable of holding the 80–120 cattle suggested by documentary evidence (*ibid.*; see section 3.3). Perhaps the nearby names of Bulling Dean, Summerdown and Bullock Down recorded on the OS 1st Edition mapping hint at earlier use of the local downland for the summer pasturing of cattle?

It is probable that the earliest valley entrenchments originated in ancient areas of seasonal pasture, spaces where the early medieval downland was still utilised as an intercommonable resource. It is possible that water in the form of dew-ponds was provided to the livestock that wandered close to the enclosures and the valley entrenchments could have been utilised in periodic round ups or collections of animals. Some were located close to important downland droves and, in the case of the enclosure at Swanborough Coombe, the associated holloway led to the meeting place of the local hundred (*P.N.Sx* 1930, 317). Such locations may have developed due to an early role in the transhumance economy. Communities may have been following a tradition of gathering together, initially for the benefit of pastoralism, later developing into meeting places used for local administration and fairs. The Old English place-name elements associated with Swanborough ('*swāna-beorg*') have the meaning of peasant's, swine-herd's or herdsman's hill (*P.N.Sx* 1930, 317; *P.N.E.* 1956b, 171) and the proximity of a valley entrenchment would be no surprise given the '*swāna*' element's pastoral connotations. On the strength of the existing evidence presented here it is, of course, impossible to be certain to what degree the enclosures were used for differing livestock types and in order to understand more fully the nature and phases of animal husbandry on the downs it is necessary to turn to other data sets. These include the study of animal bone assemblages, a category of evidence to which we will turn in the following chapter.

CHAPTER *8*

Animal bone assemblages

....

8.1 Introduction

> Let all the old and weak be drafted out before Lammas, and let them be put in good pasture to fatten, and when the best have presently mended and are fat, let them be sold to the butchers … and let all the rest of the draft beasts which cannot be sold then, be sold before Martinmas. (Oschinsky 1971, 274–75)

The tradesmen mentioned in the above passage were a relatively new phenomenon at the tail end of the 13th century when Walter of Henley's *Le Dite de Hosebondrie* was compiled. Only by the late medieval period had the butcher-grazier begun to appear in the South-East's towns, leasing land in the countryside for the fattening of meatstock (Mate 1991, 120). Prior to this time, peasant farmers would have largely processed carcasses themselves. This is supported by an earlier study of butchery marks by Grant (1987) that showed a gradual change over the medieval period from haphazard disarticulation by knife, to consistent cut patterns and cleaver-based methods of butchery. These new processes, which had begun by the 12th century (a document dated AD 1179 mentions a guild of butchers of London; *Pipe. R.* 26, 154; Jones 1976, 1), often included the splitting of animals into equal sides, evidenced by the appearance of sagitally cleaved vertebrae. In the case of cattle, this could have only been achieved with specialist equipment and purpose-built premises (Grant 1987, 56–57; Sykes 2009, 353).

This new craft, which was brought about by a late medieval increase in meat as a proportion of the diet, is depicted in a handbook describing in detail both the beneficial and harmful properties of foods (the *Tacuino Sanitatis*). The work is testament to a greater familiarity with the trade in meat, which by this time had come to be sold jointed, by the breast and side (*e.g. perna baconis*, 'a ham'; *cost*', 'a side of mutton'; Woolgar 1992). This acquaintance with animal processing and slaughter is also recorded in contemporary sermons that make reference to the butcher's dog, with its 'blody mowth', and the cries of compassion from swine and oxen for their fellows as they were slain (Owst 1933; Woolgar 2006, 90). Though such documents are relatively common for the later medieval period, survival of similar material from earlier times is often limited. In attempting to reconstruct the cattle economy of the South-East, it is the parts of animals butchers often throw away (the bones) that provides one of the most numerous and enlightening strands of evidence for studying early livestock regimes.

This chapter aims to utilise these physical remains so as to compare and contrast the bone assemblages of the three major domesticates (cattle, sheep and pig) across the different *pays* that together make up our wider study area. Despite the importance of other animals to the medieval diet and farming practice, including poultry, horses, rabbits and fish (see Grant 1988, 154–74; Banham and Faith 2014, 79–105), it is these three species 'which formed the mainstay of farming economies and contributed the vast majority of meat in the diet' (Rippon 2012, 241).

The value of zooarchaeology has long been recognised for determining the relative frequencies of species at a given site, or group of sites, and from there reconstructing diet and economy. This is often undertaken with the aim of determining whether communities based their subsistence on cattle, sheep/goats or pigs. More recent studies have, however, used this data to characterise settlements (*e.g.* Grant 1988) or explore what human–animal relationships have to offer the study of aspects of the past often thought archaeologically intangible, such as status, ethnic, religious or gender-based identity (Sykes 2009, 354). A further more recent application has been the use of bone assemblages to study the evolution of cultural landscapes with the aim of understanding variation in the character of the countryside (*e.g.* Rippon 2012; Rippon *et al.* 2015). It is primarily to study of regional variation in the farming economy that the medieval bone assemblages of the South-East will here be applied.

8.2 Methodology

As outlined in the introductory chapter, it is one of the principal aims of this work to understand the role that the cattle economy played in the shaping of the South-East's historic landscape and the evolution of its rural settlement pattern. The holistic inter-disciplinary approach that is being attempted holds much in common with previously mentioned studies. The methodology followed for the collection of data here is greatly influenced by that developed by Rippon for his *Making Sense of an Historic Landscape* (2012). Gathering of animal bone assemblages therefore began with reference to Sykes's (2007) national overview. This was followed by a search of Archaeology South-East's (UCL Institute of Archaeology) project database for sites with stratified medieval animal bone assemblages. Local society journals and published monographs were then explored, as well as the Archaeology Data Service's grey literature report library.

In compiling the data, a number of issues had to be resolved. The first of these relates to a well-known methodological problem concerning the distinguishing of goat (*Capra hircus*) remains from those of sheep (*Ovis aries*). It was thus decided to group these two species together for the purposes of this study. Within the study of animal bone assemblages, a minimum of 100 identifiable fragments are required to be statistically reliable, although assemblages of over 500 fragments are preferred. In similarity with Rippon's (2012) study, the emphasis here is to group data from each *pays* to allow comparison of regional livestock regimes and their relation to the landscape. As a result, the individual sizes of site assemblages are less important. This said, the number of assemblages of over 100 fragments in a given group are shown in the relevant tables (Tables 8.2–8.5). An average of site averages is also given (Tables 8.2, 8.4 and 8.6) to overcome the problem of large samples that are out of line with a series of smaller assemblages. When calculating the average of site averages only sites with assemblages of over 100 fragments are included.

In choosing a statistical method of collecting the data, fragment counts or Number of Identified Specimens (NISP) are the most frequently used methods of quantifying bones by species from archaeological sites, and syntheses have most often been produced on this basis (Sykes 2007, 9). These raw fragment counts usually exaggerate the importance of cattle as their large bones tend to fragment into more identifiable pieces, while estimations based on the other method of quantification, Minimum Numbers of Individuals (MNI), tend to produce a bias towards higher levels of sheep/goat and pig (Sykes 2007, 28). As the majority of animal bone reports only provide a simple fragment count or NISP, these are the data utilised here. For the reasons outlined above, a selection 'for' cattle and 'against' sheep should be assumed for all assemblages covered by this review.

The large differences in the body sizes of cattle, sheep and pigs must be taken into account when assessing the relative amount of beef, mutton and pork in the diet (Grant 1988, 162). As a meat animal, cattle's size makes them good value; more meat is returned for the labour of keeping and butchering them than from smaller livestock. Indeed, from a cultural perspective, cattle appear to have been particularly prized in the early medieval period (Banham and Faith 2014, 85–87) and their relative importance has been confirmed by past studies. The bones of cattle were more numerous than those of sheep on well over half of the Anglo-Saxon settlements investigated by Sykes (2006, 58, fig. 5.1) and both sheep and cattle were always more numerous than any other species.

Such national overviews provide the starting point for discussing the results of the medieval data gathered for the South-East. Table 8.1 shows the relative proportions of the three major domesticates from sites of differing social status. These will be compared to the results from the particular *pays* within our study area as an aid to discussion of regional variation in faunal assemblages within the South-East (for the pioneering of this approach, see Rippon 2012).

In order to facilitate comparison to these national trends, the South-East's data was categorised by site type, but the results were also placed within a chronological framework to allow analysis of change over time. As discussed previously, the medieval period has been traditionally viewed as an age when sheep were of particular importance. This is often reflected in the documentary evidence, particularly the accounts of monastic estates. These record huge flocks of up to 10,000 strong with herds of cattle and pigs being very much in the minority (Carus-Wilson 1962, 185–86). From the above archaeological data (Table 8.1) it is possible to suggest that the historical evidence puts rather more emphasis on wool production than was truly the case. During the 14th century the percentage of sheep bones in several towns actually fell, with a recovery

Site type	Cattle	Sheep/goat	Pig
A. Grant 1988, tab. 8.10. 12th/13th centuries			
towns	*c.* 42%	*c.* 42%	*c.* 16%
secular elite	*c.* 42%	*c.* 46%	*c.* 34%
rural	*c.* 33%	*c.* 46%	*c.* 21%
B. Sykes 2009, fig. 17.1			
towns	*c.* 47%	*c.* 39%	*c.* 14%
secular elite	*c.* 36%	*c.* 33%	*c.* 31%
ecclesiastical elite	*c.* 32%	*c.* 35%	*c.* 33%
rural	*c.* 37%	*c.* 46%	*c.* 17%

TABLE 8.1: Statistical analysis of the percentages of cattle, sheep/goat and pig from different categories of site in medieval Britain (Rippon 2012, tab. 12.1)

in the 15th century when beef production was also becoming increasingly important (Grant 1988, 151, 153–54). The later medieval period was a time of changing cattle husbandry practices. Animals from early medieval sites tend to derive from adults slaughtered after serving as plough animals; however, from the late 14th century calf remains are increasingly represented (Sykes 2009, 350). This suggests a growing move towards a meat and dairy economy (Albarella 1997), a change that was allied with a significant increase in animal size attributable to selective breeding. These improvements long pre-dated the Agricultural Revolution of the 18th and 19th centuries (Sykes 2009, 350), and may have been part of a suite of agrarian changes motivated by the social and economic upheaval that followed the Black Death (Thirsk 1997).

Due to these known shifts in agricultural practice the accepted divisions of the medieval period (early AD 410–1066, later AD 1066–1350 and late medieval AD 1350–1540) are not appropriate for an economic-based landscape study. As Rippon (2012, 245) has clarified, the economic and demographic changes of the 'long 8th century' (Brown and Foard 1998; Williamson 2003; Rippon 2008) meant that the southern English countryside of the 9th and 10th centuries had far more in common with the later medieval period than that which had gone before. This transformation makes the chronology developed by Rippon (2012, 246) far more appropriate to this section of our study than the traditional period boundaries found elsewhere. The landscape chronology largely adopted from Rippon (*ibid.*) is outlined below:

- Earliest medieval period (5th to the 7th centuries)
- Middle medieval period (8th century to the mid-14th century)
- Late medieval period (mid-14th to the late 15th century).

8.3 Results

Earliest medieval (5th–7th century)

Only 12 sites dating to the earliest medieval period have significant animal bone assemblages within the South-East. These were restricted to non-manorial rural settlements of which only seven produced assemblages of over 100 fragments. At the time of writing important bone reports such as that from Lyminge await full publication (Thomas forthcoming). The majority of sites were located on the North Kent Plain and, of these, many are the result of commercial infrastructure projects (*e.g.* Andrews *et al.* 2011; Dawkes 2017). The lack of excavated assemblages of this date restricts meaningful analysis and comparison of the data across the individual *pays*. Given the complete lack of earliest medieval urban and elite sites the limitations on this analysis is especially so across site types. The largest assemblage came from Northfleet on the North Kent Plain (783 fragments; Andrews *et al.* 2011) and analysis showed it was dominated by cattle (52%), with sheep being less important than pig at 19% and 29% respectively.

At Botolphs in the South Downs the assemblage (266 fragments) was dominated by cattle (42%) and pig (37%), with sheep only making up 21% of the earliest medieval assemblage (Gardiner 1990). At first this seems strange in a landscape that is traditionally viewed as sheep country. On closer inspection, however, it is clear that the Clay-with-Flints geology and riverine location of this site may have been more conducive to the keeping of cattle than the chalkland hills that characterise much of the rest of the area. The traditional dominance of sheep within this *pay* was redressed by the assemblage from Rookery Hill, Bishopstone (Bell 1977; Gebbels 1977; 114 fragments) Though this was a small assemblage, it showed the dominance of sheep (48%).

Evidence from a small number of sites on the Greensand Ridge show that this area may have been important during the early medieval period for the pasturing of cattle (Table 8.2). The collection of bones from the Early to Middle Anglo-Saxon site at Friar's Oak, Hassocks, West Sussex (Butler 2000; 411 fragments) is of interest. The area later belonged to a medieval manor called 'Wickham', which was derived from an earlier Anglo-Saxon multiple estate (Warne 2000). Friar's Oak had access to common wood-pastures at nearby Strood and the meadowland of the manor may have also been used communally (*ibid.*, 68). Warne (*ibid.*) has postulated that temporary or seasonal structures may have been associated with the use of these streamside meadows and that the sunken feature building excavated at the site could have performed such a function. Fox (2012, 140–42) has suggested that isolated examples of this type may have played a role in seasonal pastoral activities, and possible examples from elsewhere in Sussex have been interpreted in this regard (Margetts 2018, 152, 178). Overall, it can be said that during the earliest medieval period cattle appear to have comprised a significant part of the South-East's rural economy. Sheep seem to have taken a slightly inferior role to pigs, which were also well represented (see Table 8.2). The Greensand Ridge and North Kent Plain may have been particularly important for cattle as their high relative frequency is above the national average for the period (40% on rural sites; see Sykes 2009, fig. 17.1, pre-Conquest); further excavated evidence is, however, required before any more definitive interpretations can be made.

TABLE 8.2: Summary of earliest medieval bones of the three major domesticates recovered from non-manorial sites

Pays	No. assemblage () = assem. >100+	Total frags	Cattle frags	%	Ave. of ave.	Sheep nos	%	Ave. of ave.	Pigs nos	%	Ave. of ave.
Coastal Plain	0	0	0	0	0	0	0	0	0	0	0
Greensand Ridge	2 (1)	422	276	65	66	99	24	23	47	11	11
High Weald	0	0	0	0	0	0	0	0	0	0	0
Low Weald	0	0	0	0	0	0	0	0	0	0	0
North Downs	1 (0)	19	8	42	–	5	26	–	6	32	–
North Kent Plain	5 (4)	1550	788	50.8	56	340	21.9	21	422	27.2	23
Pevensey Levels	0	0	0	0	0	0	0	0	0	0	0
Romney Marsh	0	0	0	0	0	0	0	0	0	0	0
South Downs	4 (2)	528	176	33	37	178	34	34	174	33	29
Thames Basin	0	0	0	0	0	0	0	0	0	0	0
Totals	12 (7)	2519	1248	49	53	622	25	26	649	26	21

Middle medieval (8th–mid-14th century)

In comparison to the preceding 5th to the 7th centuries the middle medieval period is witnessed by an explosion of animal bone assemblages. This is partly due to the relative chronological length of the period but also demographic growth and agricultural expansion. The growth of the data is especially so for urban and non-manorial rural sites, which together contribute over 83% by site type of the gathered data. Fifty-three animal bone assemblages were investigated in total, and although monastic sites, castles and manorial settlements provided few assemblages, some of these were large (Tables 8.3 and 8.4). The *pay* with the most sites was the South Downs, a situation that reflects the historical concentration of archaeological work within the South-East. The North Kent Plain and Sussex Coastal Plain were also well represented; however, all of the sites within the latter were concentrated in the town of Chichester or the medieval port of Shoreham. The prevalence of sheep in these urban centres (the numbers of which were well above the national average) appears to confirm the documented popularity of sheep-corn husbandry for which the area is famous. The numbers of sheep from Shoreham may also be indicative of the port's importance to the wool trade as it is known that during the reign of Edward I the town, along with Seaford someway to the east, comprised the primary port for wool export in Sussex (Pelham 1934, 129).

No reliable animal bone assemblages have been produced by urban sites on the Greensand Ridge. Away from the towns, the excavated rural settlements of the Greensand were more statistically viable. Again, sheep were not particularly important, figuring well below the national average. Cattle, too, were less important than pigs, which dominated at 45% of the fragment count. The prominence of pigs within the assemblage could perhaps be expected given the proximity of the Weald and its historical association with swine pasture. It is probable that peasant communities based on the manor of Buckland, part of which yielded the largest proportion of the bone assemblage (Dawkes 2014; 123 fragments), could have taken advantage of pannage rights in nearby woodland. This large manor is recorded in Domesday as having 17 villagers, 8 smallholders, a church and 10 slaves (Domesday, 19, 14). Buckland was a parent manor and had detached settlements within the Wealden interior. These included Hartswood, which remained as a manorial detachment until the 16th century (Malden 1911, 174). The area may have been utilised for the pannage of swine prior to 1379 when John de Arundel, Lord of Buckland, received licence to 'inclose his wood of "Herteswode", and to impark 360 acres of land adjacent thereto' (*Cal. Pat.* 1377–81, 380).

Urban assemblages from the newly founded middle medieval towns of the High Weald provided surprisingly abundant results. This is probably due to the presence of exceptional preservational contexts when compared to the rural sites found in the remainder of the *pay*. The acidic ground conditions that dominate the region were less prevalent within town centre sites than elsewhere, a situation probably encouraged by deposition of bones within

TABLE 8.3: Summary of middle medieval bones of the three major domesticates from each of the pays within the study area grouped by sites of different social status

	Settlement type	No. assemblage () = assem. >100+	Total frags	Cattle		Sheep		Pig		Total
				nos	%	nos	%	nos	%	
Coastal Plain	towns	7 (3)	7309	3059	42	3655	50	595	8	7309
	monastic	0	0							
	castle	0	0							
	manorial	0	0							
	rural	0	0							
Greensand Ridge	towns	1 (0)	14	9	64	4	29	1	7	14
	monastic	0	0							
	castle	0	0							
	manorial	0	0							
	rural	2 (1)	159	51	32	37	23	71	45	159
High Weald	towns	3 (2)	480	231	48	140	29	109	23	480
	monastic	1 (0)	96	26	27	23	24	47	49	96
	castle	0	0							
	manorial	0	0							
	rural	0	0							
Low Weald	towns	2 (0)	49	24	49	14	29	11	22	49
	monastic	0	0							
	castle	0	0							
	manorial	1 (1)	135	115	85	20	15			135
	rural	1 (1)	877	456	52	351	40	70	8	877
North Downs	towns	2 (1)	12883	5012	39	6017	47	1854	14	12883
	monastic	0	0							
	castle	1 (1)	2191	665	30	883	40	643	29	2191
	manorial	1 (1)	208	47	23	130	62	31	15	208
	rural	1 (1)	227	42	19	80	35	105	46	227
North Kent Plain	towns	1 (0)	71	32	45	33	46	6	8	71
	monastic	0	0							
	castle	0	0							
	manorial	0	0							
	rural	6 (3)	1685	731	43	696	41	258	15	1685

(Continued)

TABLE 8.3: *(Continued)*

	Settlement type	No. assemblage () = assem. >100+	Total frags	Cattle		Sheep		Pig		Total
				nos	%	nos	%	nos	%	
Pevensey Levels	towns	1 (0)	20	6	30	13	65	1	5	20
	monastic	0	0							
	castle	1 (1)	998	291	29	366	37	341	34	998
	manorial	0	0							
	rural	0	0							
Romney Marsh	towns	2 (2)	492	219	44	204	42	69	14	492
	monastic	0	0							
	castle	0	0							
	manorial	0	0							
	rural	1 (1)	818	282	34	357	44	179	22	818
South Downs	towns	3 (1)	11398	4730	41	4786	42	1882	17	11398
	monastic	1 (1)	287	81	28	158	55	48	17	287
	castle	0	0							
	manorial	0	0							
	rural	7 (5)	6222	1193	19	3210	52	1819	29	6222
Thames Basin	towns	2 (1)	641	394	61	134	21	113	18	641
	monastic	0	0							
	castle	0	0							
	manorial	3 (1)	336	154	46	56	17	126	37	336
	rural	1 (0)	35	28	80	6	17	1	3	35

pits (*e.g.* at Deadman's Lane, Rye; Hopkinson 2015; 39 fragments). The town assemblages show a slightly higher than average proportion of cattle as well as high frequencies of pig. Sheep were rare at 29% confirming the traditional view of the livestock economy of the area (see Pelham 1934; Gardiner 1999, 38). While an animal bone assemblage from Tonbridge in Kent produced a High Wealden animal bone assemblage fairly evenly distributed between species (Swift and Blackmore 2010; 187 fragments) an assemblage from the town of Battle (James 2008; 254 fragments) was dominated by cattle. The bones from the latter site showed clear butchery marks and juvenile animals were recorded amongst the remains (Sibun 2008). Also in Battle, the monastic site of Battle Abbey provided a moderate sized assemblage of 96 fragments (Hare 1985). Such sites are probably the least reliable in terms of relationship to local conditions, drawing as they do upon their large ecclesiastical estates. Numerically, pig was the most important species (49%), followed by cattle (27%) and sheep (24%).

TABLE 8.4: Summary of middle medieval bones of the three major domesticates from sites of different social status from each of the pays within the study area

Settlement type	No. assemblage () = assem. >100+	Total frags	Cattle			Sheep			Pig		
			nos	%	Ave. of ave.	nos	%	Ave. of ave.	nos	%	Ave. of ave.
Towns											
Coastal Plain	7 (3)	7309	3059	42	44	3655	50	46	595	8	10
Greensand Ridge	1 (0)	14	9	64	–	4	29	–	1	7	–
High Weald	3 (2)	480	231	48	46	140	29	30	109	23	24
Low Weald	2 (0)	49	24	49	–	14	29	–	11	22	–
North Downs	2 (1)	12883	5012	39	39	6017	47	47	1854	14	14
North Kent Plain	1 (0)	71	32	45	–	33	46	–	6	9	–
Pevensey Levels	1 (0)	20	6	30	–	13	65	–	1	5	–
Romney Marsh	2 (2)	492	219	45	47	204	41	40	69	14	13
South Downs	3 (2)	11398	4730	41	43	4786	42	36	1882	17	21
Thames Basin	2 (1)	641	394	61	62	134	21	20	113	18	18
Totals	24 (11)	33357	13716	41	47	15000	45	36	4641	14	17
Monastic sites											
Coastal Plain	0	0	0	0	0	0	0	0	0	0	0
Greensand Ridge	0	0	0	0	0	0	0	0	0	0	0
High Weald	1 (0)	96	26	27	–	23	24	–	47	49	–
Low Weald	0	0	0	0	0	0	0	0	0	0	0
North Downs	0	0	0	0	0	0	0	0	0	0	0
North Kent Plain	0	0	0	0	0	0	0	0	0	0	0
Pevensey Levels	0	0	0	0	0	0	0	0	0	0	0
Romney Marsh	0	0	0	0	0	0	0	0	0	0	0
South Downs	1 (1)	287	81	28	28	158	55	55	48	17	17
Thames Basin	0	0	0	0	0	0	0	0	0	0	0
Totals	2 (1)	383	107	28	28	181	47	55	95	25	17
Castles											
Coastal Plain	0	0	0	0	0	0	0	0	0	0	0
Greensand Ridge	0	0	0	0	0	0	0	0	0	0	0
High Weald	0	0	0	0	0	0	0	0	0	0	0
Low Weald	0	0	0	0	0	0	0	0	0	0	0
North Downs	1 (1)	2191	665	31	30	883	40	40	643	29	30

(Continued)

TABLE 8.4: (Continued)

Settlement type	No. assemblage (() = assem. >100+)	Total frags	Cattle nos	Cattle %	Cattle Ave. of ave.	Sheep nos	Sheep %	Sheep Ave. of ave.	Pig nos	Pig %	Pig Ave. of ave.
North Kent Plain	0	0	0	0	0	0	0	0	0	0	0
Pevensey Levels	1 (1)	998	291	29	29	366	37	37	341	34	34
Romney Marsh	0	0	0	0	0	0	0	0	0	0	0
South Downs	0	0	0	0	0	0	0	0	0	0	0
Thames Basin	0	0	0	0	0	0	0	0	0	0	0
Totals	2 (2)	3189	956	30	29.5	1249	39	38.5	984	31	32
Manorial sites											
Coastal Plain	0	0	0	0	0	0	0	0	0	0	0
Greensand Ridge	0	0	0	0	0	0	0	0	0	0	0
High Weald	0	0	0	0	0	0	0	0	0	0	0
Low Weald	1 (1)	135	115	85	85	20	15	15	0	0	0
North Downs	1 (1)	208	47	23	23	130	62	62	31	15	15
North Kent Plain	0	0	0	0	0	0	0	0	0	0	0
Pevensey Levels	0	0	0	0	0	0	0	0	0	0	0
Romney Marsh	0	0	0	0	0	0	0	0	0	0	0
South Downs	0	0	0	0	0	0	0	0	0	0	0
Thames Basin	3 (1)	336	154	46	46	56	17	17	126	37	37
Totals	5 (5)	679	316	47	51	206	30	31	157	23	17
Non-manorial rural settlements											
Coastal Plain	0	0	0	0	0	0	0	0	0	0	0
Greensand Ridge	2 (1)	159	51	32	33	37	23	15	71	45	52
High Weald	0	0	0	0	0	0	0	0	0	0	0
Low Weald	1 (1)	877	456	52	52	351	40	40	70	8	8
North Downs	1 (1)	227	42	19	19	80	35	35	105	46	46
North Kent Plain	6 (3)	1685	731	43	40	696	41	41	258	15	19
Pevensey Levels	0	0	0	0	0	0	0	0	0	0	0
Romney Marsh	1 (1)	818	282	34	34	357	44	44	179	22	22
South Downs	7 (5)	6222	1193	19	30	3210	52	44	1819	29	26
Thames Basin	1 (0)	35	28	80	–	6	17	–	1	3	–
Totals	19 (12)	10023	2783	28	35	4737	47	36	2503	25	29

The vertebrae of ox, sheep and pig were chopped axially (Locker 1985, 183), confirming the presence of advanced butchery. Although the bones of piglet were present, some of the remains were of animals aged two to three years. The pig mandibles occasionally showed much wear, indicating their food was particularly abrasive (beech and oak mast?). It is likely that much of the meat consumed by the monks came from the abbey's own manors, but purchases were also made from Battle market (Locker 1985, 184). The bones of calves were present amongst the assemblage (*ibid.*), perhaps confirming the consumption of veal raised on the abbey's lands documented in Chapter 3.

The towns of the Low Weald produced small assemblages. More valuable is the ecclesiastical site of Stretham Moat, Henfield (Funnell 2009). Here the assemblage of 135 fragments was totally dominated by cattle at 85%, with fewer sheep and no pig remains. The site has been previously discussed in the preceding chapters and is documented for its excessive number of cows (Chapter 3; *Chi. Chart.* 1942, 223–24). It is also associated with a form of oval enclosure, field-names related to cattle and dairying and a moated site belonging to the Bishop of Chichester (Chapter 6). The number of cows were equivalent to northern vaccaries, and although too much reliance should not be placed on the limited animal bone assemblage it reinforces the notion that the manor operated as an ecclesiastical livestock concern. Such an operation could have been sited to exploit the rich pasturage on the banks of the Adur as well as nearby woodland pastures around Henfield.

One rural site was recorded in the Low Weald, at Brisley Farm, Ashford, Kent (Stevenson 2013b). This site, which is perhaps more famous for its Iron Age remains, produced a good-sized assemblage of 877 bones. Cattle dominated at 52%, which is far in excess of the national average. Sheep were also important, perhaps due to the proximity of Romney Marsh; however, pig appeared to be uncommon. Cattle were represented by both meat joints and skeletal extremities, suggesting the animals were butchered and eaten on site (Ayton 2013, 343). The relative abundance of skeletal fragments does, however, suggest that a number of beef joints were eaten and discarded elsewhere (*ibid.*). A high percentage (77% of the identifiable bone group) of cattle appear to have been slaughtered prior to reaching 2–3 years of age, although a number of mature specimens perhaps kept as a breeding herd or for traction were also recovered. The age data is thought to be representative of an emphasis on meat production as opposed to secondary products (*ibid.*, 345).

The North Downs provided some of the largest animal bone assemblages examined across the South-East. The results can therefore be claimed as a reasonably reliable representation of the middle medieval livestock economy of the area. The North Downs appears to have been important sheep country, perhaps hinting at specialisation. Assemblages from both towns and secular manorial sites showed frequencies above the national average. At Guildford Castle and Palace 40% of bones of the three major domesticates were derived from sheep (Poulton 2005; total assemblage 2,191 fragments). Pigs also appear to have been important, no doubt encouraged by the extensive woodlands that covered the Clay-with-Flints areas of downland. The low-status rural sites encountered during works associated with the A2 (Allen *et al.* 2012; 227 fragments) produced high numbers of pigs at 46% of the assemblage, a frequency more than double the national average (17%; Sykes 2009, fig. 17.1). Such evidence is valuable as low-status peasant settlements are reliable for showing local farming conditions.

Only one urban site was encountered on the North Kent Plain producing a small unreliable assemblage (Stevens 2013; 71 fragments). Six assemblages were retrieved from rural sites, with three of these producing over 100 fragments each. While sheep also appeared to be important to the low-status rural populace, the frequency was below the national average. Cattle appear to have been the more important species; however, the sites that contributed the most fragments (over 60% of the total number of bones) were both from 8th- and 9th-century deposits at Cliffsend on the Isle of Thanet (Andrews *et al.* 2015; McKinley *et al.* 2014; 793 and 242 fragments respectively). The results may therefore be indicative of a localised early medieval livestock regime rather than a reflection of the entire *pay*.

As would be expected, the coastal wetlands of the Pevensey Levels and Romney Marsh produced assemblages that showed the importance of sheep. At Pevensey Castle (Fulford and Rippon 2011; 998 fragments) a large group of bones were derived from sheep (37%), a frequency that is greater than that found for the castles of South-West England by Rippon (2012; cattle 32%; sheep 35%; pigs 33%). The number of pigs was also larger than the national average from the single low-status rural site on Romney Marsh. At Lydd Quarry the farmsteads were clearly engaged in sheep husbandry (44% of the 818 fragment assemblage), although it was the frequency of pigs that was greater than the national average (22%; Barber and Priestley-Bell 2008). At St Thomas Primary School, Winchelsea, the urban assemblage again showed the prevalence of sheep (47%) and pigs (21%) to the detriment of cattle (33%; James and Barber 2004; assemblage of 289 fragments). The numbers of pigs recorded in these wetlands is interesting as in the past the area has overwhelmingly been seen as sheep country. Though sheep were clearly the most important species, pigs appear to have played a key secondary role. This may be a significant revelation as it appears to confirm the analysis of medieval estate records that show reclaimed marshlands were important landscapes for the rearing of such animals (see Rippon 2002b, 86). The uncertainly dated but probably 13th-century assemblage from Southlands School, New Romney, was deemed unreliable as medieval finds may have been mixed with post-medieval material (Armitage 2002; Draper and Meddens 2009; 261 fragments).

Away from the coastal marshes the other iconic sheep country of the South-East is the rolling chalkland hills of the South Downs. Here the towns of Lewes and Seaford have produced bone assemblages, although the size of the former was by far the larger, with both late Anglo-Saxon (166 fragments) and later medieval (11,179 fragments) groups represented (Swift in prep.). During the late Anglo-Saxon period the assemblage from Lewes was dominated by cattle (44%), although pigs (26.5%) were also important. The number of sheep was surprisingly limited (29.5% of the assemblage), seeming to contradict the usual perception of the livestock economy of the *pay*. Look closer at the assemblage in relation to the national averages for the pre-Conquest period, however, and the results are easier to explain. The numbers of cattle were actually below the 55% recorded for urban assemblages in the period by Sykes (2009, fig. 17.1 A), whilst the numbers of pig and sheep were greater.

After the Conquest sheep became even more important at Lewes, being the most frequent species found amongst the bone assemblage (4,705 fragments), equalling the 42% of the assemblage occupied by cattle. During this period the frequencies of both sheep and pigs (42% and 16% respectively) exceeded the post-Conquest national average. Both epipyseal fusion data and mortality profiles, reconstructed with reference to tooth eruption and wear, indicate that the majority of cattle remains related to older individuals, reflecting an economy geared towards grain production rather than beef. It is likely that cattle were prized as draught animals, something confirmed by the pathology, which showed stress- and age-related arthropathic injuries (Ayton in prep.). The majority of cattle were of a small-horned type (Sykes and Symmons 2007) with just four specimens classed as 'short-horned' having an outer horn curvature greater than 145 mm (the longest of these measured 189 mm; Ayton in prep.). Analysis of the slenderness of cattle metacarpals showed that cattle found at Lewes became significantly more robust in the 13th century, either suggesting that more males were being supplied, that several types of cattle were represented (*ibid.*) or that livestock was being improved. While cattle appear to have been kept for traction and meat, sheep were kept for their wool. The presence of neo-natal pig remains suggests they were raised locally, with the majority of animals being culled between 24 and 30 months (*ibid.*). Overall the towns in this *pay* showed the importance of sheep (42%) and pigs (17%), which were both recorded at frequencies above the national average. Cattle appear to have taken an inferior role, confirming the traditional view of the area's livestock economy.

St Nicholas Hospital, also in Lewes, continued this trend with 55% of the assemblage dominated by sheep (Barber and Sibun 2010; 287 fragments). The hospital was run by Lewes Priory, which belonged to the reformed Benedictine Order of Cluny. The priory is well known as one of the wealthiest monasteries in all England, wealth that was mainly built upon the medieval trade in wool. By the 13th century the institution was the largest wool-producing monastery in the country and access to large herds of sheep could easily explain the domesticates numbers in the hospital's assemblage. The South Downs peasant also appears to have favoured the keeping of sheep (52% of the rural assemblage), but pigs were also surprisingly important at 12% above the national average. Cattle appear to have played a minor role, making up only a small proportion of peasant livestock within the *pay*.

The final *pay* to receive discussion is the Thames Basin. Here two urban sites in Southwark, Greater London provided assemblages (Sayer 2005; Haslam 2012). The Former Whitstable Day Nursery site (Haslam 2012) produced a statistically viable group of 627 bones contributing to an overall town assemblage (totalling 641 fragments) that showed the dominance of cattle; at 61%, which is 14% above the national average for post-Conquest sites recorded by Sykes (2009, fig. 17.1). Pigs were also slightly above the national average, whereas sheep made up a limited proportion of the overall urban assemblage for the *pay*. The importance of cattle in this area seems to be corroborated by post-Conquest town sites that could not be grouped with the rest of the middle medieval data due to problems with distinctions within the stratigraphic phasing. Tabard Square, also in Southwark, produced a large assemblage of 1,564 bones of which 54% were identifiable to cattle, 27% to sheep and 19% to pig (Killock 2009). A post-Conquest site in Kingston-upon-Thames (Andrews 2001; 158) again showed high proportions of cattle at 48%. The numbers of sheep were small (34%), whilst pigs appear to have been relatively common (18%).

No castle or monastic assemblages were encountered for the *pay*, although three secular elite sites were explored at Battersea Flour Mills, Greater London (Cooke 2001), Woking Palace, Surrey (Poulton 2015) and Brooklands, Weybridge (also in Surrey; Hanworth and Tomalin 1977). Together these verified the importance of cattle to the *pay* shown by the urban sites with a frequency of cattle that was 10% above the post-Conquest national average (Sykes 2009, fig. 1.17). The numbers of sheep were poor (only 17%) whereas the high-status value of pigs as a meat animal seems to have been valued at 37%. Only one rural site was encountered – a probable late 8th-century settlement at Althorpe Grove, Battersea (Blackmore and Cowie 2001), although the number of bones retrieved was small (only 35 fragments identifiable to cattle, sheep or pig), reducing the reliability of the assemblage.

Late medieval period (mid-14th to the late 15th century)

As can be seen from Table 8.5 many of the assemblages from the late medieval period were limited, producing only a small number of bones. Though these assemblages should be considered unreliable individually, they occasionally serve to reinforce the pattern of livestock economies for the various *pays* noted for the middle medieval period (*e.g.* sheep on the West Sussex Coastal Plain, cattle and pigs on the Greensand Ridge).

Of a more reliable nature was the combined assemblage of two urban sites on the Coastal Plain. This was largely derived from excavations at the former Shippham's Factory, Chichester (2,259 fragments; Taylor forthcoming). The large joint assemblage once again showed the importance of sheep within the *pay* with numbers well above the post-Conquest national average (39%; Sykes 2009, fig. 17.1). Numbers of cattle equalled the national average (43%; *ibid.*), perhaps indicating the increased importance of beef to the diet during the late medieval period.

TABLE 8.5: Summary of late medieval bones of the three major domesticates from each of the pays within the study area grouped by sites of different social status

	Settlement type	No. assemblage ()= assem. >100+	Total frags	Cattle nos	%	Sheep nos	%	Pig nos	%	Total
Coastal Plain	towns	2 (1)	2296	1072	47	989	43	235	10	2296
	monastic	0	0							
	castle	0	0							
	manorial	0	0							
	rural	1 (0)	15	2	13	10	67	3	20	15
Greensand Ridge	towns	1 (0)	21	13	62	8	38			21
	monastic	0	0							
	castle	0	0							
	manorial	0	0							
	rural	1 (0)	19	4	21	5	26	10	53	19
High Weald	towns	3 (2)	21	110	41	49	18	112	41	271
	monastic	1 (1)	164	54	33	45	27	65	40	164
	castle	0	0							
	manorial	0	0							
	rural	0	0							
Low Weald	towns	4 (1)	165	89	54	53	32	23	14	165
	monastic	0	0							
	castle	0	0							
	manorial	0	0							
	rural	0	0							
North Downs	towns	0	0							
	monastic	0	0							
	castle	1 (1)	387	149	38	96	25	142	37	387
	manorial	0	0							
	rural	0	0							
North Kent Plain	towns	1 (1)	204	78	38	98	48	28	14	204
	monastic	0	0							
	castle	0	0							
	manorial	0	0							
	rural	0	0							
Pevensey Levels	towns	0	0							
	monastic	0	0							
	castle	1 (1)	576	133	23	264	46	179	31	576
	manorial	0	0							
	rural	0	0							

(Continued)

TABLE 8.5: *(Continued)*

	Settlement type	No. assemblage ()= assem. >100+	Total frags	Cattle nos	%	Sheep nos	%	Pig nos	%	Total
Romney Marsh	towns	1 (1)	1241	835	67	320	26	86	7	1241
	monastic	0	0							
	castle	0	0							
	manorial	0	0							
	rural	1 (1)	708	293	41	241	34	174	25	708
South Downs	towns	1 (0)	68	36	53	20	29	12	18	68
	monastic	0	0							
	castle	0	0							
	manorial	0	0							
	rural	1 (0)	31	12	39	12	39	7	22	31
Thames Basin	towns	1 (1)	217	111	51	67	31	39	18	217
	monastic	0	0							
	castle	0	0							
	manorial	1 (1)	652	419	64	122	19	111	17	652
	rural	0	0							

Within the High Weald the significance of pigs appears to continue on urban sites with numbers far in excess of the post-Conquest national average. Though the traditional management of swine through the outlying pannage system is thought to have been in severe decline by this date, pigs were an important part of the late medieval townscape. Indeed, their ability to live on kitchen scraps and within small enclosed spaces makes them particularly suited to urban environments. Whilst cattle and sheep would have been brought to town on the hoof, a large proportion of swine remains recovered from late medieval urban sites were likely derived from animals raised locally in backyard plots and gardens. The high frequencies of swine found on the High Weald's urban sites may be linked to the status of those living in the settlements. Though the population of towns in the High Weald was swelled by low-status craftworkers and wage labourers in the late 13th and 14th centuries the demographic had begun to reverse by the 1370s. Population decline led to the creation of larger urban plots occupied by free tenants and an emerging mercantile class (see Gardiner 1995). By the end of the medieval period the consumption of pork amongst those higher up the social scale appears to have been in decline. Conversely, the meat's valuable fat content, ease of preservation and relative low cost of production encouraged pig keeping amongst the urban lower classes (Albarella 2006, 72–74; Jørgensen 2013, 431). This said, the frequency of pig remains found within the urban assemblage of the High Weald far outweighs what would be expected from a town of this date within much of the rest of

England. This was a time when the relative consumption of pork was low, having been steadily falling since the Norman Conquest (Albarella 2006, 74). Despite the importance of pigs raised in towns it is likely to have been the immediate rural hinterland that would have provided the majority of the livestock consumed at the urban sites.

Though monastic sites may not be reliable indicators of local conditions, the importance of pigs to the High Weald would also seem to be demonstrated by the late medieval monastic assemblage from Battle Abbey (Hare 1985; 164 fragments). Here, swine dominated the identifiable bones (7% above the post-Conquest national average), however, cattle also appear to have played an important role, the numbers being slightly larger (33%) than the post-Conquest average for elite ecclesiastical sites (32%; Sykes 2009, fig. 17.1). Though the importance of bovines in the urban assemblage was dwarfed by the numbers of pig, cattle dominated the bones recovered from Battle's Jenner and Simpson Mill site (65% of the total 106 fragments; James 2008). The implication of the town's monastic and urban evidence is that although pigs were an important part of the local livestock economy, cattle pasturing was perhaps equally significant within the wider area. Indeed, the high numbers of pigs found within the urban assemblage for the *pay* may be slightly misleading. Most of the identifiable pig fragments (85%) came from just one site; Tonbridge Stock and Cattle Market (Swift and Blackmore 2010).

The suitability of the Wealden interior for pig and cattle rearing also seems to have extended to the Low Weald clay lands. The combined late medieval assemblages from the towns of Crawley and Horsham (Stevenson 2003; Stevens 2008; 2010; Grant-Reis 2019) surpass the post-Conquest national average for cattle and equal the average for pig. In comparison to the preceding period the numbers may mark an increase in the relative proportion of cattle and a drop in the keeping of pigs. The importance of cattle during medieval times is also reflected in town assemblages from Romney Marsh, and the Thames Basin. The latter should be no surprise given the area's middle medieval results; however, Romney Marsh has been traditionally seen as sheep country. The assemblage from just one site at St Thomas Primary School, Winchelsea (James and Barber 2004) was dominated by cattle at 67% of the reasonably large assemblage (1,241 fragments). This may reflect the increased importance of beef in the diet during the late medieval period but may also be indicative of the town of New Winchelsea's geographical position. It lies on the border between the Low Weald and the marsh proper and the results may demonstrate that at this date the community was drawing its food from its Wealden hinterland rather than the nearby coastal wetlands. It may be that catastrophic floods of the later medieval period and French raids of the 14th century were disruptive to agricultural activity within the marsh. It could also be the case that Winchelsea's location also meant that it was effectively cut-off from eastward trade by the Rother estuary (Martin and Martin 2004, 25). It was the Benedictine abbey at Battle that was one of the town's principal trading partners (*ibid.*).

This said, a bone assemblage from the combined rural sites of Lydd Quarry (Barber and Priestley-Bell 2008; 708 fragments) also indicated that a wholly sheep-orientated industry may not have been the case on the marsh during the late medieval period. The frequencies of cattle and pig bones were above the post-Conquest national average with sheep actually trailing Syke's (2009, fig. 17.1) national average by 12%. Though this may reflect some reorientation of agriculture and use of reclaimed land rather than saltmarsh and waste during the period, we should be wary of drawing too many conclusions from small numbers of bone assemblages.

The importance of sheep appears to have continued within the town of Canterbury during the mid-14th to the late 15th century. At 1–7 New Dover Road (Stevens 2013; 204 fragments) the animals dominated the assemblage, while pigs were also reasonably important equalling the post-Conquest national average for urban sites. At the secular elite site of Woking Palace, in the Thames Basin (Poulton 2015; 652 fragments), however, the continued importance of cattle in this *pay* was clear. The good-sized assemblage was dominated by cattle at 64%, whilst the numbers of sheep and pig were rather poor.

8.4 Discussion and conclusions

In the opening chapters (Chapters 1–3) it was made clear how examination of documentary evidence and a traditional bias in study towards certain landscapes of the South-East has dominated perception of the medieval livestock economy of the area. The region has been consistently seen as either sheep or pig country, with the former being pastured on the iconic chalkland hills and the latter within the wooded vastness of the Weald. Whilst examination of the animal bone data has reaffirmed some of these assumptions, it has also served to clarify the importance of cattle within the medieval agriculture of the region. It appears that there was significant regionalisation in animal husbandry, with particular soils and topographies being more suited to the keeping of certain livestock types. What is most apparent was the distinct ubiquity of pigs amongst the livestock economies of the particular *pays*. While they seldom formed the most important domestic species, they were often the key secondary livestock throughout the area. Though the data was limited, the keeping of swine appears to have been more important to 6th and 7th century communities than the pasturing of sheep. The use of the Weald as a seasonal pastoral resource may have been key to the high numbers of pigs that were kept throughout the region, and this was made clear in the high numbers of these animals that were found on sites that lay close to the Weald (particularly on the Greensand). Beyond the woodlands of the South-East, urban environments and reclaimed marshlands also appear to have been important locations for the keeping or consumption of swine.

In contrast to the universal keeping of pigs, the numbers of sheep or cattle dominated the regional livestock economies to greater or lesser extents. These divergences appear to be inextricably linked to underlying environmental

TABLE 8.6: Summary of late medieval bones of the three major domesticates from sites of different social status from each of the pays within the study area

Settlement type	No. assemblage ()= assem. >100+	Total frags	Cattle		Ave. of ave.	Sheep		Ave. of ave.	Pig		Ave. of ave.
			nos	%		nos	%		nos	%	
Towns											
Coastal Plain	2 (1)	2296	1072	47	46	989	43	43	235	10	10
Greensand Ridge	1 (0)	21	13	62	–	8	38	–	0	0	–
High Weald	3 (2)	21	110	41	41	49	18	17	112	41	42
Low Weald	4 (1)	165	89	54	54	53	32	32	23	14	14
North Downs	0	0	0	0	0	0	0	0	0	0	0
North Kent Plain	1 (1)	204	78	38	38	98	48	48	28	14	14
Pevensey Levels	0	0	0	0	0	0	0	0	0	0	0
Romney Marsh	1 (1)	1241	835	66	67	320	26	26	86	8	7
South Downs	1 (0)	68	36	53	–	20	29	–	12	18	–
Thames Basin	1 (1)	217	111	51	51	67	31	31	39	18	18
Totals	**14 (7)**	**4233**	**2344**	**55**	**50**	**1604**	**38**	**33**	**535**	**13**	**17**
Monastic sites											
Coastal Plain	0	0	0	0	0	0	0	0	0	0	0
Greensand Ridge	0	0	0	0	0	0	0	0	0	0	0
High Weald	1 (1)	164	54	33	33	45	27	27	65	40	40
Low Weald	0	0	0	0	0	0	0	0	0	0	0
North Downs	0	0	0	0	0	0	0	0	0	0	0
North Kent Plain	0	0	0	0	0	0	0	0	0	0	0
Pevensey Levels	0	0	0	0	0	0	0	0	0	0	0
Romney Marsh	0	0	0	0	0	0	0	0	0	0	0
South Downs	0	0	0	0	0	0	0	0	0	0	0
Thames Basin	0	0	0	0	0	0	0	0	0	0	0
Totals	**1 (1)**	**164**	**54**	**33**	**33**	**45**	**27**	**27**	**65**	**40**	**40**
Castles											
Coastal Plain	0	0	0	0	0	0	0	0	0	0	0
Greensand Ridge	0	0	0	0	0	0	0	0	0	0	0
High Weald	0	0	0	0	0	0	0	0	0	0	0
Low Weald	0	0	0	0	0	0	0	0	0	0	0
North Downs	1 (1)	387	149	38	38	96	25	25	142	37	37
North Kent Plain	0	0	0	0	0	0	0	0	0	0	0
Pevensey Levels	1 (1)	576	133	23	23	264	46	46	179	31	31
Romney Marsh	0	0	0	0	0	0	0	0	0	0	0
South Downs	0	0	0	0	0	0	0	0	0	0	0
Thames Basin	0	0	0	0	0	0	0	0	0	0	0
Totals	**2 (2)**	**963**	**282**	**29**	**30.5**	**360**	**37**	**35.5**	**321**	**33**	**34**

(Continued)

TABLE 8.6: *(Continued)*

Settlement type	No. assemblage ()= assem. >100+	Total frags	Cattle		Ave. of ave.	Sheep		Ave. of ave.	Pig		Ave. of ave.
			nos	%		nos	%		nos	%	
Manorial sites											
Coastal Plain	0	0	0	0	0	0	0	0	0	0	0
Greensand Ridge	0	0	0	0	0	0	0	0	0	0	0
High Weald	0	0	0	0	0	0	0	0	0	0	0
Low Weald	0	0	0	0	0	0	0	0	0	0	0
North Downs	0	0	0	0	0	0	0	0	0	0	0
North Kent Plain	0	0	0	0	0	0	0	0	0	0	0
Pevensey Levels	0	0	0	0	0	0	0	0	0	0	0
Romney Marsh	0	0	0	0	0	0	0	0	0	0	0
South Downs	0	0	0	0	0	0	0	0	0	0	0
Thames Basin	1 (1)	652	419	64	64	122	19	19	111	17	17
Totals	**1 (1)**	**652**	**419**	**64**	**64**	**122**	**19**	**19**	**111**	**17**	**17**
Non-manorial rural settlements											
Coastal Plain	1 (0)	15	2	13	–	10	67	–	3	20	–
Greensand Ridge	1 (0)	19	4	21	–	5	26	–	10	53	–
High Weald	0	0	0	0	0	0	0	0	0	0	0
Low Weald	0	0	0	0	0	0	0	0	0	0	0
North Downs	0	0	0	0	0	0	0	0	0	0	0
North Kent Plain	0	0	0	0	0	0	0	0	0	0	0
Pevensey Levels	0	0	0	0	0	0	0	0	0	0	0
Romney Marsh	1 (1)	708	293	41	41	241	34	34	174	25	25
South Downs	1 (0)	31	12	39	–	12	39	–	7	22	–
Thames Basin	0	0	0	0	0	0	0	0	0	0	0
Totals	**4 (1)**	**773**	**311**	**40**	**41**	**268**	**35**	**34**	**194**	**25**	**25**

factors, which, despite not dictating the keeping of certain livestock types, nonetheless influenced medieval husbandry choices. Thus the marshland landscapes of the Pevensey Levels, Romney Marsh and parts of the North Kent Plain were exploited for their suitability for sheep, while the poor, heathy soils of the Greensand Ridge, High Weald and Thames Basin encouraged the keeping of cattle. Within the data it is easy to perceive that the dry, light soils of the Coastal Plain, North and South Downs were extensively used for the pasturing of sheep, whilst the well-watered, heavy clay lands of the Low Weald were considered cattle country. Exceptions to these rules were sometimes encountered and it is clear that certain localised environments gave rise to livestock economies that were not typical for the wider area. The most conspicuous example of this was the use of South Downs river valleys for the keeping of cattle in contrast to the sheep walk that dominated much of the rest of the *pay*. Of further interest are examples of changing husbandry choices; in Romney Marsh this was likely to have been linked to the medieval modification of the landscape, as larger areas of marshland were reclaimed a switch in emphasis may have occurred from sheep to cattle. This was possibly short-lived trend as by the post-medieval period the area would once again be famous for its sheep husbandry.

From the examination of animal bone assemblages, it is possible to suggest that cattle were an important livestock species throughout the South-East, but particularly so in certain landscapes. Plate 8.1 shows the *pays* dominated by particular domesticates in the middle medieval period. In the light of the above discussion this should not be considered a definitive map of the importance of livestock types, although when considering documentary and other evidence it does give a reasonably accurate picture of where cattle as opposed to sheep country lay. Unfortunately, similar mapping could not be produced for the earliest and late medieval South-East as the combined assemblages for particular *pays* were often not statistically reliable. What this figure serves to emphasise is how important cattle were in terms of the geographical area covered. It is the core area of the Weald and those lands that bordered the Thames Valley where cattle were favoured. Sheep dominated a much smaller land mass, although these areas have been historically considered to be amongst the most densely settled and economically advanced within the region. This contrast between landscapes utilised for sheep as opposed to cattle was so stark that livestock specialisation can be suspected and, when combined with other evidence (*e.g.* documentary; Chapter 3), sometimes even cautiously discerned (*e.g.* the manor of Stretham near Henfield). It is certain that during the medieval period sheep and cattle ranches (*Vaccaria* and *Beccaria*) existed within the counties of the South-East and during the following chapter we shall explore the likely form of a vaccary establishment.

CHAPTER 9

Wealden case studies:
the Hayworth and Wickhurst

9.1 Introduction

> They in their times have not known any other claim, to take of right any profits,
> within the waste aforesaid, but only the lord of Trubwicke their tenants, except
> waifs, strayes and that the tenants only, have common of pasture there and none
> other, and this they have heard their ancestors and forefathers say also, and this as
> they think it, has been used out of time of mind. (Taken from a dispute with the
> Barony of Lewes over common rights; BL Add. MS 5684)

The preceding sections have shown that within the South-East certain
landscapes are more suited to the pasturing of cattle than others. Documentary
place-name and archaeological evidence has highlighted that the Weald should
be considered as a stock-rearing region, and although the pannage of swine was
an important factor in the livestock economy of the area, the keeping of cattle
should be considered of at least equal importance to the keeping of pigs. This
is due to the additional effects their husbandry had on the area's settlement
evolution, nomenclature and landscape formation. Over the coming chapter we
shall explore two recently published sites from the author's own work (Margetts
2017; 2018a). The evidence concerns Wealden seasonal settlement, as well as
the traditions of early medieval outpasture and transhumance. The work will
illustrate the transition from seasonal woodland pastures to permanent manorial
establishments held in severalty and the form of a specialised vaccary complex
will be established.

The work presented here concerns two sites on the boundary between the
Low and High Weald. The first of these, the Hayworth, comprised a ring-
fenced farm of probable early type located in the historic parish of Cuckfield,
West Sussex. Along with the holdings of Bolnore and Wigperry, this comprised
part of the manor of Trubwick, a onetime subsidiary holding and 'outlier' of
the manor of Plumpton Boscage (Salzman 1940, 159). The medieval manor of
Trubwick was created by subinfeudation from Plumpton sometime between the
10th and mid-13th centuries. This fits with Everitt's (1986, 55) fourth stage of
medieval Wealden development – a time when post-Conquest farms bore the
names of their early owners. Despite the lack of bone survival, the archaeological
remains clearly relate to a farm that dealt with livestock. To date it possibly
represents the most completely excavated vaccary yet known, and certainly the
most intensively investigated example from lowland Britain.

The second archaeological site comprised Wickhurst Green, the developer's name for a large-scale residential scheme south of the village of Broadbridge Heath and west of the town of Horsham, West Sussex. It encompassed over 46 ha of investigation, resulting in 14 ha of land stripped to the archaeological horizon. To date the excavation represents the largest single archaeological investigation conducted within the Weald of West Sussex. The work took place on areas of farmland (mainly laid to pasture) that sloped gently down to the River Arun in the south and Boldings Brook in the east. The farmland was divided by mature hedgerows, many of which proved to be ancient in character. The site was situated at *c.* 30–35 m OD. To the south-east, beyond the site boundary, a prominent hill, High Wood, reaches a height of *c.* 58 m OD.

Areas of land to the north (Broadbridge Heath) and south of the site (High Wood and parts of the River Arun) lay within detached portions of Sullington parish, remaining so until 1878 when they were transferred to Horsham parish (Hudson 1986, 129). Like Plumpton above, Sullington lies on the fertile Sussex Spring-line situated at the foot of the South Downs scarp. The north–south-aligned roads, tracks and footpaths in the area were probably formed by at least the 8th century due to their suitability for seasonal pastoral usage reflected in Anglo-Saxon charters and place-name evidence.

The additional significance of the sites is signalled by their association with place-names indicative of Anglo-Saxon pastoral origins that contain Old English elements such as *wic* (Chapter 4; *P.N.E.* 1956b, 257), *worð* 'an enclosure' (*ibid.*, 273) and possibly *haga* 'a hedge, an enclosure' (*P.N.E.* 1956a, 221). These may point to the longevity of medieval livestock husbandry, both at these sites and within the Wealden region. The recovery of important palaeo-environmental remains also aids understanding of the pastoral exploitation and medieval modification of the region's woodlands.

9.2 Case study 1: the Hayworth

The Hayworth 7th to 11th century

The Hayworth excavation was located within an oval enclosure of ancient origin – postulated by local historian Heather Warne (2009) to be part of the holdings of Earl Godwin during the early 11th century. It is likely that the site existed within a unit of farmed land by the reign of Edward the Confessor (AD 1042–66; *ibid.*), and the boundaries of this oval can easily be traced on Nicholas Hardham's estate map of 1638 (Figure 9.1). The lanes that encircle 'the Hayworthe' are here named 'Halfe Streete' and 'Kinges Highwaye' and are little changed from the late medieval period. The lane that marks the oval's southern boundary also serves to separate the parishes of Cuckfield and Keymer, a detail that further corroborates the enclosure's antiquity. The site at Bolnore shows interesting similarities to that at Broadbridge Heath in that both are clearly associated with droveways, as well as oval enclosures and open areas of grazing.

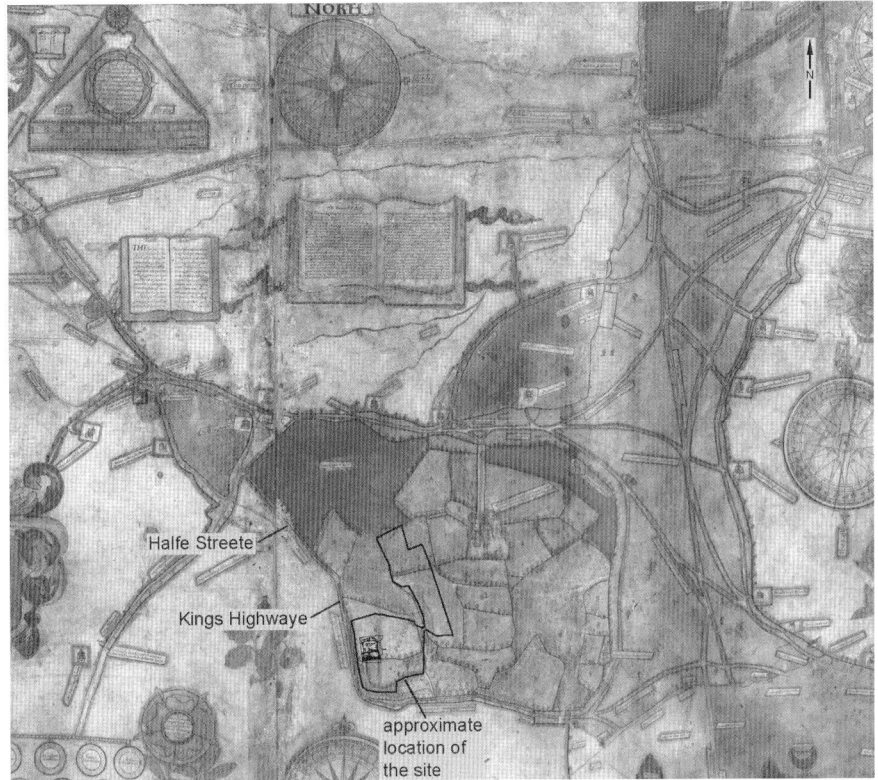

FIGURE 9.1: Nicholas Hardham Estate map, dated 1638 (WSRO Add. MS 28, 784; by F. Griffin. © Archaeology South-East, UCL).

As mentioned within Chapter 4, place-names incorporating Old English elements have the potential to illuminate early medieval settlement and land-use. Figure 9.2 shows the likely extent of the manor of Trubwick alongside what would later become the freeholds (and, in the case of Hayworth and Bolnore, manors) that descended from this territory. Trubwick itself (*Trubewica* AD 1166, *Trubwic* AD 1199) probably derives from an amalgamation of an Old English personal name *Trubba* (a possible pet form of *Trumbeorht* or *Trumbeald*) and the element *wic* (*P.N.Sx* 1929, 269; see section 4.6). Perhaps the most significant connotation of the name in a Wealden context is that concerned with dairying. This is more likely to have been associated with cows rather than sheep, which (as explained elsewhere, see sections 3.10 and 4.6) were not suited to the Weald's environment.

Haywards (*Heyworth* AD 1261, *Hayworth(e)* AD 1276) is a compound of Old English *worð* ('an enclosure') and *hege* ('a hedge, a fence') or *hēg* ('hay, mowing grass'; *P.N.Sx* 1929, 268). The name essentially means hedged enclosure (*P.N.E.* 1956b, 274–75; Glover 1975, 74) and therefore consideration of the similar element *haga* is prudent. This may derive from the same Primitive Germanic root word as *hege* (*P.N.E.* 1956a, 221, 222), and has been well studied by Hooke (1989, 123–25), who has viewed these names as a strongly fenced enclosures, enclosed woods often with royal associations, early game preserves or even

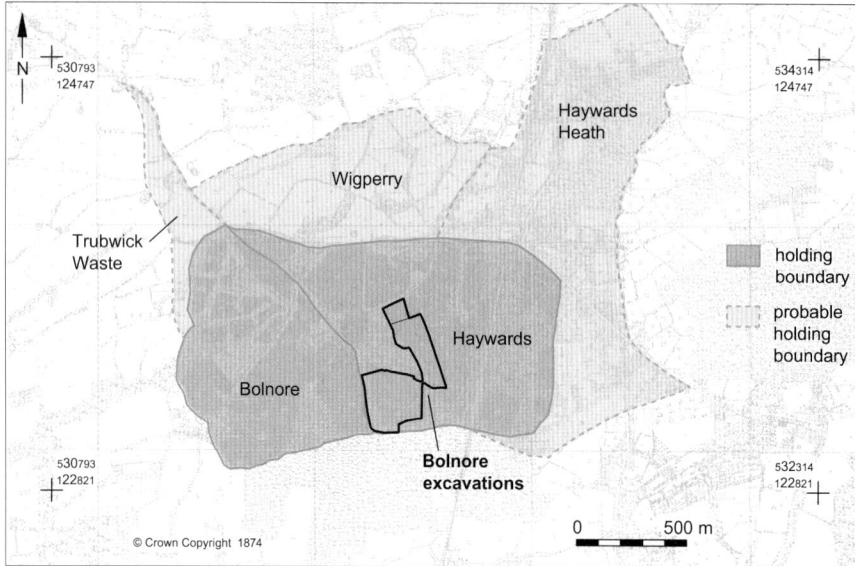

FIGURE 9.2: Plan showing the likely extent of the manor of Trubwick: and later freeholds and areas of 'waste' (by F. Griffin. © Archaeology South-East, UCL)

fortified settlements (*ibid.*). These connotations are seen by Everitt (1986, 142–43) as unlikely for a Wealden context – the names being a more likely reference to enclosed pasture with the *worð* element perhaps indicating an enclosure for stock. To Faith (2006), the 'worthys' of Devon (derived from name elements related to *worð*), were an early and distinctive type of farm, distinguished by curving boundary banks and apparently established in uncontested open landscapes (see Chapter 6).

The final two names associated with the territory of Trubwick are Bolnore (*Bulnore* AD 1559) and Wigperry (*Wyggepyrye* AD 1296, *Wygepirie* AD 1298). The former contains the Old English element *ōra*, which is understood to mean 'a border, a margin, a bank, an edge' (*P.N.E.* 1956b, 55) and often referred to features in the landscape which acted as markers for travellers (Gelling and Cole 2000, 203–05). The name may show that a dairy farm at Trubwick was associated with cattle, as it could be derived from 'bull's bank' or possibly from an Old English personal name, *i.e. Bula* (*P.N.Sx* 1929, 262). Wigperry may mean '*Wicga's* pear tree' (*ibid.*, 269).

Trubwick is known to be a detached Wealden outlier of the manor of Plumpton/Plumpton Boscage (Salzman 1940, 159; Warne 2009). As such, Trubwick would have operated within the system of seasonal transhumance known to be prevalent within the Weald during the early medieval period. The date to which the system of outpasture derives is not entirely understood and has been recognised as an important topic for further study. The Hayworth's nature as one of these detached seasonal pastures, similar to the Kentish 'denns', indicates that it would have been linked to its parent settlement by a droveway. A candidate for this route can be found in an existing sunken lane that passes close to the south and west of the site. This feature, is named as

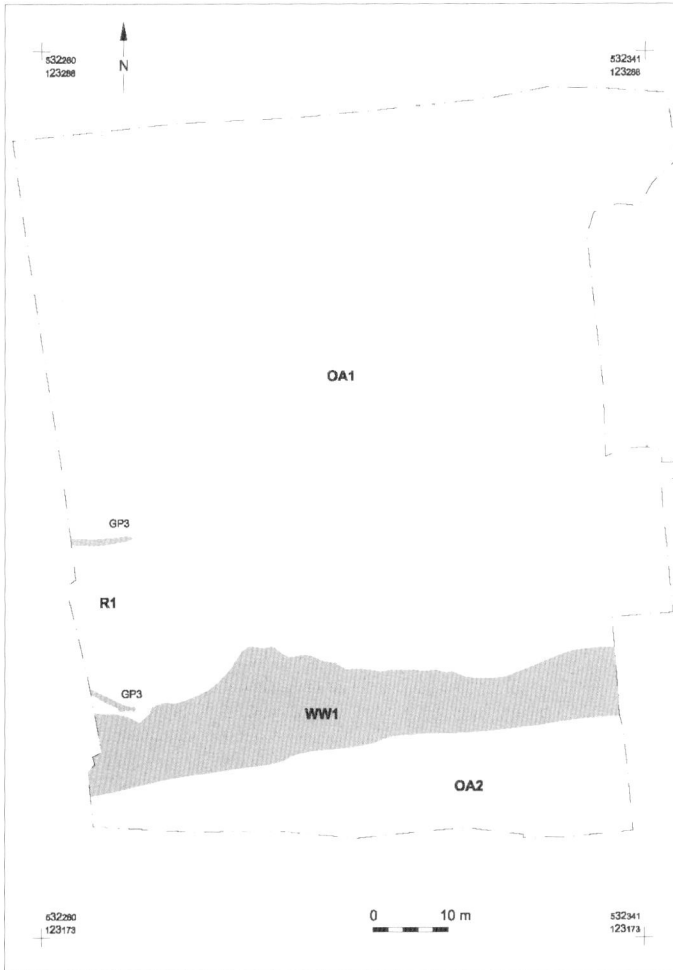

'Halfe Streete' and 'Kinges Highwaye' in 1638 (Figure 9.1). Further trackways and hedges on the northern and eastern sides indicate an oval-shaped enclosure adjacent to the open 'Haywards Heath'. Two documents referring to a King's Highway at Plumpton, dated 1639 and 1739 respectively (WSRO LYTTON/ MSS/472; ESRO SAS-N/217), may suggest the route of the current B2112 and Plumpton Lane as the most likely course linking the parent (Plumpton) with its Wealden outlier (Trubwick).

The three later freeholds of Hayworth, Bolnore and Wigperry were probably not the only portions of land that belonged to the later medieval manor of Trubwick, which clearly had its origins in the early medieval period. Areas of waste recorded on Nicholas Hardham's map were also likely parts of the manor. The waste of Trubwick was described as an elongated area of predominantly roadside waste was said to end at the Hatchgate (WSRO Add. MS 28, 784), the name of which comprises two elements that have been frequently linked with droveways and pastoral activity (Everitt 1986, 130–31).

The 'Hatchgate' name is preserved in a modern farm. The waste of 'Haywards Hoth' is also recorded, and would have been utilised as an area of unenclosed pasture where the lords of Trubwick had rights of common (BL Add. MS 5684; Salzman 1940, 160).

As well as droveways and waste, another feature of the Sussex Weald is clear arc-shaped, or sub-oval boundaries of which the Hayworth and Bolnore appear to be examples (see Chapter 6). This category of enclosure has been shown to have clear place-name associations (*i.e. wic* and *fold/falod*) and those containing the '*wic*' name element are most likely to have been linked with dairying (Chapter 6).

Period 1, phase 1: 11th century (Figure 9.3)

Following the Norman Conquest, the manor of Plumpton, as well as much of the land in the vicinity of the site, was given to William Warenne (Lord of the Rape of Lewes). Fieldwork showed that during the same century the site comprised two open areas (OA1 and OA2; Figure 9.3; probably utilised as pasture or wood-pasture) divided by a stream. Ditches of a driftway or track dated by pottery (GP 3; R1) were encountered projecting into an area north of the watercourse (WW1). These features continued beyond the western limit of the excavation probably linking with the adjacent droveway 'Halfe Streete Lane'. The watercourse was sampled for pollen analysis and radiocarbon dating. The minerogenic component comprised fine sand indicating influxes of sediment, possibly as surface run off from cleared land. The dating suggests accumulation was occurring between AD 658 and 1028, at least at the location sampled.

Period 1, phase 2: 12th century
(Figures 9.4 and 9.5)

During the 12th century there was a significant increase in activity. This related predominantly to the creation of a farmstead that included features related to livestock management, and the erection of buildings and features

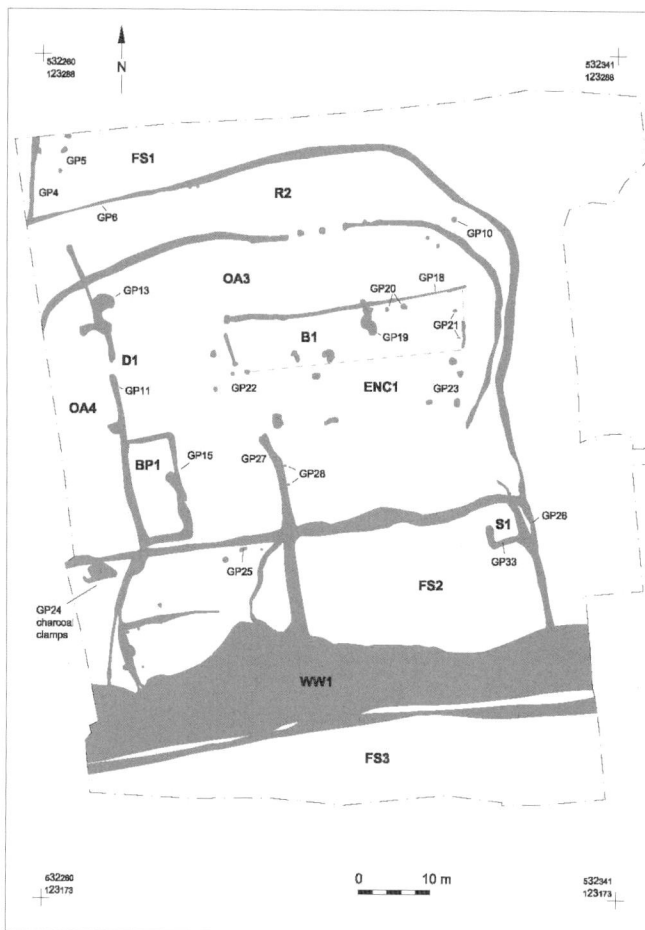

FIGURE 9.4: Period 1, phase 2 (12th century), plan of excavated features (by F. Griffin. © Archaeology South-East, UCL)

related to drainage and enclosure. The 11th-century open or wood-pasture, north of the watercourse, was converted into a field system (FS1) by means of a roughly N/S ditch and associated fence line. FS1 was orientated in relation to two parallel curvilinear ditches with associated fence lines (GP 6; R2). The feature was interpreted as a driftway or cattle race, presumably associated with the droveway to the west of the site. The narrowing to the southeast of this feature (although obscured by later recutting) may be interpreted as a cattle crush. Comparisons with modern cattle races show how a curving route was beneficial for controlled and safe livestock movement, and both races and crushes have similar dimensions to the medieval example found here.

The remains of a large building were recorded in the northern part of the site (B1) (Figure 9.4). This structure was clearly sited as the main focus of the farmstead and was positioned to take advantage of the free-draining and hardstanding properties of an underlying sandstone outcrop. The building was of two parts separated by a partition and was comprised of three lengths of foundation cut for sill walls, often terminating in substantial postholes. A lack of structural evidence on the southern side is thought to represent an open front.

Fragmentary remains of possible drystone sill walls were encountered in the base of some of the structural cuts, and pottery of 12th- and 13th-century date was retrieved from their fills. A group of postholes (GP 23) encountered to the south of the building are thought to represent a fenced exterior 'straw yard' or forstal for the cattle (ENC1; see Chapter 4).

The evidence for a second 12th-century building comprised a rectangular space devoid of features apart from a disturbed deposit of sandstone construction materials (BP1). It is presumed that little below-ground evidence of the building existed and that it was largely built upon (dry) sandstone sill walls. Finds collected from the ditches forming the enclosure included 102 sherds derived from 20 different cooking pots and a single lamp. The presence of the pottery, lamp and cooking waste indicates that the building plot comprised a dwelling. The structure and surrounding ditches fell out of use before the end of the 12th century.

A single pollen sample was recovered from a layer of 12th-century refuse and redeposited natural within the watercourse (WW1). This material was charcoal rich and suggested a period of ground consolidation achieved by depositing waste material and clay within what would have been the almost infilled stream channel. It may relate to an attempt to ford the watercourse or create a gentle, safe incline for livestock. The pollen indicated a range of taxa including wetland tree species and cereal pollen.

Period 1, phase 3: 13th century
(Figures 9.6 and 9.7)

It is largely in the 13th century when documentary evidence relating to the immediate environs of the site either begins to be produced or survives. We first learn of a John de Trobewyk who was holding a messuage and land in '*Trobewyk and Haywothe*' in 1276 (Salzman 1940, 159). A Philip of Hayworth is cited in 1265 and a Thomas of Eywrth in 1266, as suitors to the barony of Lewes court. Philip is mentioned along with a John of Bolenhore as 'pledges' for a William Winkpirie in relation to a court summons (Taylor 1940, 2). As suitors to the court, the summoned parties may be viewed as neighbours and freeholders whose lands (Hayworth, Bolnore and Wigperry) would have formed the major landholdings of the manor of Trubwick (Warne 2009, 4–7). The Trubwick and Hayworth families are mentioned in documentary evidence throughout the 13th century. The Trubwicks represented the overlords of the manor, with the Hayworths as freeholders. By AD 1358 only the Hayworths are named in accounts, the manor of Trubwick having fallen into their possession (*ibid.*, 6–8).

The 13th century is largely a story of adaptation of the existing farmstead. Ditches were remodelled or fell out of use and new buildings and enclosures were laid out. It is probable that the field-scape of the Hayworth created in the preceding phase (or earlier) continued in use during the 13th century, attested by a small number of 13th-century sherds of sand-tempered cooking pot from one of the associated ditches. During this phase, remodelling of the 12th-century driftway (R2) took place. Significant recutting of the outermost ditch occurred along its

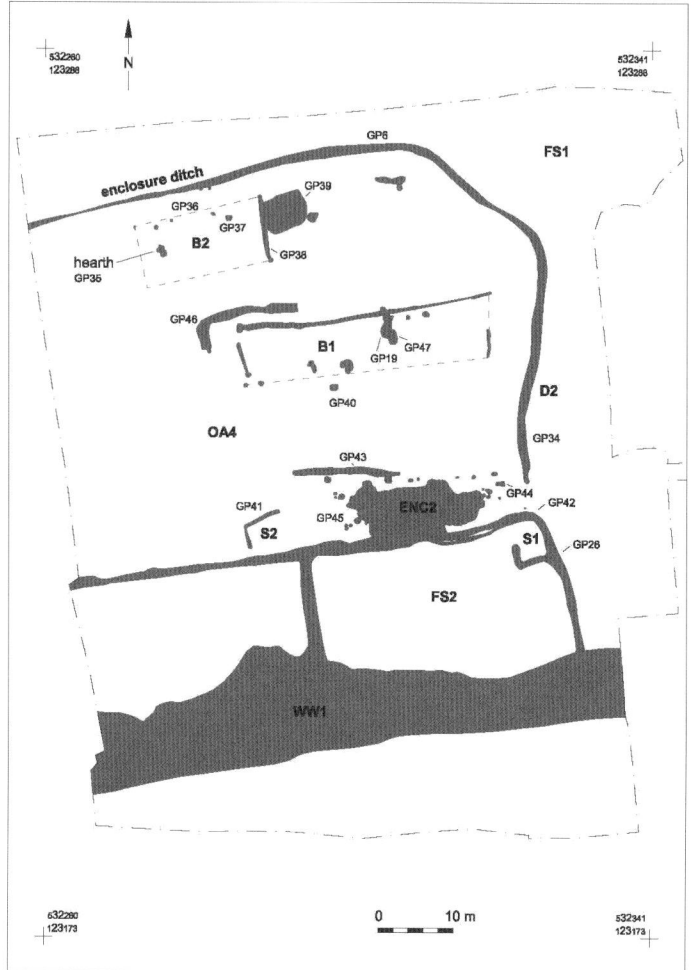

FIGURE 9.6: Period 1, phase 3 (13th century), plan of excavated features (by F. Griffin. © Archaeology South-East, UCL)

central portion, converting this feature into a fenced enclosure for the farmyard (D2; GP 34).

The main 12th-century area of the farm complex (OA4) was significantly expanded and earlier ditches were decommissioned. Dwelling (BP1) was replaced by a new structure (B2; see below). The larger (open-fronted) building (B1) continued in use, although there is a possibility that by the 13th century the eastern half of the structure may have fallen into disrepair. A pit situated close to the building contained fragmented cattle teeth as well as charcoal flecks, fired clay and 13th-century pottery.

Overlying the infilled southerly driftway ditch of R2 was a large sandstone and clay hearth (GP 35). Much *in situ* burning was recorded and the underlying clay was fire-reddened but produced little charcoal or charred macrobotanicals. Some 13th-century pottery and a single spherical hammerscale were collected from the fabric of the hearth along with chunks of fired clay and pieces of briquetage.

FIGURE 9.7: Period 1, phase 3 (13th century), reconstruction (source: author. © Archaeology South-East, UCL)

Situated close by a number of features were thought to be the partial remains of a structure associated with the hearth (B2).

The depositional processes at work in the southern half of the site changed during this phase to that of colluvial accumulation. The pollen indicates a more open grassland landscape at this stage, with occurrences of weeds and cereal in the record. The minerogenic nature of the colluvium is probably due to overall clearance of woodland in the immediate vicinity of the site, causing destabilisation of hillslope soils.

The Hayworth: a discussion

Together, archaeological and place-name evidence suggest a seasonal pasture existed here from the 7th to 11th centuries. This appears to have comprised twin oval enclosures (the Hayworth and Bolnore) associated with a large area of open grazing (Haywards Heath). Knowledge of Wealden development gained through the work of landscape historians (Witney 1976; Everitt 1986) shows the region would have originally been intercommoned; however, by the 8th century when the Hayworth began to be cleared, 'sub-commons' belonging to individual estates were being created. This process, which has been further developed by Fox (2000) for 'wold/*wald*' landscapes, accords well with the early landscape changes encountered at the site. It appears that the oval enclosure of the Hayworth was progressively (but only partially) cleared of woodland, creating an environment in which beech with oak had become the co-dominant woodland species. By the onset of the 12th and 13th centuries, the presence of grassland and cereal pollen suggests a move to a more open, cultivated landscape.

Warne (2009) has convincingly identified the Hayworth as being part of the holdings of Godwin during the 11th century. It seems possible that the archaeological remains associated with Period 1.1 originated in the late Saxon period, and were related to seasonal woodland and/or pastoral exploitation under one of England's most prominent families. This was during a stage of Wealden settlement evolution when the older commons were being subdivided to create 'manorial dens' (Witney 1976, 78–103). The, albeit sparse, 11th-century evidence may attest to seasonal usage with herders taking their stock to a well-watered and enclosed pastoral reserve.

The Old English toponymic evidence associated with the site indicates that Anglo-Saxon usage was mainly concerned with the pasturing of cattle. The name element *wic* associated with Trubwick (*P.N.Sx* 1929, 269) suggests a dairy farm (*P.N.E.* 1956b, 257–63; Coates 1999, 32). Though Anglo-Saxon dairying often involved sheep, it is possible that the area surrounding the site was suited to the pasturing of cows, implied by the place-name Bolnore. That this husbandry was connected to a hedged oval enclosure similar to the 'worthys' described by Faith (2006) and highlighted in Somerset by Rippon (2002a) is striking, and this land parcel may represent an early intake from the Wealden forest in much the same way as similar features were 'inned' from marshlands (see Rippon 2000).

Analysis of the 11th-century pottery assemblage may, however, suggest that the earliest features at the site are more representative of the beginnings of Norman exploitation (under the Warennes), rather than an inherited Anglo-Saxon outlying pastoral system. The majority of pottery encountered throughout phase 1.1 is more indicative of a post-Conquest date, suggesting perhaps an intensification of activity as Anglo-Saxon models were exploited via Norman feudal land stewardship. Indeed, some 11th-century pottery was residual in 12th- and 13th-century features supporting 11th-century origins for the farm complex. The Hayworth at this time seems to have comprised a peripheral unit of farmed land, pre-dating the nucleated village and parochial centre of Cuckfield, built to serve it and other outlying farms. Such parish-edge settlements have been linked to the ancient pastoral origins of Anglo-Saxon and earlier Wealden colonisation (Everitt 1986, 144–55), and in the Hayworth we have the indirect ancestor of the post-medieval town of Haywards Heath.

Increased activity at the site during the 12th and 13th centuries, a period long considered a time of economic advancement and agricultural innovation, surely corresponds to the creation of a farmstead related to livestock management. The main components comprised buildings and a droveway with associated enclosures. The largest building is interpreted as an open-fronted structure built on drystone sill walls with upright posts along at least part of the open front. This structure is long (up to 34 m) and narrow, facing south onto a fenced yard. The building's size was facilitated by the 13th-century innovation of building on drystone sill walls, which permitted (in areas where suitable stone existed) far more substantial buildings to be constructed than earthfast posts had allowed (Dyer 1986, 35–36). Few similar structures have so far been excavated in south-eastern England, let alone the Weald. Due to the open frontage of the building, the unsuitability of local soils and the clear pastoral bias of the excavated features, the building is interpreted as an open-fronted animal shelter. The remaining buildings may relate to an attendant herd-keeper's dwelling or, in the case of B2, perhaps a detached kitchen, dairy or industrial area.

The nearest comparable site of a similar date, Faulkners Farm, Hartfield, Sussex, revealed that a part-dairy economy was in operation (Tebbutt 1981). Interpretation of features such as enclosures, animal pens, a driftway and waterholes at the Hayworth suggests an economy based on livestock. This may account for the siting of the farmstead on a south-facing slope, close to a recognised drove route (Kinges Highway/Halfe Street Lane) and water supply. Only limited faunal remains survive to indicate the type of livestock kept, the acidic clays of the Weald being non-conducive to the preservation of bone. Some horse and cattle teeth were found close to the animal shelter and although these confirm the occurrence of these species on site, the quantity is not adequate to suggest economy. The inland presence of briquetage (from B2 and WW1) could indicate utilisation as salt licks for stock (Barford 1990), or perhaps additional processing to incorporate the resultant salt in dairy production (*i.e.* butter and cheese) (Bridbury 1955, xv; Rippon 2000, 42).

During the 12th and 13th centuries England witnessed the development of the great sheep and cattle ranches, the *beccarie* and *vaccariae* so prevalent in contemporary documentation (Dyer 1995). The high frequencies of sharpening tools in the finds assemblage would be expected on a medieval site where sheep shearing took place and the open frontage of B1 made identification of the site as a beccary possible. Nevertheless, a pastoral economy based on sheep farming is unlikely for the Hayworth. The claylands of the Weald have historically been seen as unsuitable for the grazing of this livestock type, a picture that is reflected in early 14th-century records for the Cuckfield parish where no instances of them being kept were documented (Pelham 1934, 131). Medieval sheep rearing is far more often a feature of the southern downland and marshes (Gardiner 1999b, 38; Chapter 8). Cattle ranching and dairying are more likely for this site.

The principal building of vaccary enclosures must be viewed as the cow-house. Documentary studies show these (like sheep-houses) were of significant length, for example the structure recorded at Gatesgarth vaccary, Buttermere (built in AD 1282–83) measured 20.5 m long (Winchester 2003, 114). These buildings and the area of hay meadow and/or woodland were surrounded by an enclosure (Middle English *haya*; *ibid.*, 33). This could be formed of a bank (often probably hedged) and ditch, or in stone. The purpose of these enclosures was to accommodate cattle over winter as well as to protect winter fodder in the form of hay and browse. The areas of open grazing were intended as summer pasture and would be situated on poorer upland landscapes, often comprising Forest, Chase and waste (Winchester 2010). The Hayworth may be so named due to the presence of a hedge ringing its perimeter. The presence of haw and blackthorn within the environmental assemblage and associations with the Old English name element *haga* might imply these species formed a thorny hedge, beneficial in controlling livestock and a discouragement to would-be thieves, or wolves intent on preying on the herd.

The double oval field pattern indicated by the combination of the Bolnore oval together with the Hayworth itself (see Figure 9.2) can be compared with double oval field patterns associated with vaccaries in Lancashire noted by Atkin (1985; see sections 2.6 and 6.2). These sites also share a central watercourse that would have provided an important landscape feature for the watering of stock.

Together the evidence presented here suggests that the remains encountered during the Bolnore village development almost certainly relate to a rare example of a vaccary farm. As an outlier of the manor of Plumpton, Trubwick would have been, prior to its subinfeudation, part of Earl Warenne's forest demesne. The Warenne's lands were known to be associated with vaccaries in Yorkshire, where the manorial court rolls record:

> And the officers of these vaccaries were called Instauratores and did give their yearly accounts of the Revenues of the Cattell as the Graves did give of their rents at every Audicte to the Officers of the Earlewarrenne. (Baildon 1906, xxx)

Though not a true upland region on the scale of Yorkshire and the Pennines, the Weald was certainly considered a marginal zone in the medieval period. Indeed, it would be easy to perceive parts of its landscapes (such as Ashdown Forest) as functioning similarly to the moorland and fell of northern England. Like the vaccary lands of the north, the Weald was an area of dispersed settlement with a cultural history of seasonal exploitation. The manor of Trubwick shares remarkable similarities with the northern England vaccary sites. It clearly possesses the two major landscape elements required of such an establishment, that is an enclosed plot of wood and meadow, namely the Hayworth and an expanse of open grazing on the neighbouring waste of Haywards Heath.

Only the manorial tenants of Trubwick were known to have the right to pasture animals on the wooded heath in 1567 (BL Add. MS 5684). Ford and Gabe (1981, 8) presumed that the pastured livestock would have been cattle; however, it is likely that this was not the only area of extensive grazing that the manor of Trubwick had access to. The stock funnels and droveways associated with the Hayworth potentially allowed the movement of cattle not only to the heath but also to portions of common and park in Cuckfield, as well as to St Leonard's and Ashdown Forests. These large areas of Chase would have likely been exploited as summer agistment grounds and, following payment of a fee, the lords of Trubwick and Hayworth would have been able to graze their cattle. The landholders also may have been able to exercise common rights of pasture and herbage in these forests, although no records of any such rights attached to Trubwick have been encountered.

At the Hayworth, the cluster of buildings encountered on the site may represent the dwelling of the herd keeper or *vaccarii*, as well as the largest building, which probably relates to a cow-house. The farmstead clearly would have been a specialised part of the Hayworth. John de Trobewyk was holding a messuage and land in '*Trobewyk and Haywothe*' (Salzman 1940, 159) at the time the site was in operation and it has been postulated by Warne (2009, 19) that the manorial seat of Trubwick (and later the Hayworth) would have been

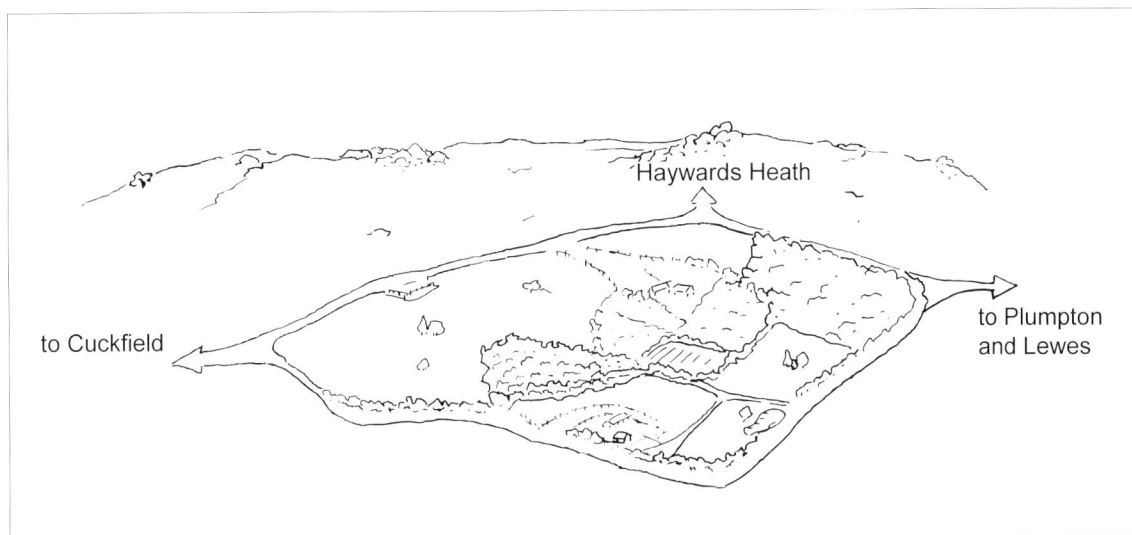

FIGURE 9.8:
Reconstruction of 'The
Hayworth', looking
north-east to Haywards
Heath (source: author.
© Archaeology South-
East, UCL)

situated at Great Haywards Farm. The small fields that represent an inner, oval core around this manorial seat (Figures 9.1 and 9.8) would probably have been utilised as the Hayworth's arable, meadow, gardens and convertible land. This may have been where the small quantities of cereal grains present at the site (including wheat, barley and possibly oat) were derived. The remaining areas outside of this 'infield' comprised a mixture of woodland, grassland pasture and wood-pasture, dominated by beech and oak, but with hedgerow species suggesting a more open habitat.

The interesting move towards a partially cleared, wooded environment where beech became the dominant species seems to have been the result of a progressive landscape change from the 7th century. Not only does this suggest development of early wooded environments (into landscapes more suitable for pastoral exploitation and therefore more permanent settlement), but also selection of tree species to aid the viability of these pastures. Acorns are known to be poisonous to cattle and a reduction in their numbers would obviously be beneficial on any pasture where cattle were kept. Beech foliage, on the other hand, can be an important fodder species, especially when forming *pollard hay* or as an early spring feed when grass is unavailable. That oak may have been deliberately reduced by the combined feeding of pigs and cattle as well as careful selection by the hand of man is a strong possibility.

Whether the family of Hayworth would have been acting as the *vaccarii* of the manor (and thus living at the site) in the time of the Trubwicks' overlordship is unknown, but interesting. The author of the *Seneschaucie* records the office of Hayward as being responsible for the woods, corn and meadows of the manor. They were also responsible for the fences and hedges of enclosures, and for preventing cattle from straying (Holt 1964, xliv; Hey 1996, 213). At this stage the principal building on the site seems to have been a cow-house. It was large, probably open-fronted, but separated into two unequal halves by a partition. It is perhaps possible that one side of this building was for the housing of cattle and that the other comprised a store. The structural evidence within this latter half could be interpreted as relating to a second storey or mezzanine, perhaps to act as a hayloft.

9.3 Case study 2: the Wickhurst

The Wickhurst mid-8th to 11th century

Mid-8th- to early 11th-century activity left little artefactual trace at this site apart from a few sherds of pottery of pre-Conquest date. This is thought to be partly due to the intermittent pastoral nature of land-use during this seasonal phase of Wealden settlement, with a low-level use of ceramics being linked to the complete unsuitability of vessels of this nature for those engaged in transhumance. Horn, leather and wooden vessels and containers were likely to have been preferred as they are lighter and less prone to breakage. The Wickhurst Green site was clearly associated with droveways (Old Wickhurst Lane, Fiveoaks Road and Mill Lane), which survive into the modern day, but also comprised a detached parochial outlier to the later medieval parent manor, parish and settlement at Sullington. Exploitation of the site during the early medieval period is thought to be related to the droveways, and possibly included important, albeit difficult to date, evidence of seasonal settlement and enclosure. By the very end of this phase (late 10th/early 11th century) a significant building, a hall or possibly a barn, was established in the west of the site adjacent to a routeway. This was possibly constructed prior to any systematic land division at the site; however, some arable agriculture was likely to have been occurring by the end of this phase.

Period 5, phase 1: AD 750–1020

The western half of the site was occupied by Landscape Area 8 (OA35) (Figure 9.9), which may have comprised an area of mixed woodland, wood-pasture and areas of grassland or scrub. This expanse of grazing land most likely became increasingly cleared over time and it is possible that some arable agriculture was taking place by the late 10th century. A number of features were encountered, including part of a sub-rectangular enclosure (ENC25). The enclosure was defined by shallow ditches, which were found to be generally sterile, apart from a single pottery sherd dated from the mid-8th to the early 11th centuries. These ditches are interpreted as an animal enclosure used for overnight corralling during periods of transhumance, or for milking and penning of stock in the summer.

Situated a little way to the north were two small sub-rectangular features interpreted as buildings or shelters (Figure 9.10). The most northerly of these, B14 (Figures 9.10 and 9.11), was a small structure defined by a wall trench.

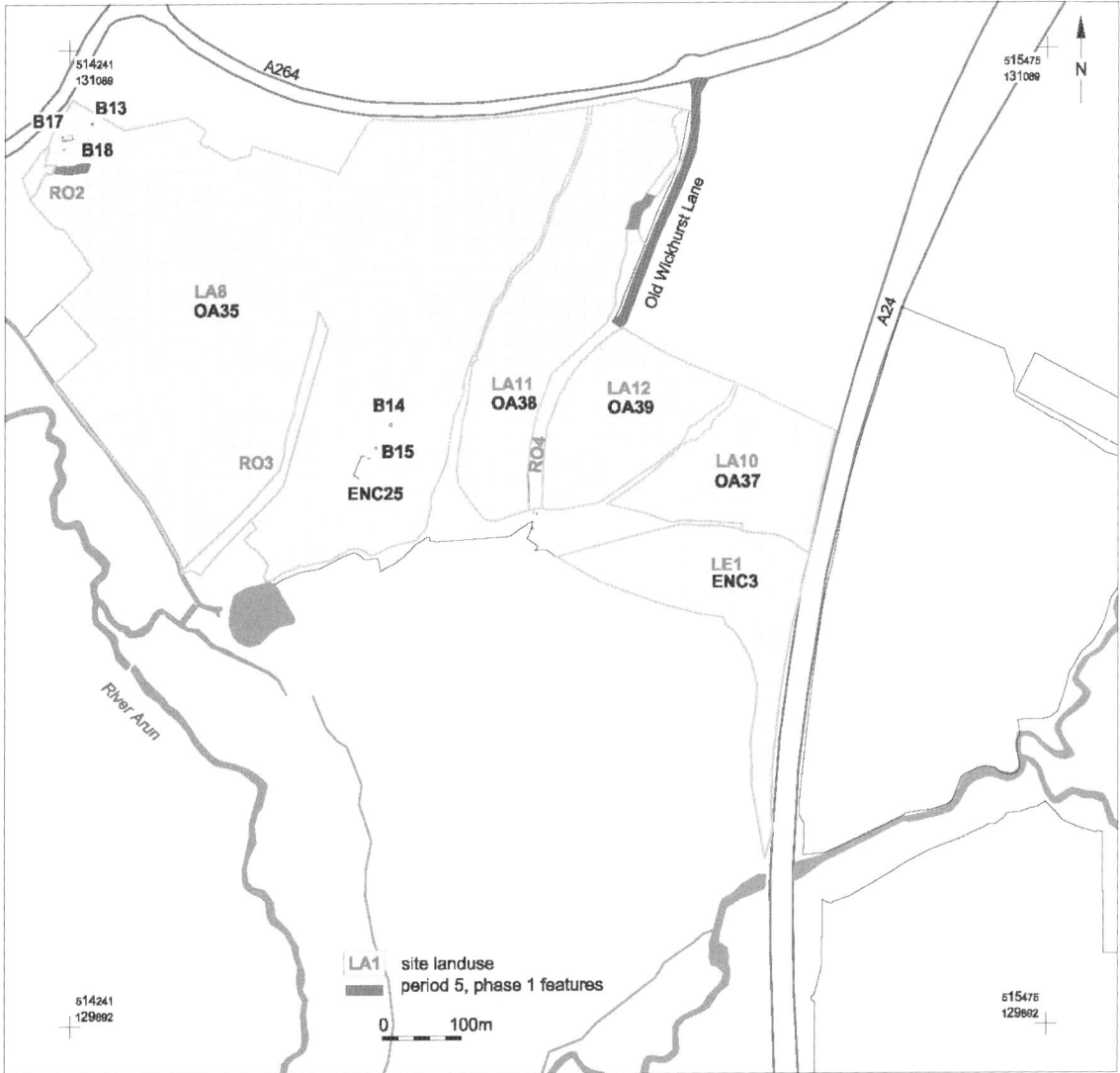

The fill deposits contained mixed finds of medieval and Roman pottery. The structure bears a passing resemblance to ancillary buildings encountered on Anglo-Saxon settlement sites (Building 20 at Springfield Lyons, for example; Tyler and Major 2005, 138–39) and the 'shielings', '*hafods/havos*' and 'booley huts' found in so-called 'marginal landscapes' in northern and western Britain and Ireland (Winchester 2000, 90–93; Gardiner 2008; Fox 2012, 27–29, 41). Place-names of the region include elements of Old and Middle English that have equivalent or similar meanings to Scandinavian words denoting summer pastures or temporary shielings in the north of England (*sætr, erg, skali/shele*). The Old English elements (*ge)sell* ('a shed, a shelter for animals, a herdsman's hut'), *scydd/scedd* ('a hovel, a shed, a pig-sty') are reasonably common elements in both Kent and Sussex (*P.N.E.* 1956b, 117–18, 115; Chapter 4) and the presence of transhumance huts would tally well with current understanding of early medieval Wealden usage.

In the north-west of OA35 was a large sub-oval 'pit' (B13) next to a smaller, circular one. The larger pit contained one of the few certain pre-Conquest sherds encountered at the site. This was found alongside a large fragment of late Roman mortarium and a piece of Roman tegula possibly used as part of the fabric of a hearth. On balance it is likely that this feature comprises a pit, although it is also possible that it represents the remains of a Saxon Sunken Feature Building. Huts with depressed floors and hearths have been related to Late Saxon seasonal grazing practices (see Gardiner 2011, 212) and this activity may be particularly relevant to the Weald at this time. The adjacent pit was backfilled by two charcoal-rich deposits. The lowest of these incorporated small fragments of fired clay, flecks of unidentifiable burnt bone and a single charred hawthorn seed as well as oak, birch, hazel and/or alder charcoal. Fragments of the latter two species returned calibrated radiocarbon dates of AD 660–770 and AD 775–970 respectively. This general area would

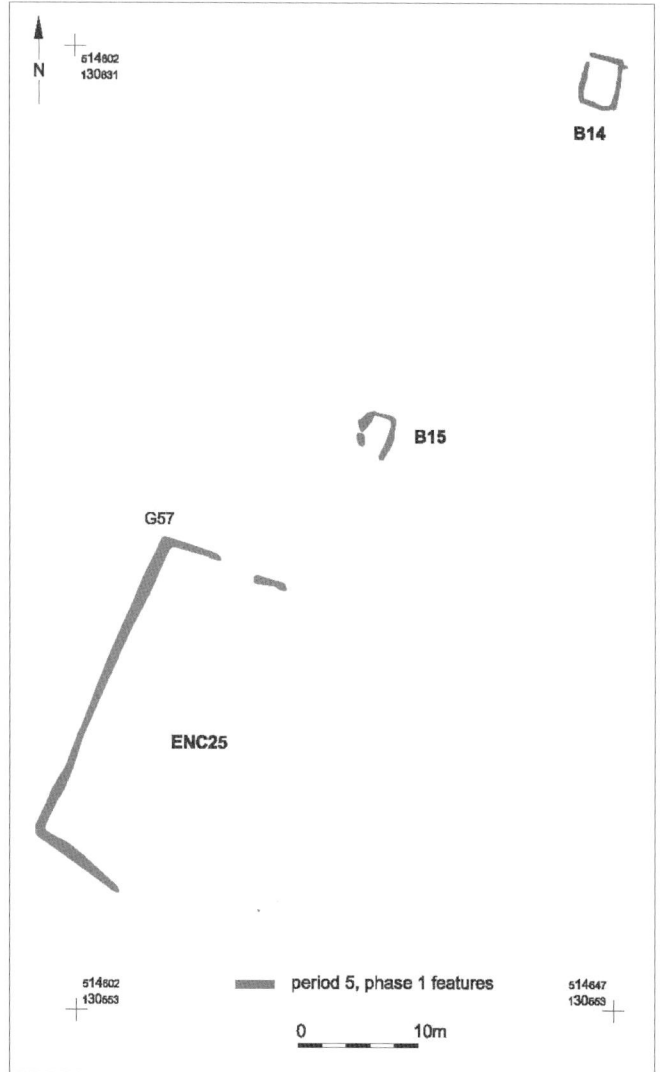

FIGURE 9.10: Plan of Enclosure 25 and Buildings 14–15 (by F. Griffin. © Archaeology South-East, UCL)

remain a focus of activity during the 11th century, but before the close of the 10th century one, possibly two, significant buildings were constructed to the west.

One of these buildings, B17, was somewhat difficult to interpret. Dating the structure also proved problematic. From all the surviving features (which were excavated in their entirety) only a single small sherd of pottery (weighing 1 g) with a late 11th- to late 12th-century date range was recovered. Despite the lack of dating material from the building itself an associated gully was filled by dark deposits which incorporated small amounts of fired clay, large amounts of charred oats, with occasional wheat grains, a weed seed and a charred hazelnut shell. The nutshell fragment and a *caryopsis* of oat were submitted for radiocarbon dating. These returned dates of cal AD 970–1040 and cal AD 970–1040 respectively. This provides a suggested construction date

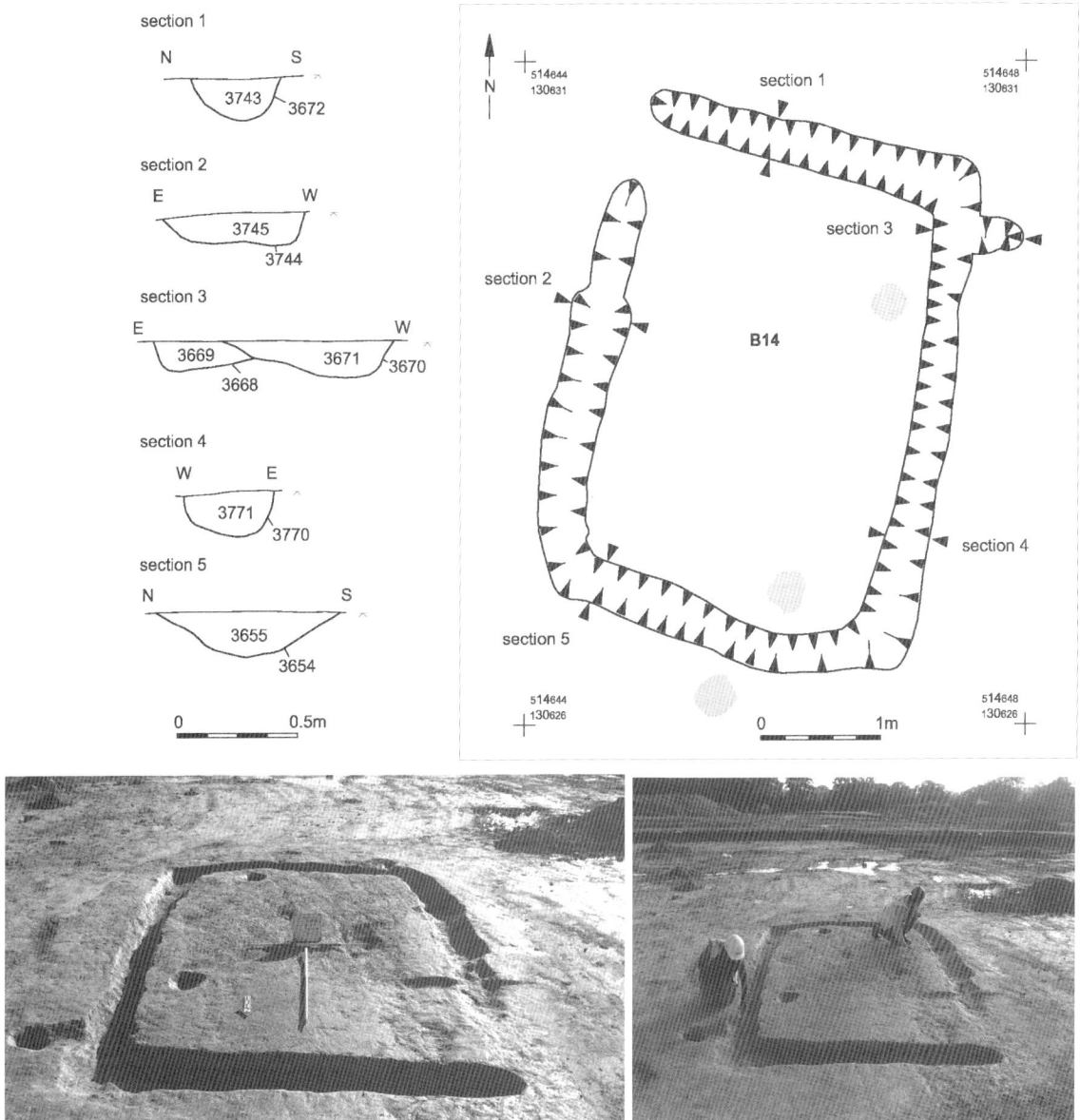

FIGURE 9.11: Detailed plan, sections and photographs of Building 14 (1.0 m scale bar) (by F. Griffin. © Archaeology South-East, UCL)

for the adjacent building of AD 970–1040 with possible continuity into the 12th century due to spatial relationships with a later surrounding enclosure and nearby 'manorial' site or estate centre (see below).

The building described above is thought to have lain adjacent to the early medieval predecessor of the Fiveoaks Road, which most likely represents the course of an early droveway utilised within a system of transhumance and seasonal pastoralism. The line of this droveway is thought to have extended into the site during the 7th to 11th century (or before). To the east, Wickhurst Lane (RO4) most likely represents part of the same droveway system as Mill Lane

(RO3), which links the detached outlier of Broadbridge with its parent settlement of Sullington at the foot of the downs (Figure 9.12). In contrast to RO3, however, a number of features were associated with the course of this droveway. The remains comprised a holloway that differed from the modern line of 'Old Wickhurst Lane', as well as droveside ditches following its course. A pond, some adjacent animal pens and a stone causeway were also encountered; however, some of these elements were dated to later periods. The stretch of holloway produced a mixed assemblage of pottery, which is most likely due to the re-worked nature of the deposits. The earliest material comprised a few fragments of Roman tegula and there were a number of intrusive post-medieval sherds. In the main, the pottery ranged from the late 11th to the early 14th centuries.

It is possible to speculate that an oval enclosure at the base of High Wood (ENC3; Figure 9.9) endured or was re-established during this phase, although no specific evidence of early medieval activity was found associated with it. Such a claim can be ventured on the basis of analogous features that have been shown to have been in use by at least the 8th or 9th centuries in the Sussex Weald (Chatwin and Gardiner 2005; Margetts 2017; Chapter 6) and elsewhere.

Period 5, phase 2: Saxo-Norman activity at Wickhurst Green (AD 1020–1175)

Activity of the mid-11th to late 12th century represents a continuation of the more sedentary occupation of the site evidenced by the construction of building B17 at the end of the preceding phase (Figure 9.13). Saxo-Norman remains were found to be associated with the laying out of field-systems (elements of which survive to the present day), accompanied by associated settlement and track ways. Two occupation foci were encountered and it has been possible to reconstruct much of the associated landscape context for these sites. Possibly the most significant area of settlement was situated in

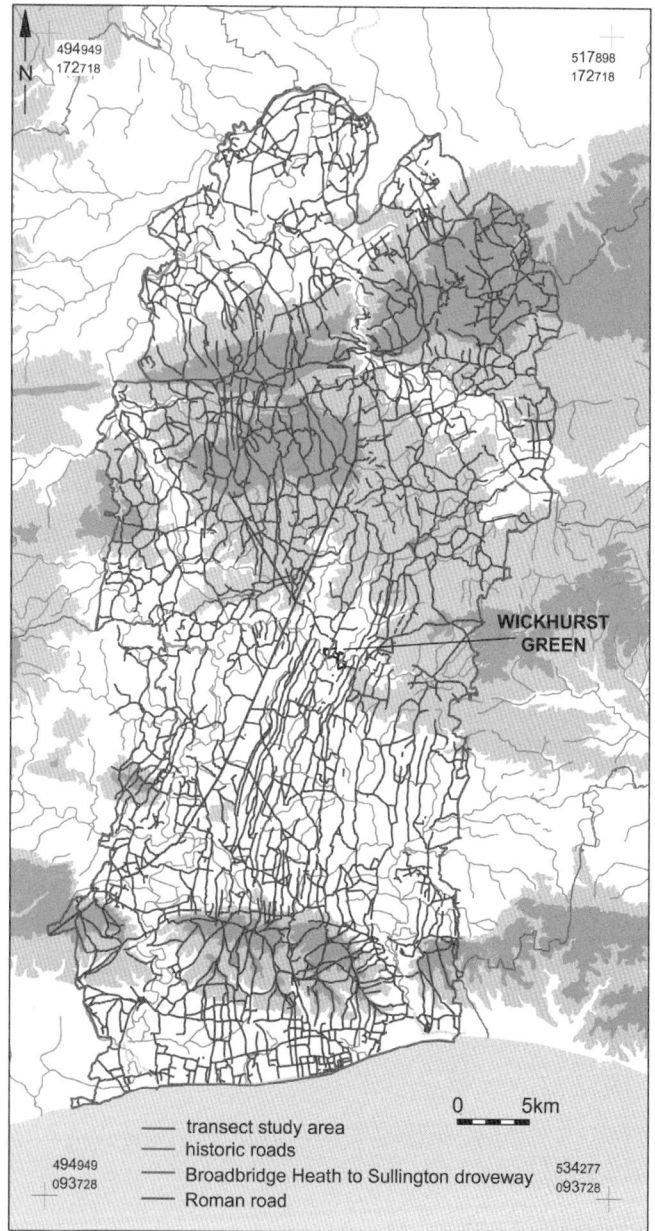

FIGURE 9.12: Wickhurst Green in relation to mapping of historic roads undertaken for Chapter 5 (illustration by the author and F. Griffin. © Archaeology South-East, UCL)

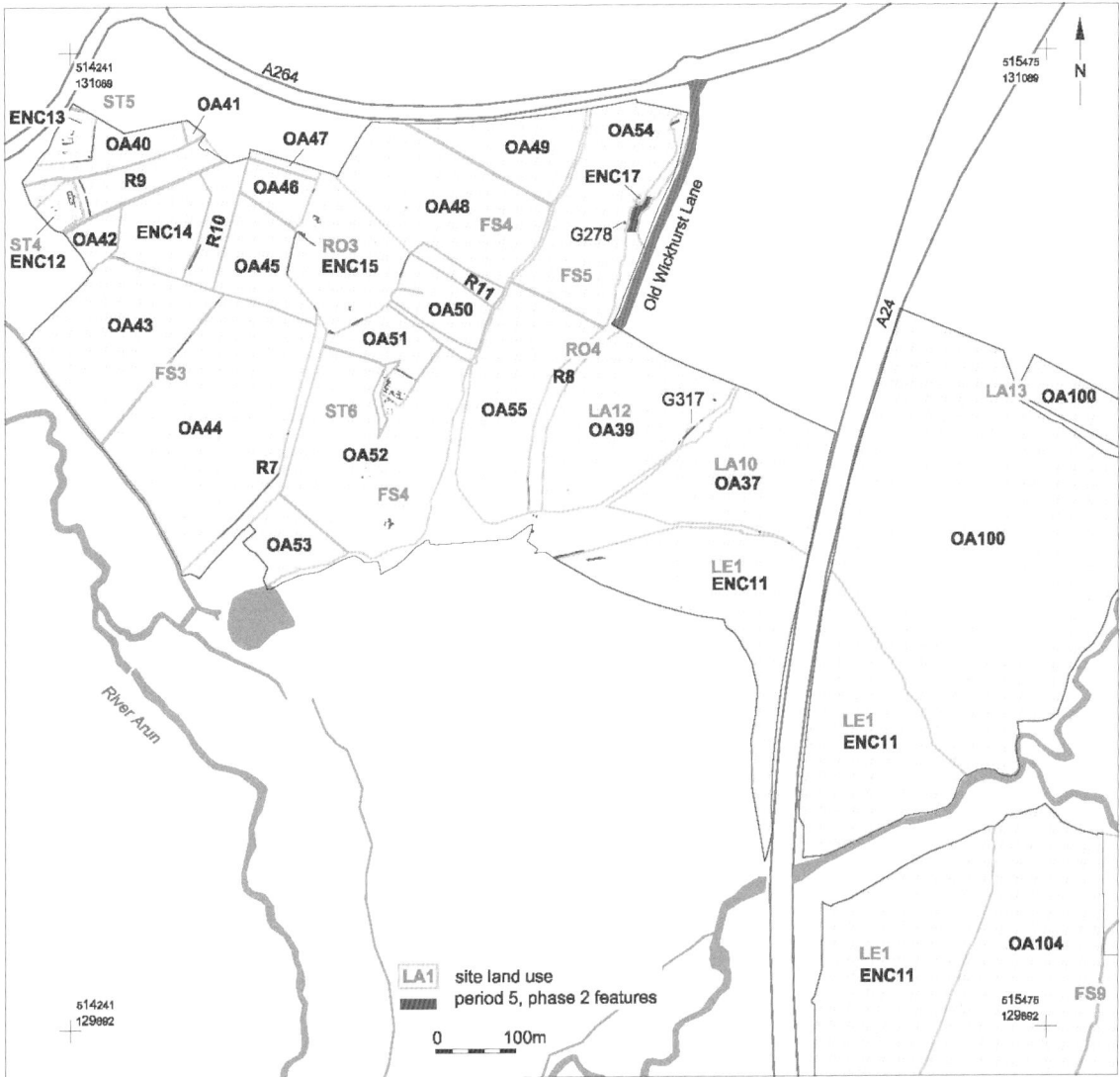

FIGURE 9.13: Plan of period 5, phase 2 features (© Archaeology South-East, UCL)

the extreme west and comprised 'high status' buildings and accompanying enclosures. These are thought to represent continued development of an area with a history of usage stretching back into the 8th century and possibly before. It is considered probable that a concerted reoccupation of the site was underway during the 10th and 11th centuries and this represents a fundamental period of Wealden development at the site.

The Wickhurst: a discussion

It is thought that from at least the 8th century the area of Broadbridge formed a Wealden sub-common or manorial *denn* belonging to a multiple estate centred at foot of the downs. The direct course of a droveway can be traced linking what would later be recorded as a parent settlement, Sullington, with its Wealden outlier, Broadbridge (Figure 9.12). The route is named as Wickhurst Lane on the tithe and OS 1st Edition maps. A Wickhurst Copse is also labelled in the area east of the lane but this droveway is alternatively named beyond the immediate vicinity of the site. The name 'Wickhurst' incorporates the Old English elements *wic* (Chapter 4) and '*hyrst*' ('a hillock, a copse'; *P.N.E.* 1956a, 276) and it seems likely that connotations as a 'wooded eminence' (*ibid.*, 277) would indicate the immediate vicinity of High Wood as 'The Wickhurst's' most likely topographic origin. Though no medieval documentation of this place-name has been traced it was in existence as an area distinct from Broadbridge in the early 19th century (1805) when records of land tax indicate William Stanford was paying £62 10s. and £2 15s. for Broadbridge and Wickhurst (WSRO MF 652). The area around Broadbridge was of poor quality, as reflected in the 'heath' place-name element suggesting soil acidification. Broadbridge Heath was named *Bradbruggesheth* during the 15th century (*P.N.Sx* 1929, 240) and is known to have been used as common pasture by the late 13th century or before (Hudson 1986, 166). The earliest surviving place-name related to Broadbridge Manor is *Brodebrig*, recorded in AD 1237 (*P.N.Sx* 1929, 225). The meaning of this name was thought by Mawer and Stenton to be self-explanatory (*ibid.*); however, it is also possible that it referred to 'broad land by a bridge'.

During the 8th to early 11th century, much of the area around Broadbridge was probably exploited as detached seasonal grazings belonging to multiple estates centred on the Sussex Spring-line or Coastal Plain. Manors such as Washington, Sullington and presumably Storrington held land within this area. The 'parent settlements' were linked to these outliers via a parallel system of droveways (see Chapter 5). As the areas controlled by Anglo-Saxon multiple estates became increasingly populated, it was necessary to define the rights of the users of land and to record boundaries more precisely (Drewett, Rudling and Gardiner 1988, 291). This process may in part have led to the increasing colonisation of the Weald as an area of 'secondary settlement' (Everitt 1986) and the need to define recently occupied holdings on the ground would have been a priority for newly established communities. The latter may be reflected in the loose coaxial boundaries and routeways that occupy much of the Sussex Low Weald (Chatwin and Gardiner 2005; Chapter 5), although the origins of these features, which were clearly utilised as manorial boundaries, may be somewhat earlier (Margetts 2018a; 2018b).

It is the 11th-century uptake of the Wealden region that reflects a fundamental phase in the evolution of the area's landscape. In the area south of Broadbridge Heath this appeared to be allied to the creation of strip manors. The early 'home farms' of these 11th-century land-holdings appear to have occupied areas close to watercourses, at roughly equidistant intervals within closely parallel routeways.

Until the 7th century, the Weald was largely utilised as an intercommoned area by communities based in more 'favourable' *pays*. After this time (7th–8th centuries) it is apparent that multiple estates were beginning to create independent '*denns*' within the forest. These comprised detached woodland

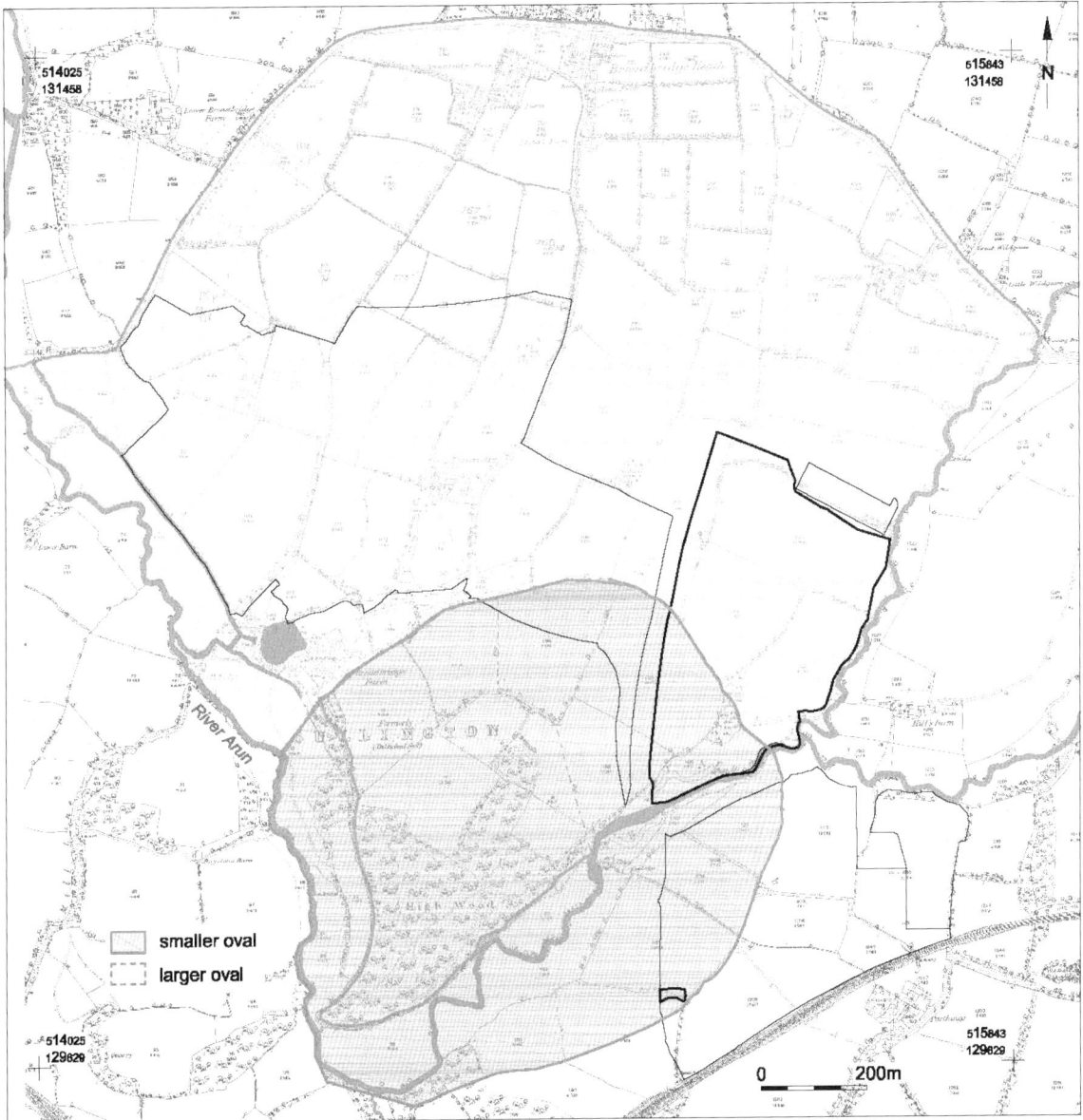

FIGURE 9.14: Map showing the double oval field pattern associated with 'The Wickhurst' at Broadbridge Heath (© Archaeology South-East, UCL)

pastures that would have originally been exploited on a seasonal basis. Evidence from the Hayworth at Bolnore shows interesting similarities to that at Broadbridge Heath in that both are clearly associated with droveways, as well as oval enclosures and open areas of grazing. In the case of the Hayworth this comprised a 'double oval' field pattern as well as Haywards Heath and 'Halfe Street Lane'. If, as is suspected, the Wickhurst was at one time utilised for seasonal dairying, this may account for the distinct similarities between the double oval field pattern encountered at the Hayworth and that at Broadbridge Heath (Figure 9.14).

What may be even more interesting is that the tradition of enclosing High Wood originated in some form during the Middle Iron Age and a similar pastoral usage has been proposed for ENC1 in that area. A further enclosure then existed in the Late Iron Age/Early Roman landscape which showed signs of possible continuity into both the historic landscape and that of today. It is probable that the enclosure was re-established by the 11th century as the local field pattern and major boundaries were also of this date. Certainly, 'The Wickhurst' was defined as an area distinct from the rest of Broadbridge by the post-medieval period (WSRO MF 652) and its name includes place-name elements of Old English origin. Wickhurst Lane, which was clearly in use by the 11th century, and probably existed by the 8th century due to its connection with a likely parent settlement at Sullington, respected this oval enclosure.

Double oval field patterns are a feature of upland landscapes in the north of England where they are often sited so that a watercourse runs through their centre. They appear to have comprised a larger pastoral unit with stock funnels leading onto upland with a smaller oval that contained field divisions intended for arable, pasture and convertible land (Atkin 1985, 173–75).

9.4 Conclusions

By the earlier 10th century a tentative landscape model can be proposed. At least some of the oval enclosures of the West Central Weald appear to be of earlier origin than the closely set system of parallel routeways that surrounded them. The ovals were established, re-established or reused within a landscape comprised of extensive areas of woodland, pasture (including heath) and wood-pasture. By this time they had come to be utilised as seasonal, often specialised areas of grazing (*denns, falolds, wics*). The routeways themselves were part of a system of transhumance, and whilst their use was widespread (and many probably originated around this time; 7th–10th centuries) they appear to have been based on, or at least influenced by, elements of an earlier, underlying network of tracks and land divisions. This roughly north-east–south-west aligned landscape may not be the result of a continuous tradition of landscape organisation, but moreover the product of a reoccurring method of dividing and traversing the Low Weald clays (Chapter 5; section 5.4). This pattern may be found elsewhere in the country and it is interesting to note that the Iron Age boundaries of the oval enclosure found at Charlton, Northamptonshire were in places respected by medieval township boundaries and the local road system (Deegan and Foard 2007, 133–34; fig. 3.29).

The parallel set of droveways had by the later 10th century come to be utilised as tenurial and administrative boundaries (see Chatwin and Gardiner 2005) and this is thought to have been linked to the burgeoning establishment of new holdings, as suggested at Wickhurst Green. These appear to have occupied the intervening spaces between parallel roads, but the older seasonal pastures (defined within oval enclosures) endured. This was probably due to the continued value placed upon these pastures by communities based at parent settlements in the south. By the 11th century numerous small farmsteads and subinfeudated manors began to encroach on the old Wealden commons (Witney 1976, 77) and this is suggested at Wickhurst Green by the appearance of 'high status' settlements in the west and central portions of the site.

The settlements at Wickhurst Green and the Hayworth are the product of 10th-/11th–12th-century colonisation of land previously utilised as seasonal pasture. It is likely this colonisation would have been encouraged by major landowners keen to extract new income from rents. These early settlers may have banded together in loose groups, in families or alliances of families. This would have been for mutual support – in hunting wolves, sharing expertise and an ox-drawn plough (Brandon 2003, 86). Adjacent peasant holdings may have been created in clearings more or less simultaneously. Properties are likely to have been reasonably large, reflecting the inferior quality of the soil and the greater acreages necessary to support a family. These original holdings would later have been subject to division caused by inheritance, alienation or purchase. Such factors may have led to additional properties, which would have been constructed on fragmented holdings (*ibid.*). The settlement sites at Wickhurst Green may signify large free tenements or customary virgates and the substantial houses encountered during the excavations may reflect such as status.

As the medieval period progressed there may be further indications of tenurial changes at the Wickhurst Green site. B17 is thought to have been a newly established holding within the Wealden interior. The 10th century was marked by a rising body of wealthy tenants and the status of the building seems to indicate a person of above average means. This would not have been an uncommon situation during the 10th and 11th centuries when it is apparent that there was a rapid upsurge in free tenants, local lords and petty bookland estates (Stafford 1989, 37–38; Reynolds 2003, 130–31).

During the 13th century the area around Broadbridge is documented as a deer park belonging to Roger Covert (Hudson 1986, 24) and it is likely that the Wickhurst Green excavations were located within the park bounds (Margetts 2018a). One of the most significant results of the fieldwork at Wickhurst Green was the degree to which the field pattern could be explored. Excavation proved that field boundaries at the site often owed their origins to the 11th century, hinting that the co-axial landscape of the western Low Weald probably reached a developed state by the Saxo-Norman period. This field-scape survived the site's imparkment. It is important not to generalise on the basis of one site; however, the results would appear to suggest that the early medieval landscape of north-east–south-west droveways and long-distance field boundaries had begun (by the 11th century) to be occupied by fields aligned in a similar direction.

The archaeological investigations discussed in these case studies have facilitated exploration of areas of woodland utilised under long-standing common rights, which evolved into manorial holdings held under rights of private property. Such transformations have been explored by Oosthuizen (2011; 2013) and the results of work connected to the Hayworth and Wickhurst Green may be important in this regard. It is arguable, however, when precisely the change occurred. What can be said with more confidence is that landscape alterations experienced at the sites ran concurrently with a period that is thought to be associated with the development of commons belonging to individual estates rather than so-called folk groups of the South Saxon kingdom. As such, it is this time (approximately the 7th–11th centuries) when a change from 'common' to 'private' was occurring. The final move towards settlements held in severalty probably did not take place until the early 11th–12th centuries, a time by which a transition from 'seasonal' to 'permanent' was complete.

The sites provided important palaeo-environmental remains and rare Wealden pollen sequences for the early and later medieval periods. At the Hayworth, prehistoric woodland, where oak, hazel and lime were the dominant species, was replaced by a closed oak and hazel habitat where holly was part of the understory. This habitat was gradually cleared from the 7th century, a process which began in what landscape historians have termed the long 8th century, a period of social and agrarian innovation that lasted from the 7th to 9th centuries (Hansen and Wickham 2000; Rippon 2008, 27). Landscape change continued until a 12th-century beech-dominated, semi-wooded environment was achieved.

As well as aiding understanding of rural landscape evolution, the excavated features provide rare insights into the likely form of early medieval transhumance huts (*(ge)sells* or *scyds*) and a 12th–13th-century cow-house (*i.e.* in the South-East similar to what is now termed an open-fronted shelter shed). Vaccaries, such as that encountered at the Hayworth, could clearly exist within a lowland context, as well as in the usual upland landscapes in which they are usually recognised. As such they may be viewed as a key element of land-use in areas of dispersed settlement such as the Weald. They are linked with the *wic*, and in this case *worð*, place-names and thus the pastoral origins of colonisation within these marginal lands. The Hayworth and vaccaries in general are connected to traditions of outpasture, transhumance and seasonal exploitation; as such, they may be of importance in understanding the origins and development of medieval colonisation of marginal wooded environs. As an early oval enclosure, the Hayworth is a primary feature in the contemporary historic landscape. It may have originated as an early medieval pound-like enclosure at a stage when the Weald was acting as an extensive area of common grazing.

CHAPTER 10

Discussion

10.1 Introduction

> 'How great on all sides is the abundance of cattle, but how strange a solitude of
> men!' says an old traveller when speaking of the Sussex Weald. (Hudson 1906, 34)

During the medieval period, South-East England was not an arable district in
the image of the Midlands or parts of East Anglia. While arable landscapes
existed, the region can, on the whole, be characterised as a pastoral zone; one
where wood-pasture, marsh and heath were of equal if not more importance
than the downland hills and sheep-corn husbandry that have dominated its
agrarian history. The pasturing of sheep and the keeping of swine were clearly
important factors in the South-East's medieval agricultural economy, but cattle
appear to have played a vital but often forgotten role in the area's economic,
cultural and social development. What has been demonstrated through this
interdisciplinary study is that, for certain landscapes, cattle husbandry has
played a crucial role in colonisation, settlement development and infrastructure.
Like the cattle economy of Dartmoor (Fox 2012, 107) what has been revealed
is an agrarian regime that was as complex as the Midland two and three field
systems.

During the early medieval period cattle were a highly valued commodity,
both economically and symbolically; 'property' and 'cattle' were closely related
concepts and essentially comprised moveable wealth (Banham and Faith 2014,
85–87). Their importance within the South-East cannot be underestimated,
as they were highly valued as food, as raw materials, as sources of manure
and as a means of traction. They were a ubiquitous element in the pastoral
economy, but were particularly numerous in certain landscapes. In terms of
this regionalisation it was the Thames valley and the huge expanse of the
Weald where cattle pasturing was most evident. To begin to conclude this
study, we shall explore cattle's role in comparison to other livestock. This will
be followed by a discussion of the presence and nature of the South-East's
vaccary establishments, themselves a product of a regionalised, environmentally
influenced, economy. What will be demonstrated is that the regional emphasis
on the study of sheep and pig husbandry has in part been misguided, a result
of the Weald's largely forgotten archaeology as well as an over-reliance on the
flawed information provided by Domesday.

10.2 Cattle's significance within the South-East

Cattle versus horses

When judging the significance of cattle within the South-East it is essential to begin with an appraisal in relation to other livestock types. In comparison to horse, cattle were clearly of paramount importance. Whilst the former were key for riding and as pack animals, the latter were absolutely essential as a plough beast utilised in the arable economy. Though both horses and cattle could perform draught duties, it was oxen that were overwhelmingly used for pulling of the plough (see section 3.4). Due to its strength the ox was at its greatest advantage on heavy soils where large teams were yoked in pairs of similar size and gait. In hilly terrain oxen could draw 'a load up a steep bank at a steady pace, whereas a horse would often rush at the work and then stop', beginning again with a snatch, 'breaking something or straining itself' (Brandon 2003, 65). Despite the speed of the horse, oxen were still favoured in Sussex not only for ploughing but, in many places, for hauling throughout the 15th century (Mate 1991, 272). Indeed, in parts of the county the ox was not overtaken by the horse until the early 19th century (Brandon 2003, 191; Figure 10.1). This continued use of oxen was a significant anomaly. By the end of the 15th century, 65%–70% of seigniorial hauling was being performed by horses, yet in Sussex very few demesnes made the switch (Mate 1991, 273). The ox was able to make up for its

FIGURE 10.1: A Sussex ox-gang working in the Weald near Hastings (ploughing the fields *c.* 1890, ESL H00464; image courtesy of East Sussex Library and Information Service)

slow speed by its ability to carry a heavier load, and although they were soon replaced by horses on the thin light soils of the downs, on the thick heavy clays of the Weald of Kent and Sussex oxen persisted into the post-medieval period (Everitt 1986, 165). Here the one arable task that a horse could perform better than an ox was harrowing, consequently, although some horses were kept, the Weald was overwhelmingly populated by oxen as a plough beast.

Apart from its heavy soils the Weald had other environmental traits that suited oxen in preference to horses. Ecologically, cattle are at an advantage where grass and hay was plentiful and cheap. It was a land-extensive animal and therefore enjoyed its greatest comparative advantage in isolated and remote areas of low to medium economic rent (Campbell 2000, 132). They could also thrive on a diet of browse, straw, roots and a little cereal; feed that would have starved a draught horse (Brandon 2003, 65). Within the South-East, the dominance of cattle as a working animal is neatly demonstrated via investigations by Campbell (2000). These showed small numbers of demesnes employing only horses, versus far greater numbers of manors relying almost exclusively on oxen for their draught needs (*ibid.*, pastoral type 1, figs 4.01, 4.02 versus pastoral types 4–6, figs 4.06–4.011). Whilst the total use of horses was restricted to parts of eastern Kent, the almost wholesale use of oxen was spread throughout the counties of Kent, Sussex and Surrey.

Despite this historic reliance on oxen, horses should not be thought of as unimportant within the region. Peasants rather than lords were the most active in the changeover to horsepower, although due to the well-known bias in the documentary record this is not always apparent. Within the Weald, later medieval smallholders were often concerned with pig-keeping and breeding cattle, although the raising of horses is also mentioned in accounts. The importance of horses to Sussex may be confirmed by way of settlement place-names recorded prior to and around the time of the Domesday Survey. During this period Hallam (1988b, 34) has shown that horse place-names were marginally more prevalent than those for cattle (8 versus 9; *ibid.*, tables 1.6 and 1.7), although as explained during Chapter 4 it does not necessarily follow that this means they were numerically dominant. It is possible that these early references to horses may indicate either trade in feral animals dependent on rough grazing rather than more formalised production within enclosed fields or the greater prestige in which horses were held. In 1086 a sokeman of the hundred of Kingston, Surrey, is recorded as being in charge of 'woodland' mares (*silvaticae equae*) belonging to the king (Domesday 22,4) and it can be speculated that the place-name of Horsham, Sussex (recorded in the 10th century) relates to an enclosure on the margins of extensive wood-pasture and heath used for breeding horses (*P.N.Sx* 1929, 225).

Allied to the production of horses, the significant dependence on oxen had implications for other parts of the cattle economy. Elsewhere in England studies have shown that, where the change from ox to horsepower was made, the cattle herd was sometimes freed up for dairying. The reduction in demand for oxen as opposed to horses often released hay and grassland necessary to support a dairy herd (Campbell 2000, 142, 145). This said, the primary function of the vaccaries of the Peak District and Derbyshire forests was the breeding of replacement oxen to pull the plough on lowland demesnes. Nevertheless, dairying was undertaken on these establishments as a by-product or secondary activity allowing the production of milk, butter and cheese that could be consumed on the manor (*ibid.*, 140). Presumably the need to keep cows in calf to produce oxen allowed a certain amount to be taken by the dairymaid or herdsman for human consumption.

Extensive pasture as well as access to fodder for overwintering was key to effective medieval cattle husbandry. In comparison to horses, pasture and fodder for cattle does not need to be of the highest quality. It has been suggested within Chapter 9 that pollard hay of beech was used as an important fodder crop on a Wealden vaccary, and ash, elm, holly and ivy were also cut to feed cattle over the winter months. This method of husbandry therefore draws a clear link between cattle and wood-pasture environments, the access to which may have been beneficial in relation to purely grassland pasture. As a ruminant, cows are able to extract more nutrition from lesser quality feeds, that is in contrast to horses, which demand valuable hay during the winter. Horses could also be pickier in relation to cereal foods and, as Walter of Henley (*c.* 1280) states, unlike cattle they would be reluctant to eat barley as 'it is too bearded and hurts the horses' mouths' (Oschinsky 1971, 330–31). Despite the differences between cattle and horses, from March to October they can act as companion grazers helping to relieve the need for pasture maintenance and by their grazing habits helping preserve the quality of the grass. Whilst cows eat longer sward and often prefer to browse, horses crop selected areas down to the ground surface. They avoid their own manure, allowing grass to regrow for cattle which eat near other species' dung but not their own. Goats can fulfil an important role within this system by clearing up any weeds or shrubs after pasturing of the other species.

Cattle versus goats

Regardless of their ability to feed on plants that would be inedible to horses or cattle and their increased browsing habit when likened to sheep, goats were never a very popular livestock type in medieval England (Dyer 2004). Once compared to the major domesticates they do not appear to have been very common. This is not simply the result of a bias in the archaeological record resulting from their skeletal similarity to sheep (Banham and Faith 2014, 93–95). The paucity of reference to them in association with small producers may be due to restrictions on smallholders taking advantage of their omnivorous eating habits (Harvey 1988, 126). Constraints on the keeping of goats is recorded in the custumals of the Sussex manors of the Archbishop of Canterbury where it is documented that the tenants of Slindon who lived in the Weald ('*Waldis*') 'have common with all their beasts everywhere except one enclosed wood of the lord. But no one shall have common with goats' (Redwood and Wilson

1958, 5). This restriction on Wealden pasturing is interesting, as goats are often associated with rough grazing and woods (Dyer 2004, 22).

In contrast to these limitations, goats did provide an important alternative to sheep and cows within the dairy economy, often being kept in districts where other livestock types could not thrive. Though the name of Gatwick 'goat-wick' (*P.N.Sr* 1934, 288) may point to early medieval goat dairies in the Weald, the animals were never popular in regions where demesnes kept large numbers of pigs instead. In Domesday Essex, where cattle were also numerous, pigs were two or three times more prevalent than goats (Harvey 1988, 126). Their tendency to spoil restricted pasture probably rendered them increasingly unpopular as the medieval period progressed (*ibid.*) and in relation to cattle and sheep their already proportionally low numbers would have decreased still further over the later Middle Ages. Due to limitations in South-East England's archaeological and documentary record (see Chapters 1–3) it is impossible to gauge goats' true importance in comparison to cattle during the medieval period. Nevertheless, the national picture suggests that goats would never have been a significant part of the pastoral economy.

Cattle versus pigs

So what of cattle's place in relation to the two other major domesticates, pigs and sheep? For the former, perhaps the biggest difference is tied to their comparative uses. While cattle were kept for traction, secondary products and reproduction, pigs were reared almost exclusively for the table. Swine are prolific breeders, with medieval sows being capable of farrowing twice a year when they produced litters with a minimum of seven piglets (*Hosbonderie*). Nevertheless, cattle's body size meant a large amount of beef could be provided from the slaughter of one animal. Feeding cattle may have been more expensive, as pigs could be raised on kitchen scraps and woodland mast, but an ox could pay for itself by work with the plough or a cow by breeding replacements for the herd (Grant 1988, 162). Of the pigs produced each year, some would be killed young for lack of winter feed, but the males would often be kept, castrated and sent to pannage before being slaughtered at Martinmas the following year (Witney 1990, 23).

As a consumer item, animal protein was often used to signify social status. We have learnt in Chapter 8 how meat formed a larger proportion of the diet for those higher up the social scale. As well as these contrasts in relative availability, the type of meat eaten by lords often differed from that of the servile tenantry. Higher-status medieval sites can often be distinguished by larger proportions of pig, deer and bird bones, animals from which meat is the primary rather than secondary product (Grant 1988, 180). During the early medieval period, high-status consumer sites tended to have more cattle and pigs, which were valued as a prestige commodity. Lower-status sites by contrast were often characterised by the keeping of sheep, valued for their secondary products: dairy, manure and wool (Sykes 2007, 37–39, fig. 38). By the end of the medieval period the status of beef seems to have been retained, whereas that of pork went into decline. Pig's low cost of production, ability to live in confined conditions and their ease of preservation, as bacon or ham, made them popular with the urban lower classes (Albarella 2006, 72–74; Jørgensen 2013b, 431). This may have affected the meat's status with those higher up the social scale. Beef, however, remained a popular foodstuff for members of the South-East's elite, who on the strength of the excavated evidence from Woking Palace, Surrey (Poulton 2015; see Chapter 8) were still avid consumers of cattle.

A comparison of the feeding habits and fodder regimes of cattle and pig is a study in the diversity of medieval husbandry practice. Pigs' omnivorous habits meant they were able to process many varieties of food including grassland pasture. Of the total of 142 settlements in Surrey mentioned in Domesday, 25 paid a rent in grass swine (Lloyd 1962, 391). Grass, of course, is also important to cattle, and no more so than for the dairy herd. Perhaps the best pasturage for the latter was found on the salt marshes of north Kent, and the Channel coast. As we have seen within Chapter 3, cows fed in this environment produced one and a half times as much milk as their wood-pasture counterparts. Despite its importance to the dairy economy, grass does not always constitute the preferred food of cattle. Browse and coarse weeds can make up a significant part of the animals' diet, something capitalised on by the Wealden farmer by the grazing of hedges and shaws. On average, modern cattle breeds pastured in woodland can consume between approximately 6 kg and 8 kg of foraged browse per day (Forestry Commission Scotland 2018) and it is probable that unimproved medieval stock could make even more use of this poor quality feed. Indeed, woodland pasture for cattle played a much more prominent role in the early agrarian economy of the South-East than we might suppose (see below).

The Kentish Domesday makes only one mention of wood-pasture without reference to pigs, at Nackington on the edge of the forest of Hardres (Domesday 5,126). Witney (1990, 25) has confidently ascribed this as a direct reference to cattle pasture, although such a leap should be noted with caution. Contrast this with the profusion of swine references in relation to woodland and we may have an answer as to why pigs in preference to cattle have been so commonly associated with the South-East's medieval livestock economy. What we must remember about Domesday, however, is that woodland was recorded in terms of the number of swine paid as an annual rent for the right of pasturage. It was a means of assessing size and value of a woodland and we should question whether it was always necessarily the case that pigs (or pigs alone) were being pastured there.

Though less nutritious than marsh, meadow or grassland there was a good deal more wood-pasture within the South-East, thanks largely to the great expanse of the Weald and the wooded parts of the downland. We have learnt within Chapter 3 of the '*hridra leah*', or cattle glades, near Petham in the Buckholt Forest (Kent) as well as the 12 oxen belonging to the '*men of la Wudecota*' in '*Godiuawuda*' (Goodwood, Sussex). These records, along with the

10th-century description of Brabourne Manor, which speaks of a hollow way going 'up over the down' to a *minnis* (from *(ge)mænnes* used of 'common land, a common holding' (Smith 1956b; possibly Stelling Minnis to the north-east)) and cowherd's wood ('*Cuwar*'), help show that areas of chalk capped with Clay-with-Flints were utilised as cattle pasture (*Recital of the crimes of Wulfbold*; Witney 1990, 26). It is apparent, too, from these accounts as well as place-name evidence and animal bone assemblages (Chapters 4 and 8) that cattle were an important feature of the woodland economy and those regions of the South-East that experienced so-called secondary settlement. Nevertheless, both pigs and cattle required careful management in order to benefit from their various advantages and so as not to disrupt the sensitive ecology of the forest. Cattle were pastured in coppice woodland once the stools had grown above browsing height and pigs were turned out in the autumn to feed on mast. The value of coppice depended on the management cycle, but generally it improved grazing by opening up the canopy, providing space and light to the woodland floor. But cattle are destructive to new growth and would be confined to plots of around five-years old. Pig grazing could be beneficial prior to stocking in woodlands by clearing up the autumn acorn crop which, if consumed in quantity by cows, can cause birth defects and even death.

Environmental evidence from the Hayworth in Sussex has shown that oak may have been deliberately reduced by the combined feeding of pigs and cattle as well as careful selection by the hand of man (Chapter 9). This alternate grazing of cattle and pigs was valuable in other ways, too, as it assisted woodland generation. This was achieved in three ways; first, by the planting and encouragement of mast-bearing trees; secondly, by the loosening of soil through the rooting activities of swine, which creates ideal germination conditions for saplings (Pott 1998, 113); and, thirdly, by the trampling of cattle, which can help reduce bracken cover.

At the time of Domesday most of the swine driven to the autumn woods were hoggasters, or yearlings. They belonged to ordinary husbandman, who might have one or two breeding sows, serviced by boars belonging to the lord or a wealthy neighbour (Witney 1990, 23). The remnants of the old forest were seasonal home to great herds of foraging swine apparent in the South-East's documentary evidence and animal bone assemblages. People who lived close to the Weald clearly took most advantage of its extensive pannage and, although the bone assemblages have limitations, the Greensand Ridge that borders the Weald appears to have been an important pig-rearing region (Chapter 8). The destination of the early medieval pig-herder was the Anglo-Saxon *denn*, so commonly and simplistically interpreted as a pasture for swine. The exploration of place-names within Chapter 4 has, however, shown that *denn* names were sometimes prefixed with cattle elements. Indeed, of all the names in *denn* and *falod* (which had a comparative meaning) explored within Chapter 4, not one is recorded as being prefixed with an element meaning swine. On the strength of this meagre etymological evidence alone it could be cautiously suggested that seasonal pasturing of cattle may have been an equally if not more important function of the *denn*'s early use. Indeed, Hallam's previous analysis of the South-East's more general toponymy indicates far fewer places derived their nomenclature from pigs (3) as opposed to cattle (8; (Hallam 1988b, tables 1.10 and 1.6 respectively). Such an assertion is, of course, over-simplistic as the meaning of *denn* may have been so intimately associated with the pasturing of pigs as to render naming one after them redundant. Nevertheless, this place-name disparity should be viewed in light of further evidence presented below (section 10.3).

By the time of Domesday, the large swine-renders recorded for Otford and Wrotham in Kent and South Malling in Sussex imply tenants' herds of 1,500–2,000 swine. Such large numbers would have been further swelled by the pigs of the demesne (Brandon 1988, 315). The Weald, too, was home to large herds of cattle as recorded on Ashdown Forest at the end of the 13th century. At this time 2,000–3,000 cattle were grazed (Penn 1984, 115). As the medieval period progressed new holdings formed through assarting encroached upon the woods, greatly reducing land available for pannage. Nevertheless, the practice continued to be an important source of revenue and the Weald of Sussex, in particular, was an immense larder of mast-fed swine. It is clear that the Crown regarded Ashdown Forest and Tonbridge South Frith as great store-houses of pig meat, a resource to be used whenever the king campaigned in Ireland or the Continent (Brandon 1988, 315–16).

The difficulties of herding pigs, the conflation of pannage with transhumance and the distance between some outlying pastures and their parent settlements has led to a questioning of our understanding of the element *denn* and how valid use of seasonal wood-pastures for swine pannage really was (Turner 1997, 10; Turner and Briggs 2016). Added to this, some authorities have played down the national importance of pannage as a method of livestock production. Rackham (1986, 122), for instance, has stated how the customs were often jocular, fanciful or even deliberately prohibitive, and that to breed animals with the aim of utilising such an unpredictable resource as the mast crop was completely impractical. This said, the density of tree cover within the Weald meant that wood-pasture for swine was extensive enough for it to still be worthwhile into the later medieval period. That pannage involved the seasonal transhumance of swine and their keepers has also been upheld upon close inspection (Turner and Briggs 2016).

The presence of skilled swineherds and the difference between the hairy, long-legged pigs of the Middle Ages and those of today go some way to explaining the possibility of herding swine over some distance (*ibid.*). Nevertheless, it should be considered whether the deeply incised and wide droves of the Weald could really be the result of a form of husbandry that was on the strength of available evidence predominantly restricted to the 10th and 11th centuries. Exploration of the region's roads (Chapter 5) has shown how the droveways were often linked to infrastructure in the form of watering places, greens and pounds as well as stock funnels and strategically placed common. Would these facilities have been needed by medieval swineherds? The nature of their task is recalled in a late 18th-century observation by William Gilpin of pig-herders within the New Forest. Gilpin describes how all that is needed to control pigs on their 'migration' was trees in plenty of mast, a slight circular fence covered with boughs and a horn for calling the animals to feed (Gilpin 1791, 113–15). Most commentators state that the pannage season ran between August and December; however, after the Conquest an October to November date became the norm (Albarella 2006, 79).

It is clear within the documents explored for Chapter 3 that the Wealden pannage season was preceded by a period of summering. This is suggested by instances such as the record of William Trancheuent and John Burgays who were obliged to take their beasts from Amberley to Pephurst Wood near Drungewick, Sussex, and common with them from Candlemas to Holyrood Day (early February to mid-September; Peckham 1925, 54). The fact that Wealden place-names such as Milkstead, Somerden and Summerlees have also been linked to a phase of early medieval dairying strengthen the case for the yearly movement of cattle (Chapter 4; Everitt 1986, 31, 122). The value placed on these seasonal sites is testified by the distance covered in the annual journey to the commons. Analysis undertaken here (Chapters 4 and 5) has shown that an area where potential cattle-related place-names were prevalent was the destination of the West Sussex droveways. This was a region occupied by oval enclosures linked to seasonal pastoral agriculture. They relate to a stage of colonisation when older intercommonable pastures were being appropriated. They took advantage of well-watered sites near extensive grazing and can be perceived as the equivalent of the Kentish *denns* (Chapter 6). Though the autumnal pannage of swine was important, this study makes clear that the enclosures use may have owed as much (if not more) to the seasonal grazing of cattle.

During this study the Weald has emerged as a highly important landscape for the pasturing of both pigs and cattle. As the medieval period progressed, however, swine may have gradually decreased in prominence as cattle's importance grew. As larger swathes of the Weald were turned over to settled agriculture and increased assarting ate into the old remnants of the forest, the seasonal movement of swine went into decline. It can be postulated, too, that the summering of cattle would have been curtailed, although the species had by this time become essential to the settled Wealden farmer. On sufficiently documented estates the method of production adopted by these 'pioneers' was a form of convertible husbandry or infield outfield. A relatively small acreage near the main barns was generously manured and almost permanently cropped with a mixture of either wheat, oats or leguminous crops such as beans (Brandon 1988, 315; 2003, 56). Cattle to the Wealden farmer had become what sheep were to the downsman, a walking source of manure that facilitated an arable crop. Not only that, but prior to mechanisation the Sussex ox was the only beast capable of ploughing the intractable Wealden clays.

Cattle versus sheep

Cattle's place within the Wealden economy was partly due to the region's environmental conditions, the soil being generally too wet for the folding of sheep (Brandon 1988, 313). Within the South-East sheep were kept in areas where grassland pasture was abundant or where salt marsh existed; the latter environment acting as an aid to milk production and as a preventative to foot rot and liver fluke (Chapters 3 and 4). As a generalisation, 'there were fewer sheep where there was most wood' (Harvey 1988, 124) and the animals can be considered uncommon on the Wealden claylands. Here, where flocks did exist they often numbered under 100 animals (Pelham 1934; Mate 1991, 134). On the sandy landscapes of the High Weald sheep were similarly uncommon (Gardiner 1999, 38) and during the medieval period they were completely excluded from Ashdown Forest (Brian Short, pers. comm.).

Other heathlands, by contrast, were grazed by both cattle and sheep, although where heather was the predominant vegetation cattle were less successful (Campbell 2000, 81). The heathlands of the Thames Basin appear to have been exploited for cattle pasturing during the early medieval period (Chapter 4); however, it is possible that the animals grazed here would have been woefully underfed. Though some oats may have been available, hay was often located at a distance, alongside the Thames or in the upper reaches of the River Wey (Lloyd 1962, 391, fig. 113). It is probable that cattle pastured on the most remote of the Surrey heathlands would have got by on forage as well as cuttings of gorse and holly to see them through the winter.

Whilst *tree* or *pollard hay* was an important feed during the Middle Ages, cattle keeping in contrast to sheep was often inextricably linked to meadow. By the later medieval period the vast majority of demesnes had access to meadowland, which was highly prized as it helped support the greatest stocking densities. Hay production required well-drained and watered grassland and in much of lowland England it comprised an improved land-use, ditches and embankments being required to protect the crop and prevent seasonal flooding (Campbell 2000, 72–73). Only after the hay was mown were meadows used for grazing, and this often communal activity would have been undertaken in the late summer and early autumn. Where hay was scarce, but land fertile, such as in northern and eastern Kent, demesne managers adopted the growing of vetches as an alternative fodder crop (*ibid.*, 75). On the Sussex Coastal Plain, spring sown vetch was the main leguminous crop before nourishing grass could be provided, and was a useful feed in times of shortage such as after hard winters when it could be used to give energy to the plough-team (Brandon 1988, 319). This use of vetch for the feeding of cattle was occasionally utilised in the Weald by the monks of Battle Abbey (Mate 1991, 270), this despite the fact that legumes for pottage yielded higher food-extraction rates than those grown for fodder (Campbell 2000, 12).

Regardless of the availability of alternative winter feeds, a lack of hay was still an impediment to the keeping of cows. On the meadow-deficient chalklands of

Hampshire and Wiltshire to the west, demesne managers reserved their hay for draught oxen. They kept few other cattle (buying in replacement plough beasts from elsewhere), concentrating their pastoral resources on the raising of sheep, which require far less hay, gaining most of their food from grass (Campbell 2000, 75). It is probable that a similar situation influenced the choice to raise sheep on the downlands of the South-East; however, it should be noted that the chalk here was not as remote from meadowland as the downland of central southern England. The South Downs in particular are cut by significant river valleys and peripheral downland locations with access to freshwater have been highlighted as locations suitable for cattle pasturage (Chapters 4 and 7).

Both cattle and sheep were valued for their secondary products and studies of sites such as Portchester Castle (Hants) indicate that wool became increasingly important from the 8th century (Grant 1982, 106; 1988, 151). The production of wool was a land-extensive activity, reliant on vast permanent pastures such as the downland sheepwalk. It was a high-value product relative to its bulk and, if stored properly, it could be kept for long periods without serious deterioration. During the later medieval period, wool was among England's chief international exports (Campbell 2000, 156–57) and this economic importance has influenced the historical evidence, which tends to put rather more emphasis on sheep and wool production than is shown by the zooarchaeological data, cattle bones often outnumbering sheep (Grant 1988, 151; Sykes 2006). Flocks were kept for their fleece but also as dairy animals and as walking sources of manure. Within parts of the South-East, such as the West Sussex Coastal Plain and Sussex Spring-line, the sheepfold was the main method of maintaining fertility. On the downland, the practice of folding aided the capacity for production but also helped consolidate the light chalky soils which would otherwise be unsuitable for extensive cultivation (Brandon 1988, 323). Individually, sheep were of far less value than cattle, and although kept for meat and wool they were also kept for milk production. According to Trow-Smith (1957, 122–23) the yield of the medieval ewe was between 7 and 12 gallons per year whereas that of the cow was somewhere around 120 to 150 gallons. These calculations were based on analysis of well-managed estates and the yields of cows in particular would have been markedly affected by the quality of their feed (*ibid.*).

It is often stated that the place of the cow as a dairy animal was secondary to that of the ewe, female cattle being primarily needed to supply replacement plough oxen. Nevertheless, though medieval cattle dairies would have been extravagant affairs, due to demands on winter fodder, there does appear to have been a tradition of such establishments within the marshes of the South-East and certain parts of the Weald and downland (Chapters 3, 4 and 7). A reference to Archbishop Wulfred's payment for 'the king's cow-land' in the marshes near Faversham (*Cinges culand*; Sawyer 1615) is often interpreted as being linked to a dairy (*e.g.* Witney 1990, 26) and explicit references to later medieval tithes of calves and cheese are known from the Weald and western South Downs of Sussex (Chapter 3; Peckham 1942, 64; Hudson 1987, 26). Excessive numbers of cows on Wealden sites close to water (Drungewick and Stretham) may also be an allusion to dairy herds (or possibly breeding stations; Chapter 3) and it is apparent that the amount of meadow available to Sussex manors was significantly expanded in the later medieval period. On manors where cattle were kept this would have allowed more intensive stocking and greater milk yields. The growth of meadow was largely due to reclamation of wetlands, but also the expansion of settlement within the Wealden region. An example of this process can be seen at Sullington in the Sussex Downs. Here only 6 acres of meadow were recorded at Domesday (Domesday 13,12), although by 1298 there were 10 acres at Sullington and 27 acres at its detached Wealden holding of Broadbridge (Cooper 1903, 174).

In terms of numbers and importance, sheep and cattle compete to be the most significant livestock type throughout the medieval period. Beyond the South-East, national-scale analysis of animal bone assemblages has shown that cattle bones were more numerous on archaeological sites of the early medieval period than those of sheep, although this was likely a product of collection bias (Sykes 2006, 58, fig. 5.1; see Chapter 8). This archaeological evidence is contrary to the historical picture gleaned from Domesday, which gives larger quantities of sheep than cattle (over 285,000 and *c.* 24,000 respectively in the eight counties where livestock were recorded; Darby 1977, 164). There are problems with this data, however, as the numbers exclude plough oxen and the given total of cows and bulls are unrealistic (*ibid.*, 165; Banham and Faith 2014, 87). This is not to overemphasise the reliability of animal bone data, because, as is acknowledged within Chapter 8, assemblages based on NISP tend to exaggerate the importance of cattle due to the species large and robust bones. At an aggregate level it is probable that sheep outnumbered cattle but this does not necessarily translate into relative importance. During the 11th century cattle were valued higher than sheep (ox 30d, cow 3s, sheep 2–2.5d; Harvey 1988, table 2.1) and it is likely these prices take the various animals' size, secondary products and agricultural roles into account. Unfortunately, the animal bone analysis presented in Chapter 8 has some limitations in its contribution to national debates over the relative importance of sheep and cattle. This is due to a general lack of available assemblages for the earliest medieval period.

By the 12th and 13th centuries, population pressure and the intensification of arable production led to the ploughing up of land that had previously been laid to cattle pasture (Grant 1988, 156). In the South-East, increased Wealden assarting and the pushing up of arable land onto peripheral virgin downland was a response to these demographic changes and this in turn had an effect on the amount of available pasture. Increasingly, more marginal areas began to be used as grazing land, a situation that favoured the keeping of sheep over cattle due to their lower nutritional requirements. Medieval oxen and cows were expected to eat between five and eight times as much as a ewe and over ten times as much as a lamb (Campbell 2000, 105). These economic benefits

	Cattle	*Sheep*	*Pigs*
South-East combined later medieval bone assemblages	*c.* 38%	*c.* 45%	*c.* 17%
National medieval combined assemblages (Sykes 2009, fig. 17.1)	*c.* 38%	*c.* 38%	*c.* 24%

		Cattle		*Sheep*		*Pig*		*Total*
		nos	*%*	*nos*	*%*	*nos*	*%*	
South-East combined assemblages	Total middle medieval	17878	38	21373	45	8380	17	47631
	Total late medieval	3410	48	2399	35	1226	17	7035

and an international demand for wool meant that in England seigniorial sheep farming gained in relative importance to cattle over the later medieval period, reaching a peak in the early 14th century (*ibid.*, 157, 160).

The importance of sheep in the South-East is exemplified by the annual amount of wool shipped from Sussex at this time. The total was around 300 sacks and 9,000 wool-fells, representing the produce of nearly 100,000 animals (Pelham 1934, 130). Zooarchaeological data collected for Chapter 8 also demonstrates this regional importance of sheep with numbers 7% above the national average for the medieval period (Table 10.1). It should be noted, however, that it was not cattle who lost out to sheep in comparison to the national data, but pigs.

During the later medieval period cattle made up a proportion of the South-East's animal bone assemblages equal to that of the national average. Despite the historical importance placed on swine pannage, the numbers of pig bones fell below what would be considered normal nationally. By the late 14th and 15th centuries cattle's importance began to grow. The decline in population as a result of the demographic changes of the mid-14th century meant that a switch in emphasis from arable to pastoral farming became the norm. There was increased land available for grazing and beef began to be a popular meat for human consumption. The late medieval importance of cattle relative to sheep is demonstrated by the animal bone data collected for Chapter 8 (Table 10.2). This shows that between the mid-14th to the late 15th century cattle gained in importance by 10% relative to sheep. This difference, contrary to the national trend shown by Grant (1988, 154, fig. 8.2), was no doubt exacerbated by a decline in demand for wool as well as regional environmental factors. 'In soils and situations where alternative forms of pastoral husbandry are possible, sheep farming is one of the least productive methods of producing human food' (Campbell 2000, 155). In pastoral areas, such as the Weald, where cattle were already dominant due to environmental influences, their importance became overwhelming.

10.3 A regionalised economy

The increased late medieval importance of cattle had its basis in a highly regionalised economy. Though it is true to say that while cows and oxen were the *ubiquitous others* of the South-East's medieval pastoralism, in certain landscapes and at certain times cattle were the dominant species kept. Such a view is contrary to our historic perception of the area's livestock economy, biased as it has been to the study of pigs and sheep. As a feature of both seigniorial and peasant agriculture, cattle were, however, present from the Thames to the Channel coast. The varied landscapes that together form the region place a differing emphasis on cattle and various aspects of their husbandry over the period in question. These differences, although noticeable, were clouded by agricultural interdependencies that faded over time but were never completely removed. They were dynamic landscapes, ones that could be radically transformed by human agency and their suitability for cattle altered; something exemplified in particular by the reclamation of coastal marshlands (see below). In turning to the various *pays* that together make up our wider study area we shall begin to discuss the regionalised economy, how it operated and where cattle as opposed to other livestock were most important.

The West Sussex Coastal Plain

The West Sussex Coastal Plain can overwhelmingly be considered an arable region. Nevertheless, it was reliant on other *pays* for the provision of key resources that helped facilitate an emphasis on crop production. Though the growing of cereals was the major enterprise, this was aided by the method of sheep-corn husbandry. Here, during the later medieval period, it was the lord's custom to lease his sheepfold so it could improve the soil of the tenants' arable land. A shepherd would be elected by the community to supervise the sheep as they were brought off the downland to manure the strips of fallow or arable stubbles. That the pastoral element of the *pays* agriculture was based on sheep was reflected in the animal bones analysis undertaken for Chapter 8. The subordinate role of cattle during the middle medieval period (8th–mid-14th century) within the Coastal Plain was also demonstrated through a general lack of cattle place-names recorded prior to AD 1100 (Chapter 4). This was not, however, true of all place-names potentially associated with the economy. A number of '*wic*' sites occurred in the area, although it is arguable whether these were connected to cattle dairying, being more likely linked to salt production or sheep dairies (*e.g.* Shopwyke; Chapter 4).

Despite sheep's dominance throughout much of the *pay*, there were areas where cattle pasturing occurred. They were sometimes kept on meadows or marshes around the major rivers or silting creeks (*rifes*). They were also grazed on the fallows of the open fields. It was the agriculturally poor wooded commons of the Manhood Peninsula, however, which held the greatest concentration of the Coastal Plain's cattle. Here, their pasturing has been proven by place-names and documentary evidence (Chapters 3 and 4) and it is likely that at least some breeding stations occurred to supply draught oxen for the nearby arable.

Larders of cattle were also kept, sometimes within parks such as that at Aldingbourne (Chapter 6). Nevertheless, despite the presence of ecclesiastical establishments such as Cakeham (Chapters 3 and 6), the Coastal Plain was overwhelmingly reliant on other areas for supply of its draught oxen. At Domesday, the coastal strip of Sussex possessed the highest concentration of plough-teams within the county (King 1962, 432, fig. 124); however, the area did not contain the extensive pasture that would enable production of the required number of oxen. From the earliest Middle Ages until the 13th and 14th centuries the Coastal Plain's manors must have exploited their Wealden holdings for production of plough beasts. Likely examples can be shown in the early detached relationships between Drungewick and its parent settlement of Durrington as well as Broadwater and its Wealden outlier of Sedgewick. At the latter, the bones of cattle have been recovered (along with sheep) during archaeological excavations (Winbolt 1925, 109–10) and the medieval park, which probably replaced an earlier seasonal pasture (associated with a pond), was also used as cattle grazing (Hudson 1987, 98; Chapter 6).

At Drungewick the large documented numbers of cattle have been highlighted throughout this book as a likely vaccary pursuing either production of plough beasts or a dairying function at the headwaters of the River Arun (Chapters 3, 4 and 6). Again the site was linked to an oval enclosure (Hale/Pephurst Wood) that would have originated in the early medieval period as a seasonal pastoral reserve (Chapter 6). Not until the widespread switch was made to draught horses could the area's arable thrive without Wealden oxen. By this time cattle farmers' fortunes on the Coastal Plain had begun to change. The benefits of an increased fodder crop caused by the adoption of the round course system allowed far more intensive livestock husbandry than had gone before (Brandon 1971, 129; 1988, 318–20). Cattle, sometimes stalled in barns, could now be fed upon leguminous crops or surplus grain and this intensive husbandry may be witnessed in the increasing number of cattle bones found in urban contexts dated to the late medieval period (Chapter 8). The earlier method of production should not be thought of as in some way backward. On the contrary, it represented a sophisticated way of exploiting extensive estates. It provided a means of maximising early agricultural yields by exploiting areas in terms of their most suited agriculture. Pastoral areas could be used for the grazing of animals to allow locations with the best soils to take fuller advantage of arable cultivation.

The North Kent Plain

A further area noted for its cereals was the North Kent Plain. Together with the Thames Estuary it has emerged as an area that was important both for sheep and cattle (Chapter 8). This mixed pastoral economy is likely to have been influenced by the area's underlying environmental factors as the varied geologies of the area have given rise to diverse landscapes such as marshes, chalk ridges (as on the Isle of Thanet) and heavy clay vales, all suited to different livestock types. As such, the area was home to highly localised livestock regimes matched to the different environments and influenced by local custom. The pastoral economy of the North Kent Plain and Thames Estuary could be seen to be contrary to any idea of a regionalised economy. Here, it was choices at the restricted level of the individual farm that may have been important. This said, the *pays* of the South-East are notoriously difficult to define (Gardiner 2012b, 100–07) and it could be argued that it was the *pay*'s very diverse nature that made it distinctive. The area is, nevertheless, well furnished with demesnes that practised Campbell's (2000, fig. 4.03) pastoral type 2 during the period of High Farming indicating an emphasis on cattle usually for breeding or dairying. These sites are mainly situated along the edges of the former Wantsum Channel or the North Kent Marshes, areas where a ready supply of water, salt and rich grazing would have been beneficial to the economy. These environments were available at the important early estate of Milton Regis which was heavily involved with cattle production and dairying indicated by documentary evidence. It is certain that the area possessed a vaccary (probably at Tunstall) as well as a number of early shieling grounds or outlying cattle and dairy farms indicated by 'stock' names (Chapters 3 and 4).

The Thames Basin

The Thames Basin has also emerged as an area where cattle were of some importance, with bone assemblages indicating the species' significance, particularly to a burgeoning London (Chapter 8). The area is characterised by heavy clays and thin sands as well as riverside meadows and pastures. The greatest concentrations of meadow, facilitating greater cattle stocking densities, were situated in the valleys of the Thames, Wandle, Wey and Mole (Lloyd 1962, 391), rivers which potential cattle-related place-names seem to favour (Chapter 4). The middle Wey valley also benefited from areas of woodland (*ibid.*, 389), which, as discussed, assisted cattle grazing and overwintering. Largely bereft of meadow, however, were the extensive heaths of the Bagshot Sands (*ibid.*, 391). These dry areas, with poor fodder, were more suited to the pasturing of sheep than cattle, a fact that possibly accounts for the lack of related place-names within the *pay* recorded away from the principal watercourses (Chapter 4). This said, an early cattle farm is likely associated with the oval or 'lobe-shaped' enclosure of Cowshot Manor which likely existed from at least the 7th century as a primary settlement or initial intake within an open landscape of far-reaching heaths (Chapter 4). The site was not far (<850 m) from a tributary of the Wey, however, and although grazing in the area may have been poor, water appears to have been readily available.

The importance of meadows and riverine pastures, particularly to the cattle economy, seems to have influenced the road system of the *pay*, which account for livestock movement along watersheds to the Thameside pastures

(Chapter 5). Cattle were also moved across the Thames itself from an early date, as indicated by the place-name Rotherhithe (Chapter 4). This embarkation point was obviously utilised to take cattle to London and it is probably true to say that as the city's importance and population grew its demands on the cattle economy were greater than could be supplied from its immediate hinterland. The meat markets and craft workers of the city would have been reliant on the cattle products of a far wider geographical area than the Thames Basin could provide, resulting in great cattle drives from areas such as the Wash, the Welsh Marches or the Wealden fringe (Chapter 3; Campbell 2000, 140–43).

The South Downs

The South Downs are rightly synonymous with sheep keeping and it can be stated with some confidence that the extensive dry pasture which largely characterised the *pay* was used fairly intensively for this purpose during the medieval period. The importance of sheep is reflected in a number of demesnes which specialised in their husbandry (Campbell 2000, figs 4.06 and 4.07), as well as by the combined animal bone assemblage explored in Chapter 8. By the 13th century ecclesiastical establishments such as Lewes Priory had built a considerable degree of wealth upon the medieval trade in wool and they, as well as the great lay lords, had reinvested capital into specialised downland sheep enterprises, such the sheepcote of the Earl of Arundel on the edge of the tithing of West Dean (Peckham 1942, 35). It is noticeable, however, that a greater number of the South Downs demesnes explored by Campbell (2000, figs 4.04 and 4.05) employed mixed regimes of sheep and cattle. Though it is possible that the cattle kept by these manors were pastured elsewhere, such as holdings situated within the Weald, the numbers indicate that the dominance of sheep within the *pay* may not be straightforward. There are instances of *wic* names situated in the eastern, more open, southern downland (Chapter 4) and it is probable that if these farms were associated with dairying they were employing sheep rather than cattle to produce milk and cheese. This is indicated by the different species' water requirements when lactating (Chapter 7) and areas of seasonal pasture used in common, such as that at Thornwick in the central downland, could have operated as summer sheep dairies. Certainly, livestock on the manor of Angmering were dominated by sheep in the late 14th century when cattle numbered 55 and sheep 1243 (Mark Gardiner, pers. comm.).

Where there was access to water, such as the 'mere' settlements of the scarp foot, the river valleys that cut the downland or areas where chalkland streams existed (such as Sompting Brook), cattle dairying may have been more viable. A record of dairy cows at Sompting in the reign of Edward III (Chapter 5) and the nomenclature of Keymer ('cow pond, lake, pool'; *P.N.Sx* 1930, 276) are illustrative of these points. Wherever river valleys penetrated the chalk downland villages had access to meadow. This was such an important commodity for the medieval keeping of cattle that it can be considered essential for any establishment linked to dairying. The meadows located on the substantial alluvial flats of the Ouse valley were particularly important during the Domesday period and here Hamsey, Iford and South Malling all possessed significant amounts of 200 or more acres (King 1962, 449). Where the downland faced the wetlands of the Pevensey Levels an important record of cattle collection following a period of open pasturing has been encountered (Chapter 3) and the so-called valley entrenchments that were provided with water and allied to long-distance droveways cannot easily be disentangled from this type of cattle husbandry (Chapter 7). Though it is clear that the South Downs can be considered primarily as sheep country in certain peripheral and localised landscapes cattle pasturing was at times more important than has been hitherto realised.

The North Downs

That cattle establishments existed in chalkland settings has been previously demonstrated by Everitt's (1986) work on the North Downs of Kent. At Marden, place-names indicate that cattle and sheep were fed off the browse of the downland woods and this custom of woodland pasture was a major factor behind clearance and colonisation within the *pay* (*ibid.*, 31). In Surrey, where Clay-with-Flints also capped the chalk, woodland existed. The nature of the Domesday evidence means it is difficult to judge the degree of correlation between the geology and woods, at least during the 11th century (Lloyd 1962, 389). By this time the North Downs economy had become generally independent of areas of primary settlement and it seems agriculture was chiefly based on specialised vaccaries and sheep-farms (Everitt 1986, 125). It was not possible to test whether cattle and sheep establishments dominated the area during the preceding 5th to 7th centuries due to the area's lack of excavated zooarchaeological evidence (Chapter 8). By the 'middle medieval period' (8th century to the mid-14th century), however, bone analysis indicates that sheep had become dominant within the *pay*. Though no vaccary sites are currently identifiable via bone assemblages in the North Downs, this in no way implies they did not exist. Indeed, a high-status site at Randall Manor has recently produced a bone assemblage completely dominated by cattle (Andrew Mayfield, pers. comm.).

The Pevensey Levels and Romney Marsh

While cattle dairying played a peripheral role in the downland, it may have been of more importance to the South-East's key wetland areas of the Pevensey Levels and Romney Marsh. Settlement in these *pays* originated as detached seasonal sites prized for their grazing and access to salt. It was shown within Chapter 3 that the quality of salt-marsh was appreciated in the medieval period when it was known that a cow would produce three times as much milk than animals fed elsewhere. On Romney Marsh these detached holdings were known as *seota* with the sites probably acting as the equivalent of the Wealden *denns* (Rippon 2000, 165). *Wic* sites also occurred on the marshland, and their nomenclature has revealed that cattle as well as sheep were pastured on the South-East's wetlands (*ibid.*, 205).

Though cattle grazing in these *pays* appears to have been a significant factor in the medieval economy, the importance may have been dwarfed by their use for sheep, at least at an early date. This situation, which was influenced by underlying environmental factors (*e.g.* salt preventing the occurrence of foot rot; *ibid.*, 39), was corroborated by the areas' 'middle medieval' animal bone assemblages, which showed sheep were by far the most numerous species (Chapter 8). By the late medieval period the situation had changed, however, with the growing importance of cattle notable in the zooarchaeological evidence of Romney Marsh (Chapter 8). It is probable that the salt-marsh, so important for sheep dairying, had become much reduced through 13th- and 14th-century reclamation and an additional factor would have been the more settled rather than seasonal nature of the marsh's occupation. This would have acted as a restriction on access of the wetlands for commoning of foreign sheep and the more settled, partly arable economy would have allowed far greater use of the area for cattle. This change may be reflected in the demesnes that fringed the marsh explored by Campbell (2000, figs 4.03, 4.06 and 4.07) that showed an emphasis on a specialised cattle as opposed to sheep economy. This change was not ubiquitous, however, as is exemplified by the records of the manors of Denge and Lydd. Here, the documents remind us that the economy of these *pays* could be radically transformed overtime. Denge in 1356–57 possessed 20 horses, 96 cattle, 178 sheep and 39 swine, but by the late 15th century the adjoining manor of Lydd was overwhelmingly dominated by sheep flocks (Mark Gardiner, pers. comm.).

The Greensand Ridge

An area that was settled somewhat earlier than Romney Marsh or the Pevensey Levels was the Greensand Ridge. Here, a pattern of droveways led deep into the Wealden interior and it is certain that these ancient routes were used for the seasonal movement of stock. Nevertheless, it is probable that the extensive commons found within this area were also utilised in the cattle economy, as may be shown by the animal bone assemblage from Friar's Oak, Hassocks (Chapter 8). What was more striking during this investigation, however, was the degree to which the medieval use of the outlying pannage system may be witnessed in the Greensand's excavated archaeological evidence. Peasant communities, such as those of the manor of Buckland, Surrey, appear to have been exploiting swine pasture rights in the Wealden interior and the evidence of pig bones indicates the regional importance of the system (Chapter 8). The evidence presented here may, however, cause a re-evaluation of the Weald's use for swine pannage. Though pigs may have been pastured in the Weald proper during the autumn mast season, we sometimes forget that it was the areas that fringed the Weald where they were kept for the remainder of the year, and consumed after slaughter. It is debatable, therefore, just how important the pasturing of swine was for the Weald as the practice had a fairly restricted time frame (its probable peak being the 10th and 11th centuries) and was long survived by a contemporaneous use for cattle. The latter had, by the 12th century, transitioned from the seasonal summering of herds to become a key permanent part of the *pays* settled economy (Chapter 11).

The Weald

In the discussion above it has been demonstrated just how regionalised the pastoral economy of the South-East really was. The nature of this regionalism was intimately linked to the area's banded resources and underlying environmental factors such as geology and hydrology. It was a number of the latter variables that made both the High and Low Weald uniquely suited to the pasturing of cattle. The heavy, sometimes wet clay of the *pays* was not appropriate for sheep, a fact reflected in the species' early 14th-century distribution (Pelham 1934). The area's environmental conditions also gave rise to extensive woodlands that were advantageous to the keeping of goats and pigs, but the former were never a particularly widespread domesticate and had legal restrictions on their grazing (Dyer 2004; see section 10.2 above). The custom of swine pannage, while being an important factor in the area's early settlement and land-use, was limited chronologically (perhaps being mainly restricted to the 10th and 11th centuries) and overwhelmingly seasonal in its application (being reliant on the autumnal mast of oak and beech). It has been argued above that pig keeping can be considered important beyond the geographical confines of the *pays*.

Economic conditions also favoured the keeping of Wealden cattle; although the area's roads were of poor quality, it was close to markets, including London. Its eastern portion also had access to a number of ports such as Rye, which was well placed to export the pastoral products of the Rother valley (Campbell 2000, 88). The Weald's land was only ever of low to medium value and vast tracts were given over to woodland, wood-pasture and grassland; a situation that favoured the reasonably land-extensive cattle economy. At a national level, exceptional extents of pasture existed in the Wey valley of west Surrey (an important supplier of fat animals to the capital), the Isle of Oxney in the valley of the eastern Rother (Kent) and the 'Forests' of Ashdown and St Leonard's, deep in the wooded core of the Sussex Weald (Campbell 2000, 88–89). Lay subsidy assessments are a good way of judging the agricultural interests and wealth of an area and a good example of a Wealden hundred can be found in Henhurst, East Sussex, detailed in the subsidy roll for AD 1332. The area had a profusion of milk cows and calves, as well as oxen, steers, horses and pigs, but very few sheep (Salzman 1961, 17; Hallam 1988d, 818–19).

Though wood-pasture was less nutritious than marsh meadow or fescue grassland, it was significant because in the Weald it was so extensive (Witney 1990, 25). Such habitats may not have been suited to dairying as the quality of feed severely affected milk yields and acorn consumption was hazardous to both the unborn calf and its mother. Woodland grazing was likely, but not exclusively, utilised for producing the plough oxen required by areas of greater arable potential or the beef steers required by the market. Dairies could exist within the river valleys and probable examples have been identified at Stretham and Drungewick (Chapters 3, 4 and 6). It was the area encompassing the upper reaches of the Arun and Wey valleys, however, which can be considered the real heartland of the South-East's cattle economy. Though a specialized economy existed within the High Weald (see section 10.4 below), it was here that a number of factors came together to imply cattle's importance. It was an area where documentary evidence has shown high numbers of cows were kept (*e.g.* Drungewick), it was well provided with commons, and was on the edge of extensive wood-pasture in the form of St Leonard's Forest. Here, tithes of calves and cheese are known from the 13th century (Hudson 1987, 26) and the Chase was fringed by parks and detached holdings engaged in pastoralism (Chapters 5 and 6). The area's manors possessed rich grazings on streamside pastures of the upper tributaries of the Rivers Wey and Mole, but by the later medieval period they also possessed quantities of meadow that sometimes dwarfed those of the so-called original lands (*e.g.* Broadbridge versus Sullington; see section 10.2 above). It was an area of oval pastoral enclosures and a dense corpus of place-names that are potential indicators of the economy (Chapters 4 and 6). It was the destination of a closely aligned set of parallel droveways (Chapter 5) and was known to produce fat-stock for the capital in the later medieval period (Campbell 2000, 88–89).

10.4 The specialised economy – the presence and nature of vaccaries

It is often the case that where highly regionalised pastoral economies existed specialised establishments flourished. One of the key aims of this book was to highlight the presence of the South-East's medieval cattle farms or vaccaries and the work undertaken has not only shown them to exist but has also succeeded in identifying individual examples. The exploration below will demonstrate their components and function, together with their development and date. Whilst it is primarily the Weald that has emerged as cattle country, vaccaries occurred in many of the *pays* of the South-East (Plate 10.1). This is due to the length of time over which they developed and also the distinct environments that encouraged their distribution. Though they principally appear as landscape elements in areas of secondary settlement, they also occurred in areas considered 'original lands'. On closer inspection such examples (*e.g.* Amberley and Milton Regis) were intimately associated with river valleys and low-lying marshes, areas at the margins of settlement prone to seasonal flooding. Whilst the map of noted vaccaries (Plate 10.1) is useful, it should by no means be considered a reliable reflection of distribution. It is likely that more vaccary establishments existed within the South-East, particularly in landscapes which have been shown to be highly engaged with the cattle economy.

One of the most certain vaccary establishments brought to light was that belonging to the manor of Milton Regis, Kent. The demesne was an early possession of the Crown, being so since before Domesday, and this royal patronage may have facilitated the extravagant demands on hay and other resources that cattle dairying required. That the manor was in possession of a cattle dairy is not specifically recorded until the 14th century, when a Report of Inquisition was compiled. It showed the presence of a *vaccaria* with a cow-house, part of which was called 'Somerhous', a building undoubtedly linked to the dairying activities performed by tenants of the manor (Chapter 3; CCA-DCc-ChAnt/M/244A). That dairying occurred on the estate was also recorded at Domesday when 56.5 weys of cheese appeared in the entry for nearby Newington. These were as a due from the manor of Milton Regis (Domesday 13,1; Campbell 1962, 556). This production of cheese was perhaps wrongly assigned to sheep by Harvey (1988, 126) as it is certain the north Kent marshes of the wider area were also engaged in early cattle dairying. We only have to consider Archbishop Wulfred's high payment for a tract of marshland between Faversham Creek and Graveney known as 'the king's cow-land' (AD 805; Sawyer 1615) to view Harvey's assumption as a product of the regional emphasis on the sheep economy. It is probable that one of the chief vaccary enclosures in the area was south of Milton Regis at Tunstall, which is also mentioned in Domesday (see Chapter 4) when it was recorded as possessing a salt-house useful in the dairy process (see section 2.5; Domesday 5,115). Likewise, the settlement of Milstead is likely to have originated as a place where cattle were milked (Chapter 4). The landscape here is crossed by aligned north-east–south-west droveways that reach up to the North Downs and on towards the extensive marshes on the River Swale and Milton Creek. Place-names indicate that the subsidiary sites of Woodstock, Bistock, Pistock/Pitstock and Stockbury originated as shieling grounds and were situated on these droveways at the edge of nearby downland. While beginning as seasonal sites, they would later develop into dependent outlying dairy or cattle farms (Chapter 4; Figure 10.2). Being situated in a downland gap near the tidal reaches of the River Arun, it is possible that areas around Amberley operated in a similar way, although the association of sites here are far less certain due to tenurial separations and other manors in the area were known to operate a sheep-based economy (*e.g.* Bury in the early 14th century; Mark Gardiner, pers. comm.).

Though the earliest medieval vaccaries, especially those engaged in dairying, may have been royal preserves, by the later medieval period great lay and ecclesiastical lords as well as monastic institutions were pursuing this specialised form of husbandry. At Stretham and Drungewick, Sussex, the Bishop of Chichester owned establishments documented for their high numbers of cows (Chapter 3; Figure 10.3) and in the Ashdown Forest the Augustine monks of Michelham Priory operated Chelwood Vetchery. This was separated from the open forest beyond by a ring-fenced oval enclosure (Chapter 6; Figure 10.4). A similar site existed at nearby Haywards Heath, where the Hayworth, a vaccary on the manor of Trubwick, originated as a seasonal enclosure belonging to the powerful Godwin's. After the Conquest it fell to William Warenne. Under his

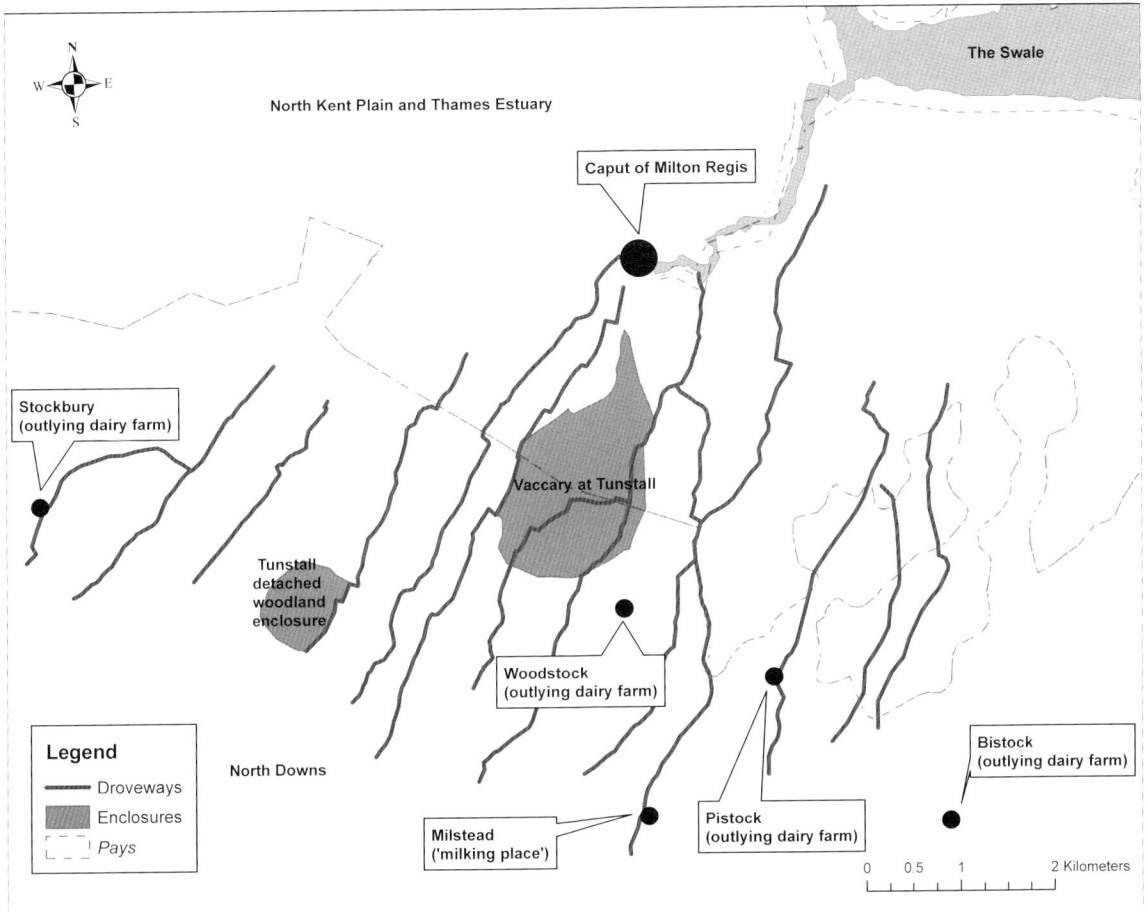

FIGURE 10.2: Vaccary elements and the droveway system at Milton Regis. The routeways link the woodland grazings on the North Downs with rich summertime pastures on the marshes bordering the Swale and Thames (illustration by the author)

baronial patronage, the manor of Trubwick evolved from a pasture in the forest to a fully functioning *vaccaria*. Despite these aristocratic origins, by the 13th or 14th century the establishment was in the possession of a petty sub-infeudated 'lord' (Chapter 9).

Whilst the social position of vaccary owners varied, gradually diminishing in status overtime, the workers engaged in these enterprises are likely to have remained relatively constant. Prior to the evolution of permanent vaccaries, summer pasturing of cattle was the task of slaves, herdsmen and amateur dairymaids. At the summer shieling grounds the production of butter and cheese was undertaken by the community's young women, the errand perhaps being an important rite of passage (Herring 2012, 98–99). Such locations are recognisable from their association with 'maiden' names (Fox 2012, 155–56), but after Domesday dairymaids began to fulfil a specific manorial role. The anonymous writer of *Hosebonderie* records that as well as dairy produce they would also be responsible for the small livestock of the demesne, the role granting them particular obligations and rights. The presence of these women and the inclusion of a separate dairy account within

To Cowfold (woodland enclosure)

Henfield

Location of Wicks
(outlying dairy farm)

Vaccary enclosure
at Rye Farm

Riverside pastures and meadow

Stretham Manor (moated site)

Location of Wykham (outlying dairy farm)

manorial records is one of the surest signs of a specialist interest in dairying (Campbell 2000, 148).

A glimpse of how the vaccaries which fringed the Forests and Chase of the South-East may have operated is contained in the records of the Forests of Yorkshire, Rossendale and Blackburnshire. Here, the officers of vaccaries were known as '*instauratores*' (Baildon 1906, xxx; Tupling 1927, 23) and they were responsible for the proper housing, feeding and pasturing of the herd (Tupling 1927, 23). They looked after vaccaries implanted at well-watered sites on the Forest edge, with 'summer lodges' on the old shieling grounds of the high moors above (Tupling 1927, 23–25; Trow-Smith 1957, 107–08). The vaccary keepers each had to report to a Chief Instaurator who organised the distribution of cattle and their transfer from vaccary to vaccary. He would also inspect the stock from time to time to monitor their welfare, making sure those that belonged to his lord were marked and that animals requiring culling were disposed of (Tupling 1927, 23, 25). A glimpse of this aspect of husbandry is recorded by the *Seneschaucie* (284–85)(Oschinsky 1971):

> And every year, from each vaccary, cause the old cows with bad teeth, and the barren, and the draft of the young avers that do not grow well to be sorted out that they may be sold in the way aforesaid.

Herds on the vaccaries of Rossendale were comprised of some 37 to 40 cows, one bull, five to six steers, five to six heifers, 13 yearlings and 14 to 16 calves

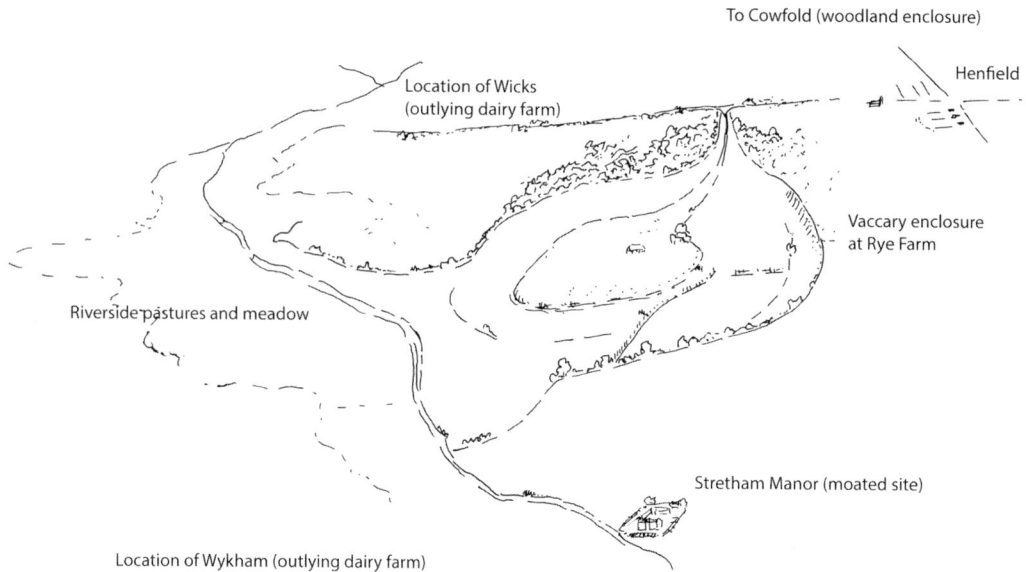

FIGURE 10.3: Vaccary elements on the manor of Stretham (alias Henfield). A vaccary enclosure was located at Rye Farm which could exploit the rich grazings on the banks of the Adur as well as rougher pasture on commons south and east of Henfield (illustration by the author)

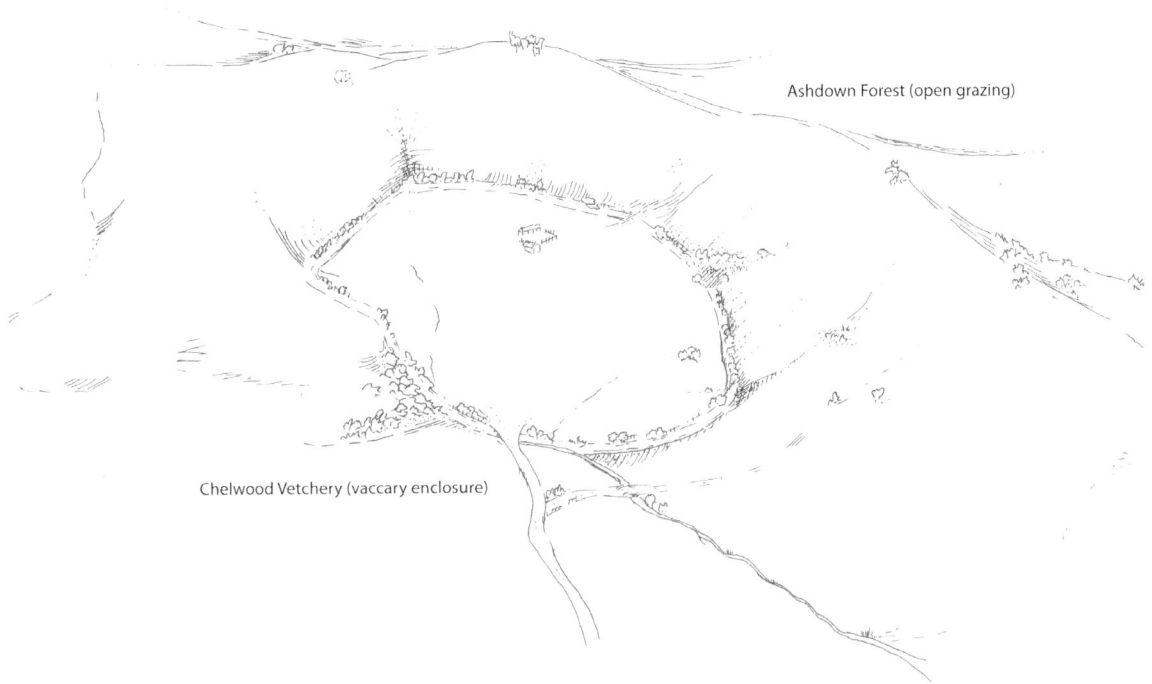

Ashdown Forest (open grazing)

Chelwood Vetchery (vaccary enclosure)

FIGURE 10.4: A suggested reconstruction of the ecclesiastical vaccary enclosure at Chelwood Vetchery on the Ashdown Forest (illustration by the author)

(Trow-Smith 1957, 107–08). In the Wyresdale Forest, Lancashire, each stock keeper was responsible for one bull and between 21 and 44 cows. In Blackburnshire the number of cows was also high (40 to one or two bulls; Winchester 2010, 114–15).

Numbers on lowland vaccaries are somewhat harder to establish. Nevertheless, in the valley of the River Wensum, north-west of Norwich, a series of 13th-century dairy accounts survive that reveal the workings of a demesne engaged in the large-scale production of butter and cheese. Here, a cowman tended a herd of 25 to 30 milk cows and the dairying was the duty of a full-time maid (Campbell 2000, 148). Within the South-East, establishments with numbers of cows comparable to the northern vaccaries have been encountered (Chapter 3) and at Stretham the numbers exceeded those on the dairy near Norwich. Despite the size of these units it is likely that the majority of South-Eastern vaccaries pastured in the region of 20 cows, with perhaps half as many followers, a bull and a variable number of oxen.

It has already been stated that vaccaries had a close association with areas of Forest and Chase, originating as elite institutions as part of the lord's forest demesne. What can be seen from Figure 10.5, however, is that they were also intimately tied to river valleys, whether that be the main channel or headwaters

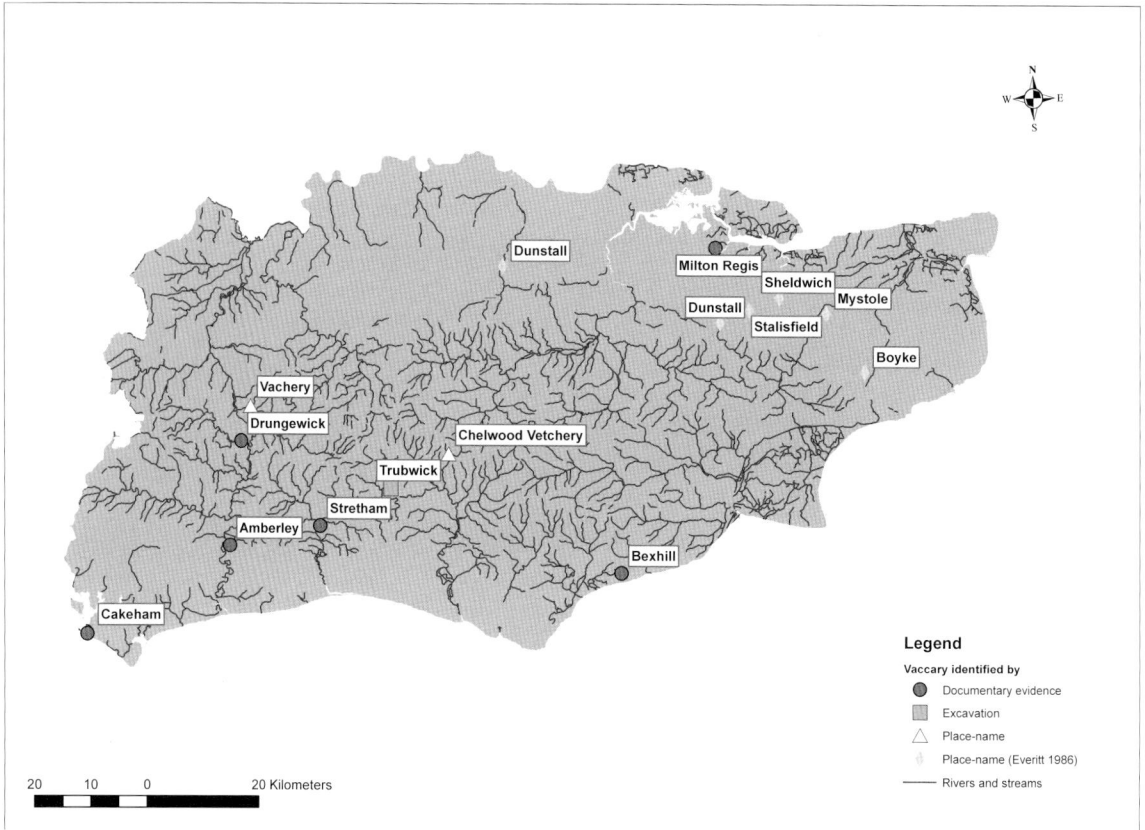

FIGURE 10.5: Highlighted vaccaries and the hydrology of the South-East. The vaccary sites are distinguished by their primary means of identification (vaccaries identified by documentary evidence were the most confidently recognised followed by excavation and place-names; drawn by the author. Contains material covered by © Crown copyright and database rights 2019 Ordnance Survey, Educational Service Provider licence number v2.1)

and tributaries. This is largely a product of the species water requirements (Chapter 7) but is also linked to the presence of meadow (see sections 10.2 and 10.3 above). Even the driest *pays* of the South-East, the chalkland hills, showed evidence of vaccaries largely where watercourses cut the Chalk. The vaccaries first highlighted by Everitt (1986) existed along the Great Stour, River Darent and the Nailbourne. He also recorded a number of sites away from watercourses, although these may have been influenced by the impermeable nature of the underlying geology, a factor that allowed stock ponds to be dug in the downland woods.

Apart from Cakeham, on the Sussex Coastal Plain, all the vaccaries identified here were associated with the slopes of rising land (Figure 10.6). This site stands out for other reasons, primarily its large number of oxen (46 in AD 1220) but also its association with a medieval park belonging to the Bishop of Chichester. It is possible that the park enclosure operated as a vaccary prior to a hunting preserve and the 20 cows recorded for the manor (Peckham 1942, 61–62) may have produced some, but not all, of the plough teams needed for the episcopal grain factories of the wider Coastal Plain. It is possible that a portion of the oxen pastured here were stocked as a larder for the Bishop's estate, but they

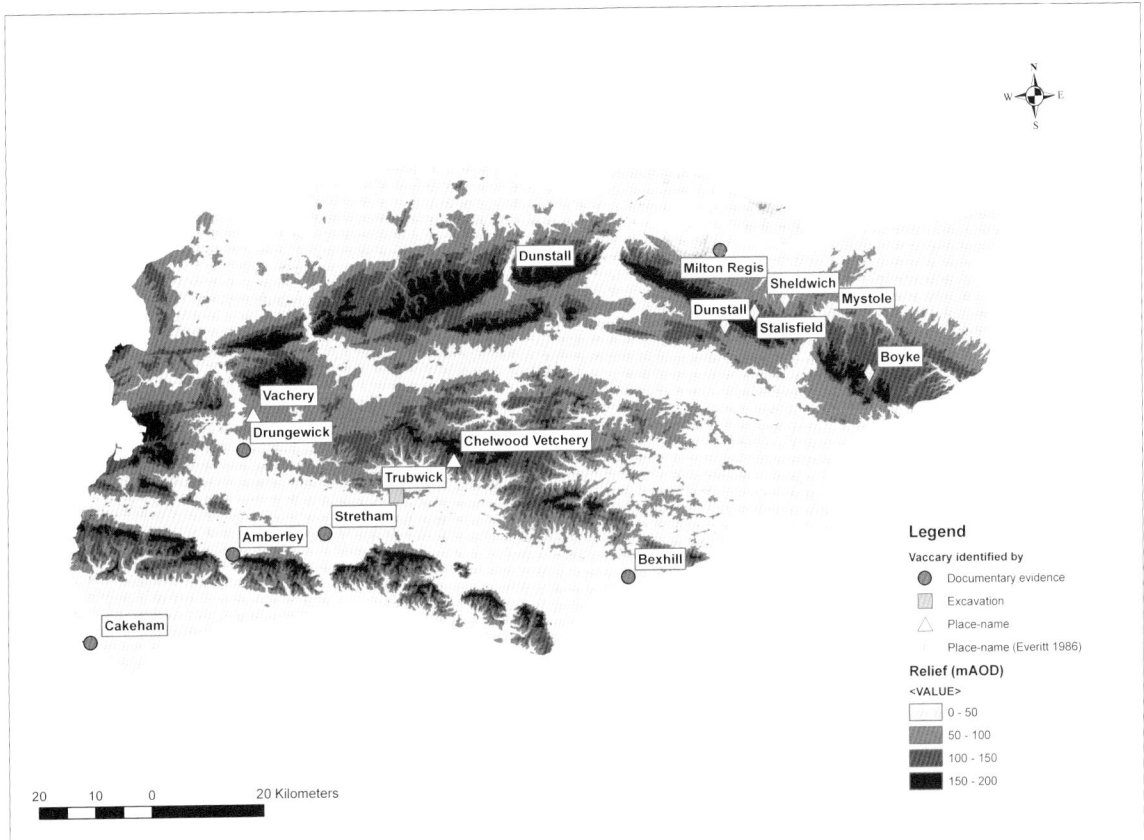

FIGURE 10.6: Highlighted vaccaries and the topography of the South-East. The vaccary sites are distinguished by their primary means of identification (vaccaries identified by documentary evidence were the most confidently recognised followed by excavation and place-names; drawn by the author. Contains material covered by © Crown copyright and database rights 2019 Ordnance Survey, Educational Service Provider licence number v2.1)

may also represent animals grazed following a journey from elsewhere within the South-East. The oxen could have been here gathering their strength prior to working on ecclesiastical demesnes. The manor was favoured with access to the marshes of Chichester Harbour as well as the woodlands and waste of the Manhood Peninsula.

The association of vaccaries with areas of common and waste can be demonstrated using data gathered for Chapter 5. Of the vaccaries that were located in the most intensively studied part of the South-East, the transect study area, all were within 2 km of an area of common or waste (Figure 10.7). Though these are likely to represent smaller fragments of once larger commons, it is probable they only afforded a portion of the open pastures available to medieval vaccaries. It was areas of Forest and Chase that provided the most extensive grazing exploited by the South-East's cattle enterprises. It was the large baronial Chases of St Leonard's and Ashdown Forests where the vaccary herds of the Weald wandered during the summer (Figure 10.8). These large areas of wood-pasture and heath facilitated the large stocking densities recorded on the well-watered and ring-fenced pastures of the vaccary proper.

FIGURE 10.7: Vaccaries of the transect study area in relation to common and waste surviving in the 19th century (drawn by the author)

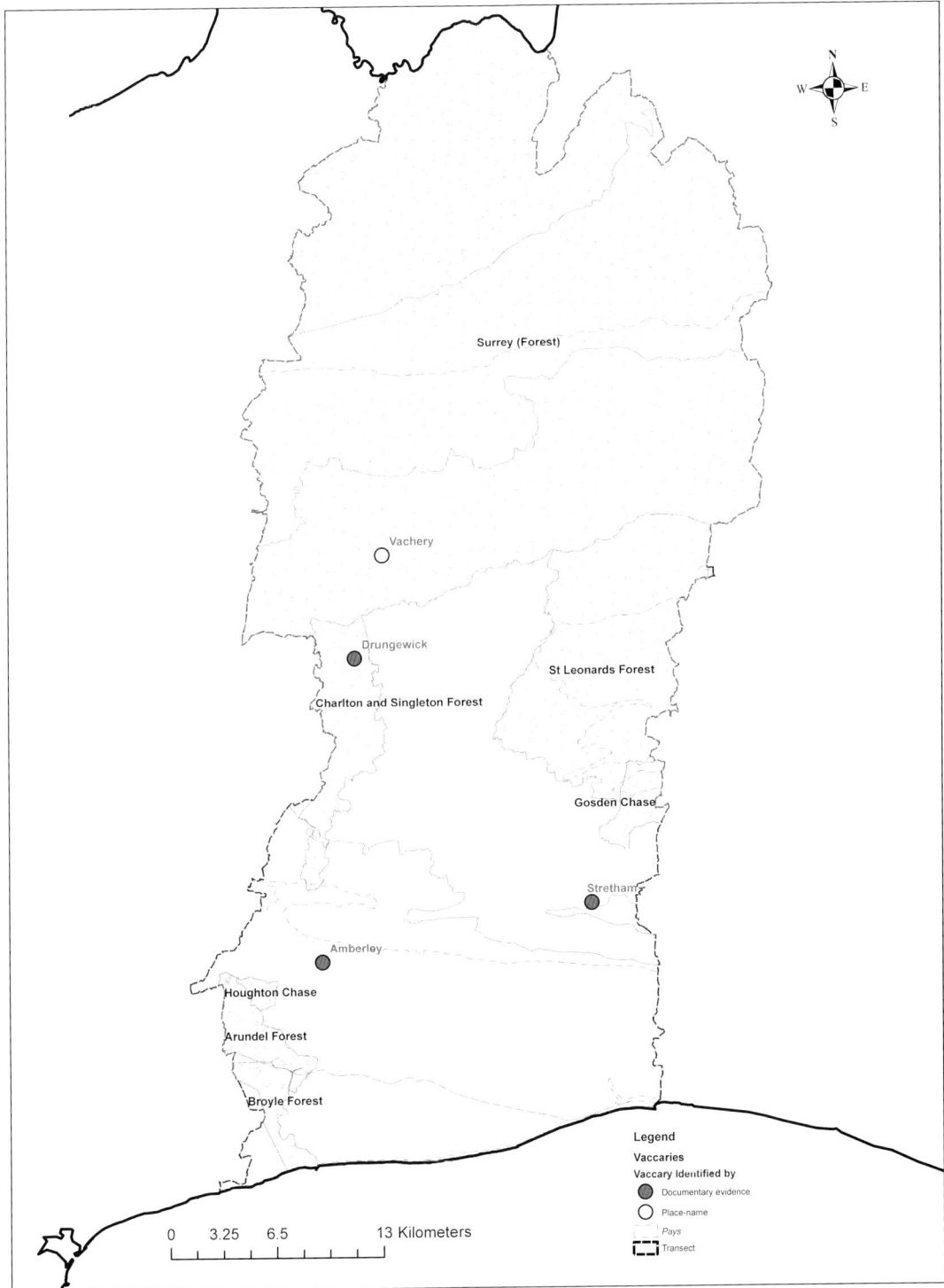

FIGURE 10.8: Vaccaries of the transect study area in relation to the Forest and Chase (drawn by the author, Forest and Chase after Langton and Jones 2010, fig. 1)

During the winter, when cattle were pastured in these large enclosures, they would sometimes be stalled in cow-houses. These were the most important in a group of vaccary buildings and comprised large, sometimes open-fronted structures (Margetts 2017). Documentary studies show cow-houses to have been of considerable length, for example at Gatesgarth vaccary, Buttermere (Cumbria), the 13th-century cow-house measured 67 feet (20.5 m) long (Winchester 2003, 114). Some appear to have had multiple components, as indicated by the 'Cowhous' in the manor of Milton Regis, Kent, which had a part called 'Somerhous' 18 feet wide (*c.* 5.48 m) and 48 feet long (14.6 m; CCA-DCc-ChAnt/M/244A). An ox-house at Kensworth (Bedfordshire) was 33 feet long (10 m) and 12 feet wide (3.65 m; Trow-Smith 1957, 113), whereas the cow-house excavated at the Hayworth was 34 m in length and *c.* 6.5 m in width, facing onto a fenced yard (Chapter 9). It had a clear division, perhaps hinting at the compartmentalisation mentioned above, and its straw-yard was reminiscent of the *forstals* of Kent which appear to have been areas adjoining the cow-house used for overwintering and milking (Chapter 4). Though cow-houses were the chief building of a vaccary it was not just cattle that dwelt within the enclosures. The vaccary keeper and his family, too, were supplied with a dwelling (Margetts 2017). Things may not have been so comfortable for the cowherd, however, who appears to have bedded down with his charges amongst the litter or ferns (Oschinsky 1971, 284–85).

The vast majority (75%) of vaccaries highlighted here (*i.e.* excluding those identified by Everitt) were situated in the Weald. All located within the transect study area were within areas of irregular road patterns on the fringes of the aligned pattern of parallel droveways (Figure 10.9) and were within 2 km of an oval enclosure or park explored within Chapter 6. The association with these landscape elements, as well as concentrations of potentially associated place-names (Figure 10.10), illuminates how the South-East's vaccaries evolved and functioned over time. The association with oval enclosures is best discussed in relation to settlement development (see Chapter 11 below), but it is clear from Figure 10.9 that the Sussex examples are all related to long-distance droveways coming from the south, whereas the Surrey example of Vachery is related to a road heading from the foot of the North Downs. This betrays the establishment's medieval date as well as links with markets and parent settlements. The road system was utilised at the local level to move livestock between pasture including enclosed winter quarters, with protected grassland, meadow and browse, as well as open summer grazings, whether that be in grassland, wood-pasture or heath. It is likely that these Wealden vaccaries represent a second phase of vaccary development. The first examples existed during the early medieval period at the fringes of areas of so-called primary settlement. Only later would vaccaries be implanted in the Weald, as replacements for seasonal pastures and as a seigniorial response to maximising resources and livestock production.

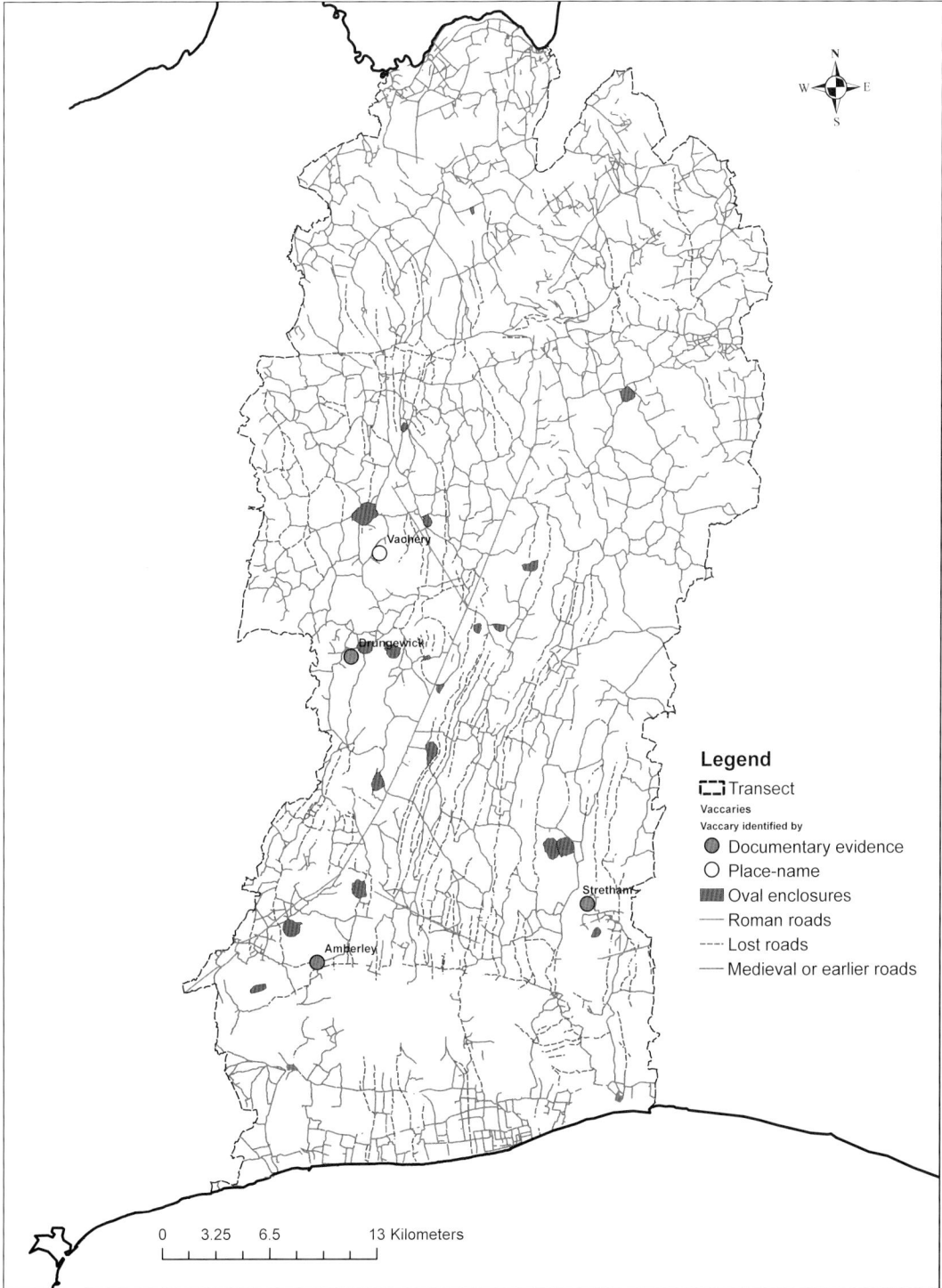

FIGURE 10.9: Vaccaries of the transect study area in relation to the medieval road system and oval enclosures identified within Chapter 6 (drawn by the author)

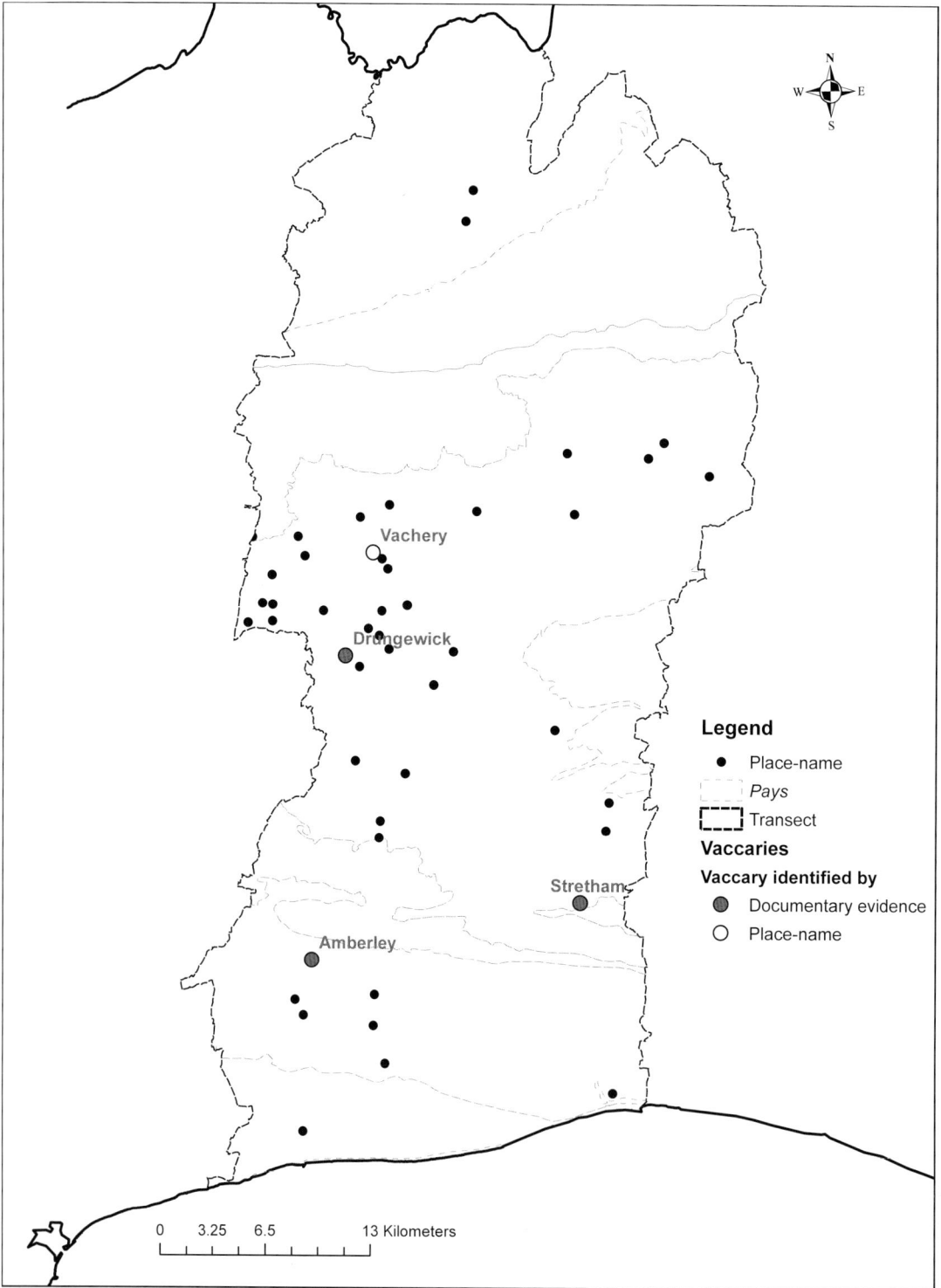

FIGURE 10.10: Vaccaries of the transect study area in relation to potential cattle-related place-names explored within Chapter 4 (drawn by the author)

CHAPTER 11

Conclusion

11.1 Cattle and colonisation

> The rights and customs of a pastoral society have thus had a profound effect on the evolution of Kentish settlement. They had their origins on the heavily wooded nature of the county, and their consequences have continued to affect the character of the county until very recently. (Everitt 1986, 32)

The interdisciplinary nature of this study has allowed an uncommon glimpse of perhaps the greatest significance of the cattle economy within the South-East, that is its influence on the region's historic settlement pattern and landscape development. As a driver of 'colonisation' and as a facilitator of both seasonal and permanent exploitation of so-called marginal areas, cattle husbandry has played a central role in the evolution of the region's historic landscape. More than this, however, these influences are still eminently traceable in the place-names, road-systems and field-pattern of some of the most archaeologically understudied parts of the country. What has been shown is that unless the nature of the cattle economy is grasped then it is impossible to comprehend the history of the Weald in particular, but also the wider region and medieval England in general. The cattle economy played a central role in the movement from the seasonal countryside utilised via transhumance to permanently settled dispersed farms where an emphasis on the production of cattle allowed additional outputs such as the growing of an arable crop or the effective management of woodland. It was the process of matching cattle to particular underlying environmental variables that made them such an asset to medieval husbandmen, lords and estates. By examining some of the evidence provided by recent excavations (Margetts 2017; 2018a) as well as the wider contribution of the work undertaken here, a speculative model of landscape evolution, one heavily reliant on cattle husbandry, can be proposed.

Much of the foundation of the medieval cattle economy lies in the intercommonable countrysides of the late 5th and 6th centuries. These are likely to have been very extensive, taking in such landscapes as the Manhood Peninsula (*mæne-wudu* P.N.Sx 1929, 79), the North and South Downs, the coastal and estuarine marshes, much of Surrey, and the entirety of the Weald. It is likely that the use of these areas was dependent on the fluctuating hegemonies of various communities and kingdoms of the earliest medieval period. Nevertheless, it is entirely probable that areas used in common were being defined at an early date, landscapes conceivably being inherited from as far back as later prehistory (Oosthuizen 2011; 2013). The endurance of these landscapes can be postulated as the result of environment and tradition rather than any political continuity. An example of one of these ancient customary commons is perhaps identifiable in the converging administrative boundaries and parochial detachments that exist near Thornwick, Barpham Week and Lee Farm on the South Downs (Chapter 5). Though these landscape elements, and the noted oval enclosure (Chapter 6), clearly relate to historic use of this remote portion of downland, it is interesting to note the proximity of the prehistoric enclosure at Harrow Hill (Figure 11.1). Hillforts are thought to have played a role in uniting dispersed communities as well as in management of livestock and communal seasonal grazing (Cunliffe 2005; Hamilton 2007, 85–86), and, although such geographical associations may be mere coincidence, it should not prevent us from theorising on the origins and nature of communal landscapes.

Following the intercommoning phase, in the late 6th and 7th centuries particular areas began to be appropriated by communities through customary usage. Though it is important not to dismiss areas of so-called secondary settlement as entirely uninhabited (Margetts 2018a), folk-groups of the kingdoms of Kent and Sussex started to identify parcels of land as their own. Such areas can be witnessed in the Weald of the men of Wye, the *Weowerawealde*, or the folk-commons and royal outlands of the *Limenwarowealde* or the *Bēadingas*

FIGURE 11.1: The Thornwick oval enclosure in relation to the prehistoric enclosure at Harrow Hill. Other oval enclosures were found in proximity to hillforts at Langham Wood and Hazel Hall (OS 1st Edition, 1876, with labelling by the author)

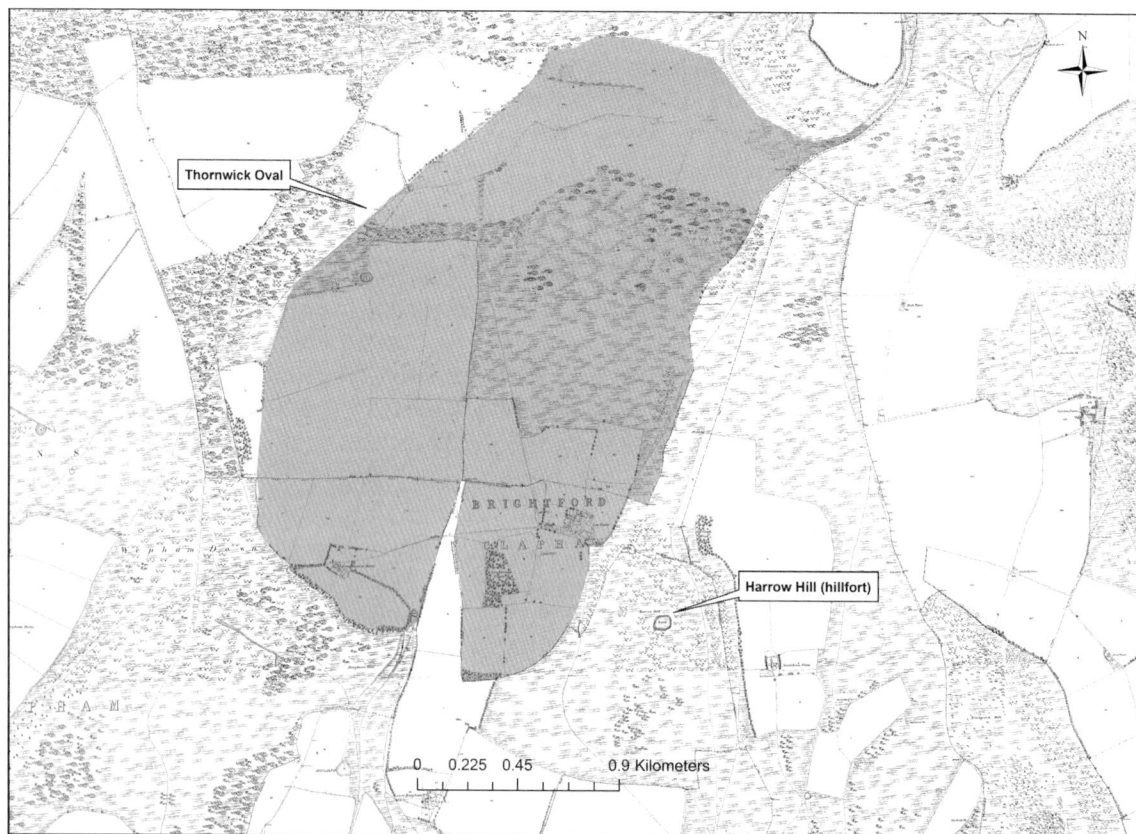

(Chapter 5). It is likely that these areas were exploited for their natural resources in the form of timber, stone and iron, but primarily as summer cattle grazings and perhaps autumn swine pastures. The commons were portions of the greater *Andredesweald* and were exploited via a phase of 'personal transhumance', whereby people moved with their livestock on a seasonal basis (see Fox 2012). During periods of cattle summering herders would have dwelt in crude shelters or shielings similar to the transhumance huts of upland areas in the north and west of Britain and in parts of Ireland. The difference with the South-East's examples is that they were primarily built of timber rather than in stone. They were largely of a type identified as *(ge)sells* or *scydds*, although sunken feature buildings may have additionally featured in such a role (Margetts 2018a; Chapter 9).

In the 7th and 8th centuries, as appropriation of marginal landscapes gathered pace, there was an increasing need to define smaller seasonal pastures within the wider commons. These were the origins of the *denns*, *wics* and *falods* of Kent, Sussex and Surrey. They were created by multiple estates as dependent outlying pastures, carved out of the open landscapes beyond. These early seasonal pastures, the 'folk-dens' (Witney 1976), appear to have occupied the choicest, south-facing slopes close to water and were the destination of an aligned pattern of droveways that penetrated the Wealden interior. These early *denns* can be identified via the place-name record where direct links can be distinguished between folk-groups of the original lands and these outlying pastures (*e.g.* Drungewick, *Dēoringa wīc*, and Clemsfold, Climpe's *falod*; *P.N.Sx* 1929, 131, 159). They were often clustered around earlier wood-pasture commons (*lēah*; *e.g.* Goringlee 'the clearing of the *Gāringas*'; *P.N.Sx* 1929, 181) or more open '*feld*' (*e.g.* Itchingfield 'open land of the people of Ecci'; *P.N.Sx* 1929, 176), these areas representing land used in-common, parcelled out from the older forest of *Andred*.

The final fragments of the old intercommonable Weald possibly survived as Anglo-Saxon free outland or as royal preserves, the '*communi pastura*' and '*sylvia regalis*' named in early charters. It can be postulated that at this early date the *lēahs* and *feld* were primarily utilised as cattle shieling grounds or as pastures for woodland mares; as indicated by instances of names like Rotherfield (*hrydera-feld* 'open land of the cattle'; *P.N.Sx* 1930, 376–77) or Horsley, Sussex (*hors*, *leah*; *P.N.Sx* 1930, 388). Though that Wealden rarity, sheep, also feature in association with *lēah and feld* (Shipley and Sheffield, Sussex; *scēap*; *P.N.Sx* 1929, 188–89; 1930, 347) nowhere are pigs named in conjunction. It may be as Turner (1997, 10) hypothesised, that swine pasture was not the original function of Wealden commons, but a '10th-century use of the woodlands adjacent to them', the areas that would become 'swine-dens' or specialised cattle enclosures of the manorial phase (see below).

As the medieval period progressed there was an increasing tendency for the multiple estates to begin to fragment, lords rather than kings started to take responsibility for regulating the use of the forest and the customary tradition of the early *denns* gave way to management via obligations or rights. From the 8th century the *denns* were increasingly defined by boundaries and encroachment on older commons can only have served to restrict the amount of open pasture (or wood-pasture) available for cattle. The oval or arc-shaped boundaries explored in this book (Chapter 6) can most confidently be assigned to this phase of Wealden development; however, it is probable that they began to emerge by the 7th century and many could be based on survivals or re-establishments of even earlier enclosures (Margetts 2018a). Though open pasture was in decline, it is probable that the ring-fenced nature of the manorial *denns* now afforded greater opportunities for enclosed autumn swine-pannage and the overwintering of cattle, factors that would have acted as an encouragement to more permanent occupation. From the 8th to 11th centuries, transhumance in the Weald increasingly became one of an 'impersonal' nature, tenants more frequently being elected or obliged to drive animals to the old outlying pastures. The use of the *denns* as detached pasture continued into the 13th century, and, as a right, pannage sometimes remained even into the 14th and 15th centuries (Chapter 6). As the later medieval period progressed, however, obligations were increasingly substituted for payments and pasture rights were commonly challenged, surrendered or ignored.

By the 10th and 11th centuries, the largely seasonal use of the Weald steadily gave way to more permanent occupation. This stage of Wealden colonisation has frequently been postulated by landscape historians (Witney 1976; Everitt 1986; Brandon 2003, 50) but has recently been proven via large-scale excavation combined with a programme of radiocarbon dating (Margetts 2018a). Key in the process of moving from a seasonal to permanent countryside was the manorial granting of land rights and subinfeudation of detached Wealden pastures, creating new permanent holdings within the South-East's interior. The latter really began to gather pace in the 12th and 13th centuries as population pressure encouraged expansion onto more marginal areas of land. During the early part of this period vaccaries featured as high-status specialised establishments implanted on the edge of areas of medieval Forest and Chase, although earlier 8th- and 9th-century royal examples also existed at the margins of original settlement (*e.g.* Milton Regis/Tunstall). They were initially run for the benefit of the lord or a monastic institution, although by the 12th and 13th centuries subinfeudation led to their parcelling off from larger estates. Vaccaries of the South-East had their origins in the seasonal pastures and manorial *denns* of the early medieval period, and in the case of the Hayworth it has been shown how an earlier oval enclosure was adopted for this purpose (Chapter 9). It is clear that oval enclosures were a particular feature of the South-East's vaccary establishments and, whilst many reflect expedient, more intensive, use of earlier pastures, some may have been created anew. At *The Vachery*, Surrey, however, a different process was apparent, one where a Wealden cattle enterprise was converted into a hunting park for deer, the switch perhaps being encouraged by a pre-existing oval enclosure (Chapter 6).

By the late medieval period the Weald had evolved into the countryside we would recognise today. The old stages of colonisation had led to varied archipelagos of cattle and swine pastures, enclosures and folds, commons and heath, all surrounding an ever-diminishing inner core of the drastically changed (but nonetheless surviving) earlier forest. Whilst these elements were still recognisable, they had by the 15th century been superseded by a more heavily utilised countryside of enclosed fields and well-managed shaws. This was the final stage of medieval Wealden colonisation, when new and old landholders alike were reliant on raising cattle to provide milk for the dairy and beef for the market, but also for their dung and use in traction; the latter factors being absolutely essential for growing an arable crop. From the end of Roman rule until the ushering in of the early modern era, cattle pasturing had provided a major impetus to the formation and colonisation of one of the most important landscapes in England. It can be claimed with some confidence that the settlement pattern, economy and environment of the Weald had all been profoundly influenced by its suitability for the raising of cattle.

11.2 Lessons for the landscape: cattle's place in the modern South-East

The medieval agriculture discussed here has relevance to modern landscape management and farming. Forgotten aspects of cattle husbandry and the animals' beneficial role for ecology and habitat regeneration hold potential value for conservation grazers and husbandmen. The fact that the medieval cattle economy of the South-East was of more importance than has hitherto been realised, and that the Weald in particular was a significant cattle-raising area, has particular relevance to our understanding and future management of landscape. There are several reasons why the South-East's wooded core is particularly suited to the husbandry of cattle as opposed to other livestock types, all of which have been discussed above (Chapter 10). One of the most important, however, was woodland, and in particular wood-pasture's value, for early cattle husbandry. Such habitats are increasingly becoming targets for restoration, although without a full appreciation of the historical context of wood-pasture management it should be questioned how successful such initiatives can be?

The fact that the Weald has not been sufficiently recognised for the significance of cattle is reflected in the research of forest ecology. That the cattle husbandry of the South-East is an often forgotten aspect of the region's past is detectable in statements that recognise the tradition of woodland grazing in areas which have been well-studied for their historic cattle-economy (*e.g.* Cumbria: Winchester 2000), but not in southern England where woodland cattle grazing has been dismissed as a 'recent interest' rather than any historic persistence (Armstrong *et al.* 2003, 26). This is certainly not the view of the current author who has for decades witnessed modern pasturing of cattle within woodlands and shaws across the Weald and beyond (Plate 11.1).

There are a number of conservation reasons for keeping cattle in woodlands. These include the benefits to biodiversity by reducing tree and scrub regeneration, maintaining open habitats and by decreasing dominant plant species (Armstrong *et al.* 2003, 26–27). How these management assets are best employed are, however, dependent on the aims of the particular project or the degree to which a holistic integrated approach is employed. All too often conservation management or restoration is undertaken from a purely economic or ecological perspective without sufficient thought to the historic landscape. The dominance of ecology within landscape restoration is exemplified by the influence of Vera's (2000) ideas on wood-pasture. Essentially, he claimed that this type of eco-system was a natural occurrence in Europe and was not a product of human intervention. Though the argument has some merit in terms of dismissing earlier ideas that the Mesolithic landscape was one of closed forest system, it fails to grasp the highly managed nature of medieval wood-pasture and its total removal from primeval wilderness of the pre-Neolithic age (Szabó 2009).

The importance of conservation and the need to manage landscapes for nature sometimes leads to a myopic approach whereby landscape stasis and curation is the outcome rather than biodiversity. Landscape preservation of course holds value, but it should sometimes be appreciated that it is the mono-cultures of intensively farmed post-medieval countrysides that are often being preserved rather than the more biodiverse, medieval and earlier landscapes reported on here. Within this environment Britain's conservation bodies have come under attack for managing landscapes for the benefit of the few rather than the many and for facilitating ecological wastelands caused by overgrazing, ones that bear little relationship to traditional custom and practice (*e.g.* Monbiot 2017; 2018).

One of the Weald's great assets for cattle keeping is the extent of its surviving tree-cover. The feeding of tree hay, in winter, has fallen from favour in modern cattle husbandry; however, during the medieval period the resource would have proven highly beneficial, particularly at times when other fodder was scarce. Consumption of twigs and leaves potentially has medicinal effects on cattle, although apart from the benefits of willow evidence is scarce; the area still requires in-depth research and study (Peter Aspin, pers. comm.). Despite the dearth of scientific evidence, the health benefits of browsing to cattle can possibly be traced in the calving and vigour of the free-grazing longhorn herd of the Knepp estate in the Sussex Weald. This rewilding project has shown statistics for both factors that are better than most conventional farms (Tree 2018, 103). Whilst the art of feeding pollard hay has largely been lost, modern stockmen continue to appreciate the benefits of trees for preventing erosion, providing shelter and shade. Southern England is amongst three areas in the UK to show slightly higher densities of cattle grazing in woodland sites, the others being Cumbria and Argyll (Armstrong *et al.* 2003, 26).

Though the benefits of tree-cover are being increasingly realised (Woodland Trust 2015) there are a number of aspects of medieval practice that should be considered in light of current approaches to landscape management and conservation. Trees can regenerate within cattle-grazed woodlands, although the degree of regeneration declines as grazing pressure increases (Armstrong *et al.* 2003, 27). Subsequent advice for conservation managers who wish to encourage a range of ancient and semi-natural woodland types has therefore encouraged lower stocking densities (usually a stocking around 0.5 livestock units per hectare; Mayle 1999; Woodland Trust 2012; Scottish Forestry 2018), something that was clearly managed by medieval farmers by way of stints, small herd sizes and restrictions on the month and length of grazing. For restoration of lowland wood-pasture and maintenance of parkland environments, however, a higher grazing intensity is usually recommended (Mayle 1999). The grazing of enclosed spaces was a particular feature of the medieval period within the South-East and it is important to consider the varying environments that would have existed within ring-fenced areas including seasonal grazed *denns* and the more heavily cropped vaccaries and deer parks of the early and later medieval periods.

Palaeoenvironmental studies are key to future understanding of the habitats that flourished within such environments and should provide the templates for considering the aims of conservation and restoration initiatives. An important first step is provided by the results of the palynological work at the Hayworth enclosure, West Sussex. Here, from the 7th century an enclosed seasonal pasture was gradually cleared of woodland until by the 11th century a wood-pasture type environment in which beech with oak had become the co-dominant woodland species was achieved. By the onset of the 12th and 13th centuries the presence of grassland and cereal pollen suggests a move to a more open, cultivated landscape concurrent with the enclosure's use for a more settled and intensively worked vaccary (Margetts 2017). The details of the pollen record and the charred environmental remains provide key indications of the habitats and species present within the enclosure, which itself was probably formed of thorny species present in the environmental record and indicated by the site's place-name (*ibid.*; see section 9.2). Cattle and other large herbivores are known to prefer browsing certain species rather than others with a declining order of preference comprising oak, goat willow, [Scots pine, birch, ash], hazel, beech, alder, rowan, holly and hawthorn (Armstrong *et al.* 2003, 27–28). The low predilection for holly and hawthorn supports theories that the species can regenerate under higher browsing pressures than others (*ibid.*). In light of such information it is easy to see how consideration of pollen records can inform historic landscape restoration, but this can only be achieved via an integrated holistic approach.

It is likely that the long-term study of innovative 'restoration' projects such as that at Knepp have far more to offer understanding of medieval landscapes than the pre-Neolithic wilderness of lowland Europe that they were originally set up to imitate (for the original aims of this project, see Kernon and Deane 2007). The creation of wood-pasture in enclosed pastoral reserves should be considered in the light of this study, for only through a greater appreciation of the nature of the medieval cattle economy can the development of our current countryside be understood.

11.3 Final thoughts

It was the intention of this work to highlight the importance of the cattle economy within the South-East of England and to redress the historical imbalance between an agrarian history dominated by the study of the later medieval wool trade, and to a lesser extent the swine pannage of the 10th and 11th centuries. It has been shown how important the species were to medieval farming, colonisation and culture, whilst highlighting significant aspects of past environment and husbandry that have noteworthy implications for how we manage the landscape today. The author hopes that the study will be of interest to archaeologists, landscape historians and geographers, agricultural writers, farmers and conservationists. It is his intention to pursue similar studies in other regions, ones that also experienced the fundamental influence of *the wandering herd*.

Bibliography

Adams, C. 1999: 'Medieval administration', in K. Leslie and B. Short (eds), *An Historical Atlas of Sussex*. Chichester: Phillimore and Co., 40–41

Adams, R.F. 1995: *Dairy Reference Manual*. Ithaca, New York: Northeast Regional Agricultural Engineering Service, Cooperative Extension

Albarella, U. 1997: 'Size, power, wool and veal: zooarchaeological evidence for late medieval innovations', in De G. Boe and F. Verhaeghe (eds), *Environment and Subsistence in Medieval Europe*. Brugge: Institute for the Archaeological Heritage of Flanders, 19–30

Albarella, U. 2006: 'Pig husbandry and pork consumption in medieval England', in C.M. Woolgar, D. Serjeantson and T. Waldron (eds), *Food in Medieval England: Diet and Nutrition*. Oxford: Oxford University Press, 72–87

Albarella, U. and Davis, S.J.M. 1996: 'Mammals and birds from Launceston Castle, Cornwall: decline in status and the rise of agriculture', *Circaea*, vol. 12(1), 1–156

Allen, M.J. 2005: 'Beaker and Early Bronze Age activity, and a possible Beaker valley entrenchment, in Cuckoo Bottom, near Lewes, East Sussex', *Sussex Archaeological Collections*, vol. 143, 35–45

Allen, T. 2004: 'Swine, salt and seafood: a case study of Anglo-Saxon and early medieval settlement in north-east Kent', *Archaeologia Cantiana*, vol. 124, 117–35

Allen, T., Donnelly, M., Hardy, A., Hayden, C. and Powell, K. 2012: *A Road Through the Past: Archaeological Discoveries on the A2 Pepperhill to Cobham Road-Scheme in Kent*. Oxford: Oxford Archaeology Monograph 16

Andrews, P. 2001: 'Excavation of a multi-period settlement site at the former St John's Vicarage, Old Malden, Kingston upon Thames', *Surrey Archaeological Collections*, vol. 88, 161–224

Andrews, P. 2004: 'Kingston – Saxon royal estate centre to post-medieval market town: the contribution of archaeology to understanding towns in Surrey', in J. Cotton, G. Crocker and A. Graham (eds), *Aspects of Archaeology and History in Surrey: Towards a Research Framework for the County*. Guildford: Surrey Archaeological Society, 169–85

Andrews, P., Mepham, L., Schuster, J. and Stevens, C.J. 2011: *Settling the Ebbsfleet Valley, High Speed 1 Excavations at Springhead and Northfleet, Kent, The Late Iron Age, Roman, Saxon and Medieval Landscape, vol 4: Saxon and Later Finds and Environmental Reports*. Oxford: Oxbow Books

Andrews, P., Booth, P., Fitzpatrick, A.P. and Welsh, K. 2015: *Digging at the Gateway: Archaeological Landscapes of South Thanet*. Oxford: Oxbow Books

Armstrong, H.M., Poulsom, L., Connolly, T. and Peace, A. 2003: *A Survey of Cattle-Grazed Woodlands in Britain*. Woodland Ecology Branch and 2 Statistics and Computing Branch, Forest Research

ASE 2004: *Excavations at the Former Site of Tribe's Yard, Bersted Street, Bognor Regis, West Sussex*. Archaeology South-East unpublished report

Aston, M. 1993: *Monasteries in the Landscape*. Stroud: Amberley Publishing

Aston, M. and Rowley, T. 1974: *Landscape Archaeology: An Introduction to Fieldwork Techniques on Post-Roman Landscapes*. Newton Abbot: David and Charles

Atkin, M.A. 1985: 'Some settlement patterns in Lancashire', in D. Hooke (ed.), *Medieval Villages: A Review of Current Work*. Oxford: Oxford University Committee for Archaeology Monograph 5, 171–86

Atkin, M.A. 1993: 'Sillfield Preston Patrick: a double-oval type of field pattern', *Transactions of the Cumberland Westmorland Antiquarian and Archaeological Society*, vol. 93, 145–53

Atkin, M.A. 1994: 'Land use and management in the upland demesne of the De Lacy estate of Blackburnshire c.1300', *Agricultural History Review*, vol. 42(1), 1–19

Attenborough, F.L. (ed.) 1922: *The Laws of the Earliest English Kings*. London: Cambridge University Press

Ayton, G. 2013: 'The animal bone from Brisley Farm', in J. Stevenson, *Living by the Sword: The Archaeology of Brisley Farm, Ashford, Kent*. Portslade: SpoilHeap Monograph 6

Ayton, G. in prep: 'The animal bone', in D. Swift, *Excavations in Lewes*. SpoilHeap Monograph series

Baildon, W.P. (ed.) 1906: *Court Rolls of the Manor of Wakefield, Vol II, 1297 to 1309*. Leeds: The Yorkshire Archaeological Society

Bailey, M. 1982: *A Marginal Economy? East Anglian Breckland in the Later Middle Ages*. Cambridge: Cambridge University Press

Baker, A.R.H. 1973: 'Field systems of southeast England', in A.R.H. Baker and R.A. Butlin (eds), *Studies of Field Systems in the British Isles*. Cambridge: Cambridge University Press, 377–429

Baker, C.R. and Herbert, A.N. 2008: 'Excavation of a Medieval Settlement at Pond Field, Littlebrook, Dartford', *Archaeologia Cantiana*, vol. 128, 281–300

Ballard, A. (ed.) 1920: *Records of the Social and Economic History of England and Wales. vol. 4, II: An Eleventh Century Inquisition of St Augustine's, Canterbury*. London: Published for the British Academy by H. Milford

Banham, D. and Faith, R. 2014: *Anglo-Saxon Farms and Farming*. Oxford: Oxford University Press

Barber, L. and Priestley-Bell, G. 2008: *Medieval Adaptation, Settlement and Economy of a Coastal Wetland: The Evidence from around Lydd, Romney Marsh, Kent*. Oxford: Oxbow Books

Barber, L. and Sibun, L. 2010: 'The medieval hospital of St Nicholas, Lewes, East Sussex: Excavations 1994', *Sussex Archaeological Collections*, vol. 148, 79–109

Barber, L., Gardiner, M. and Rudling, D. 2002: 'Excavations at Eastwick Barn', in D. Rudling (ed.), *Downland Settlement and Land-use: The Archaeology of the Brighton Bypass*. London: Archetype Publications, 107–40

Barford, P.M. 1990: 'Briquetage finds from inland sites', in A.J. Fawn, K.A. Evans, I. McMaster and G.M.R. Davies, *The Red Hills of Essex: Salt-Making in Antiquity*. Colchester: Colchester Archaeological Group Annual Report 30, 79–80

Barrowman, S. 2012: *An Assessment of an Archaeological Excavation at 4–19 Stockwell Street, Greenwich, London, SE10 9BD*. Pre-Construct Archaeology unpublished report

Bedwin, O. 1983: 'Miss P.A.M. Keef's excavations at Harting Beacon and nearby sites 1948–52', *Sussex Archaeological Collections*, vol. 121, 199–202

Bedwin, O. 2009: 'The animal remains', in J. Funnell, 'A medieval moated site at Streatham near Henfield, West Sussex', *Sussex Archaeological Collections*, vol. 147, 92

Bell, M. 1977: 'Excavations at Bishopstone, Sussex: the Anglo-Saxon period', *Sussex Archaeological Collections*, vol. 115, 193–241

Bell, M. 1983: 'Valley sediments as evidence of prehistoric land-use on the South Downs Itford Bottom; Kiln Combe; Chalton', *Proceedings of the Prehistoric Society*, vol. 49, 119–50

Bell, M. 2020: *Making One's Way in the World: The Footprints and Trackways of Prehistoric People*. Oxford: Oxbow Books

Biddick, K. 1989: *The Other Economy: Pastoral Husbandry on a Medieval Estate*. Berkeley: University of California Press

Birch, W. de G. (ed.) 1885: *Cartularium Saxonicum: A Collection of Charters Relating to Anglo-Saxon History. Vol. 1, AD 430–839*. London: Whiting and Co.

Bird, J. and Bird, D.G. (eds) 1987: *The Archaeology of Surrey to 1540*. Guildford: Surrey Archaeological Society

Bishop, B.J. and Bagwell, M. 2005: *Iwade: Occupation of a North Kent Village from the Mesolithic to the Medieval Period*. London: Pre-Construct Archaeology Monograph 3

Blaauw, W.H. 1850: 'Letters to Ralph de Nevill, Bishop of Chichester (1222–24) and Chancellor to King Henry III', *Sussex Archaeological Collections*, vol. 3, 35–76

Blackmore, L. and Cowie, R. 2001: 'Saxon and Medieval Battersea: Excavations at Althorpe Grove, 1975–8', *Surrey Archaeological Collections*, vol. 88, 67–92

Blair, J. 1989: 'Frithuwold's kingdom and the origins of Surrey', in S. Bassett (ed.), *The Origins of the Anglo Saxon Kingdoms*. Leicester: Leicester University Press, 97–107

Blair, J. 1991: *Early Medieval Surrey: Landholding, Church and Settlement before 1300*. Stroud: Alan Sutton Publishing and Surrey Archaeological Society

Blair, J. and Ramsey, N. (eds) 1991: *English Medieval Industries: Craftsmen, Techniques, Products*. London: The Hambledon Press

Booth, P., Champion, T., Foreman, S., Garwood, P., Glass, H., Munby, J. and Reynolds, A. 2011: *On Track: The Archaeology of High Speed 1 Section 1 in Kent*. Oxford and Salisbury: Oxford Wessex Archaeology Monograph 4

Bradley, R. 1970: 'The excavation of a beaker settlement at Belle Tout, East Sussex, England', *Proceedings of the Prehistoric Society*, vol. 36, 312–79

Bradley, R. 1971: 'An Iron Age promontory fort at Belle Tout', *Sussex Archaeological Collections*, vol. 109, 8–19

Brandon, P. 1963: *The Common Wastes of Sussex*. Birkbeck (University of London) unpublished Ph.D. thesis

Brandon, P. 1971: 'Demesne arable farming in coastal Sussex during the later Middle Ages', *Agricultural History Review*, vol. 19, 113–34

Brandon, P. 1974: *The Sussex Landscape*. London: Hodder and Stoughton

Brandon, P. (ed.) 1978: *The South Saxons*. London and Chichester: Phillimore and Co.

Brandon, P. 1988: 'Farming techniques: south-eastern England', in H.E. Hallam (ed.), *The Agrarian History of England and Wales: Vol II, 1042–1350*, Cambridge: Cambridge University Press, 312–24

Brandon, P. 1998: *The South Downs*. Chichester: Phillimore and Co.

Brandon, P. 2003: *The Kent and Sussex Weald*. Chichester: Phillimore and Co.

Brandon, P. 2005: *The North Downs*. Chichester: Phillimore and Co.

Brandon, P. and Short, B. 1990: *The South East from AD 1000*. London: Longman

Bridbury, A.R. 1955: *England and the Salt Trade in the later Middle Ages*. Oxford: Clarendon Press

Bright, D. 2010: 'The Pilgrims' Way revisited: the use of the North Downs main trackway and the Medway crossings by medieval travellers', *Kent Archaeological Society eArticle*. Available at: <http://www.kentarchaeology.ac/authors/DerekBright01.pdf> [Accessed 16 December 2019]

Bright, D. 2012: 'The Pilgrims' Way: fact and fiction of an ancient trackway', *Archaeologia Cantiana*, vol. 132, 361

Britnell, R.H. 1977: 'Finchfield Park under the plough, 1341–42', *Essex Archaeology and History*, vol. 9, 107–12

Brookes, S.J. 2007: *Economics and Social Change in Anglo-Saxon Kent AD 400–900: Landscapes, Communities and Exchange*. Oxford: Archaeopress, British Archaeological Reports British Series, 431

Brooks, N. 1989: 'The creation and early structure of the kingdom of Kent', in S. Bassett (ed.), *The origins of Anglo-Saxon Kingdoms*. Leicester: Leicester University Press, 55–74

Brown, T. and Foard, G. 1998: 'The Saxon landscape: a regional perspective', in P. Everson and T. Williamson (eds), *The Archaeology of Landscape*. Manchester: Manchester University Press, 67–94

Butler, C. 1994: 'The excavation of a medieval site at Muddleswood, near Hurstpierpoint, West Sussex', *Sussex Archaeological Collections*, vol. 132, 101–14

Butler, C. 2000: *Saxon Settlement and Earlier Remains at Friars Oak, Hassocks, West Sussex*. Oxford: Archaeopress, BAR British series 295

Cam, H.M. 1963: *Liberties & Communities in Medieval England: Collected Studies in Local Administration and Topography*. London: Merlin Press

Camden, W. 1722: *Britannia: or a chorographical description of Great Britain and Ireland, together with the adjacent islands*. London: Awnsham Churchill

Campbell, B.M.S. 2000: *English Seigniorial Agriculture: 1250–1450*. Cambridge: Cambridge University Press

Campbell, E.M.J. 1962: 'Kent', in H.C. Darby and E.M.J. Campbell (eds), *The Domesday Geography of South-East England*. Cambridge: Cambridge University Press, 483–562

Cannon, H.L. 1908: *The Great Roll of the Pipe for the Twenty-Sixth Year of the Reign of King Henry the Second, AD 1179–1180*. London: The Pipe Roll Society, vol. XXIX

Cantor, L. 1983: *The Medieval Parks of England: A Gazetteer*. Loughborough: Dept of Education, Loughborough University of Technology

Carpenter, E., Small, F., Truscoe, K. and Royall, C. 2016: *South Downs National Park the High Woods from above NMP*. Portsmouth: Historic England Research Report Series no. 14-2016. Available at: <https://www.southdowns.gov.uk/wpcontent/uploads/2016/08/The HighWoodsfromaboveNationalMapping Programme.pdf> [Accessed 16 December 2019]

Carus-Wilson, E.M. 1962: 'The medieval trade of the ports of the Wash', *Medieval Archaeology*, vol. 6(1), 182–201

CDC 2006: *Report on an Archaeological Excavation at Bramshott Bottom, near Beacon Hill, Harting, West Sussex*. Chichester District Council unpublished report

Chatwin, D. and Gardiner, M. 2005: 'Rethinking the early medieval settlement of woodlands: evidence from the western Sussex Weald', *Landscape History*, vol. 27, 31–49

Clough, M. 1969: *Two Estate Surveys of the Fitzalan Earls of Arundel, 14th Century*. Lewes: Sussex Record Society, vol. 67

Coates, R. 1999: 'Place-names before 1066', in K. Leslie and B. Short (eds), *An Historical Atlas of Sussex*. Chichester: Phillimore and Co., 32–33

Cooke, N. 2001: 'Excavations at Battersea Flour Mills, 1996–7: the medieval and post-medieval manor houses and later Thames-side industrial sites', *Surrey Archaeological Collections*, vol. 88, 93–131

Cooper, A. 2000: 'The king's four highways: legal fiction meets fictional law', *Journal of Medieval History*, vol. 26(4), 351–70

Cooper, J.H. 1903: 'The Coverts: part I', *Sussex Archaeological Collections*, vol. 46, 170–80

Costen, M.D. 2011: *Anglo-Saxon Somerset*. Oxford: Oxbow Books

Cowgill, J., de Neergaard, M. and Griffiths, N. 1987: 'Knives and scabbards', *Medieval Finds from Excavations in London 1*. Woodbridge, Suffolk: Boydell Press

Cullen, P. and Jones, R. 2012: 'Manure and middens in English place- names', in R. Jones (ed.), *Manure Matters: Historical, Archaeological and Ethnographical Perspectives*. Farnham: Ashgate Publishing, 97–108

Cunliffe, B.W. 2005: *Iron Age Communities in Britain*, 4th edition. Abingdon: Routledge

Cunliffe Shaw, R. 1956: *The royal forest of Lancaster*. Preston: Guardian Press

Curwen, E. and Curwen, E.C. 1920: 'The earthworks of Rewell Hill, near Arundel', *Sussex Archaeological Collections*, vol. 61, 20–30

Curwen, E. and Curwen, E.C. 1922: 'Notes on the archaeology of Burpham and the neighbouring downs', *Sussex Archaeological Collections*, vol. 63, 1–53

Curwen, E. and Curwen, E.C. 1923: 'Sussex lynchets and their associated field-ways', *Sussex Archaeological Collections*, vol. 64, 1–65

Curwen, E. and Curwen, E.C. 1928: 'Earthworks in Gobblestubbs Copse, Arundel', *Sussex Archaeological Collections*, vol. 69, 223

DAERA 2017: *Water Advice for Livestock Farmers*. Department of Agriculture, Environment and Rural Affairs, Northern Ireland. Available at: <https://www.daera-ni.gov.uk/articles/water-advice-livestock-farmers> [Accessed 04 December 2017]

Daniel-Tyssen, J.R. 1873: 'The Parliamentary Surveys of the county of Sussex, AD 1649–1653', *Sussex Archaeological Collections*, vol. 25, 23–61

Darby, H.C. 1954: 'Some early ideas on the agricultural regions of England', *The Agricultural History Review*, vol. 2, 30–47

Darby, H.C. 1977: *Domesday England*. Cambridge: Cambridge University Press

Darby, H.C. and Campbell, E.M.J. (eds) 1962: *The Domesday Geography of South-East England*. Cambridge: Cambridge University Press

Davies, E. 1985: '*Hafod* and *lluest*: the summering of cattle and upland settlement in Wales', *Folk Life*, vol. 23(1), 76–96

Davis, H.W.C. 1914: 'The Chronicle of Battle Abbey', *The English Historical Review*, vol. 29, 426–34

Dawkes, G. 2014a: *Archaeological Excavations at Tower Street Car Park, Chichester, West Sussex. Final Report and Updated Project Design for Publication*. Archaeology South-East unpublished report

Dawkes, G. 2014b: *Archaeological Post-Excavation Assessment and Updated Project Design Report. Outwood to Buckland Strategic Water Main, Surrey*. Archaeology South-East unpublished report

Dawkes, G. 2016: *Archaeological Excavations at Pocock's Field, King's Drive, Eastbourne, East Sussex, BN21 2PB. A Post-Excavation and Updated Project Design Report*. Archaeology South-East unpublished report

Dawkes, G. 2017: *Between Thames and Medway: Archaeological Excavations on the Hoo Peninsula and its Environs*. Portslade: SpoilHeap Monograph 13

Dawkes, G., Grant, K., Hart, D. and Swift, D. 2019: *Beyond the Wantsum: Archaeological Investigations in South Thanet, Kent*. Portslade: SpoilHeap Monograph 22

Deegan, A. and Foard, G. 2007: *Mapping Ancient Landscapes in Northamptonshire*. Swindon: English Heritage

Ditchfield, P.H. and Page, W. (eds) 1906. *The Victoria County History of Berkshire Volume I*. London: Archibald Constable

Dodgson, J.M. 1966: 'The significance of the distribution of the English place-names in *-ingas*, *-inga-* in South-east England', *Medieval Archaeology*, vol. 10, 1–29

Dodgson, J.M. 1978: 'Place-names in Sussex: the material for a new look', in P. Brandon (ed.), *The South Saxons*. Chichester: Phillimore and Co., 54–88

Dodgson, J.M. and Khaliq, P. 1970: 'Addenda and corrigenda to the Survey of English Place-Names', *Journal of the English Place-Name Society*, vol. 2, 18–74

Doherty, A. 2014a: *Archaeological Excavations at Monk's House, Rodmell. A Post-Excavation Assessment and Updated Project Design Report*. Archaeology South-East unpublished report

Doherty, A. 2014b: *An Archaeological Watching Brief at 145 Vale Avenue, Patcham. A Post-Excavation Assessment and Updated Project Design Report*. Archaeology South-East unpublished report

Doherty, A. and Greatorex, C. 2016: *Excavations on St Anne's Hill: A Middle/Late Iron Age Site and Anglo-Saxon Cemetery at St Anne's Road, Eastbourne, East Sussex*. Portslade: SpoilHeap Monograph 11

Douglas, D.C. (ed.) 1944: *Domesday Monachorum of Christchurch, Canterbury*. London: The Royal Historical Society

Drewett, P. 1982: *The Archaeology of Bullock Down, Eastbourne, East Sussex: The Development of a Landscape*. Lewes: The Sussex Archaeological Society

Drewett, P., Rudling, D. and Gardiner, M. 1988: *The South-East to AD 1000*. Longman: London

Du Boulay, F.R.H. 1961: 'Denns, droving and danger', *Archaeologia Cantiana*, vol. 76, 75–87

Du Boulay, F.R.H. 1966: *The Lordship of Canterbury: An Essay on Medieval Society*. London: Nelson

Dumville, D.N. 1992: *Wessex and England from Alfred to Edgar: Six Essays in Political, Cultural and Ecclesiastical Revival*. Woodbridge: Boydell Press

Dunster, S. (ed.) 2013: *The Medway Towns: River, Docks and Urban Life*. Chichester: Phillimore and Co.

Dyer, C. 1986: 'English peasant buildings in the later Middle Ages (1200–1500)', *Medieval Archaeology*, vol. 30, 19–45

Dyer, C. 1995: 'Sheepcotes: evidence for medieval sheepfarming', *Medieval Archaeology*, vol. 39, 136–64

Dyer, C. 2004: 'Alternative agriculture: goats in medieval England', in R.W. Hoyle (ed.), *People, Landscape and Alternative Agriculture: Essays for Joan Thirsk*. Exeter: The British Agricultural History Society, 20–38

Eddison, J. (ed.) 1995: *Romney Marsh: The Debatable Ground*. Oxford: Oxford University Committee for Archaeology Monograph 41

Eddison, J. and Green, C. (eds) 1988: *Romney Marsh: Evolution, Occupation, Reclamation*. Oxford: Oxford University Committee for Archaeology

Ekwall, E. 1960: *The Concise Oxford Dictionary of English Place-Names*. Oxford: Clarendon Press

England, J. 2012: *'There's more here than you think': A Detailed History of Broadbridge Heath*. Horsham: Friends of Horsham Museum

English, J. 1997: 'A possible early Wealden settlement type', *Medieval Settlement Research Group Annual Report*, vol. 2, 5–6

English Heritage 2006a: *Historic Farmsteads, Preliminary Character Assessment: South East Region*. Cheltenham: University of Gloucestershire, English Heritage and the Countryside Agency

English Heritage 2006b: *Historic Farmsteads, Preliminary Character Assessment: North East Region*. Cheltenham: University of Gloucestershire, English Heritage and the Countryside Agency

Evans, N. and Yarwood, R. 1995: 'Livestock and landscape', *Landscape Research*, vol. 20, 141–46

Everitt, A. 1976: 'The making of the agrarian landscape of Kent', *Archaeologia Cantiana*, vol. 92, 1–31

Everitt, A. 1977: 'River and wold: reflections on the historical geography of regions and *pays*', *Journal of Historical Geography*, vol. 3, 1–20

Everitt, A. 1986: *Continuity and Colonization: The Evolution of Kentish Settlement*. Leicester: Leicester University Press

Faith, R. 2006: 'Worthys and enclosures', *Medieval Settlement Research Group Annual Report*, no. 21, 9–14

Faith, R. 2012: 'Some Devon farms before the Norman Conquest', in S. Turner and B. Silvester (eds), *Life in Medieval Landscapes*. Oxford: Windgather Press, 73–88

Faith, R. and Fleming, A. 2012: 'The Walkhampton enclosure (Devon)', *Landscape History*, vol. 33(2), 5–28

Finberg, H.P.R. 1972a: 'Anglo-Saxon England to 1042', in H.P.R. Finberg (ed.), *The Agrarian History of England and Wales: Volume I. AD 43–1042*. London: Cambridge University Press, 385–525

Finberg, H.P.R. (ed.) 1972b: *The Agrarian History of England and Wales: Volume I. AD 43–1042*. London: Cambridge University Press

Fleming, A. 2006: 'Post-processual landscape archaeology: a critique', *Cambridge Archaeological Journal*, vol. 16(3), 267–80

Fleming, A. 2012: 'Working with wood-pasture', in S. Turner and B. Silvester (eds), *Life in Medieval Landscapes*. Oxford: Windgather Press, 15–31

Fleming, A. and Ralph, N. 1982: 'Medieval settlement and land use on Holne Moor, Dartmoor: the landscape evidence', *Medieval Archaeology*, vol. 26, 101–37

Fleming, L. (ed.) 1960: *Chartulary of Boxgrove Priory, 12th–14th Centuries*. Lewes: Sussex Record Society vol. 59

Ford, W.K. and Gabe, A.C. 1981: *The Metropolis of Mid-Sussex: A History of Haywards Heath*. Haywards Heath: Charles Clark

Forestry Commission Scotland 2018: *How to Calculate the Forage Intake of Livestock and Wild Herbivores*. Available at: <https://scotland.forestry.gov.uk/woodland-grazing-toolbox/grazing- management/grazing-regime/season/forage-intake> [Accessed 16 April 2019]

Fox, H. 2000: 'The wolds before 1500', in J. Thirsk (ed.), *The English Rural Landscape*. Oxford: Oxford University Press, 50–61

Fox, H.S.A. 2001: *The Evolution of the Fishing Village: Landscape and Society along the South Devon Coast, 1086–1550*. Oxford: Leopard's Head Press

Fox, H.S.A. 2008: 'Butter place-names and transhumance', in O.J. Padel and N. Parsons (eds), *A Commodity of Good Names: Essays in Honour of Margaret Gelling*. Donington: Shaun Tyas, 352–64

Fox, H.S.A. 2012: *Dartmoor's Alluring Uplands: Transhumance and Pastoral Management in the Middle Ages*. Exeter: University of Exeter Press

French, C. 1996: 'Molluscan analysis', in R.P.J. Jackson and T.W. Potter, *Excavations at Stonea, Cambridgeshire, 1980–85*. London: British Museum, 639–54

Froese, C. and Small, D. 2001: *Water Consumption and Waste Production during Different Production Stages in Hog Operations*. DGH Engineering Presented to Manitoba Livestock Manure Management Initiative Inc.

Fulford, M. and Rippon, S. 2011: *Pevensey Castle Sussex: Excavations in the Roman Fort and Medieval Keep, 1993–95*. Salisbury: Trust for Wessex Archaeology, Wessex Archaeology Report 26

Fuller, G.J. 1953: 'The development of roads in the Surrey-Sussex Weald and coastlands between 1700 and 1900', *Transactions and Papers (Institute of British Geographers)*, vol. 19, 37–49

Funnell, J. 2009: 'A medieval moated site at Streatham near Henfield, West Sussex', *Sussex Archaeological Collections*, vol. 147, 77–95

Gardiner, M. 1984: 'Saxon settlement and land division in the western Weald', *Sussex Archaeological Collections*, vol. 122, 75–83

Gardiner, M. 1985: 'Planned medieval land division in Withyham, East Sussex', *Sussex Archaeological Collections*, vol. 123, 109–14

Gardiner, M. 1988: 'Early, middle and late Anglo-Saxon periods', in P. Drewett, D. Rudling and M. Gardiner, *The South-East to AD 1000*. Longman: London, 246–341

Gardiner, M. 1990: 'An Anglo-Saxon and Medieval Settlement at Botolphs, Bramber, West Sussex', *The Archaeological Journal*, vol. 147, 216–75

Gardiner, M. 1993: 'The excavation of a late Anglo-Saxon settlement at Market Field, Steyning, 1988–9', *Sussex Archaeological Collections*, vol. 131, 21–67

Gardiner, M. 1995a: 'Aspects of the history and archaeology of medieval Seaford', *Sussex Archaeological Collections*, vol. 133, 189–212

Gardiner, M. 1995b: *Medieval Settlement and Society in the Eastern Sussex Weald before 1420*. University College London unpublished Ph.D. thesis

Gardiner, M. 1996a: 'The geography and peasant rural economy of the eastern Sussex High Weald, 1300–1420', *Sussex Archaeological Collections*, vol. 134, 125–39

Gardiner, M. 1996b: 'Excavations at Lewes Friary, 1985 and 1988–9', *Sussex Archaeological Collections*, vol. 134, 71–123

Gardiner, M. 1997a: 'The colonisation of the Weald of South-East England', *Medieval Settlement Research Group*, vol. 12, 6–8

Gardiner, M. 1997b: 'Archaeological Excavations in Steyning, 1992–95: further evidence for the evolution of the Late Saxon small town', *Sussex Archaeological Collections*, vol. 135, 143–71

Gardiner, M. 1998: 'The characterisation of medieval Wealden settlements: excavations at Ivenden, Combe Farm, Mayfield, East Sussex', *Sussex Archaeological Collections*, vol. 136, 95–110

Gardiner, M. 1999a: 'Late Saxon Sussex *c.*650–1066', in K. Leslie and B. Short (eds), *An Historical Atlas of Sussex*. Chichester: Phillimore and Co., 30–31

Gardiner, M. 1999b: 'The medieval rural economy and landscape', in K. Leslie and B. Short (eds), *An Historical Atlas of Sussex*. Chichester: Phillimore and Co., 38–39

Gardiner, M. 2001: 'Medieval fishing and settlement on the Sussex coast', *Medieval Settlement Research Group*, vol. 16, 6–7

Gardiner, M. 2003: 'Economy and landscape change in post-Roman and early medieval Sussex, 450–1175', in D. Rudling (ed.), *The Archaeology of Sussex to AD 2000*. King's Lynn: Heritage Marketing and Publications, 151–60

Gardiner, M. 2008: 'A preliminary list of booley huts in the Mourne Mountains, County Down', *Ulster Journal of Archaeology*, vol. 67, 142–52

Gardiner, M. 2011: 'Late Anglo-Saxon settlements', in H. Hamerow, D.A. Hinton and S. Crawford (eds), *The Oxford Handbook of Anglo-Saxon Archaeology*. Oxford: Oxford University Press, 198–217

Gardiner, M. 2012a: 'Time regained: booley huts and seasonal settlement in the Mourne Mountains, County Down, Ireland', in S. Turner and B. Silvester (eds), *Life in Medieval Landscapes*. Oxford: Windgather Press, 106–24

Gardiner, M. 2012b: 'South-East England: forms and diversity in medieval rural settlement', in

N. Christie and P. Stamper (eds), *Medieval Rural Settlement: Britain and Ireland, AD 800–1600*. Oxford: Windgather Press, 100–17

Gardiner, M. and Rippon, S. 2009: 'Looking to the future of medieval archaeology', in R. Gilchrist and A. Reynolds (eds), *Reflections: Fifty Years of Medieval Archaeology, 1957–2007*. Leeds: Maney Publishing, Society for Medieval Archaeology, 65–75

Gardiner, M. and Warne, H. 1999: 'Domesday Settlement', in K. Leslie and B. Short (eds), *An Historical Atlas of Sussex*. Chichester: Phillimore and Co., 34–35

Gardiner, M., Jones, G. and Martin, D. 1991: 'The excavation of medieval aisled hall at Park Farm, Salehurst, East Sussex', *Sussex Archaeological Collections*, vol. 129, 81–97

Gebbels, A. 1977: 'Excavations at Bishopstone, Sussex: the animal bones', *Sussex Archaeological Collections*, vol. 115, 277–84

Gelling, M. 1984: *Placenames in the Landscape*: The *Geographical Roots of Britain's Place-Names*. London: J.M. Dent & Son

Gelling, M. and Cole, A. 2000: *The Landscape of Place-Names*. Stamford: Shaun Tyas

Gelling, M. and Probert, D. 2010: 'Old English *stoc* "place"', *Journal of the English Place-Name Society*, vol. 42, 79–85

Gerrard, C. and Aston, M. 2007: *The Shapwick Project, Somerset: A Rural Landscape Explored*. Leeds: Society for Medieval Archaeology Monograph 25

Gilpin, W. 1791: *Remarks on Forest Scenery, and Other Woodland Views, Volume II*. London: R. Blamire

Glasscock, R.E. 1965: 'The distribution of lay wealth in Kent, Surrey, and Sussex, in the early fourteenth century', *Archaeologica Cantiana*, vol. 80, 61–68

Glover, J. 1975: *The Place Names of Sussex*. London: B.T. Batsford

Graham, D., Graham, A. and Taylor, D. 2005: 'Trial trenching on a probable moated site at Downside Farm, Cobham', *Surrey Archaeological Collections*, vol. 92, 217–29

Grant, A. 1982: 'The use of tooth wear as a guide to the age of domestic ungulates', in B. Wilson, C. Grigson and S. Payne (eds), *Ageing and Sexing Animal Bones from Archaeological Sites*. Oxford: BAR British Series, vol. 109, 91–108

Grant, A. 1987: 'Some observations on butchery in England from the Iron Age to the medieval period', *Anthropozoologica Premier Numéro Spécial*, 1, 53–58

Grant, A. 1988: 'Animal resources', in G. Astill and A. Grant (eds), *The Countryside of Medieval England*. Oxford: Blackwell Publishers, 149–85

Grant-Reis, K. 2019: 'Archaeological investigations at the former Sussex House Site, High Street, Crawley, West Sussex: evidence of medieval and post-medieval occupation on the periphery of the historic core', *Sussex Archaeological Collections*, vol. 157, 149–71

Greatorex, C. 2005: *An Archaeological Excavation Undertaken on Land Located to the West of Post Office Cottage, High Street, Pevensey, East Sussex*. C.G. Archaeology unpublished report

Gurrey, P. 1931: 'The place-names of Sussex by A. Mawer; F.M. Stenton', *The Review of English Studies*, vol. 7(28), 459–62

Hall, H. (ed.) 1903: *The Pipe Roll of the Bishopric of Winchester: for the fourth year of the pontificate of Peter des Roches, 1208–1209*. London: P.S. King and Son

Hallam, H.E. (ed.) 1988a: *The Agrarian History of England and Wales: Volume II. AD 1042–1350*. London: Cambridge University Press

Hallam, H.E. 1988b: 'England before the Norman Conquest', in J. Thirsk (ed.), *The Agrarian History of England and Wales: Volume II. 1042–1350*. Cambridge: Cambridge University Press, 1–44

Hallam, H.E. 1988c: 'Farming techniques: southern England', in J. Thirsk (ed.), *The Agrarian History of England and Wales: Volume II. 1042–1350*. Cambridge: Cambridge University Press, 341–68

Hallam, H.E. 1988d: 'The life of the people', in J. Thirsk (ed.), *The Agrarian History of England and Wales: Volume II. 1042–1350*. Cambridge: Cambridge University Press, 818–53

Hamilton, S. 2007: 'Cultural choices in the "British Eastern Channel Area"', in C. Haselgrove and T. Moore (eds), *The Later Iron Age in Britain and Beyond*. Oxford: Oxbow Books, 81–106

Hann, A. (ed.) 2009: *The Medway Valley: A Kent Landscape Transformed*. Chichester: Phillimore and Co.

Hansen, I.L. and Wickham, C. (eds) 2000: *The Long Eighth Century: Production, Distribution and Demand*. Leiden: Brill

Hanworth, R. and Tomalin, D.J. 1977: *Brooklands Weybridge: The Excavation of an Iron Age and Medieval Site 1964–5 and 1970–71*. Guildford: Surrey Archaeological Society research vol. 4

Hare, J.N. 1985: *Battle Abbey: The Eastern Range and the Excavations of 1978–80*. London: Historic

Buildings and Monuments Commission for England Archaeological report no. 2

Harvey, S. 1985: 'Taxation and the ploughland in Domesday Book', in P.H. Sawyer (ed.), *Domesday Book: A Reassessment*. London: Edward Arnold, 86–103

Harvey, S. 1988: 'Domesday England', in J. Thirsk (ed.), *The Agrarian History of England and Wales: Volume II. 1042–1350*. Cambridge: Cambridge University Press, 45–138

Harvey, S. 2014: *Domesday: Book of Judgement*. Oxford: Oxford University Press

Haselgrove, D. 1978: 'The Domesday record of Sussex', in P. Brandon (ed.), *The South Saxons*. Chichester: Phillimore, 190–220

Haslam, A. 2012: *An Archaeological Excavation at the Former Whitstable Day Nursery, Stevens Street, London Borough of Southwark, London SE1*. Pre-Construct Archaeology unpublished report

Hasted, E. 1797: *The History and Topographical Survey of the County of Kent: Volume 3*. Canterbury: W. Bristow

Hearne, T. (ed.) 1720: *Textus Roffensis*. Oxford

Hemming, J. 2002: '*Bos Primigenius* in Britain: or, why do fairy cows have red ears?', *Folklore*, vol. 113, 71–82

Herring, P. 1996: 'Transhumance in medieval Cornwall', in H.S.A. Fox (ed.), *Seasonal Settlement*. Leicester: University of Leicester Department of Adult Education

Herring, P. 2012: 'Shadows of ghosts: early medieval transhumants in Cornwall', in S. Turner and B. Silvester (eds), *Life in Medieval Landscapes*. Oxford: Windgather Press, 89–105

Hey, D. 1996: *The Oxford Companion to Local and Family History*. Oxford: Oxford University Press.

Higham, M.C. 1968: *Excavation on the Site of the Medieval Vaccary of Goldshaw Booth, Sabden Fold, Lancashire*. Unpublished report

Higham, N.J. and Ryan, M.J. 2013: *The Anglo-Saxon World*. New Haven and London: Yale University Press

Hindle, P. 2012: *Medieval Roads and Tracks*, 3rd edition. Oxford: Shire Publications

Hines, J. 2004: '*Sūpre-gē* – the foundations of Surrey', in J. Cotton, G. Crocker and A. Graham (eds), *Aspects of Archaeology and History in Surrey: Towards a Research Framework for the County*. Guildford: Surrey Archaeological Society, 91–102

Hinton, D.A. 1997: 'The "Scole-Dickleburgh field system" examined', *Landscape History*, vol. 19, 5–12

Hodges, R. 1982: *Dark Age Economics: The Origins of Towns and Trade, AD 600–1000*. London: Duckworth

Holden, E.W. 1963: 'Excavations at the deserted medieval village of Hangleton, part 1', *Sussex Archaeological Collections*, vol. 101, 54–181

Holden, E.W. 1976: 'Excavations at Old Erringham, Shoreham: part one, a Saxon weaving hut', *Sussex Archaeological Collections*, vol. 114, 306–21

Holt, N.R. (ed.) 1964: *The Pipe Roll of the Bishop of Winchester 1210–11*. Manchester: Manchester University Press

Hooke, D. 1987: 'Anglo-Saxon estates in the Vale of the White Horse', *Oxoniensia*, vol. 52, 129–43

Hooke, D. 1988: 'Regional variation in southern and central England in the Anglo-Saxon period and its relationship to land units and settlement', in D. Hooke (ed.), *Anglo-Saxon Settlements*. Oxford: Basil Blackwell, 123–51

Hooke, D. 1989: 'Pre-Conquest woodland: its distribution and usage', *Agricultural History Review*, vol. 37, 113–29

Hooke, D. 1998: *The Landscape of Anglo-Saxon England*. London: Leicester University Press

Hooke, D. 2008: 'Early medieval woodland and the place-name term *léah*', in O.J. Padel and D.N. Parson (eds), *A Commodity of Good Names: Essays in Honour of Margaret Gelling*. Donington: Shaun Tyas, 365–76

Hooke, D. 2012: '*Wealdbæra* and *swina mæst*', in S. Turner and B. Silvester (eds), *Life in Medieval Landscapes*. Oxford: Windgather Press, 15–41

Hooke, D. 2013: 'Old English *wald*, weald in place-names', *Landscape History*, vol. 34(1), 33–49.

Hopkinson, D. 2008: *An Archaeological Evaluation at St Nicholas' School, New Romney, Kent*. Archaeology South-East unpublished report

Hopkinson, D. 2015: *Archaeological Excavations at Deadmans Lane, Rye, East Sussex. A Post-Excavation Assessment and Updated Project Design Report*. Archaeology South-East unpublished report

Hoskins, W.G. 1952: 'The making of the agrarian landscape', in W.G. Hoskins and P.R. Finberg (eds), *Devonshire Studies*. London: Jonathan Cape, 289–333

Hoskins, W.G. 1955: *The Making of the English Landscape*. London: Hodder and Stoughton

Hudson, T.P. (ed.) 1980: *A History of the County of Sussex: Victoria County History Volume VI, part 1*. London: Oxford University Press

Hudson, T.P. (ed.) 1986: *A History of the County of Sussex: Victoria County History Volume VI, part 2.* London: Oxford University Press

Hudson, T.P. (ed.) 1987: *A History of the County of Sussex: Victoria County History Volume VI, part 3.* London: Oxford University Press

Hudson, T.P. (ed.) 1997: *A History of the County of Sussex: Victoria County History Volume V, part 1.* Oxford: Oxford University Press

Hudson, W.H. 1906: *Nature in Downland.* London: Longmans, Green and Co.

Jackson, J.W. 1955: 'Animal bones and shell', in R. Musson, 'A thirteenth-century building at Bramble Bottom, Eastbourne', *Sussex Archaeological Collections*, vol. 93, 169–70

James, R. 2008: 'Excavations at the Jenner and Simpson Mill site, Mount Street, Battle, East Sussex', *Sussex Archaeological Collections*, vol. 146, 149–73

James, R. 2015: 'Archaeological investigations at Pevensey and Westham CE School, High Street, Westham, East Sussex', *Sussex Archaeological Collections*, vol. 153, 73–81

James, R. and Barber, L. 2004: *St Thomas' CE Primary School, Winchelsea, East Sussex. Post-Excavation Assessment and Project Design.* Archaeology South-East unpublished report

Johnson, M. 2007: *Ideas of Landscape.* Oxford: Blackwell Publishing

Jolliffe, J.E.A. 1933: *Pre-feudal England: The Jutes.* Oxford: Oxford University Press

Jones, G. 2010: 'A "common of hunting"? Forests, lordship, and community before and after the Conquest', in J. Langton and G. Jones (eds), *Forests and Chases of Medieval England and Wales c.1000–c.1500.* St John's College and Oxbow Books, 36–67

Jones, G.R.J. 1961: 'Settlement patterns in Anglo-Saxon England', *Antiquity*, vol. 35(139), 221–32

Jones, G.R.J. 1979: 'Multiple estates and early settlement', in P.H. Sawyer (ed.), *English Medieval Settlement.* London: Edward Arnold, 9–34

Jones, R. 2009: 'Manure and the medieval social order', in M.J. Allen, N. Sharples and T. O'Connor (eds), *Land and People: Papers in Honour of John G. Evans.* Oxford: Oxbow Books, Prehistoric Society Research Paper 2, 215–25

Jones, R. 2012: 'Why manure matters', in R. Jones (ed.), *Manure Matters: Historical, Archaeological and Ethnographical Perspectives.* Farnham: Ashgate Publishing, 1–12

Jones, R. and Hooke, D. 2012: 'Methodological approaches to medieval rural settlements and landscapes', in N. Christie and P. Stamper (eds), *Medieval Rural Settlement: Britain and Ireland, AD 800–1600.* Oxford: Oxbow Books, 31–42

Jørgensen, D. 2013a: 'Pigs and pollards: medieval insights for UK wood pasture restoration', *Sustainability*, vol. 5, 387–99

Jørgensen, D. 2013b: 'Running amuck? Urban swine management in late medieval England', *Agricultural History*, vol. 87, 429–51

Keef, P.A.M., Wymer, J.J. and Dimbleby, G.W. 1965: 'A Mesolithic site on Iping Common, Sussex, England', *Proceedings of the Prehistoric Society*, vol. 31, 85–92

Keeling, S.M. and Lewis, C.P. 1984: *A History of the County of Sussex: Index to Volumes I–IV, VII, and IX.* Oxford: Oxford University Press

Kernon, T. and Deane, R. 2007: *An Holistic Management Plan for a Naturalistic Grazing Project on the Knepp Castle Estate, Sussex: Feasibility Assessment.* Kernon Countryside Consultants and Land Use Consultants unpublished report

Killock, D. 2009: *An Assessment of an Archaeological Excavation at Tabard Square, 34–70 Long Lane and 31–47 Tabard Street, London SE1, London Borough of Southwark.* Pre-Construct Archaeology unpublished report

King, A.C. 1975: 'A medieval town house in German Street, Winchelsea', *Sussex Archaeological Collections*, vol. 113, 124–45

King, S.H. 1962: 'Sussex', in H.C. Darby and E.M.J. Campbell (eds), *The Domesday Geography of South-East England.* Cambridge: Cambridge University Press, 407–82

Kipling, R. 1902: *Sussex*

Kissock, J. 2001: 'The upland dimension: further conjectures on early medieval settlement in Gower', *Morgannwg*, vol. 45, 55–68

Kurath, H. (ed.) 2007: *Middle English Dictionary.* Michigan: The University of Michigan Press

Lamond, E. (ed.) 1890: *Walter of Henley's Husbandry.* London: Royal Historical Society

Langton, J. and Jones, G. (eds) 2010: *Forests and Chases of Medieval England and Wales c.1000–c.1500.* Oxford: St John's College and Oxbow Books

Lawson, T. 2004: 'Anglo-Saxon Kent: settlement of the Weald', in T. Lawson and D. Killingray (eds), *An Historical Atlas of Kent.* Chichester: Phillimore and Co., 29–30

Leach, P.E. (ed.) 1982: *Archaeology in Kent to AD 1500*. London: CBA, Council for British Archaeology Research Report 48

Leslie, K. and Short, B. (eds) 1999: *An Historical Atlas of Sussex*. Chichester: Phillimore and Co.

Lewis, C.P. 2009: *A History of the County of Sussex: Victoria County History Volume V, part 2*. London: Booth

Lewis, E., Roberts, E.V. and Roberts, K. 1988: *Medieval Hall Houses of the Winchester Area*. Winchester: Winchester City Museum

Liddiard, R. (ed.) 2007: *The Medieval Park: New Perspectives*. Macclesfield: Windgather Press

Lister, J. (ed.) 1917: *Court Rolls of the Manor of Wakefield, Vol. III: 1313 to 1316, and 1286*. Leeds: Yorkshire Archaeological Society

Lloyd, C.W. 1962: 'Surrey', in H.C. Darby and E.M.J. Campbell (eds), *The Domesday Geography of South-East England*, 364–406

Lloyd, J. 2013: 'The Origin of the Lathes of east Kent', *Archaeologia Cantiana*, vol. 133, 83–114

Locker, A. 1985: 'The animal and plant remains', in J.N. Hare, *Battle Abbey: The Eastern Range and the Excavations of 1978–80*. London: Historic Buildings and Monuments Commission for England, Archaeological report no. 2, 183–89

Long, A., Hipkin, S. and Clarke, H. (eds) 2002: *Romney Marsh: Coastal and Landscape Change through the Ages*. Oxford: University of Oxford, School of Archaeology

Lovell, J. 2001: 'Excavations on a medieval site at Little High Street, Worthing, West Sussex, 1997', *Sussex Archaeological Collections*, vol. 139, 133–45

Loyn, H.R. 1962: *Anglo-Saxon England and the Norman Conquest*. London: Longmans

Malden, H.E. (ed.) 1902: *The Victoria County History of the County of Surrey: Volume I*. London

Malden, H.E. (ed.) 1905: *The Victoria County History of the County of Surrey: Volume II*. London

Malden, H.E. (ed.) 1911: *The Victoria County History of the County of Surrey: Volume III*. London: Constable and Co.

Malden, H.E. (ed.) 1912: *The Victoria County History of the County of Surrey: Volume IV*. London: Constable and Co.

Malden, H.E. (ed.) 1914: *Index to: The Victoria County History of the County of Surrey*. London: Constable and Co.

Maltby, M. 2007: 'Chop and change: specialist cattle carcass processing in Roman Britain', *TRAC 2006. Proceedings of the Sixteenth Annual Theoretical Roman Archaeology Conference*, 59–76

Manley, J. (ed.) 2016: *Secrets of the High Woods: Revealing Hidden Landscapes*. Midhurst: South Downs National Park Authority

Mansion, J. 1931: 'The Place-Names of Sussex', *English Studies*, vol. 13, 200–01

Margary, I.D. 1947: 'Roman communications between Kent and the East Sussex iron-works', *Sussex Archaeological Collections*, vol. 86, 22–41

Margary, I.D. 1948: *Roman Ways in the Weald*. London: Phoenix House

Margary, I.D. 1950: 'The development of turnpike roads in Sussex', *Sussex Notes and Queries*, vol. 13, 49–53

Margetts, A. 2017: 'The Hayworth: a lowland vaccary site in South-East England', *Medieval Archaeology*, vol. 61(1), 117–48

Margetts, A. 2018a: *Wealdbǣra: excavations at 'Wickhurst Green', Broadbridge Heath and the Landscape of the West Central Weald*. Archaeology South-East (UCL) and Surrey County Archaeological Unit, Spoilheap Monograph 18

Margetts, A. 2018b: 'A world of summer and autumn: the Romano-British to early medieval Weald and signs of continuity', *Archaeology International*, vol. 21(1), 89–94

Marshall, W. 1798: *The rural economy of the Southern Counties; comprising Kent, Surrey, Sussex, the Isle of Wight, the chalk hills of Wiltshire, Hampshire, [etc.], and including the culture and management of hops in the districts of Maidstone, Canterbury and Farnham, Vol. II*. London: Nicol

Martin, D. 1989: 'Three moated sites in North-East Sussex. part 1: Glottenham', *Sussex Archaeological Collections*, vol. 127, 89–122

Martin, D. 1990: 'Three moated sites in north-east Sussex. part 2: Hawksden and Bodiam', *Sussex Archaeological Collections*, vol. 128, 89–116

Martin, D. and Martin, B. (eds) 2004: *New Winchelsea, Sussex: A Medieval Port Town*. London: University College London, Field Archaeology Unit and English Heritage

Mate, M. 1987: 'Pastoral farming in South-East England in the fifteenth century', *Economic History Review*, vol. 40(4), 523–36

Mate, M. 1991: 'Farming practice and techniques: Kent and Sussex', in J. Thirsk (ed.), *The Agrarian History of England and Wales: Volume III, 1348–1500*. Cambridge: Cambridge University Press, 268–84

Mawer, A. and Stenton, F.M. (eds) 1929: *The Place-Names of Sussex: Part 1*. Cambridge: Cambridge University Press, English Place-Name Society, vol. 6

Mawer, A. and Stenton, F.M. (eds) 1930: *The Place-Names of Sussex: Part 2*. Cambridge: Cambridge University Press, English Place-Name Society, vol. 7

Mawer, A. and Stenton, F.M. (eds) 1934: *The Place-Names of Surrey*. London: English Place-Name Society, vol. 11

Maxwell Lyte, H.C. (ed.) 1898: *Calendar of Close Rolls Preserved in the Public Record Office. Edward III. AD 1333–1337*. London: Her Majesty's Stationary Office

Maxwell Lyte, H.C. (ed.) 1903: *Calendar of the Charter Rolls Preserved in the Public Record Office. Vol. 1, Henry III. AD 1226–1257*. London: His Majesty's Stationary Office

Maxwell Lyte, H.C. (ed.) 1908: *Close Rolls of the Reign of Henry III Preserved in the Public Record Office, Vol. III. AD 1234–1237*. London: His Majesty's Stationary Office

Maxwell Lyte, H.C. (ed.) 1910: *Calendar of Inquisitions Post Mortem and Other Analagous Documents. Preserved in the Public Record Office, Vol. VI. Edward II*. Hereford: His Majesty's Stationary Office

Maxwell Lyte, H.C. (ed.) 1916: *Close Rolls of the Reign of Henry III Preserved in the Public Record Office. AD 1242–1247*. London: His Majesty's Stationary Office

Mayle, B. 1999: *Domestic Stock Grazing to Enhance Woodland Biodiversity*. Forestry Commission information note

McKinley, J.I., Leivers, M., Schuster, J., Marshall, P., Barclay, A. and Stoodley, N. 2014: *Cliffs End Farm Isle of Thanet, Kent: A Mortuary and Ritual Site of the Bronze Age, Iron Age and Anglo-Saxon Period*. Salisbury: Wessex Archaeology Report 31

Mileson, S. 2009: *Parks in Medieval England*. Oxford: Oxford University Press

Miller, E. (ed.) 1991: *The Agrarian History of England and Wales: Volume III. AD 1348–1500*. Cambridge: Cambridge University Press

Miller, R. 1967: 'Shiels in the Brecon Beacons', *Folk Life*, vol. 5(1), 107–10

Monbiot, G. 2017: 'The Lake District as a world heritage site? What a disaster that would be', *The Guardian*, 9 May 2017. Available at: <https://www.theguardian.com/commentisfree/2017/may/09/lake-district-world-heritage-site-george-monbiot> [Accessed 29 May 2019]

Monbiot, G. 2018: 'Britain's national parks are a farce: they're being run for a tiny minority', *The Guardian*, 28 February 2018. Available at: <https://www.theguardian.com/commentisfree/2018/feb/28/britain-national-parks-reclaim-rewild> [Accessed 29 May 2019]

Moorhouse, S. 2003: 'Anatomy of the Yorkshire Dales: decoding the medieval landscape', in T.G. Manby, S. Moorhouse and P. Ottaway (eds), *The Archaeology of Yorkshire: An Assessment at the Beginning of the 21st Century*. Leeds: Yorkshire Archaeological Society, Occasional Paper no. 3, 293–362

Moorhouse, S. 2007: 'The medieval parks of Yorkshire: function, contents and chronology', in J. Langton and G. Jones (eds), *Forests and Chases of Medieval England and Wales c.1000–c.1500*. Oxford: St John's College and Oxbow Books, 99–127

Morris, J. (ed.) 1975: *Domesday Book: Surrey*. Chichester: Phillimore and Co.

Morris, J. (ed.) 1976: *Domesday Book: Sussex*. London and Chichester: Phillimore and Co.

Morris, J. (ed.) 1983: *Domesday Book: Kent*. Chichester: Phillimore and Co.

MSU 2016: *Do Sheep Always Need Access to a Fluid Water Source?*. Michigan State University Extension. Available at: <http://msue.anr.msu.edu/news/do_sheep_always_need_access_to_a_fluid_water_source> [Accessed 4 December 2017]

Munnery, T. 2016: *A Bronze Age Ring-Ditch and Mesolithic and Medieval Activity at Waitrose, South Street, Dorking, Surrey*. SpoilHeap Occasional Paper 7

Musson, R. 1955: 'A thirteenth-century building at Bramble Bottom, Eastbourne', *Sussex Archaeological Collections*, vol. 93, 157–70

National Research Council 1985: *Nutrient Requirements of Sheep*, 6th revised edition. Washington, D.C: Subcommittee on Sheep Nutrition, Committee on Animal Nutrition, Board on Agriculture, Nation Research Council, National Academy Press

National Research Council 2000: *Nutrient Requirements of Beef Cattle*, 7th revised edition, update 2000. Washington, DC: The National Academies Press

Newman, C. 2006: 'Medieval period resource assessment', in M. Brennand (ed.), *The Archaeology of North West England: An Archaeological Research Framework for the North West Region*. Council for British Archaeology North West, 115–43

Nicholson, R. and Worley, F. 2006: *Animal Bone from Saltwood Tunnel, Kent*. Oxford Wessex Archaeology: CTRL Specialist Report Series. Available at: <http://archaeologydataservice.ac.uk/archives/view/ctrl/downloads.cfm?group=1001> [Accessed 16 December 2019]

NRAES 1998. *Dairy Feeding Systems: Management, Components, and Nutrients: Proceedings from the Dairy Feeding Systems – Management, Components, and Nutrients Conference, December 8–10, 1998, Camp Hill, Pennsylvania.* Ithaca, New York: Northeast Regional Agricultural Engineering Service, Cooperative Extension

O'Connor, T. 2011: 'Animal husbandry', in H. Hamerow, D.A. Hinton and S. Crawford (eds), *The Oxford Handbook of Anglo-Saxon Archaeology.* Oxford: Oxford University Press, 363–78

OMAFRA 2017: *Water Requirements of Livestock.* Ontario Ministry of Agriculture, Food and Rural Affairs. Available at: <http://www.omafra.gov.on.ca/english/engineer/facts/07-023.html> [Accessed 4 December 2017]

Oosthuizen, S. 2011: 'Archaeology, common rights, and the origins of Anglo-Saxon identity', *Early Medieval Europe*, vol. 19 (2), 153–181

Oosthuizen, S. 2013: *Tradition and Transformation in Anglo-Saxon England: Archaeology, Common Rights and Landscape.* London: Bloomsbury Academic

Oschinsky, D. (ed.) 1971: *Walter of Henley and Other Treatises on Estate Management and Accounting.* Oxford: Clarendon Press

Owst, G.R. 1933: *Literature and Pulpit in Medieval England: A Neglected Chapter in the History of English Letters and of the English People.* Cambridge: Cambridge University Press

Page, W. (ed.) 1905: *The Victoria History of the County of Sussex Volume I.* London: Archibald Constable and Co.

Page, W. (ed.) 1907: *The Victoria History of the County of Sussex Volume II.* London: Archibald Constable and Co.

Page, W. (ed.) 1908: *The Victoria History of the County of Kent Volume I.* London: Archibald Constable and Co.

Page, W. (ed.) 1926: *The Victoria History of the County of Kent Volume II.* London: The St Catherine Press

Page, W. (ed.) 1932: *The Victoria History of the County of Kent Volume III.* London: The St Catherine Press

Page, W. (ed.) 1973: *A History of the County of Sussex: Victoria County History Volume II.* London: Published for the University of London Institute of Historical Research

Parfitt, K. and Sweetinburgh, S. 2009: 'Further investigation of Anglo-Saxon and medieval Eastry', *Archaeologia Cantiana*, vol. 129, 313–32

Parfitt, K., Corke, B. and Cotter, J. 2006: *Townwall Street, Dover: Excavations 1996.* Canterbury: Canterbury Archaeological Trust

Partida, T., Hall, D. and Foard, G. 2013: *An Atlas of Northamptonshire: The Medieval and Early-Modern Landscape.* Oxford: Oxbow Books

Peckham, W.D. (ed.) 1925: *Thirteen Custumals of the Sussex Manors of the Bishop of Chichester.* Lewes: Sussex Record Society, vol. 31

Peckham, W.D. (ed.) 1942: *The Chartulary of the High Church of Chichester.* Lewes: Sussex Record Society, vol. 46

Pelham, R.A. 1934: 'The distribution of sheep in Sussex in the early fourteenth century', *Sussex Archaeological Collections*, vol. 75, 130–36

Penn, R. 1984: *Portrait of Ashdown Forest.* London: Robert Hale

Pipe, A. 2006: *The Animal Bones from Tonbridge Stock and Cattle Market, Bank Street, Tonbridge, Kent.* Museum of London Archaeology unpublished report

Pitt-Rivers, A.H. 1887: *Excavations in Cranborne Chase, near Rushmore, on the Borders of Dorset and Wilts, 1880–1896. Vol. IV.* London: Harrison and Sons

Pollard, A.J. 1990: *North-eastern England during the Wars of the Roses: Law Society, War, and Politics 1450–1500.* Oxford: Clarendon Press

Porter, V. 2001: *British Cattle.* Oxford: Shire Publications

Postan, M.M. 1972: *The Medieval Economy and Society.* London: Weidenfeld and Nicholson

Pott, R. 1998: 'Effects of human interference with the landscape with special reference to the role of grazing livestock', in M.F. Wallis de Vries, J.P. Bakker and S.E. Van Wieren (eds), *Grazing and Conservation Management.* Dordrecht: Kluwer Academic Publishers, 107–34

Poulton, R. 1998: 'Excavation between Castle Street and Bear Lane, Farnham', *Surrey Archaeological Collections*, vol. 85, 133–43

Poulton, R. 2005: *A Medieval Royal Complex at Guildford: Excavations at the Castle and Palace.* Guildford: Surrey Archaeological Society Monograph

Poulton, R. 2015: *The Moated Medieval Manor and Tudor Royal Residence at Woking Palace. Excavations between 2009 and 2015.* Woking: SpoilHeap Monograph 16

Powell, A.B., Barnett, C. and Grimm, J. 2009: 'A medieval enclosure and bakery or brewhouse at Fulston Manor, Sittingbourne', in P. Andrews, K. Egging Dinwiddy, C. Ellis, A. Hutcheson, C. Philpotts, A.B. Powell and J. Schuster (eds), *Kentish*

Sites and Sites in Kent. Salisbury: Wessex Archaeology Monograph 24, 175–98

Priestley-Bell, G. 2008: *The Excavation of Prehistoric, Medieval and Post-Medieval Remains at St Bartholomew's Close, Chichester, West Sussex.* Archaeology South-East unpublished report

Rackham, O. 1986: *The History of the Countryside.* London: Dent

Rackham, O. 1990: *Trees and Woodlands in the British Landscape. The Complete History of Britain's Trees, Woods and Hedgerows*, revised edition. London: Phoenix Press

Rackham, O. 2003: *The Illustrated History of the Countryside.* London: Weidenfeld & Nicolson

Rackham, O. 2006: *Woodlands: New Naturalist vol. 100.* London: Harper Collins

Rady, J. 2010: *Excavations at Thanet Earth 2007–2008.* Canterbury Archaeological Trust unpublished report

Rady, J. forthcoming: *Excavations at Thanet Earth: The Medieval Period.* Canterbury Archaeological Trust

Ramm, H.G., McDowall, R.W. and Mercer, E. 1970: *Shielings and Bastles.* London: HMSO, RCHME

Rathbone, S. 2012: 'Booley houses, hafods and sheilings: a comparative study of transhumant settlements from around the northern basin of the Irish Sea', in A. Horning and N. Brannon (eds), *Ireland and Britain in the Atlantic World.* Dublin: Wordwell, Irish Post-medieval Archaeology Group Proceedings 2, 111–29

Redwood, B.C. and Wilson, A.E. 1958: *Custumals of Sussex Manors of the Archbishop of Canterbury, 1285–1330.* Lewes: Sussex Record Society, vol. 57

Reynolds, A. 2003: 'Boundaries and settlements in later sixth- to eleventh century England', in D. Griffiths, A. Reynolds and S. Semple (eds), *Boundaries in Early Medieval Britain.* Oxford: Oxbow Books, 98–136

Richardson, A. 2007: '"The King's chief delights": a landscape approach to the royal parks of post-Conquest England', in R. Liddiard (ed.), *The Medieval Park: New Perspectives.* Macclesfield: Windgather Press, 27–48

Rippon, S.1996: 'Roman and medieval settlement on the north Somerset Levels: survey and excavation at Banwell and Puxton, 1996', *Archaeology in the Severn Estuary*, vol. 7, 39–52

Rippon, S. 1997a: *The Severn Estuary: Landscape Evolution and Wetland Reclamation.* London: Leicester University Press

Rippon, S. 1997b: 'Roman and medieval settlement on the north Somerset Levels: second season of

survey and excavation at Banwell and Puxton, 1997', *Archaeology in the Severn Estuary*, vol. 8, 41–54

Rippon, S. 2000: *The Transformation of Coastal Wetlands,* Oxford: Oxford University Press

Rippon, S. 2002a: 'Infield and outfield: the early stages of marshland colonisation and the evolution of medieval field systems', in T. Lane and J. Coles (eds), *Through Wet and Dry: Essays in Honour of David Hall*, Sleaford and Exeter: Lincolnshire Archaeology and Heritage Report Series 5, WARP Occasional Paper 17, 54–70

Rippon, S. 2002b: 'Romney Marsh: evolution of the historic landscape and its wider significance', in A. Long, S. Hipkin and H. Clarke (eds), *Romney Marsh: coastal and Landscape Change through the Ages.* Oxford: Oxford University School of Archaeology Monograph 56, 84–100

Rippon, S. 2004: *Historic Landscape Analysis: Deciphering the Countryside.* York: CBA, Council for British Archaeology Practical Handbooks in Archaeology no. 16

Rippon, S. 2006: *Landscape, Community and Colonisation: The North Somerset Levels during the 1st to 2nd Millennia AD.* York: Council for British Archaeology Research report no. 152

Rippon, S. 2008: *Beyond the Medieval Village: Diversification of Landscape Character in Southern Britain.* Oxford: Oxford University Press

Rippon, S. 2012: *Making Sense of an Historic Landscape.* Oxford: Oxford University Press

Rippon, S. 2013: 'Historic Landscape Character and Sense of Place', *Landscape Research*, vol. 38(2), 179–202

Rippon, S., Smart, C. and Pears, B. 2015: *The Fields of Britannia.* Oxford: Oxford University Press

Roberts, B.K. and Wrathmell, S. 2000: *An Atlas of Rural Settlement in England.* London: English Heritage

Rodwell, W. 1978: 'Relict landscapes in Essex', in H.C. Bowen and P.J. Fowler (eds), *Early Land Allotment.* Oxford: BAR British series, 48, 89–98

Roffe, D. 2000: *Domesday: The Inquest and the Book.* Oxford: Oxford University Press

Roman Britain 1938: 'Roman Britain in 1937, sites explored', *Journal of Roman Studies*, vol. 28(2), 169–206

Rose, S. 2018: *The Wealth of England: The Medieval Wool Trade and its Political Importance 1100–1600.* Oxford: Oxbow Books

Rotherham, I.D. 2007: 'The historical ecology of medieval parks and the implications for conservation', in R. Liddiard (ed.), *The Medieval Park: New Perspectives*. Macclesfield: Windgather Press, 79–96

Salvagno, L. 2015: *The Neglected Goat: A Methodological Approach to the Understanding of the Role of this Species in English Medieval Husbandry*. University of Sheffield unpublished Ph.D. thesis

Salzman, L.F. (ed.). 1903: *An Abstract of Feet of Fines Relating to the County of Sussex, from 2 Richard I to 33 Henry III*. Lewes: Sussex Record Society, vol. 2

Salzman, L.F. (ed.). 1904: *A Calendar of Post Mortem Inquisitions Relating to the County of Sussex, 1 to 25 Elizabeth*. Lewes: Sussex Record Society, vol. 3

Salzman, L.F. (ed.). 1908: *An Abstract of Feet of Fines Relating to the County of Sussex, from 34 Henry III to 35 Edward I*. Lewes: Sussex Record Society, vol. 7

Salzman, L.F. (ed.). 1916: *An Abstract of Feet of Fines Relating to the Ccounty of Sussex, from 1 Edward II to 24 Henry VII*. Lewes: Sussex Record Society, vol. 23

Salzman, L.F. (ed.). 1923: *The Chartulary of the Priory of St Peter at Sele*. Cambridge: Heffer

Salzman, L.F. (ed.). 1933: *The Chartulary of the Priory of St Pancras of Lewes: Part 1*. Lewes: Sussex Record Society, vol. 38

Salzman, L.F. (ed.). 1934: *The Chartulary of the Priory of St Pancras of Lewes: Part 2*. Lewes: Sussex Record Society, vol. 40

Salzman, L.F. (ed.) 1935: *A History of the County of Sussex: Victoria County History Volume III*. Oxford: Oxford University Press

Salzman, L.F. (ed.) 1937: *A History of the County of Sussex: Victoria County History Volume IX*. Oxford: Oxford University Press

Salzman, L.F. (ed.) 1940: *A History of the County of Sussex: Victoria County History Volume VII*. Oxford: Oxford University Press

Salzman, L.F. (ed.) 1953: *A History of the County of Sussex: Victoria County History Volume IV*. Oxford: Oxford University Press

Salzman, L.F. 1961: 'Early taxation in Sussex', *Sussex Archaeological Collections*, vol. 99, 1–19

Sambrook, P. 2006: 'Deserted rural settlements in south-west Wales', in K. Roberts (ed.), *Lost Farmsteads: Deserted Medieval Settlements in Wales*. York: Council for British Archaeology, CBA Research Report 148, 83–110

Saunders, M.J. 1998: 'Archaeological investigations on the route of the Crawley High Street relief road, Crawley, West Sussex', *Sussex Archaeological Collections*, vol. 136, 81–94

Sawyer, P.H. 1968: *Anglo-Saxon Charters: An Annotated List and Bibliography*. London: Royal Historical Society

Sayer, K. 2006: *An Assessment of an Archaeological Excavation at 52–56 Lant Street, London Borough of Southwark, LTU 03*. Pre-Construct Archaeology unpublished report

Scargill-Bird, S.R. (ed.) 1887: *Custumals of Battle Abbey: In the reigns of Edward I and Edward II 1283–1312*. London: The Camden Society

Scottish Forestry 2018: *Determining Stocking Density and Duration of Grazing*. Available at: <https://forestry.gov.scot/woodland-grazing-toolbox/grazing-management/ grazing-regime/stocking-density-and-duration> [Accessed 29 May 2019]

Searle, E. (ed.) 1980: *The Chronicle of Battle Abbey*. Oxford: Clarendon Press

Searle, E. and Ross, B. (eds) 1967: *The Cellarers' Rolls of Battle Abbey: 1275–1513*. Lewes: Sussex Record Society, vol. 65

Sellick, J. and Yarwood, R. 2013: 'Placing livestock in landscape studies: pastures new or out to graze?', *Landscape Research*, vol. 38(4), 404–20

Semple, J. 2008: 'The medieval deer parks of Wrotham', *Archaeologia Cantiana*, vol. 128, 179–210

SERF 2008: *South East Research Framework*. Maidstone: Kent County Council

Shennan, S. 1985: *Experiments in the Collection and Analysis of Archaeological Survey Data: The East Hampshire Survey*. Sheffield: University of Sheffield

Shields, G. 2005: 'The Roman roads of the Portslade/ Aldrington area in relation to a possible Roman port at Copperas Gap', *Sussex Archaeological Collections*, vol. 143, 135–49

Short, B. 2006: *England's Landscape: The South-East*, London: Collins for English Heritage

Sibun, L. 2008: 'The animal bone', in R. James, 'Excavations at the Jenner and Simpson Mill site, Mount Street, Battle, East Sussex', *Sussex Archaeological Collections*, vol. 146, 167–68

Smith, A.H. 1956a: *English Place-Name Elements: Part 1, the Elements A–IW, Maps*. Cambridge: English Place-Name Society, vol. 25

Smith, A.H. 1956b: *English Place-Name Elements: Part 2, the Elements JAFN–YTRI, Index and Maps*. Cambridge: English Place-Name Society, vol. 26

Smith, A.H. 1961: *The Place-Names of the West Riding of Yorkshire. Part III: Morley Wapentake*. London: Cambridge University Press, English Place-Name Society, vol. 32

Smith, N. 1999: 'The earthwork remains of enclosures in the New Forest', *Proceedings of the Hampshire Field Club and Archaeological Society*, vol. 54, 1–56

Smith, N. 2007: 'The location and operation of demesne cattle farms in Sowerby Graveship circa 1300', *Transactions of the Halifax Antiquarian Society*, vol. 15 new series, 17–32

Smith Ellis, W. 1885: *The parks and forests of Sussex, ancient and modern*. Lewes: H. Wolff

Stafford, P. 1989: *Unification and Conquest: A Political and Social History of England in the Tenth and Eleventh Centuries*. Oxford: Oxford University Press

Stevens, S. 1997: 'Excavations at the Old Post Office site, 15–17 High Street, Crawley, West Sussex', *Sussex Archaeological Collections*, vol. 135, 193–208

Stevens, S. 2004: 'Excavations at 1–3 High Street, Seaford, East Sussex', *Sussex Archaeological Collections*, vol. 142, 79–92

Stevens, S. 2007: 'Archaeological investigations on the A27 Polegate Bypass, East Sussex', *Sussex Archaeological Collections*, vol. 145, 119–35

Stevens, S. 2008: *Archaeological Investigations in The Vicarage Garden, Causeway, Horsham, West Sussex*. Archaeology South-East unpublished report

Stevens, S. 2009a: *Archaeological Investigations at the Former Site of Highdown School, Durrington Lane, Worthing, West Sussex*. Archaeology South-East unpublished report

Stevens, S. 2009b: 'Excavations at No. 5 John Street, Shoreham-By-Sea, West Sussex', *Sussex Archaeological Collections*, vol. 147, 97–109

Stevens, S. 2010: *Archaeological Investigations at 29–35 High Street, Crawley, West Sussex*. Archaeology South-East unpublished report

Stevens, S. 2011: 'Archaeological investigations at the Ropetackle site, Shoreham-by-Sea, West Sussex', *Sussex Archaeological Collections*, vol. 149, 59–158

Stevens, S. 2013: *Archaeological Investigations at 1–7 New Dover Road, Canterbury. Post-Excavation Assessment and Updated Project Design*. Archaeology South-East unpublished report

Stevenson, J. 2003: *The Former King and Barnes Brewery Site, Horsham, West Sussex*. Archaeology South-East unpublished report

Stevenson, J. 2013a: *Archaeological Investigations at 15 Knightrider St, Maidstone, Kent*. Archaeology South-East: Kent Archaeological Reports online. Available at: <http://www.kentarchaeology.org.uk/10/027.pdf> [Accessed 16 December 2019]

Stevenson, J. 2013b: *Living by the Sword: The Archaeology of Brisley Farm, Ashford, Kent*. Portslade: SpoilHeap Monograph 6

Straker, E. 1941: 'The Vachery ironworks', *Surrey Archaeological Collections*, vol. 47, 48–51

Svensson, E. and Gardiner, M. 2009: Introduction: marginality in the preindustrial European countryside', in J. Klápště and P. Somer (eds), *Arts and Crafts in the Medieval Rural Environment*. Turnhout: Brepols Publishers, Ruralia VII, 21–25

Sweetinburgh, S. (ed.) 2010: *Later Medieval Kent, 1220–1540*. Woodbridge: Boydell and Brewer

Swift, D. and Blackmore, L. 2010: *Archaeological Investigations at the Site of the Former Capitol Cinema, High Street, Tonbridge, Kent*. Museum of London Archaeology: Kent Archaeological Reports online. Available at: <http://www.kentarchaeology.org.uk/10/027.pdf> [Accessed 16 December 2019]

Swift, D. in prep: *Between the Twittens: from Iron Age occupation to County Town, archaeological excavations in Lewes, East Sussex*. SpoilHeap Monograph series

Sykes, N. 2009: 'Animals, the bones of medieval society', in R. Gilchrist and A. Reynolds (eds), *Reflections: 50 Years of Medieval Archaeology, 1957–2007*. Leeds: Maney Publishing, The Society for Medieval Archaeology Monograph 30, 347–61

Sykes, N.J. 2006: 'From *cu* and *sceap* to *beffe* and *motton*', in C.M. Woolgar, D. Serjeantson and T. Waldron (eds), *Food in Medieval England: Diet and Nutrition*. Oxford: Oxford University Press, 56–71

Sykes, N.J. 2007: *The Norman Conquest: A Zooarchaeological Perspective*. Oxford: Archaeopress, BAR International Series 1656

Sykes, N. and Symmons, R. 2007: 'Sexing cattle horn-cores: problems and progress', *International Journal of Osteoarchaeology*, vol. 17(5), 514–23

Szabó, P. 2009: 'Open woodland in Europe in the Mesolithic and in the Middle Ages: can there be a connection?', *Forest Ecology and Management*, vol. 257, 2327–30

Taylor, A.J. (ed.) 1940: *Records of the Barony and Honour of the Rape of Lewes*. Lewes: Sussex Record Society, vol. 44

Taylor, C. 2007: 'England's landscape: a review article', *Landscape History*, vol. 29, 93–99

Taylor, J. forthcoming. *Archaeological Investigations at the Former Shippam's Factory and Shippam's Social Club, East Walls, Chichester, West Sussex*. Pre-Construct Archaeology Monograph Series

Tebbutt, C.F. 1981: 'A deserted medieval farm settlement at Faulkner's Farm, Hartfield', *Sussex Archaeological Collections*, vol. 119, 107–16

Thirsk, J. 1987: *Agricultural Regions and Agrarian History in England, 1500–1750*. Basingstoke: Palgrave Macmillan

Thirsk, J. 1997: *Alternative Agriculture: A History. From the Black Death to The Present Day*. Oxford: Oxford University Press

Thirsk, J. 2002: 'The British Agricultural History Society and *The Agrarian History of England and Wales*: new projects in the 1950s', *The Agricultural History Review*, vol. 50(2), 155–63

Thomas, G. 2005: 'Refining the biography of a marketplace tenement: a recent excavation and archaeological interpretative survey at "The Marlipins", Shoreham-by-Sea, West Sussex', *Sussex Archaeological Collections*, vol. 143, 173–204

Thomas, G. 2010: *The Later Anglo-Saxon Settlement at Bishopstone: A Downland Manor in the Making*. York: Council for British Archaeology, CBA Research Report 163

Thomas, G. 2019: *Resource Assessment and Research Agenda for the Anglo-Saxon Period*. South East Research Framework. Available at: <https://www.kent.gov.uk/data/assets/pdf_file/0008/93176/South-East-Research-Framework-Resource-Assessment-and-Research-Agenda-for-the-Anglo-Saxon-period.pdf> [Accessed 28 August 2019]

Thomas, G. forthcoming: *Excavations at Lyminge*

Thornton, M. 2012: 'Lord's man or community servant? The role, status and allegiance of village Haywards in fifteenth-century Northamptonshire', in S. Turner and B. Silvester (eds), *Life in medieval landscapes*. Oxford: Windgather Press, 213–24

Toms, H.S. 1907: *Prehistoric Valley Entrenchments, near Falmer*. Brighton: Brighton and Hove Archaeology Club

Toms, H.S. 1912: 'Excavations at the Belle Tout valley entrenchments', *Sussex Archaeological Collections*, vol. 55, 41–55

Toms, H.S. 1913: 'A record of the valley-side entrenchment in Bramble Bottom, Eastdean', *Transactions and Journal of the Eastbourne Natural History, Photographic and Literary Society*, vol. 5(4), 58–62

Toms, H.S. 1924: 'Valley entrenchments west of the Ditchling Road', *Brighton and Hove Archaeologist*, vol. 2, 57–72

Toms, H.S. 1926: 'Valley entrenchments east of the Ditchling Road', *Brighton and Hove Archaeologist*, vol. 3, 42–61

Topley, W. 1873: 'On the relation of the parish boundaries in the South-East of England to great physical features, particularly to the chalk escarpment', *The Journal of the Anthropological Institute of Great Britain and Ireland*, vol. 3, 32–56

Tree, I. 2019: *Wilding: The Return of Nature to a British Farm*. London: Picador

Trow-Smith, R. 1957: *A History of British Livestock Husbandry to 1700*. London: Routledge and Kegan Paul

Tupling, G.H. 1927: *The Economic History of Rossendale*. Manchester: Manchester University Press

Turner, D. 1987: 'The archaeology of Surrey, 1066–1540', in J. Bird and D.G. Bird (eds), *The Archaeology of Surrey to 1540*. Guildford: Surrey Archaeological Society, 223–61

Turner, D. 1997: 'Thunderfield Surrey: central place or shieling?', *Medieval Settlement Research*, vol. 12, 8–10

Turner, D. and Briggs, R. 2016: 'Testing transhumance: Anglo-Saxon swine pastures and seasonal grazing in the Surrey Weald', *Surrey Archaeological Collections*, vol. 99, 165–93

Turner, S. and Young, R. 2007: 'Concealed communities: the people at the margins', *International Journal of Historical Archaeology*, vol. 11, 297–303

Tyler, S. and Major, H. 2005: *The early Anglo-Saxon cemetery and later Saxon settlement at Springfield Lyons, Essex*. Chelmsford: Essex County Council, East Anglian Archaeological Report no. 111

Vanderzee, G. (ed.) 1807: *Nonarum inquisitiones in curia scaccarii. Temp. Regis Edwardi III*. London

Vera, F.W.M. 2000: *Grazing, Ecology and Forest History*. Wallingford: CABI Publishing

Wade-Martins, P. 1980: *Fieldwork and Excavation on Village Sites in the Launditch Hundred, Norfolk*. Dereham: The Norfolk Archaeological Unit, East Anglian Archaeology, no. 10

Wallenberg, J.K. 1934: *The Place-Names of Kent*. Uppsala: Appelbergs boktryckeriaktiebolag

Ward, A. 1997: 'Transhumance and settlement on the Welsh uplands: a view from the Black Mountain', in N. Edwards (ed.), *Landscape and Settlement in Medieval Wales*, Oxford: Oxbow Monograph 81, 97–111

Warne, H. 'Friar's Oak: the historical context', in C. Butler, *Saxon Settlement and Earlier Remains at Friars Oak, Hassocks, West Sussex*. Oxford: Archaeopress, BAR British series 295, 65–71

Warne, H. 2009: *'Hayworthe' and 'Trobewyk': An Assessment of the Early History of Hayworth and Trubwick in Haywards Heath.* Haywards Heath: S. Meier

Warner, P. 1996: *The Origins of Suffolk.* Manchester: Manchester University Press

Watson, M. 1891: *On the Downs*

Watts, G. 2003: 'Identifying drove roads in southern England', *Proceedings of the Hampshire Field Club and Archaeological Society*, vol. 40, 18–19

Watts, V. 2004: *The Cambridge Dictionary of English Place-Names.* Cambridge: Cambridge University Press

Webster, C.J. 2008: 'South West archaeological research framework: a research agenda for archaeology in South West England', in C.J. Webster (ed.), *The Archaeology of South West England.* Somerset County Council, 269–91

Weekes, J. 2012: *Resource Assessment and Research Agenda for the Medieval Period.* South-East Research Framework. Available at: <https://shareweb.kent.gov.uk/Documents/leisure-and-culture/heritage/SERF%20Medieval.pdf> [Accessed 14 February 2014]

Welch, M. 2007: 'Anglo-Saxon Kent to AD 800', in J. Williams (ed.), *The Archaeology of Kent to AD 800.* Woodbridge: The Boydell Press, 187–248

White, G. 1836: *The Natural History of Selbourne.* London: Allan Bell and Co.

White, S. 1999: 'Early Saxon Sussex c.410–c.650', in K. Leslie and B. Short (eds), *An Historical Atlas of Sussex.* Chichester: Phillimore and Co., 28–29

Williams, J. (ed.) 2007: *The Archaeology of Kent to AD 800.* Woodbridge: The Boydell Press

Williamson, T. 1987: 'Early co-axial field systems on the East Anglian Boulder Clays', *Proceedings of the Prehistoric Society*, vol. 53, 419–31

Williamson, T. 1998: 'The "Scole-Dickleburgh field system" revisited', *Landscape History*, vol. 20, 19–28

Williamson, T. 2003: *Shaping Medieval Landscapes: Settlement, Society, Environment.* Bollington: Windgather Press

Williamson, T. 2006: 'Mapping field patterns: a case-study from eastern England', *Landscapes*, 7(i), 55–67

Williamson, T. 2007: *Rabbits, Warrens and Archaeology.* Stroud: Tempus Publishing

Williamson, T. 2008: 'Co-axial landscapes: time and topography', in P. Rainbird (ed.), *Monuments in the Landscape.* Stroud: Tempus, 123–35

Williamson, T. 2013: *Environment, Society and Landscape in Early Medieval England. Time and Topography.* Woodbridge: The Boydell Press

Williamson, T., Liddiard, R., Partida, T., Foard, G., Hall, D. and McClain, A. 2011: *A GIS Aided Study of Agriculture and Landscape in Midland England* [dataset]. York: Archaeology Data Service [distributor] (doi:10.5284/1000151)

Wilson, A.E. 1961: *Custumals of the Manors of Laughton, Willingdon, and Goring.* Lewes: Sussex Record Society, vol. 60

Winbolt, S.E. 1925: 'Sedgewick Castle', *Sussex Archaeological Collections*, vol. 66, 83–110

Winchester, A.J.L. 1987: *Landscape and Society in Medieval Cumbria.* Edinburgh: John Donald Publishers

Winchester, A.J.L. 2000: *The Harvest of the Hills: Rural Life in Northern England and the Scottish Borders, 1400–1700.* Edinburgh: Edinburgh University Press

Winchester, A.J.L. 2003: 'Demesne livestock farming in the Lake District: the vaccary at Gatesgarth, Buttermere, in the later thirteenth century', *Transactions of the Cumberland and Westmorland Antiquarian & Archaeological Society*, vol. 3, 3rd series, 109–18

Winchester, A.J.L. 2010: 'Vaccaries and agistment: upland medieval forests as grazing grounds', in J. Langton and G. Jones (eds), *Forests and Chases of medieval England and Wales c.1000–c.1500*, 109–24

Winchester, A.J.L. 2012: 'Seasonal settlement in northern England: shieling place-names revisted', in S. Turner and B. Silvester (eds), *Life in Medieval Landscapes.* Oxford: Windgather Press, 125–49

Windrum, A. 1978: *Horsham: An Historical Survey.* Chichester: Phillimore and Co.

Witney, K.P. 1976: *The Jutish Forest: A Study of the Weald of Kent from 450 AD to 1380 AD.* London: Athlone Press

Witney, K.P. 1990: 'The woodland economy of Kent, 1066–1348', *The Agricultural History Review*, vol. 38, 20–39

Woodland Trust 2012: *Woodwise: Conservation Grazing in Woodland Management.* Available at: <http://www.woodlandtrust.org.uk/mediafile/100263349/pg-wt-2014-woodwise-2012autumn.pdf?cb=435a97b193f048419903e8a34c51ea8a> [Accessed 29 May 2019]

Woodland Trust 2015: *Trees Provide Cover and Boost Production.* Available at: <https://www.woodlandtrust.org.uk/media/1786/trees-provide-fodder-and-boost-production.pdf> [Accessed 29 May 2019]

Woolgar, C.M. 1992: *Household Accounts from Medieval England: Part 1*. Oxford: Oxford University Press, Records of Social and Economic History, new series XVII

Woolgar, C.M. 2006: 'Meat and dairy products in late medieval England', in C.M. Woolgar, D. Serjeantson and T. Waldron (eds), *Food in Medieval England: Diet and Nutrition*. Oxford: Oxford University Press, 88–101

Woolgar, C.M., Serjeantson, D. and Waldron, T. (eds), *Food in Medieval England*. Oxford: Oxford University Press, 88–101

Wormald, P. 1985: *Bede and the Conversion of England: The Charter Evidence*. Jarrow Lecture 1984

Wormald, P. 1999: *The Making of English Law: King Alfred to the Twelfth Century*. Oxford: Blackwell

Yorke, B.A.E. 1983: 'Joint kingship in Kent *c.* 560 to 785', *Archaeologica Cantiana*, vol. 99, 1–20

Zell, M. 1994: *Industry in the Countryside: Wealden Society in the Sixteenth Century*. Cambridge: Cambridge University Press